REINACH AND THE FOUNDATIONS OF PRIVATE LAW

This volume introduces the legal philosopher Adolf Reinach and his contributions to speech act theory, as well as his analysis of basic legal concepts and their relationship to positive law. Reinach's thorough analysis has recently garnered growing interest in private law theory, yet his 'phenomenological realist' philosophical approach is not in line with contemporary mainstream approaches. The essays in this volume resuscitate and interrogate Reinach's unique account of the foundations of private law, situating him in contemporary private law theory and broader philosophical currents. The work also makes Reinach's methods more accessible to those unfamiliar with early phenomenology. Together these contributions prove that while Reinach's perspective on private law shares similarities and points of departure with trends in today's legal theory, many of his insights remain singular and illuminating in their own right. This title is also available as Open Access on Cambridge Core.

Marietta Auer is Professor of Law and Director at the Max Planck Institute for Legal History and Legal Theory in Frankfurt.

Paul B. Miller is the Robert and Marion Short Professor of Law and Associate Dean for International and Graduate Programs at Notre Dame Law School, where he directs the Notre Dame Program on Private Law.

Henry E. Smith is the Fessenden Professor of Law at Harvard Law School, where he directs the Project on the Foundations of Private Law.

James Toomey is Associate Professor of Law at the University of Iowa. Previously, he was an assistant professor of law at the Elisabeth Haub School of Law at Pace University, New York.

Reinach and the Foundations of Private Law

Edited by

MARIETTA AUER

Max Planck Institute for Legal History and Legal Theory

PAUL B. MILLER

University of Notre Dame

HENRY E. SMITH

Harvard Law School

JAMES TOOMEY

University of Iowa

CAMBRIDGE
UNIVERSITY PRESS

CAMBRIDGE
UNIVERSITY PRESS

Shaftesbury Road, Cambridge CB2 8EA, United Kingdom

One Liberty Plaza, 20th Floor, New York, NY 10006, USA

477 Williamstown Road, Port Melbourne, VIC 3207, Australia

314–321, 3rd Floor, Plot 3, Splendor Forum, Jasola District Centre, New Delhi – 110025, India

103 Penang Road, #05–06/07, Visioncrest Commercial, Singapore 238467

Cambridge University Press is part of Cambridge University Press & Assessment, a department of the University of Cambridge.

We share the University's mission to contribute to society through the pursuit of education, learning and research at the highest international levels of excellence.

www.cambridge.org
Information on this title: www.cambridge.org/9781009446006

DOI: 10.1017/9781009446013

First published 2025

A catalogue record for this publication is available from the British Library

A Cataloging-in-Publication data record for this book is available from the Library of Congress

ISBN 978-1-009-44600-6 Hardback
ISBN 978-1-009-44599-3 Paperback

For my teacher Claus-W. Canaris

– MA

For Stella, Serena, and Kieran

– PBM

For my teacher Karl S. Guthke

– HES

For Cristina, and my parents

– JT

Contents

Contributors

Marietta Auer, Managing Director, Max Planck Institute for Legal History and Legal Theory

Kimberly Baltzer-Jaray, Lecturer, King's University College, University of Western Ontario

Andrew S. Gold, Professor of Law, University of California, Irvine

Lorenz Kaehler, Professor for Private Law, Civil Procedure, and Philosophy of Law, University of Bremen

Stephan Kirste, University Professor for Philosophy of Law and Social Philosophy, University of Salzburg

Olivier Massin, Full Professor of General Philosophy, University of Neuchâtel

Paul B. Miller, Robert and Marion Short Professor of Law and Associate Dean for International and Graduate Programs, University of Notre Dame

Crescente Molina, Assistant Professor of Law, Rutgers University

Alessandro Salice, Senior Lecturer, University College Cork

Henry E. Smith, Fessenden Professor of Law, Harvard University

Sandy Steel, Professor of Law and Philosophy of Law, University of Oxford

Emma Tieffenbach, Postdoctoral Researcher, University of Zurich and Università della Svizzera italiana

James Toomey, Associate Professor of Law, University of Iowa

Acknowledgements

This volume grew out of a conference, 'Reinach and the Foundations of Private Law', held at the Max Planck Institute for Legal History and Legal Theory, in Frankfurt in August 2023. The editors sincerely thank the generosity of the Max Planck Institute for Legal History and Legal Theory for hosting the conference, alongside support from Harvard Law School and the University of Notre Dame. In addition, the editors thank Harvard Law School for making publication in an Open Access format possible.

Introduction

James Toomey[*]

Adolf Reinach (1883–1917) was a philosopher. Before his battlefield death at the age of thirty-three, his philosophical career was brief; the corpus he left slim.[1] Today, he is best known for developing a theory of social acts thought to be an independent precursor to the speech act theories of John Austin and others later in the century.[2] He is cited in certain branches of philosophy for his contributions on speech act theory and other contributions to metaphysics, including the mode of existence of states-of-affairs, their relationship to other features of our world, and the role of 'phenomenology' in epistemology.[3] In short, Reinach is taken today as a rather obscure metaphysician with a limited body of work.

But Reinach was also a *legal* philosopher. He wrote and thought a great deal about the law and legal philosophy,[4] and, uniquely in the philosophical circles in which he moved, he had trained as a lawyer.[5] Indeed, just as Austin would later draw

* Associate Professor of Law, University of Iowa College of Law; previously Assistant Professor of Law, Elisabeth Haub School of Law at Pace University. Thanks to my co-editors on this volume, Marietta Auer, Paul Miller, and Henry Smith, for helpful comments and feedback on this Introduction.

1 Adolf Reinach, *Gesammelte Schriften* (M Niemayer 1951); Karl Schuhmann and Barry Smith, 'Adolf Reinach: An Intellectual Biography', in Kevin Mulligan (ed), *Speech Act and Sachverhalt: Reinach and the Foundations of Realist Phenomenology* (Nijhoff 1987) 25.

2 John F Crosby, 'Adolf Reinach's Discovery of the Social Acts' (1983) 3 Aletheia 143; Kevin Mulligan (ed), *Speech Act and Sachverhalt: Reinach and the Foundations of Realist Phenomenology* (Nijhoff 1987).

3 Jan Woleński, 'Adolf Reinach, Negative States of Affairs and the Concept of Omission' (2020) 90 Folia Iuridica 5; Barry Smith, 'On the Cognition of States of Affairs', in Kevin Mulligan (ed), *Speech Act and Sachverhalt: Reinach and the Foundations of Realist Phenomenology* (Nijhoff 1987) 189; Kimberly Baltzer-Jaray, 'Bogged Down in Ontologism and Realism. Reinach's Phenomenological Realist Response to Husserl', in Rodney KB Parker (ed), *The Idealism-Realism Debate Among Edmund Husserl's Early Followers and Critics* (Springer 2021); Denis Seron, 'Adolf Reinach's Philosophy of Logic', in Bruno Leclercq, Sebastien Richard, and Denis Seron (eds), *Objects and Pseudo-Objects: Ontological Deserts and Jungles from Brentano to Carnap* (De Gruyter 2015).

4 ibid.

5 Baltzer-Jaray (Chapter 4, this volume).

on legal examples in his own discussion of speech acts,[6] Reinach's social act theory is presented in, but takes up only a portion of, the most substantial publication of his life – the 1913 monograph *The A Priori Foundations of the Civil Law.*[7] The *Foundations* is a substantial work of legal philosophy that theorizes about basic constituents of private law – promise, obligation, claim, right, property, representation, and more – as social acts.[8]

In the century since his death, Reinach's substantive legal philosophy – that is, the *rest* of the *Foundations* – has fallen by the wayside.[9] Until recently, you could search in vain for citations to Reinach in the law reviews. While Reinach's contributions to philosophy have undergone a renaissance in certain branches of ontology in the past forty years, his *legal* philosophy has not been the focus.[10] And even as private law theory has turned greater attention to Kant and other moral philosophers in recent decades,[11] if you wanted to discuss Reinach at an English-speaking conference on jurisprudence, you would at best be looked at with befuddlement.

Granted, given what Reinach argued about the law, his dismissal from the Anglophone jurisprudential canon makes some sense. As the title of his monograph suggests (the *A Priori Foundations*), Reinach argued that the basic legal concepts that structure private law are metaphysically real constituents of the universe, accessible *a priori* by something called the 'phenomenological method' – '[w]e shall show that the structures which one has generally called specifically legal have a being of their own just as much as numbers, trees, or houses, that this being is

6 JL Austin, *How to Do Things with Words* (JO Urmson and Marina Sbisà, eds, 2d edn Harvard University Press 1975); 57.

7 Hereinafter *The Foundations* or *Foundations.* Citations throughout the volume are to John F Crosby's most recent English translation, except where otherwise noted by individual authors. Adolf Reinach, 'The Apriori Foundations of the Civil Law' (John F Crosby tr, 1983) 3 Aletheia 1, reprinted in Adolf Reinach, *The Apriori Foundations of the Civil Law Along with the Lecture 'Concerning Phenomenology'* (John F Crosby ed, Ontos Verlag 2012), originally published as Adolf Reinach, 'Die apriorischen Grundlagen des bürgerlichen Rechtes', 1(2) *Jahrbuch für Philosophie und phänomenologische Forschung* (Max Niemeyer 1913) 685–847.

8 ibid.

9 Of course, not entirely. Neil Duxbury, 'The Legal Philosophy of Adolf Reinach' (1991) 77 Archives for Philosophy of Law and Social Philosophy 314; Stanley L Paulsen, 'Demystyifying Reinach's Legal Theory', in Kevin Mulligan (ed), *Speech Act and Sachverhalt: Reinach and the Foundations of Realist Phenomenology* (Kluwer 1987). And indeed, while engagement with Reinach's work has become rare in English-language legal philosophy, it has been the subject of a small but consistent literature in German. Sophie Loidolt, *Einführung in die Rechtsphänomenologie* (Mohr Siebeck 2010); Christoph J Lüttenberg, 'Über das Sein des Sollens – Die rechtlichen Gebilde in der Rechtsphänomenologie Adolf Reinachs' (2020) 11 Zeitschrift für rechtswissenschaftliche Forschung 9; Kai Purnhagen, 'Grundlagen der Rechtsphänomenologie – Eine kritische Darstellung der Rechtsphänomenologie von Adolf Reinach und Wilhelm Schapp zu den apriorischen Grundlagen des Privatrechts' (2009) 31 JURA – Juristische Ausbildung 661.

10 Barry Smith, 'Adolf Reinach: An Annotated Bibliography', in Kevin Mulligan (ed), *Speech Act and Sachverhalt: Reinach and the Foundations of Realist Phenomenology* (Nijhoff 1987); Jeff Mitscherling, Tanya DiTommaso, and Aref Nayad, *The Author's Intention* (Lexington 2004) 5.

11 Ernest J Weinrib, *The Idea of Private Law* (Harvard University Press 1995); Arthur Ripstein, 'Private Order and Public Justice: Kant and Rawls' (2006) 92 Virginia L Rev 1391.

independent of its being grasped by men, that it is in particular independent of all positive law.'[12] '[T]he positive law', Reinach boldly proclaims, '*finds* the legal concepts which enter into it; *in absolutely no way does it produce them*.'[13]

In the century since Reinach wrote, there is perhaps no proposition of legal theory more widely taken for granted than that, whatever legal concepts are, they are not what Adolf Reinach thought.[14] Most famously and enduringly associated with the contributions of American Legal Realism, various forms of nominalism about legal concepts – that, say, the legal concepts of 'contract' and 'ownership' are more or less arbitrary exercises in policymaking, often *sub silentio* – have been gospel in the legal academy for over a hundred years.[15] As the slogan has it, 'we are all legal realists now'.[16] In analytical jurisprudence, neither HLA Hart nor Ronald Dworkin thought legal concepts have a determinate metaphysical existence.[17] And whatever the Law and Economics and Critical Legal Studies movements disagree about, it isn't this.[18]

But perhaps now is the time to start engaging with Reinach – and his provocative metaphysical realism about legal concepts, sharp analysis of those concepts, and epistemic confidence in 'phenomenological' discernment – once again in legal philosophy. In the past few decades, theorists, particularly of the 'New Private Law' school, have grown increasingly skeptical of the hegemonic picture of private law concepts as exercises in boundless policy invention and reinvention.[19] Many of these scholars again take seriously private law's internal point of view, sometimes including that perspective's notorious solicitude for conceptual reasoning, while acknowledging a variety of interdisciplinary, external perspectives.[20] And indeed, in the past few years, legal theorists have begun to engage with Reinach's work in private law theory and adjacent areas of philosophy.[21]

12 Reinach (n 7) 4.
13 ibid.
14 Frederick Schauer, 'The Limited Domain of the Law' (2004) 90 Virginia L Rev 1909.
15 Karl N Llewellyn, *The Common Law Tradition: Deciding Appeals* (Little, Brown & Co. 1960) 180–81; Felix S Cohen, 'Transcendental Nonsense and the Functional Approach' (1935) 35 Columbia L Rev 809; Scott Brewer, 'On the Possibility of Necessity in Legal Argument: A Dilemma for Holmes and Dewey' (2000) 34 John Marshall L Rev 9, 39.
16 Joseph William Singer, 'Legal Realism Now' (1988) 76 California Law Review 465, 467.
17 Ronald Dworkin, *Law's Empire* (Harvard University Press 1986) 83; HLA Hart, *The Concept of Law* (3rd ed Oxford University Press 2012) 129–29; Jules L Coleman, 'Truth and Objectivity in Law' (1995) 1 Legal Theory 33, 47.
18 Guido Calabresi and A Douglas Melamed, 'Property Rules, Liability Rules, and Inalienability: One View of the Cathedral' (1972) 85 Harvard L Rev 1089; Duncan Kennedy, 'Form and Substance in Private Law Adjudication' (1976) 89 Harvard L Rev 168; Gary Peller, 'The Metaphysics of American Law' (1985) 73 California L Rev 1151.
19 Andrew S Gold, John CP Goldberg, Daniel B Kelly, Emily Sherwin, and Henry E Smith (eds), *The Oxford Handbook of the New Private Law* (Oxford University Press 2020).
20 ibid.
21 James Toomey, 'Property's Boundaries' (2023) 109 Virginia L Rev 131; Olivier Massin, 'The Metaphysics of Ownership: A Reinachian Account' (2017) 27 Axiomathes 577; Manuela Massa, 'Property and *Nuda Potestas* as Constitutions of Reinach's Philosophy of Law' (2020) 90 Folia Iuridica 75.

In this context, Reinach's account of the *a priori* foundations of civil law offers valuable insights – perhaps *uniquely* valuable insights – to both proponents and detractors of a conceptualist, formalist turn in private law theory. For one thing, unlike many earlier proponents of legal formalism and natural law theory, Reinach *knew* he was defending a contrarian view against rising (and ultimately ubiquitous) positivist nominalism.[22] He framed his thesis against a view 'on which there is general agreement', that 'all legal propositions are *creations* of the lawmaking factors'.[23] And by taking seriously and engaging with nominalism on its own terms, his arguments might merit more credence than earlier theorists who assumed worldviews no longer widely accepted – say what you will about Reinach, he is no easily dismissed pre-Darwinian natural law theorist building jurisprudence on partisan theology. Indeed, he is no traditional natural law theorist at all, because although he took core legal concepts like promise to be metaphysically real, he also believed them normatively inert, and the positive law free to deviate from their *a priori* entailments in the name of morality or expedience.[24]

Moreover, Reinach's enthusiastic embrace of *metaphysical* realism in private law can help both illuminate and challenge debates around legal concepts today. For those sympathetic to a role for conceptual reasoning or analysis in legal discourse, Reinach might offer a theory of legal concepts' nature – supported by his broader 'Realist Phenomenology' theory of the universe, a general account of metaphysics and epistemology that has been revisited in philosophy in the past few decades.[25] Or, as several contributions in this volume suggest in different ways, it might be that his *analysis* of legal concepts is illuminating even if his particular *theory* of their existence is not – he may have done valuable work making sense of the entailments of legal concepts that exist in some other, less difficult, way.[26]

At the same time, to skeptics of law's internal point of view, or of the determinacy of legal concepts, Reinach might be saying the quiet part of any sort of legal conceptualism out loud. Nominalists about legal concepts have long suspected their opponents of (at least) closet Platonism – of being committed to law as a 'brooding omnipresence in the sky',[27] consisting of a 'heaven for legal concepts',[28] notwithstanding the interdisciplinary efforts of New Private Law theorists to avoid these sorts

[22] Reinach (n 7), 4.

[23] ibid.

[24] ibid 45.

[25] Barry Smith, 'Realistic Phenomenology', in Lester Embree (ed), *Encyclopedia of Phenomenology* (Springer 1997) 586; Baltzer-Jaray, 'Bogged Down' (n 3) 156.

[26] Andrew S Gold and Henry E Smith (Chapter 5, this volume); Marietta Auer (Chapter 1, this volume); James Toomey (Chapter 2, this volume); Paul B Miller (Chapter 7, this volume); Lorenz Kaehler (Chapter 3, this volume); Sandy Steel (Chapter 6, this volume).

[27] *S Pac Co v Jensen* [1917] 244 U.S. 205, 222 (Holmes, J., dissenting).

[28] Rudolf von Jhering, 'In the Heaven for Legal Concepts: A Fantasy' (Charlotte L Levy, tr, 1985) 58 Temple L Q 799.

of commitments.[29] From that perspective, at least Reinach *doesn't* shy away from bold work in metaphysics, but rather embraces it wholeheartedly – perhaps raising the possibility that, at bottom, and in one of its best articulations, maybe conceptual analysis in legal reasoning *does* demand faith in something like the World of Legal Forms.[30]

In this volume, we bring together papers by American and European legal theorists and philosophers on Reinach's work and its implications for private law. In so doing, we aspire to both resuscitate and interrogate Reinach's legal theory, to situate Reinach's theories alongside their alternatives and make sense of their relationship to debates in contemporary private law scholarship. Moreover, we hope that this volume will serve as a resource for private law scholars hoping to learn more about Reinach, philosophers and scholars of Reinach who plan to engage more with the legal aspects of his work, and students coming upon Reinach for the first time.

The contributions are arranged in three parts. In the first, Marietta Auer, James Toomey, Lorenz Kaehler, and Kimberly Baltzer-Jaray write about issues related to Reinach's philosophical methodology. In Part II, Andrew Gold and Henry Smith, Sandy Steel, Paul Miller, and Olivier Massin discuss connections between Reinach's legal philosophy and contemporary private law theories. And finally, Stephan Kirste, Emma Tieffenbach, Alessandro Salice and Olivier Massin, and Crescente Molina draw on Reinach's approach in making novel arguments about *particular* legal concepts – from the concept of legal time to that of agreement.

This introduction is similarly arranged. After setting the scene with a brief biography of Adolf Reinach, we introduce each of the three parts, and summarize the chapters, in turn.

I.1 A BRIEF LIFE OF ADOLF REINACH

Adolf Bernhard Philipp Reinach was born in 1883 to a prominent and well-established Jewish family in Mainz, near Frankfurt, then of the German Empire.[31] His interest in philosophy began in his teenage years at *Ostergymnasium* at Mainz,

[29] Paul B Miller, 'The New Formalism in Private Law' (2021) 66 American Journal of Jurisprudence 175; Henry E Smith, 'On the Economy of Concepts in Property' (2012) 160 University of Pennsylvania L Rev 2097; John Gardner, *From Personal Life to Private Law* (Oxford University Press 2018) 11–12; Jules L Coleman, 'The Practice of Corrective Justice' (1995) 37 Arizona L Rev 15, 22.

[30] Granted, it is controversial whether Reinach's account is properly described as 'Platonist'. Kimberly Baltzer-Jaray, 'Adolf Reinach Is Not a Platonist' (2009) 13 Symposium: Canadian J Continental Philosophy 100; Smith, 'Cognition of States of Affairs' (n 3) 201. As far as legal philosophers go, however, he was clearly *something like* a Platonist.

[31] John F Crosby, 'A Brief Biography of Adolf Reinach', in John Crosby (ed), *The Aprior Foundations of the Civil Law: Along with the Lecture 'Concerning Phenomenology'* (Ontos Verlag 2012).

where he was introduced to Plato, who would remain one of his most significant influences throughout his life.[32]

In 1901, Reinach started at the University of Munich, where he studied philosophy and psychology under Theodor Lipps, who was famous for interdisciplinary research in both fields.[33] While Reinach's heart clearly lay in philosophy and its intersection with empirical psychology, he also studied law and jurisprudence; indeed, he earned a PhD in philosophy in 1904 with a dissertation on the concept of causality in criminal law.[34] During his years in Munich, Reinach fell in with a broad group of other students of Lipps, who would largely form his intellectual network for the rest of his life, many of whom were or would go on to be important philosophers in their own right – Johannes Daubert, Dietrich von Hildebrand, Max Scheler, Moritz Geiger, Theodor Conrad, Alexander Pfänder, and more.[35]

While Reinach was beginning his intellectual journey in Munich, Edmund Husserl, already established, was working in Göttingen, on, among other things, the foundations of logic, and the relationship between logic and psychology.[36] In his 1901 work *Logical Investigations*, Husserl argued against the view (much in vogue, and embraced by philosopher-psychologists like Lipps) that logic was reducible to psychology, and propounded a new method, which he called 'phenomenology', as an alternative.[37] Reinach's circle in Munich began reading Husserl in the early years of the twentieth century, and its members were particularly attracted by the emphasis in *Logical Investigations* on the metaphysical realism of logic, as contrasted with the views of their mentor, Lipps.[38] In 1905, Reinach and several of his friends from Munich began moving to Göttingen to work with Husserl directly – the so-called 'Munich invasion of Göttingen'.[39]

Evidently, however, in a familiar tale, Reinach's parents found disputes about the ontological status of logic rather frivolous (or at least unemployable), and insisted he return to his legal studies.[40] He did so in 1906, taking courses in Munich and Tübingen, most influentially from the legal theorist Ernst Beling, whose account of criminal law saw it as composed of 'delict-types', through which certain sets of facts were held to constitute specified legal forms – not unlike Reinach's own later views in civil law.[41] And though clearly he had little interest in practicing law, Reinach's

32 Anna Reinach, sketch of a 'Lebenslauf', in the Bavarian State Library, Ana 379 D II1 (quoted in Schuhmann and Smith (n 1) 2.
33 Schuhmann and Smith (n 1) 2.
34 Adolf Reinach, 'On the Concept of Causality in the Criminal Law' (tr. Berit Brogaard) (2009) 1 Libertarian Papers 1; Schuhmann and Smith (n 1) 5.
35 Alessandro Salice, 'The Phenomenology of the Munich and Göttingen Circles' in Edward N Zalta (ed), *Stanford Encyclopedia of Philosophy* (online 2020).
36 Stefania Centrone, *Logic and Philosophy of Mathematics in the Early Husserl* (Springer 2010).
37 Edmund Husserl, *Logical Investigations, Vol. I* (JN Findlay tr, Routledge 2001).
38 Salice (n 35); Schuhmann and Smith (n 1) 6.
39 Salice (n 35).
40 Crosby, 'A Brief Biography' (n 31) viii.
41 Schuhmann and Smith (n 1) 7–8; Baltzer-Jaray (Chapter 4, this volume).

legal studies were not without characteristic intellectual enthusiasm – he boasted to his friends that he had memorized large portions of the Imperial German Code of Civil Procedure[42] and commented favourably on the insight of many of his teachers.[43] In 1907, he sat for and passed the state law exams, before promptly returning to philosophy.[44]

In 1909, once more firmly working on philosophical issues, Reinach habilitated at Göttingen with Husserl's support, with a thesis on the nature of judgement, and began teaching as a *Privatdozent*.[45] His teaching – something he had done informally among his philosophical peers for a long time – was rather legendary;[46] 'the Göttingen students . . . of this period refer to Reinach, not to Husserl, as their real teacher in phenomenology;'[47] observing that he was 'brilliant in directing philosophical seminars'.[48]

During these years, Reinach worked closely with Husserl as an assistant, helping to revise and prepare the second edition of *Logical Investigations*, which was to be published in 1913, and helping to edit Husserl's new journal *Yearbook for Philosophy and Phenomenology Research*, which would become the preeminent publication of the phenomenological movement in the following decades.[49] In 1912, Reinach married Anna Stettenheimer, among the first women to obtain a PhD in physics from the University of Tübingen.[50]

At the same time, Reinach was hard at work on his own contributions. In 1913, in the first edition of the *Yearbook*, he published his masterwork, *The A Priori Foundations of the Civil Law*.[51] Connecting his legal training with his philosophical thinking, the monograph argues that, rather than inventions of positive law, foundational legal concepts like promise and property are metaphysically real, and knowledge about them is accessible *a priori*.[52] Specifically, these legal forms are *social acts*, which Reinach took to be an ontological kind not sufficiently recognized in philosophy.[53] Similar to John Austin's later theory of speech acts, this 'discovery' of social acts in the *Foundations* is what Reinach is best known for today.[54] But in the remainder of the work, Reinach seeks to illustrate the realism of legal concepts by

42 Quoted in Schuhmann and Smith (n 1) 8.
43 ibid.
44 Crosby, 'A Brief Biography' (n 31) viii.
45 Schuhmann and Smith (n 1) 12–13.
46 Salice (n 35); Schuhmann and Smith (n 1) 14; Crosby, 'A Brief Biography' (n 31) ix.
47 Herbert Spiegelbert, *The Phenomenological Movement* (3rd ed, Springer 1994) 191.
48 Edmund Husserl, *Briefe an Roman Ingarden* (Nijjoff 1968) 114.
49 Schuhmann and Smith (n 1) 12–16.
50 Kimberly Baltzer-Jaray, 'Happy 104th Wedding Anniversary, Adolf & Anna!', https://reinach.ophen.org/2016/09/15/happy-104th-wedding-anniversary-adolf-anna/.
51 Reinach, 'Foundations' (n 7).
52 ibid 4.
53 ibid 18–28.
54 Sources cited in note 2, above.

reasoning to synthetic *a priori* judgements about them – that, say, a promise need not be accepted; a claim dissolves once waived.[55]

In the same edition of the *Yearbook* in which the *Foundations* appeared, Husserl also published his next great work, *Ideas*, advocating for phenomenology grounded not in metaphysical realism but transcendental idealism.[56] The contiguity of this work with Husserl's realism about logic in *Logical Investigations* has long been controversial, and Reinach and his fellow travelers in metaphysical realism took it as a substantial departure – 'the *Ideas* ... provided young phenomenologists with an opportunity to renew their commitment to a robust form of metaphysical realism, which was perceived as incompatible with Husserl's transcendental idealism.'[57] Indeed, while it may have been 'something of an exaggeration'[58] to claim that after *Ideas* 'Reinach and, following him, the others broke away from the new developments',[59] an important intellectual rift had opened among self-identified 'phenomenologists,' and Reinach and Husserl were beginning to disagree about the basic foundations of philosophy.[60]

Any further intellectual divergence (or reconciliation) between Reinach and Husserl was, however, not to be. In August 1914, Europe descended into general war.[61] The notorious, now-mystifying war fever that swept Europe that fateful month did not pass Reinach by – he volunteered immediately and was in France by September, alongside his younger brother Heinrich, also a lawyer, who would later be imprisoned on *Kristallnacht* and escape to Brazil.[62] While at the front, Reinach continued thinking about philosophy – corresponding with his friends on philosophical topics and announcing lecture courses he would never give.[63] In 1916, Reinach converted to Christianity and, while on leave, he and Anna were baptized into the Protestant Church.[64] His final writings were sketches on the phenomenology of religion, written from the battlefield.[65] Adolf Reinach died in the service of the German Empire on 16 November 1917, at the age of thirty-three.[66]

Back in Germany, Edmund Husserl eulogized Reinach in *Kant Studies* – 'German philosophy has suffered a heavy loss as a result of Adolf Reinach's early

55 Reinach, 'Foundations' (n 7).

56 Schuhmann and Smith (n 1) 20; Edmund Husserl, *Ideas: General Introduction to Pure Phenomenology* (originally published 1913) (Routledge 2012).

57 Salice (n 35).

58 Schuhmann and Smith (n 1) 21.

59 D Cairns, *Conversations with Husserl and Fink* (Nijhoff 1976) 10.

60 Salice (n 35); Crosby, 'A Brief Biography' (n 31) ix; Rodney KB Parker (ed), *The Idealism-Realism Debate Among Edmund Husserl's Early Followers and Critics* (Springer 2021).

61 Barbara W Tuchman, *The Guns of August: The Outbreak of World War I* (Penguin 1994).

62 Schuhmann and Smith (n 1) 23; 2.

63 ibid 24.

64 ibid 24; Crosby, 'A Brief Biography' (n 31) ix–x.

65 Schuhmann and Smith (n 1) 24; Crosby, 'A Brief Biography' (n 31) ix–x.

66 Schuhmann and Smith (n 1) 24.

death.'[67] Reinach had left his unpublished papers with Anna, with instructions to destroy them in the event of his death.[68] Several previously unpublished fragments nevertheless appeared in the *Collected Writings* of Adolf Reinach, published in 1921 and edited and arranged by Edith Stein and other students, with an introduction by Hedwig Conrad-Martius;[69] other writings were finally destroyed when Anna Reinach fled Germany in 1942, in the face of Nazi persecution.[70]

I.2 REINACH AND HIS METHOD

To modern philosophical eyes, Reinach is a difficult philosopher to place. On the one hand, he writes like an analytical philosopher – he is engaged in an exercise that looks a lot like conceptual analysis, tosses variables around, and routinely invokes the philosophy of mathematics. On the other, he called his method 'phenomenology' and was a prime assistant to ur-Continental Edmund Husserl. Was Reinach an 'analytical' philosopher or a 'Continental' one? The answer, perhaps, is both, and neither.

Indeed, Reinach's life, and his work, sits right at the point of departure of these schools. The Husserl of *Logical Investigations* was influenced by Gottlob Frege, often taken to be the founder of analytical philosophy, and was preoccupied with the foundations of mathematics and logic, just like Russell, Carnap, and the early Wittgenstein.[71] It was this Husserl that Reinach, and the other 'Munich Realists' were drawn to and worked with.[72] This began to change after *Ideas*, as Husserl took a turn into transcendental idealism, and Reinach and his friends doubled down in their realist commitments.[73] Before the War, Reinach remained Husserl's closest assistant.[74] After, Husserl obviously needed a new one.[75] He settled on a former seminary student named Martin Heidegger;[76] and the rest, as they say, is history.

But before you jump to the conclusion that Reinach is *just* some sort of crypto-analytic, that isn't quite right either. It was very important to him that his method was 'phenomenological', and he insisted on claims such as that '[i]n immersing ourselves in the essence of [legal] entities, we spiritually see what holds for them'.[77]

67 Edmund Husserl, 'Obituary notice (entire)' in John Crosby (ed), *The Apriori Foundations of the Civil Law: Along with the Lecture 'Concerning Phenomenology'* (Ontos Verlag 2012) xi, originally published in (1919) 13 Kant-Studien 147.

68 Schuhmann and Smith (n 1) 25.

69 Adolf Reinach, *Gesammelte Schriften* (Niemeyer 1921); Schuhmann and Smith (n 1) 25.

70 Schuhmann and Smith (n 1) 25.

71 Salice (n 35).

72 ibid.

73 ibid.

74 Schuhmannn and Smith (n 1) 21.

75 Salice (n 35).

76 Edmund Husserl, *Edmund Husserl Briefwechsel, Vol. 2 Die Münchener Phänomenologen* (Elisabeth Schuhmann and Karl Schuhmann, eds, Kluwer 1994)

77 Reinach (n 7).

Indeed, it might be best to say that the moment of 'Realist Phenomenology' Reinach occupied with his friends from Munich was its own bounded moment in philosophy – then eclipsed after twenty years of turmoil by the linguistic turn in English and existentialism on the Continent. The survivors of the moment – Roman Ingarden, Max Scheler, Hedwig Conrad-Martius, Dietrich von Hildebrand, Edith Stein – carried on the legacy of Realist Phenomenology in more religious philosophy.[78]

The chapters in the first part of the book address questions raised by Reinach's philosophical method, his relationship to other philosophical schools, and the implications of his philosophical position for his jurisprudence. In 'Promising, Owning, Enacting: Adolf Reinach's Phenomenology of Legal Speech Acts', Marietta Auer draws out the nature of Reinach's phenomenological theory of private law by examining it in light of both the German civil law tradition and mid-century language philosophy. As noted earlier, Reinach was trained in the law, and the *Foundations* reflects a deep knowledge of the German Civil Code. This knowledge of German law shapes some of Reinach's analysis but, at other times, offers a foil for his views. Those views rest on a theory of social speech acts – legal relations arise when actors engage in various social speech acts. Reinach concentrates in particular on promising and owning. Auer shows how deeply linguistic Reinach's approach is and draws out its etymological background. Promising involves speaking (*versprechen*), and owning involves hearing and obeying (*gehören*). Even enactment is a social speech act (*bestimmen*) with etymological linguistic overtones.

This confluence of tools and goals in Reinach's phenomenology of private law allows him to avoid some of the pitfalls of established schools of thought, Auer argues. His approach is not wholly positivist, and nor is it moralist (natural law) or nominalist (as in Legal Realism and its relatives). Reinach can, from this perspective, be interpreted as eschewing metaphysics where it is not necessary. Promisors are obligated to perform because they have promised, rather than because of positive law, promisee reliance, good consequences from promise keeping, and the like. Reinach thus solves notorious problems – such as justifying the bindingness of promises and the nature of ownership as more than a bundle of rights – by stopping philosophical analysis when it reaches the '*a priori*' bedrock in the law. In this way, Reinach does not overclaim about what ought to be from what is, and thereby avoids the common pitfalls of 'ontologism'.

In 'Darwin's Reinach', James Toomey argues that Reinach's approach to basic legal concepts can be embraced on the basis of evolutionary psychology rather than Reinach's own strong metaphysical views. Reinach thought that basic legal

78 As discussed above, Reinach, too, converted to Christianity during the First World War. Crosby, 'A Brief Biography' (n 31) x. It is perhaps fair to critique Realist Phenomenology as demanding a faith in the abstract and immaterial closely compatible with religion and mysticism. On the other hand, at least in Reinach's case, it is hard to disentangle the influence of his combat experiences from his own turn to religion. Husserl, 'Obituary' (n 67) xiv; Schuhmann and Smith (n 1) 24.

concepts existed outside the law, that positive law could deviate from them, and that both are distinct from morality. This combination of positions is very unusual and was a path not much trodden in the twentieth century. However, later developments in evolutionary psychology bear some resemblance to Reinach's position – legal concepts are anchored in reality, because adaptive fitness is necessarily constrained by external reality of some kind. Evolution and an evolved modular mind produce concepts very much like those explored by Reinach. Toomey points out that there is some irony in this, in that Reinach wrote at a time when controversy raged over whether concepts and reasoning were psychological or more firmly grounded ontologically. With Edmund Husserl and Gottlob Frege, Reinach took the ontological side and was at great pains to distance himself from the 'psychologism' of his mentor Theodor Lipps. By contrast to the psychology of his day, modern evolutionary psychology is not as plastic and arbitrary and so is surprisingly compatible with Reinach's *a priori*, without being a full-blown *a priori* in the metaphysical sense.

Although a strongly ontological and an evolutionary psychological take on concepts are in principle distinct, Toomey argues that for practical purposes they are very close, and closer than Reinach and his contemporaries thought. Reinach, Husserl, and Frege made arguments for ontological robustness of concepts and reasoning that were contested at the time. The domain most amenable to their approach was mathematics. Reinach's subject matter, the law, presents difficulties because law is inherently social – no people, no law. Reinach took his concepts to be timeless and equally applicable to any beings capable of engaging in social acts, but experience only offers people as such agents, and in this domain, Toomey argues, evolutionary psychology points in the same directions as Reinach's methodology. Thus, one can accept that Reinachian concepts exist as features of human psychology without taking them to exist as metaphysically distinct basic concepts as Reinach did.

Lorenz Kaehler, in 'Is There a Legal A Priori? On Necessary, Essential, and Non-positive Propositions in Reinach's Theory', interrogates Reinach's central thesis in the *Foundations* – that there indeed exist *a priori* legal propositions independent of all positive law. Kaehler maintains that, although Reinach has convincingly shown that there are *non-positive* propositions of law with truth value – that is, legal propositions that are true not solely by reference to positive law – he has not demonstrated the more ambitious claim that these propositions are in fact epistemically *a priori*. Indeed, as Kaehler points out, there are a variety of ways in which legal propositions could be non-positive but not *a priori* – they might be presupposed by positive law, perhaps grounded in minimal morality, or at least partially justifiable with reference to experience.

From Kaehler's perspective, Reinach's arguments for insisting that the non-positive propositions he is discussing, indeed all plausible arguments for insisting that non-positive propositions are *a priori*, are unavailing. Drawing on more recent work in epistemology and metaphysics, Kaehler suggests that there are many necessary, essential, and intuitive propositions that depend on experience – and to the extent those are the only arguments in favor of the *a priori* status of Reinach's legal propositions (and they seem to be) they do not get us to that conclusion. And yet, according to Kaehler, the fact that Reinach has not proven the central thesis of the *Foundations* does not mean that his analysis is unimportant. Though Reinach *thought* he had discovered an *a priori* sphere of right, Kaehler grants he conducted important analysis of something like a *non-positive* sphere of right, a significant domain of legal propositions thus far inadequately theorized.

In 'Adolf Reinach, Negation, and Law,' Kimberly Baltzer-Jaray connects Reinach's legal philosophy and training to broader aspects of his ontology. Among contemporary ontologists, Reinach is known for the controversial view that 'negative states-of-affairs' – the rose's *not* being blue, for instance – have the same ontological status as positive ones – the rose's *being* red. This position was received with skepticism by many of Reinach's fellow travelers in phenomenological realism, including Johannes Daubert and Roman Ingarden, who insisted that the ontological status of positive states of affairs is always primary; negative ones are at best derivative, and, at worst, purely psychological or linguistic.

But Baltzer-Jaray argues that there might be something to Reinach's position, and that it was Reinach's legal studies – unique among his philosophical peers – that helped him see it. As Baltzer-Jaray points out, apparently negative states-of-affairs – the *absence* of due care, say – routinely play a role in constituting legal conclusions as much as positive ones do. Negative states of affairs, in other words, often appear *legally* on a par with positive states. This ubiquitous structure of legal reasoning, Baltzer-Jaray argues, helped Reinach consider the role of negation in ontology in a way that was unavailable to his contemporaries, and revealed to him an ontological significance in negative states of affairs that others did not appreciate. Moreover, Baltzer-Jaray suggests that Reinach's views on negative states-of-affairs might have implications for a range of contemporary social and ethical problems, and that linking his legal philosophy to his ontology can help make sense of him as a unified philosophical thinker.

I.3 REINACH AND PRIVATE LAW THEORY

If you're looking for contemporary legal theorists, who, like Reinach, claim to be outlining the *a priori* foundations of private law, you'll be looking a long time. But that hardly means that Reinach doesn't bear resemblance – in sharing certain concerns, conclusions, and methods – to many important threads in contemporary private law theory. To be sure, Reinach's careful parsing of the entailments of concepts like 'promise', 'enactment', and 'obligation' divorced (at least aspirationally) from any consideration of the positive law are about as far away from the nominalist view of legal concepts still fashionable in traditional Law and Economics and Critical Legal Studies. But the last two decades or so have seen a resurgence in private law theory outside of these schools.

This work has come from a variety of points of entry. Some of it draws on moral philosophy, and a turn towards something more like metaphysical and moral realism in analytical philosophy.[79] Other scholars think that legal concepts, regardless of their moral or ontological status, serve necessary functions – economic, psychological, semantic – in packaging information across domains.[80] And still others simply *do* doctrinal analysis, taking it seriously as a project.[81] Traveling under the heading of 'New Private Law', these disparate threads have argued that there is a place for the internal conceptual structure of traditional legal reasoning.[82]

Reinach's legal philosophy offers important points of connection with this intellectual movement, as well as significant contrasts. And the chapters in Part II engage with these sorts of connections – laying bare and critiquing Reinach's theories of legal philosophy or comparing and contrasting Reinach's positions with those of other theorists.

Andrew Gold and Henry Smith, in 'Legal Concepts as a Deep Structure of the Law: Reinach's A Priori in Action', argue that regardless of the ontological status of the legal concepts Reinach analyses, his methods and conclusions are clearly on to *something*, and on to something of value to both sides to various persistent dichotomies in private law theory. Taking Reinach's discussion of property, transfer, and representation as case studies, they reveal how Reinach's analysis captures general intuitions behind common forms in many positive legal systems, often more plausibly than alternative accounts. Gold and Smith analogize Reinach's *a priori* domain of right to the role that 'deep structure' plays in generative grammar theory – a consistent, robust structure presupposed by, and which indeed makes possible,

79 Weinrib (n 11); Rebecca Stone, 'Private Liability Without Wrongdoing' (2023) 73 University of Toronto LJ 53; Scott Hershovitz, 'The End of Jurisprudence' (2015) 124 Yale LJ 882; Steven Schaus, 'A Simple Model of Torts and Moral Wrongs' (2022) 97 Notre Dame L Rev 1029; Charles Fried, *Contract as Promise: A Theory of Contractual Obligation* (2nd ed Oxford University Press 2015); Seana Valentine Shiffrin, 'The Divergence of Contract and Promise' (2007) 120 Harvard L Rev 708; John Gardner, 'What Is Tort Law For? Part I. The Place of Corrective Justice' (2011) 30 Law and Philosophy 1, 50.

80 Thomas W Merrill and Henry E Smith, 'Optimal Standardization in the Law of Property: The Numerus Clausus Principle' (2000) 110 Yale LJ 1; John CP Goldberg and Benjamin C Zipursky, 'Torts as Wrongs' (2010) 88 Texas L Rev 917; Henry E Smith, 'Property as the Law of Things' (2012) 125 Harvard L Rev 1691; Shyamkrishna Balganesh and Gideon Parchomovsky, 'Structure and Value in the Common Law' (2015) 163 University of Pennsylvania L Rev 1241; Jeremy Waldron, '"Transcendental Nonsense" and System in the Law' (2000) 100 Columbia L Rev 16; Felipe Jiménez, 'A Formalist Theory of Contract Law Adjudication' (2021) 2020 Utah L Rev 1121.

81 Ben McFarlane and Robert Stevens, 'The Nature of Equitable Property' (2010) 4 Journal of Equity 1; Danielle D'Onfro, 'Contract-Wrapped Property' (2024) 137 Harvard L Rev 1061; Lawrence M Solan, 'Contract as Agreement' (2007) 83 Notre Dame L Rev 353.

82 Andrew S Gold, John CP Goldberg, Daniel B Kelly, Emily Sherwin, and Henry E Smith (eds), *The Oxford Handbook of the New Private Law* (Oxford University Press 2020).

variation in surface structure. And just as with deep structure in linguistics, Reinach's *a priori* might be consistent with a range of theories of its ontological grounding – perhaps it is onto something metaphysically real, but it could just be psychologically universal, or conventional in response to consistent functional needs, all three, or other things.

Seeing Reinach's theory in this light, Gold and Smith argue, has several benefits, and helps cut through contemporary polarities in private law theory. Reinach's account is 'internal' in the sense that it takes seriously the law's conceptual vocabulary, yet 'external' insofar as it is agnostic to the positive law; it is 'holist' in refusing to theorize primitives away, but 'reductionist' in revealing how complex positive legal mechanisms can be built from a deeper, smaller array of primitives. Moreover, reckoning with the deep structure of law can have benefits in purely functional terms, taking stock of the kinds of legal propositions people will find intuitive, and those that require greater cognitive load to enshrine and enforce. Reinach, Gold and Smith take it, is thus doing – or at least compatible with – New Private Law.

In 'Private Law beyond the Law', Sandy Steel tackles one of the most puzzling aspects of Reinach's legal theory – the relationship between his analysis of *a priori* legal concepts and the inevitable normativity of the positive law, in the demands it makes of us and the reasons to which it is answerable. Steel does so in two ways. First, he observes that, while many contemporary private law theorists do not *say* they are seeking something as mysterious as the '*a priori* foundations of the civil law', it often looks as though that is what they are doing. Where most contemporary such theorists depart from Reinach, however, is in that they appear to be studying the *a priori moral* foundations of private law, as, say, contemporary neo-Kantians. In contrast, Reinach's approach to descriptive analysis carries unique benefits in clarity, but unique risks of conflating that which *a priori is* with that which the positive law *ought* to do, a risk of which Reinach himself was acutely aware.

Second, Steel synthesizes Reinach's scattered, and perhaps not altogether clear, remarks about normativity in the *Foundations*. At once, Reinach maintains that promises generate, *a priori*, obligations, but that these obligations are not *moral* obligations; that positive law has the capacity to create genuine oughts; and yet at the same time that positive law might be answerable to extrinsic moral considerations. Steel finds provocative points of comparison in contemporary private law theory and case law, while at the same time questioning whether Reinach in fact held a coherent, thorough theory about the relationship between his *a priori*, normativity, and the positive law. In short, Steel argues that Reinach's unique phenomenology of legal concepts at once clarifies and elides the normativity of positive law.

Paul Miller, in 'Reinach on Personality and Representation', juxtaposes what he takes to be one of Reinach's most insightful contributions – his analysis of representation – with an admirable failure – his incomplete analysis of legal personhood. Unlike many contemporary private law theorists and legal philosophers, Miller observes, Reinach was well aware that his theory demanded an account of legal personhood, and throughout the *Foundations* he gestures obliquely to the conditions and prerequisites of personhood – an admirable aspiration. At the same time, Miller finds Reinach's discussion incomplete, alluding to rather than substantiating a thorough theory of personhood. And Reinach's failure to connect his theory of legal concepts to a theory of persons who use them and for whom they are used, Miller holds, renders Reinach's claims to have discovered universal truths accessible to all intelligence implausible.

Where Reinach's discussion of personhood was incomplete, Miller describes his analysis of representation as something of a triumph – an account second only to Hobbes' and distinguished by its own genuine insights. Some of these innovations include Reinach's distinction between authentic and inauthentic representation, drawing on his view of social acts as having authentic and inauthentic forms, and his account of passive representation. At the same time, Miller argues that Reinach's theory of representation is ultimately limited by his failure to connect it to a general account of legal personhood. As elsewhere, Reinach acknowledges that representation is intimately tied up with legal personality. But without a theory of legal personality, his theory of representation must necessarily be limited.

Olivier Massin, in 'The Ontology of Liberties: Reconciling Reinach and Hohfeld' situates Reinach alongside his more influential contemporary – Wesley Hohfeld. Working independently through their brief, contemporaneous lives in Germany and the United States, respectively, Massin points out many similarities in the legal ontologies of Reinach and Hohfeld – both sought to elucidate the obscure, essential conceptual substructure of legal reasoning, clarifying legal discourse at its atomistic base level. And in so doing, Reinach and Hohfeld settle on many of the same essential distinctions – between claim rights and liberty rights, between possession and ownership, between legal powers and legal rights, and more.

At the same time, Reinach and Hohfeld disagree significantly on the nature of legal liberties. Hohfeld claims such rights correspond to correlative 'no rights' held by others. Reinach rejects this – liberty rights, he claims, are *absolute* rights, which essentially lack correlatives of any kind. Massin argues that both theorists are on to something. Reinach is right, he suggests, insofar as *some* liberties are absolute and uncorrelative. But he is wrong that all are – and as Hohfeld argued, Massin contends that *some* liberties do indeed have no-right correlatives. Taking Reinach and Hohfeld together, in other words, helps illuminate a thorough ontology of liberty rights that accommodates both relative and absolute liberties.

I.4 REINACH AND LEGAL CONCEPTS

Reinach's most famous philosophical position is his discovery of social acts. His most controversial is metaphysical realism about legal concepts. But neither of these positions occupies most of Reinach's time and attention in the *Foundations*. Most of the *Foundations* is dedicated to careful analysis of specific legal concepts – promise, claim, obligation, property, lien, enactment, and more. To take Reinach seriously, then, is not merely to interrogate his phenomenological realism, nor to situate him among contemporary currents in legal theory. It is, at least in part, to *do* what he did – to theorize about the law and its concepts along the lines that he does, inspired by some aspect of his analysis, whether what he has to say about particular legally significant concepts, or guided by his commitment to concepts' realism and primitive atomism.

The chapters in Part III do just that – tackling a particular legal concept either directly on Reinach's terms, or in a method broadly inspired by his. Stephan Kirste, in 'Adolf Reinach and Gerhart Husserl on the Foundations of Legal Phenomenology and the Temporality of Law', offers a thorough examination of the legal concept of time in Reinach's work as compared to that of Gerhart Husserl, son of Edmund and a later phenomenologist. In so doing, Kirste reveals important similarities and disagreements between Reinach's Pre-War Realist Phenomenology, and Gerhart Husserl's transcendental idealist perspective drawing on the later work of his father and of Heidegger. As Kirste points out, Reinach believed that legal concepts like promises, in their general form, are timeless and *a priori*, but that particular instances of promises, and the claims and obligations they give rise to, are inherently temporal and in a peculiar way under-appreciated in philosophy – they are entities that come into being with the promise, and disappear from the world with its fulfilment or waiver.

According to Kirste, this suggests that Reinach understood that the law to some extent relies on its own internal temporal structure, in principle distinct from the general flow of chronological time – a promise creates its own 'extended present' within which it could be accepted. Working within the idealist phenomenology of later decades, untethered from a timeless *a priori* realm, Gerhart Husserl took a similar notion further, suggesting that law, a work of will of the population, expresses its own abstract temporal consciousness in the decisions of particular judges. But Kirste argues that neither Reinach nor Gerhart Husserl fully appreciated the extent to which law indeed regulates its own past, present, and future, and thus creates its own temporality, each offering a less-than-complete theory of the relationship between law and time.

In 'How to Make Gifts with Words', Emma Tieffenbach employs Reinach's theory of social speech acts and his analysis of promise to evaluate theories of gifts. Analytic philosophers disagree over basic questions about the nature of gifts. Does the recipient of a gift need to know about a gift for it to occur? Does the recipient have to accept the gift? Does a physical transfer have to occur? Some other kind of transfer? Reinach never treated gift in any detail, but his general theory and its application to promises suggests that a declaration that the gifter is (thereby) transferring ownership is required. No act on the part of the recipient is needed, although a recipient can by an affirmative act prevent the gift from being completed.

A gift need not be taken up but can be refused. Key to this analysis is the idea that the transfer is of ownership, not of the thing itself.

This 'Ownership View of Gift' that Tieffenbach endorses carries a number of advantages. Although in common parlance gifts are treated as transfers of things, a close look at gifts in Reinachian fashion reveals that the structure of gifts is based on transfer of ownership. Gifts are not bilateral even though they can be blocked by the recipient. Moreover, linguistic usage and borderline scenarios reveal that uptake is not required and that it is ownership that is transferred. Moreover, Tieffenbach suggests that her view helps explain the surprisingly wide variety of speech acts that can result in such a transfer of ownership. These include the familiar speech acts involving transfer of ownership directly but also embrace the granting of a right to revoke a promise to pay for a thing and the waiver of a right to an amount of money owed for a thing. That such specific insights into gifts flow from a close look into the metaphysics of the social speech acts involved in gifting is quite Reinachian in spirit.

In 'So Close and Yet So Far: Reinach and Gilbert on Promises', Alessandro Salice and Olivier Massin compare Reinach's theory of promises to the more recent theory of Margaret Gilbert, noting striking similarities, but ultimately endorsing Reinach's theory as stronger where they come apart. Like Reinach, and unlike most of today's theorists, Gilbert maintains that promises, even immoral ones, inevitably give rise to obligations, that these obligations are non-moral and relational, and that theories of promissory obligation that seek to ground the binding character of promise in expectation, trust, or other functional concerns are off on the wrong foot. Unlike Reinach, however, who insists that promise is an *a priori* primitive that by its nature generates obligations, disclaiming the need for further grounding, Gilbert situates promises as a form of joint commitment – the promisor and promisee jointly committing to endorse as a body the promisor's plan of action.

For a variety of reasons, Salice and Massin argue that Gilbert's account is not a plausible theory of our ordinary concept of promise. It suggests, for example, that a promise is something a promisor and promisee do together, and for which a promisee bears some moral responsibility, while we generally think of promises as an act of a promisor themselves, for which they bear sole responsibility. The failure of Gilbert's account in these ways, notwithstanding its admirable solicitude for taking ordinary social concepts seriously, Salice and Massin maintain, suggests that Reinach's view might be on to something – perhaps the concept of promise is simply a primitive that generates obligations by virtue of its very nature, such that accounts that seek further grounding for that fact are doomed to failure.

Finally, Crescente Molina, in 'The Conceptual Foundations of Contract Formation', offers a novel account of contract formation in a thoroughly Reinachian spirit. Molina starts from the premise – the 'Necessity of Agreement Axiom' – that contracts presuppose the mutual assent of at least two people to some sort of agreement. Taking this widely accepted intuition about the essential nature of contract, Molina argues, expands our account of the possibilities of contract formation. While the traditionally taught ritual of 'offer' and 'acceptance' is surely *one* way parties can reach the required agreement, this traditional framing obscures another – 'contractual subscription', or agreement to a pre-existing set of legal entailments in legislation, custom, or elsewhere.

Assuming the Necessity of Agreement Axiom, Molina considers the kinds of social acts that can or must constitute contracts. He suggests, contrary to the longstanding assumption of the common law world, that the social act of promise is the wrong place to start. Bare promises can *unilaterally* generate obligations. If a promise is to create a bilateral agreement, as demanded by the Necessity of Agreement Axiom, it must be in a particular form – a *promissory offer* that by its terms only becomes binding on acceptance. It is not the social act of promising *simpliciter*, then, but only a particular species, that could give rise to contract. But Molina, indeed, thinks the Necessity of Agreement Axiom pushes us even further – to recognizing that contracts could be formed without any social act at all. In some cases of contractual subscription, Molina holds, a contract comes into being with only *internal* assent; assent that fulfills the Necessity of Agreement Axiom, but is not a *social* act, in Reinachian terms, at all.

BIBLIOGRAPHY

Auer M (Chapter 1, this volume)

Austin JL, *How to Do Things with Words* (JO Urmson and Marina Sbisà, eds, 2d edn Harvard University Press 1975)

Balganesh S and G Parchomovsky, 'Structure and Value in the Common Law' (2015) 163 University of Pennsylvania L Rev 1241

Baltzer-Jaray K (Chapter 4, this volume)

'Bogged Down in Ontologism and Realism. Reinach's Phenomenological Realist Response to Husserl', in RKB Parker (ed), *The Idealism-Realism Debate among Edmund Husserl's Early Followers and Critics* (Springer 2021)

'Happy 104th Wedding Anniversary, Adolf & Anna!', https://reinach.ophen.org/2016/09/15/happy-104th-wedding-anniversary-adolf-anna/

'Adolf Reinach Is Not a Platonist' (2009) 13 Symposium: Canadian J Continental Philosophy 100

Brewer S, 'On the Possibility of Necessity in Legal Argument: A Dilemma for Holmes and Dewey' (2000) 34 John Marshall L Rev 9

Cairns D, *Conversations with Husserl and Fink* (Nijhoff 1976)

Calabresi G and AD Melamed, 'Property Rules, Liability Rules, and Inalienability: One View of the Cathedral' (1972) 85 Harvard L Rev 1089

Centrone S, *Logic and Philosophy of Mathematics in the Early Husserl* (Springer 2010)

Cohen FS, 'Transcendental Nonsense and the Functional Approach' (1935) 35 Columbia L Rev 809

Coleman JL, 'The Practice of Corrective Justice' (1995) 37 Arizona L Rev 15

'Truth and Objectivity in Law' (1995) 1 Legal Theory 33

Crosby JF, 'A Brief Biography of Adolf Reinach', in J Crosby (ed), *The Apriori Foundations of the Civil Law: Along with the Lecture 'Concerning Phenomenology'* (Ontos Verlag 2012)

'Adolf Reinach's Discovery of the Social Acts' (1983) 3 Aletheia 143

D'Onfro D, 'Contract-Wrapped Property' (2024) 137 Harvard L Rev 1061
Duxbury N, 'The Legal Philosophy of Adolf Reinach' (1991) 77 Archives for Philosophy of Law and Social Philosophy 314
Dworkin R, *Law's Empire* (Harvard University Press 1986)
Fried C, *Contract as Promise: A Theory of Contractual Obligation* (2nd ed Oxford University Press 2015)
Gardner J, *From Personal Life to Private Law* (Oxford University Press 2018)
'What Is Tort Law For? Part I. The Place of Corrective Justice' (2011) 30 Law and Philosophy 1
Gold AS, JCP Goldberg, DB Kelly, E Sherwin and HE Smith (eds), *The Oxford Handbook of the New Private Law* (Oxford University Press 2020)
Gold AS and HE Smith (Chapter 5, this volume)
Goldberg JCP and BC Zipursky, 'Torts as Wrongs' (2010) 88 Texas L Rev 917
Hart HLA, *The Concept of Law* (3rd ed Oxford University Press 2012)
Hershovitz S, 'The End of Jurisprudence' (2015) 124 Yale LJ 882
Husserl E, 'Obituary notice (entire)', in J Crosby (ed), *The Apriori Foundations of the Civil Law: Along with the Lecture 'Concerning Phenomenology'* (Ontos Verlag 2012) xi, originally published in (1919) 13 Kant-Studien 147
Ideas: General Introduction to Pure Phenomenology (originally published 1913) (Routledge 2012)
Logical Investigations, Vol. I (tr. JN Findlay) (Routledge 2001)
Edmund Husserl Briefwechsel, Vol. 2 Die Münchener Phänomenologen (Elisabeth Schuhmann and Karl Schuhmann, eds, Kluwer 1994)
Briefe an Roman Ingarden (Nijhoff 1968)
von Jhering R, 'In the Heaven for Legal Concepts: A Fantasy' (tr. Charlotte L Levy) (1985) 58 Temple L Q 799
Jiménez F, 'A Formalist Theory of Contract Law Adjudication' (2021) 2020 Utah L Rev 1121
Kaehler L (Chapter 3, this volume)
Kennedy D, 'Form and Substance in Private Law Adjudication' (1976) 89 Harvard L Rev 168
Llewellyn KN, *The Common Law Tradition: Deciding Appeals* (Little, Brown & Co. 1960)
Loidolt S, *Einführung in die Rechtsphänomenologie* (Mohr Siebeck 2010)
Lüttenberg DJ, 'Über das Sein des Sollens – Die rechtlichen Gebilde in der Rechtsphänomenologie Adolf Reinachs' (2020) 11 Zeitschrift für rechtswissenschaftliche Forschung 9
Massa M, 'Property and *Nuda Potestas* as Constitutions of Reinach's Philosophy of Law (2020) 90 Folia Iuridica 75
Massin O, 'The Metaphysics of Ownership: A Reinachian Account' (2017) 27 Axiomathes 577
McFarlane B and R Stevens, 'The Nature of Equitable Property' (2010) 4 Journal of Equity 1
Merrill TW and HE Smith, 'Optimal Standardization in the Law of Property: The *Numerus Clausus* Principle' (2000) 110 Yale LJ 1
Miller PB (Chapter 7, this volume)
'The New Formalism in Private Law' (2021) 66 American Journal of Jurisprudence 175
Mitscherling J, T DiTommaso, and A Nayad, *The Author's Intention* (Lexington 2004)
Mulligan K (ed), *Speech Act and Sachverhalt: Reinach and the Foundations of Realist Phenomenology* (Nijhoff 1987)
Parker RKB (ed), *The Idealism-Realism Debate among Edmund Husserl's Early Followers and Critics* (Springer 2021)
Paulsen SL, 'Demystyifying Reinach's Legal Theory', in K Mulligan (ed), *Speech Act and Sachverhalt: Reinach and the Foundations of Realist Phenomenology* (Kluwer 1987)

Peller G, 'The Metaphysics of American Law' (1985) 73 California L Rev 1151
Purnhagen K, 'Grundlagen der Rechtsphänomenologie – Eine kritische Darstellung der Rechtsphänomenologie von Adolf Reinach und Wilhelm Schapp zu den apriorischen Grundlagen des Privatrechts' (2009) 31 JURA – Juristische Ausbildung 661
Reinach A, *Gesammelte Schriften* (Niemayer 1951)
'The Apriori Foundations of the Civil Law' (tr. JF Crosby) (1983) 3 Aletheia 1–142, reprinted in A Reinach, *The Apriori Foundations of the Civil Law: Along with the lecture 'Concerning Phenomenology'* (JF Crosby ed, Ontos Verlag 2012), originally published as A Reinach, Die apriorischen Grundlagen des bürgerlichen Rechtes, 1(2) *Jahrbuch für Philosophie und phänomenologische Forschung* (Max Niemeyer 1913), 685–847
'On the Concept of Causality in the Criminal Law' (tr. B Brogaard) (2009) 1 Libertarian Papers 1
Ripstein A, 'Private Order and Public Justice: Kant and Rawls' (2006) 92 Virginia L Rev 1391
S. Pac. Co. v. Jensen, 244 U.S. 205, 222 (1917) (Holmes, J., dissenting)
Salice A, 'The Phenomenology of the Munich and Göttingen Circles', in EN Zalta (ed), *Stanford Encyclopedia of Philosophy* (online 2020)
Schauer F, 'The Limited Domain of the Law' (2004) 90 Virginia L Rev 1909
Schaus S, 'A Simple Model of Torts and Moral Wrongs' (2022) 97 Notre Dame L Rev 1029
Schuhmann K and B Smith, 'Adolf Reinach: An Intellectual Biography', in K Mulligan (ed), *Speech Act and Sachverhalt: Reinach and the Foundations of Realist Phenomenology* (Nijhoff 1987)
Seron D, 'Adolf Reinach's Philosophy of Logic', in B Leclercq, S Richard, and D Seron (eds), *Objects and Pseudo-Objects: Ontological Deserts and Jungles from Brentano to Carnap* (De Gruyter 2015)
Shiffrin SV, 'The Divergence of Contract and Promise' (2007) 120 Harvard L Rev 708
Singer JW, 'Legal Realism Now' (1988) 76 California Law Review 465
Smith B, 'Realistic Phenomenology', in L Embree (ed), *Encyclopedia of Phenomenology* (Springer 1997) 58
'Adolf Reinach: An Annotated Bibliography' in K Mulligan (ed), *Speech Act and Sachverhalt: Reinach and the Foundations of Realist Phenomenology* (Nijhoff 1987)
'On the Cognition of States of Affairs', in K Mulligan (ed), *Speech Act and Sachverhalt: Reinach and the Foundations of Realist Phenomenology* (Nijhoff 1987)
Smith HE, 'On the Economy of Concepts in Property' (2012) 160 University of Pennsylvania L Rev 2097
'Property as the Law of Things' (2012) 125 Harvard L Rev 1691
Solan LM, 'Contract as Agreement,' (2007) 83 Notre Dame L Rev 353
Spiegelbert H, *The Phenomenological Movement* (3rd ed Springer 1994)
Steel S (Chapter 6, this volume)
Stone R, 'Private Liability Without Wrongdoing' (2023) 73 University of Toronto LJ 53
Toomey J (Chapter 2, this volume)
'Property's Boundaries' (2023) 109 Virginia L Rev 131
Tuchman BW, *The Guns of August: The Outbreak of World War I* (Penguin 1994)
Waldron J, '"Transcendental Nonsense" and System in the Law' (2000) 100 Columbia L Rev 16
Weinrib EJ, *The Idea of Private Law* (Harvard University Press 1995)
Wolenski J, 'Adolf Reinach, Negative States of Affairs and the Concept of Omission' (2020) 90 Folia Iuridica 5

PART I

Reinach and His Method

1

Promising, Owning, Enacting

Adolf Reinach's Phenomenology of Legal Speech Acts

*Marietta Auer**

1.1 INTRODUCTION

If the reader of this chapter were asked to single out the most-disputed or least-understood features of contemporary private law, two good responses – for common and civil law backgrounds alike – come to mind. First, how does the binding power of contract arise out of a promise? In the common law of contracts, the promise classically needs to be backed by consideration in order to become binding for the promisor, even if the consideration is only nominal, for example, a dollar or a cent. But what is the deeper meaning of the consideration requirement beyond this proverbial 'peppercorn theory'?[1] If the binding power of the contract is not derived from the promise, where does it come from? The 'will theory'? Reliance? Equity? Morality?[2] Or, to argue from the other side, as law and economics scholars have proposed under the provocative heading of 'efficient breach', why shouldn't the parties to a contract simply break free of its bonds if a better, more efficient opportunity for contracting arises?[3] These questions are indicative of the ongoing debates in contract theory in the common law world. But the civil law of contracts

* I am grateful for comments from my co-editors Paul B Miller, Henry Smith and James Toomey as well as for comments from James Thompson on two earlier drafts.

1 See, e.g., Arthur L Corbin, 'The Effect of Options on Consideration' (1925) 34 Yale LJ 571; Lon L Fuller, 'Consideration and Form' (1941) 41 Colum L Rev 799, 820. For the substantive bases of contract liability, see ibid 806–813.

2 See, e.g., Charles Fried, *Contract as Promise: A Theory of Contractual Obligation* (2nd edn, Oxford University Press 2015); Anthony T Kronman, 'A New Champion for the Will Theory' (1981) 91 Yale LJ 404.

3 The wide range of views on the topic of 'efficient breach' cannot be exhausted here. See initially Robert L Birmingham, 'Breach of Contract, Damage Measures, and Economic Efficiency' (1970) 24 Rutgers L Rev 273. A recent variant is the 'dual performance hypothesis' proposed by Daniel Markovits and Alan Schwartz; see Daniel Markovits and Alan Schwartz, 'The Myth of Efficient Breach: New Defenses of the Expectation Interest' (2011) 97 Va L Rev 1939.

doesn't fare much better. While it avoids the quandaries of the consideration doctrine by founding the binding power of the contract on mutual declarations of will, it is nevertheless faced with the same problem: Why are contractual parties bound to what they consented to do?[4]

Second, as if the intricacies of contract law weren't enough, there is property law and the century-old debate whether property should be conceived as an absolute right to a thing or as a mere 'bundle of sticks' of relative rights against other persons.[5] As simple as this restatement of the notorious 'bundle theory' of property may sound, it is still one of the focal points of common law debates on property. The antipodes of 'thing' versus 'bundle' recur across the theoretical spectrum from legal doctrine through law and economics to political theory and legal philosophy.[6] Here again, the civil law seems to offer an easy way out, since its codified structure still reflects the ancient Roman dualism between *rights in rem* and *rights in personam*, thus preserving the structural divide between rights to things and rights against persons within present-day doctrine.[7] Yet, the preservation of an ancient systematic ideal can hardly count as a sufficient reason to insulate civil law property against the structural challenge posed by the bundle theory. But what follows from this? Is the German Civil Code simply wrong in conceptually separating rights to things from obligations? Or might there be some deeper reason for this distinction that could, in turn, help common law property theorists deal with the 'bundle challenge'?

This chapter aims to answer these questions by reconstructing Adolf Reinach's phenomenological theory of private law as developed in *The Apriori Foundations of the Civil Law*[8] against the dual background of the German civil law tradition, wherein Reinach

4 On the formation of contracts through mutual declarations of will, see §§ 145ff BGB [Bürgerliches Gesetzbuch] (German Civil Code, 1900). For theories of the binding power of contracts, see, e.g., Franz Bydlinski, *Privatautonomie und objektive Grundlagen des verpflichtenden Rechtsgeschäftes* (Springer 1967); Claus-Wilhelm Canaris, *Die Vertrauenshaftung im deutschen Privatrecht* (CH Beck 1971); Reinhard Singer, *Selbstbestimmung und Verkehrsschutz im Recht der Willenserklärungen* (CH Beck 1995); Claus-Wilhelm Canaris, 'Wandlungen des Schuldvertragsrechts – Tendenzen zu seiner "Materialisierung"' (2000) 200 Archiv für die civilistische Praxis 273, 279–280.

5 See, e.g., James E Penner, 'The Bundle of Rights Picture of Property' (1996) 43 UCLA L Rev 711.

6 See, e.g., Thomas W Merrill and Henry E Smith, 'What Happened to Property in Law and Economics?' (2001) 111 Yale LJ 357; Henry E Smith, 'Property as the Law of Things' (2012) 125 Harvard L Rev 1691; Joseph W Singer, 'Property as the Law of Democracy' (2014) 63 Duke LJ 1287.

7 The German Civil Code preserves this dualism, inter alia, in the conceptual distinction between the law of obligations (*Schuldrecht*) and property law (*Sachenrecht*). For the common law discussion, see Wesley N Hohfeld, 'Fundamental Legal Conceptions as Applied in Judicial Reasoning' (1917) 26 Yale LJ 710; Albert Kocourek, 'Rights in Rem' (1920) 68 U Penn L Rev 322; Arthur L Corbin, 'Jural Relations and Their Classification' (1921) 30 Yale LJ 226; Albert Kocourek, 'Polarized and Unpolarized Legal Relations' (1921) 9 Kentucky LJ 131.

8 Adolf Reinach, 'The Apriori Foundations of the Civil Law' (John F Crosby tr, 1983) 3 Aletheia 1, reprinted in Adolf Reinach, *The Apriori Foundations of the Civil Law Along with the Lecture 'Concerning Phenomenology'* (John F Crosby ed, Ontos Verlag 2012), originally published as Adolf Reinach, 'Die apriorischen Grundlagen des bürgerlichen Rechtes', in 1(2) *Jahrbuch für*

received his legal training, and modern language philosophy. Both viewpoints complement each other and will prove equally indispensable to reading Reinach. It is impossible to overlook the deep influence of German private law doctrine on Reinach's theory. Thus, to gain access to Reinach's thought, a promising path is to assess his theoretical claims against the backdrop of the civil law tradition. On this basis, the cultural as well as linguistic situatedness of some of Reinach's claims of apriority will become apparent, thus making his theory a valuable resource for cross-system theory comparisons. Yet, such a doctrinal reading of Reinach alone obviously cannot do justice to his original philosophical endeavour. Building on existing work, this chapter thus brings Reinach's phenomenology into further dialogue with modern language philosophy.[9] The following sections will take up these issues in greater depth. Section 1.2 will explore Reinach's concept of a priori foundations of private law and will use John L Austin's concept of 'performative verbs'[10] to understand it as a phenomenology of the performative foundations of legal language. Sections 1.3, 1.4 and 1.5 will, in turn, explore the three most important performative verbs in Reinach's theory against the background of their original etymologies and legal connotations in German private law: 'promising', 'owning' and 'enacting'. I conclude by arguing that what Reinach has to offer today's private law theorists is a slim and remarkably timeless theory of linguistically defined social acts as the basis of legal meaning. This theory merits further consideration, even if the question of its potentially stronger ontological or epistemological readings is left open.

1.2 REINACH'S A PRIORI AS A PHENOMENOLOGY OF PERFORMATIVE LEGAL LANGUAGE

The story of Reinach's brief career and untimely death is largely a story of what could have been the path of German legal philosophy had it not been for the

Philosophie und phänomenologische Forschung (Max Niemeyer 1913), 685–847 [hereinafter Reinach, 'Foundations']. References to the German original are made to Adolf Reinach, 'Die apriorischen Grundlagen des bürgerlichen Rechtes', in Karl Schuhmann and Barry Smith (eds), *Adolf Reinach. Sämtliche Werke. Textkritische Ausgabe in 2 Bänden* vol 1 (Philosophia 1989) [hereinafter Reinach, 'Grundlagen'].

9 John L Austin, *How to Do Things with Words* (James O Urmson and Marina Sbisà eds, 2nd edn, Harvard University Press 1975); John R Searle, *Speech Acts. An Essay in the Philosophy of Language* (Cambridge University Press 1969). For interpretations of Reinach in the context of speech act theory, see, e.g., John F Crosby, 'Adolf Reinach's Discovery of the Social Acts' (1983) Aletheia III 143; Kevin Mulligan, 'Promisings and other Social Acts: Their Constituents and Structure', in Kevin Mulligan (ed), *Speech Act and Sachverhalt. Reinach and the Foundations of Realist Phenomenology* (Kluwer 1987); Klaus Hoffmann, 'Reinach and Searle on Promising: A Comparison', in ibid; Jean-Louis Gardies, 'Adolf Reinach and the Analytic Foundations of Social Acts', in ibid; James M Brown, 'Reinach on Representative Acts', in ibid; Barry Smith, 'On the Cognition of States of Affairs', in ibid; Armin Burkhard, *Soziale Akte, Sprechakte und Textillokutionen. A. Reinachs Rechtsphilosophie und die moderne Linguistik* (Max Niemeyer 1986); John F Crosby, 'Speech Act Theory and Phenomenology', in Reinach, 'Foundations' (n 8) 167.

10 See Austin (n 9) 151–164.

atrocities of the twentieth century.[11] Reinach, born into an affluent Jewish family in Mainz on 23 December 1883, enrolled at the law faculty of the University of Munich in 1901, but ended up spending most of his time studying philosophy with Theodor Lipps. At that time one of the leading German philosophers, Lipps was committed to employing the newly developed methods of psychology to the philosophy of mind. Reinach, however, did not stay long within this intellectual circle. After the completion of his dissertation in 1904, and as part of a migration of students later known as the 'Munich invasion of Göttingen',[12] he moved to Göttingen and in 1909 obtained his *habilitation* with Edmund Husserl, Lipps' anti-psychological opponent. In 1913, Reinach was among the founders of Husserl's *Yearbook for Philosophy and Phenomenological Research*, in which *The Apriori Foundations of the Civil Law* appeared in the same year,[13] four years prior to the author's untimely death on the battlefields of World War I outside Diksmuide in Flanders on 16 November 1917.

Though a constant temptation, it is nevertheless pointless to speculate about what Reinach might have achieved had he lived to develop a mature scholarly body of work out of his youthful first attempt at legal philosophy. The theoretical path Reinach explores is remarkably different from virtually all other paths of legal philosophy or jurisprudence that came to fruition in the twentieth century and eventually went on to form the core of the discourse. At the historical point in time when Reinach was writing, there were three main epistemic paradigms within jurisprudence to choose from.[14] First, legal positivism, analyticism and a non-philosophical 'general theory of law' flourished both in England and on the continent. A second, opposing tendency was the simultaneous movement towards free law, jurisprudence of interests, legal realism and sociological jurisprudence. Third and finally, there was the idealist counter-position to the latter expressed in value philosophies, renewed natural law theories and an idealistically turned Neo-Kantianism or Neo-Hegelianism. Reinach's legal phenomenology, however, did not fit into any of these camps.[15] He posited the extra-legal existence of legal

[11] On Reinach's biography, see his self-testimonies and the editor's report in Schuhmann and Smith (eds), *Adolf Reinach. Sämtliche Werke* (n 8) vol 1, 636; vol 2, 665–672, 713; Karl Schuhmann and Barry Smith, 'Adolf Reinach: An Intellectual Biography', in Kevin Mulligan (ed), *Speech Act and Sachverhalt. Reinach and the Foundations of Realist Phenomenology* (Kluwer 1987).

[12] Schuhmann and Smith, 'Adolf Reinach: An Intellectual Biography' (n 11) 8.

[13] For the editions used here, see n 8. For the publication history and original sources, see the editor's report in Schuhmann and Smith (eds), *Adolf Reinach. Sämtliche Werke* (n 8) vol 2, 676–679.

[14] On the twentieth-century history of legal epistemologies, see Marietta Auer, 'A Genealogy of Private Law Epistemologies', in Thilo Kuntz and Paul B Miller (eds), *Methodology in Private Law Theory: Between New Private Law and Rechtsdogmatik* (Oxford University Press 2024).

[15] On Reinach's legal theory, see Stanley L Paulson, 'Demystifying Reinach's Legal Theory', in Kevin Mulligan (ed), *Speech Act and Sachverhalt. Reinach and the Foundations of Realist Phenomenology* (Kluwer 1987); Karl Larenz, *Methodenlehre der Rechtswissenschaft* (6th edn,

concepts without committing to positivism, realism or idealism. His ontology of legal objects was neither merely nominalist, as legal realism would have it, nor idealist in the sense that it implied a transcendental a priori of legal morality. Yet, Reinach's rejection of a moral a priori of the law did not commit him to legal positivism as a theory of jurisprudence either. On the contrary, he emphatically defended the independence between what he perceived as the a priori foundations of private law and the positive law:[16]

> We shall show that the structures (*Gebilde*) which one has generally called specifically legal (*spezifisch rechtlich*) have a being on their own just as much as numbers, trees, or houses, that this being is independent of its being grasped by men, that it is in particular independent of all positive law. It is not only false but ultimately meaningless to call legal entities and structures creations of the positive law, just as meaningless as it would be to call the founding of the German empire or some other historical event a creation of the historical science. We really do find what one has so emphatically denied: the positive law *finds* the legal concepts which enter into it; *in absolutely no way does it produce them*.[17]

What is, then, the essence of Reinach's legal a priori? The phenomenological shibboleth 'back to the things themselves'[18] demands going back to the things *as* they are given to us in experience. According to the phenomenological view, the object *itself* – and not just its representation – becomes accessible to the perceiving consciousness. Consciousness is not *in* the mind; it performs itself through being conscious of something *other* than itself.[19] In Reinach's phenomenology of law, apriority thus serves to describe the irreducible structures of human consciousness as the basis of cognitive acts, to the extent they are foundational for legal meaning. By building his concept of apriority on the perception of legally foundational cognitive acts, Reinach arrives at the contention that a priori foundations of the law in fact *exist* and can be grasped as an immediate object of phenomenological perception. But what are legally foundational cognitive acts? This point represents a

Springer 1991) 111–113; Neil Duxbury, 'The Legal Philosophy of Adolf Reinach' (1991) 77 ARSP 314 (part 1), 466 (part 2); Andreas Funke, *Allgemeine Rechtslehre als juristische Strukturtheorie* (Mohr Siebeck 2004) 37–38.

[16] For further discussion, see infra Section 1.5 at n 100 and accompanying text.

[17] Reinach, 'Foundations' (n 8) 4.

[18] Adolf Reinach, 'Über Phänomenologie' (1914), in Schuhmann and Smith (eds), *Adolf Reinach. Sämtliche Werke* (n 8) vol 1, 538; see also Anthony J Steinbock, 'Back to the Things Themselves' (1997) 20 Human Studies 127. On Reinach's phenomenology, see John F Crosby, 'Adolf Reinach's Discovery of the Social Acts' (1983) Aletheia III 143; Kimberly Baltzer-Jaray, 'Phenomenological Jurisprudence: A Reinterpretation of Reinach's Jahrbuch Essay', in J Edward Hackett and J Aaron Simmons (eds), *Phenomenology for the Twenty-First Century* (Palgrave Macmillan 2016); Kimberly Baltzer-Jaray, 'Bogged Down in Ontologism and Realism: The Phenomenology of Adolf Reinach' in Rodney K B Parker (ed), *The Idealism-Realism Debate among Edmund Husserl's Early Followers and Critics* (Springer 2021).

[19] Edmund Husserl, *Formal and Transcendental Logic* § 94 (D Cairns trans, Springer 1969).

theoretical crossroads from which several possible interpretations of Reinach's phenomenology emanate.

A thick metaphysical reading of Reinach implies a commitment to the epistemological and ontological premises of phenomenology. At the very least, the phenomenological unity of transcendence and experience demands a theory of consciousness that reflects an objective reality beyond individual perception – a reality governed by structural laws independent of the psychic constitution of the human mind. Such structural laws exist; the laws of logic provide an example. With Edmund Husserl, the problem of phenomenology can thus be reformulated as follows: Are the laws of logic a function of human psychology, or is human psychology, on the contrary, a function of the laws of logic? Reinach, siding with Husserl against his early academic mentor Theodor Lipps in this core question of the *fin-de-siècle Psychologismusstreit*, clearly insisted on the latter, emphasising the logical as well as ontological priority of the elementary structures of consciousness.[20] Yet, this reading will hardly convince an anti-metaphysical audience versed in the legal theories of the late twentieth and early twenty-first centuries. But Reinach does not actually need a final answer to the psychologism challenge in order to make a philosophically meaningful statement about the foundations of the law. Another plausible reading of his theory avoids the baggage of philosophical phenomenology by restricting Reinach's claim to a proto-language philosophy of the law. On this – much slimmer – reading, the core of Reinach's theory lies in the simple claim that cognitive acts are, at least in many cases if not *pro tanto*, social acts performed through language. Reinach's a priori thus translates into a phenomenology of the performative foundations of legal language. That the law is, generally speaking, a linguistic social praxis is all one needs to know in order to grasp the essence of its foundations.

This is where Reinach's phenomenology lends itself to an interpretation along the lines of modern speech act theory.[21] Half a century prior to J L Austin's *How to Do Things with Words*, Reinach had already conceptualised his core concept of the 'social act', defined as a 'spontaneous act in need of being heard',[22] in terms of a proto-Austinian performative utterance. Indeed, some parallels between the speech act theory developed by mid twentieth-century philosophers of language, on the one hand, and Reinach's theory of linguistically defined social acts as the legal a priori, on the other, are so striking that they raise the question of a direct influence of Reinach on Austin.[23] Where Reinach conceptualises legal acts as essentially social acts and other-directed utterances 'in need of being heard', Austin distinguishes

[20] See Edmund Husserl, *Logische Untersuchungen* vol 1, §§ 17–20 (Elmar Holenstein ed, Springer 1975) 63–71. On this debate, see James Toomey, 'Darwin's Reinach', Chapter 2 in this volume.

[21] See n 9 for references.

[22] Reinach, 'Foundations' (n 8) 19–20: 'We designate the spontaneous acts which are in need of being heard, social acts. […] The turning to another subject and the need of being heard is absolutely essential for every social act.'

[23] On Reinach's potential influence on speech act theory, see Mulligan (n 9) 33–34 at n 5.

between declarative and performative utterances and points to the fundamental irreducibility of the performative character of the latter.[24] This is not to argue that all social acts constitute speech acts, that all speech acts qualify as social acts, or that all legal acts necessarily presuppose either speech acts or Reinachian social acts. If we put aside the considerable theoretical differences,[25] there is nonetheless a significant overlap between the three groups of acts, which makes it a fruitful enterprise to use Austin's speech act theory as an interpretive aide when coming to terms with Reinach's phenomenology.

Two features of Austin's theory appear particularly well suited to illuminate Reinach's legal theory. First, Austin's distinction between the truth conditions for declarative and performative utterances has direct implications for assessing the binding power of legal acts independently of their truth value. While declarative utterances can be true or false, performative utterances, according to Austin, may only 'succeed' or 'fail', that is, be 'happy' or 'unhappy'.[26] For Austin, happiness or unhappiness thus replaces truth or falsehood in the realm of performative (or illocutionary) speech acts. One way to read this insight is as a restatement of the non-naturalist metaethical position that the truth criteria applicable to statements of natural facts do not apply to moral statements, or, for that matter, to the assessment of legal acts. But Austin's insight goes even further than this by pointing to the pervasive power of the social performance of normativity, which supplants and supervenes natural laws even where they seem to govern. Reinach formulates a remarkably similar intuition in rejecting the classical project of natural law while, at the same time, rescuing it in the form of a phenomenology of social performativity. Thus, for Reinach, it is not the eternal truth of contractualism but the performative happiness of the very act of contracting that constitutes its normative power:

> When Hobbes and other natural law philosophers posit contracts and derive from them claims, obligations, and other legal consequences, they are altogether in the right. For these consequences are grounded, as we have shown, *in the essence of the performed acts.*[27]

Second, it is no accident that Reinach uses the example of contracting to illustrate his more general point. As we will see shortly, the binding contract, a result of the

[24] See Austin (n 9) 12: 'to *say* something is to *do* something; or [...] *by* saying or *in* saying something we are doing something'. Later in his work, Austin replaces the concept of performative utterances by the three-pronged distinction between locutionary, illocutionary and perlocutionary acts. Within this triad, the performative utterance is represented in the illocutionary act, defined as 'performance of an act *in* saying something as opposed to performance of an act *of* saying something'; see ibid 99–100.

[25] On the fundamentally different theoretical points of departure, see Mulligan (n 9) 31: Whereas Reinach's concept of language aims at a representation of the mind, Austin's ordinary language philosophy opposes logical conceptions of language.

[26] Austin (n 9) 133: '(1) the performative should be doing something as opposed to just saying something; and (2) the performative is happy or unhappy as opposed to true or false.'

[27] Reinach, 'Foundations' (n 8) 137; emphasis added.

performative power of mutual promises, comprises one of the centrepieces of Reinach's private law theory and opens up another avenue of productive dialogue with Austin's theory of performative verbs.[28] Reinach, too, relies on performative verbs such as 'commanding [...], requesting, warning, questioning, informing, answering and [...] still many other acts'[29] to describe the innumerable multitude of legally relevant performative social acts. The similarities to Austin, who distinguishes five classes of performative verbs constituting a plethora of social interactions, are striking. According to Austin's classification, 'verdictives' comprise all verbs that mean 'giving a verdict', such as convicting, acquitting, grading or assessing.[30] 'Exercitives' describe the exercise of powers or rights through appointing, voting, ordering, advising or warning, to which Reinach's case of 'enacting' also belongs.[31] Another important class for the matter at hand is 'commissives', which commit the speaker to doing something and, in particular, contain Reinach's central case of 'promising'.[32]

With this analytical background mastered, the stage is now set for a reconstruction of Reinach's private law theory along the lines of Austin's theory of performative verbs. In the following part, I will explore the performative phenomenology of the arguably most important concept in Reinach's theory – namely, 'promising' (*versprechen*). This concept is fundamental to Reinach's understanding of the performativity of contracts and the entire law of obligations.

1.3 PROMISING AND SPEAKING (*VER-SPRECHEN*)

The promise, or, more precisely, the social act of promising lies at the core of Reinach's theory of obligations. Reinach offers a comprehensive theory of the law of obligations centred on the act of promising. He identifies the promise as the exclusive origin of claims and obligations as relative rights within the bipolar legal relation between promisor and promisee. On this basis, Reinach draws several a priori conclusions for the structure of the law of obligations. He departs from the question whether the promise needs to be accepted in order to be binding, then offers an exposition of possible modes of termination for promises and obligations and concludes by addressing the fundamental problem of why promises are binding at all.

28 Austin (n 9) 151–164.

29 Reinach, 'Foundations' (n 8) 19–20.

30 Austin (n 9) 153–155.

31 ibid 155–157. For 'enacting', see infra Section 1.5 at n 95 and accompanying text.

32 ibid 157–160. For the sake of completeness, Austin's 'behabitives' indicate social behaviour and comprise verbs like apologising, congratulating or condoling, while 'expositives' refer to utterances in the course of a conversation: replying, arguing, assuming or postulating. See ibid 160–164.

Let us first examine Reinach's theory of promising as the source of obligation. For Reinach, 'it lies in the essence of this act [sc. promising] to bring forth claims and obligations.'[33] But why is this the case? And how can Reinach claim the apriority of the effect of promising – assuming it exists at all? The answer directly follows from Reinach's definition of the social act. As discussed above, the social act is performative precisely in its 'need of being heard', that is, in its linguistic other-directedness as such. This means that the question of how the obligation arises from the promise cannot be further reduced or permits any further analysis; indeed, it would be a mistake to search for further grounds of the obligation *beyond* the social performativity of the promise. Under the premise that the socially irreducible is identical with the a priori, it follows that the promise *as such* – as opposed to its content, the promisor's intention, or the 'informative expression of a resolution of will'[34] – is the decisive reason for the emergence of the obligation arising from the promise. Reinach particularly stresses the difference between a mere 'expression of intending', on the one hand, and the promise as 'an independent spontaneous act which in turning without, expresses itself',[35] on the other. He thus establishes a sharp distinction between 'intending' and 'promising' as the a priori basis of the legal distinction between a declaration of will as opposed to a promise by pointing to the incommensurable performativity of both acts. The upshot of this argument is a critique of the construction of the formation of contracts through matching declarations of will under the German Civil Code:[36]

> We now see clearly how thoroughly mistaken und untenable is the usual conception of promising as an expressing of intention or of will. An expression of will runs like this: I intend. If it is directed to someone, then it is an informing, which is indeed a social act but no act of promising. And of course it does not become a promise by being directed to the one who will profit from the intended action. Promising is neither intending nor the expression of intending; it is rather an independent spontaneous act which in turning without, expresses itself. [. . .] It is not – as one had thought – through impotent declarations of intention that relations of right are constituted but rather through the strictly apriori efficacy of the social acts.[37]

But is this argument, as Reinach contends, sufficient to establish the very act of promising as the a priori foundation of the law of obligations? The answer is that Reinach's argument is surprisingly efficient because it provides the best possible *irreducible* interpretation of the emanation of the obligation from the promise under

[33] Reinach, 'Foundations' (n 8) 26.
[34] ibid.
[35] ibid.
[36] §§ 145ff BGB; see also supra Section 1.1 at n 4. On Reinach's critique of the declaration of will as the basis of contract in the German Civil Code, see also infra Section 1.4 at n 90 and accompanying text.
[37] Reinach, 'Foundations' (n 8) 26.

the condition that promising exists as a practice in private law. But how do we know that this explanation of the obligatory power of the obligation is indeed irreducible? Here, no further argument can be given. But this is precisely the point where Reinach's philosophy reveals its striking modernity and ability to work on several levels apart from the thicker metaphysical assumptions of both phenomenology and language philosophy. In the reading proposed here, Reinach's a priori of promising essentially amounts to an application of Ockham's razor to contract theory, a discursive reduction that releases the latter from the search for further explanations for the binding power of contracts where none can be given.[38] Read this way, Reinach's argument closely resembles Wittgenstein's picture in the *Philosophical Investigations* of the spade turning upon reaching hard bedrock: 'Once I have exhausted the justifications, I have reached bedrock, and my spade is turned. Then I am inclined to say: "This is simply what I do."'[39] Reinach is also looking for the irreducible forms of law which neither require nor even allow for further definition or analysis. Apriority, for Reinach, neither requires transcendental conditions of knowledge or truth, nor priority of cognition over experience. It simply requires grasping the constituent, irreducible elements of human consciousness in the limited realm of legal acts – understanding the elements that, within the law, permit no further questioning. Having hit bedrock, the spade is turned and every further philosophical effort is rendered futile.

The next question Reinach raises is whether the promise needs to be accepted in order to be binding. His argument sets out from the observation that the concept of acceptance – another performative act – is ambiguous, if not polysemous. Reinach distinguishes no less than five meanings on what 'acceptance of an offer' could mean: (1) the outward expression of a positive response to the promise, irrespective of how it is performed; (2) the substantive content of the positive response; (3) the promisee's inner experience of 'saying yes'; (4) the outward expression of this inner acceptance; and finally, (5) the acceptance as 'a social act in its own right which is not reducible to an informing.'[40] These distinctions might at first glance seem captious. Yet, by introducing them, Reinach again highlights the crucial difference between the performative power of the promise as a speech act and the diverging

[38] Indeed, it is Reinach's conviction that weak philosophical thought exposes itself through the search for definitions where none can be given. See ibid 65: 'It is a sign of a philosophically misshapen mind to demand definitions where none are possible or have any value. We have characterized promising as a social act and have unfolded its distinctive presuppositions and effects. But what distinguishes promising as such from other social acts such as commanding or requesting, can indeed be seen (*erschauen*) and made evident to others, but it can no more be defined than one can define that which distinguishes red from other colors.' The quote continues by citing Descartes: 'perhaps one of the main errors which one can commit in the sciences [is] to try to define what can only be seen through itself.'

[39] Ludwig Wittgenstein, *Philosophical Investigations* § 217 (GEM Anscombe, PMS Hacker and J Schulte trans, PMS Hacker and J Schulte eds, 4th edn, Wiley-Blackwell 2009) 91. Interestingly, the argument is part of Wittgenstein's treatment of rule following.

[40] Reinach, 'Foundations' (n 8) 29.

construction of the binding contract in the positive law. A common fallacy among jurists familiar with the positive law of contracts, he argues, is to jump from the a priori performativity of the binding promise to the instrumental, a posteriori conclusion that there can be no binding contract without offer and acceptance:

> It is now clear how ambiguous is the question whether a promise needs to be accepted in order to be efficacious. In raising this question one is mainly thinking about the principle of the positive law that onesided acts of intention usually do not produce claim and obligation, and that some 'meeting of the minds' (*Willenseinigung*) is usually required, that is, to put it in our language, an agreement which is constituted by mutual social acts.[41]

Yet, such an identification between the binding power of promising and the rules for binding contracts would be rash, Reinach argues. The a priori performativity of the promise has nothing to do with the acceptance required for a binding contract under positive law. The promise should no more be confused with the contractual offer required by law than the acceptance can be reduced to the first, formal, contractual meaning stated above. Instead, Reinach is only interested in the question whether the speech act of promising needs to be accepted in the second, substantive sense in order to become efficacious, and he clearly answers this question in the negative: 'We are only asking whether *promising* needs a (material) acceptance in order to be efficacious.'[42] Since the acceptance of a promise cannot amount to another promise – due to the resulting infinite regress of mutual promising – the promise must carry its binding power in itself, that is, in the very performativity of promising:

> The accepting of a promise, however, cannot itself be a vowing or a promising. For then we would fall into a fallacious *regressus in infinitum*, inasmuch as this new promise would also need acceptance, etc. This also shows clearly how thoroughly different [*from promising*] the supposed analogates [*requesting and commanding*] are. With them it is a question of imposing an obligation on the addressee of the social act, and this of course really does need some acceptance. But in the case of promising the performer of the act assumes the obligation himself; on the side of the addressee there arise only claims, and we do not see why any social act on his part should be necessary. And so we are entitled to say: claim and obligation are grounded in promising as such.[43]

It goes without saying that this analytical conclusion – which excludes the possibility of a priori binding promises vis-à-vis third persons[44] – is incongruous with

41 ibid 30.

42 ibid.

43 ibid 31.

44 ibid: 'We put forward the apriori law that the claim can only arise in the person of the addressee. It is apriori impossible that a person to whom the promise is not directed should acquire a claim from it. Of course the positive law deals with contracts with third-party

both the civil law of obligations, which construes the binding power of contract through offer and acceptance, thus bypassing the concept of promise altogether, and with the common law and the doctrine of consideration. While Reinach does not deal with the doctrine of consideration, it follows from his treatment of the a priori binding power of the promise that the consideration doctrine can only be regarded a positive, a posteriori contingency of contract law and not as a part of its a priori essence.

From this understanding of the promise as binding per se and the one-sided emergence of obligation and claim right, Reinach deduces further consequences for the fulfilment, violation and termination of both promise and obligation. He distinguishes two ways of dissolving an obligation: realisation (i.e., fulfilment) and waiver. The natural – 'destined' – way of dissolving an obligation is 'the realization of its content by the promisor.'[45] If the realisation does not occur at the time and in the way it should, the claim is 'violated'. For Reinach, the violation – even in cases of impossibility – does not terminate the obligation; again, a consequence at odds with the doctrine of impossibility under the German Civil Code.[46] Other than realisation, the only other way to dissolve an obligation is through waiver by the promisee. Reinach takes pains to distinguish the waiver of the claim by the addressee from the revocation of the promise itself through the promisor. Whereas the waiver 'is grounded immutably in the essence of the claim',[47] the revocation requires 'a legal capacity or power (*rechtliches Können*)'[48] that can only be conferred on the promisor by the promisee. Reinach describes this granting of the legal power to revoke as a separate social act that necessarily cannot be a promise. A promise would only create another obligation for the promisee to waive the claim but does not confer any immediate power on the promisor to revoke the promise. The latter distinction relies heavily on the structure of German private law, wherein the difference between obligation (*Verpflichtung*) and disposition over a right based on an underlying legal power to dispose (*Verfügung, Verfügungsmacht*) is so fundamental as to amount to apriority.[49]

Finally, Reinach returns to the core question of why promises – or, for that matter, contracts – are binding at all. His ultimate answer to this question consists in refuting three alternative approaches to his own theory by showing that none of them can provide further reasons for the binding power of promises, hence delivering indirect proof of his own assumption that no such reasons can be given. The first approach, exemplified by David Hume's nominalist and conventionalist theory of

beneficiaries. [...] For now let us just remark that it is surely no accident that contracts with third-party beneficiaries were in some legal codes established so late, if at all.'

45 ibid 32.

46 See § 275 BGB.

47 Reinach, 'Foundations' (n 8) 33.

48 ibid 34.

49 See in more detail infra Section 1.4 at nn 85 ff and accompanying text.

moral obligation, holds that the binding power of the promise does not stem from the promise itself but from 'the *willing* of the *obligation*, which arises from the promise'.[50] According to Hume, restated by Reinach, this internal motivation on the part of the promisor to be bound is, in turn, experienced as binding by the promisor because a social convention that promises should be binding exists. Thus, the binding power of the promise can be construed in two ways. Either the social convention that promises should be binding directly implants an 'ought' into the perceived intention of the promisor, because promises cannot be thought of other than as conventionally binding, or the conventional explanation of the binding power of promising refers to an external category of social utility, which demands that promises be binding because it is useful that they should be so. In both cases, the reasoning is circular or begging the question. If the promisor regards his promise as binding because convention says so, no advancement is made beyond the starting point why promises should be binding at all. If conventional reasoning regards promises as binding because it is socially useful that they are, the same question arises on a higher level: Why should the 'ought' of the binding power of promises follow from a conventional experience of social utility – which may or may not apply to a particular promise without presupposing that, as a *promise*, it has a good reason to be binding in its own right?

The second theory Reinach opposes is the psychologistic explanation of moral obligation proposed by his early teacher Theodor Lipps.[51] In Reinach's reading, Lipps' theory appears as the paradigmatic case of an extreme internalist theory which directly traces the binding power of the promise back to the promisor's intention to be bound. This reading thus even goes beyond the internalist reading of Hume stated above in that it does not even purport to rely on a social convention to explain the binding power of contract. Instead, it directly places the burden of explanation on the inner psychic state arising out of promising that the promisor experiences as an 'ought' to hold himself bound by the promise. This path of argumentation, however, actually exacerbates the difficulties of providing independent reasons for the binding power of promise experienced above. To argue that the will to be bound creates a psychic state from which emerges the imperative that the promisor 'ought' to be bound by a promise does not at all imply that such an 'ought' in fact exists, unless – again – the binding power of the promise is already presupposed.

Finally, Reinach discusses the same problem from the standpoint of consequentialism, exemplified by the 'uitilitarian theory' (*Erfolgstheorie*) of the now mostly

[50] Reinach, 'Foundations' (n 8) 35–38, with reference to David Hume, *A Treatise of Human Nature: Being an Attempt to Introduce the Experimental Method of Reasoning into Moral Subjects* (John Noon 1739/40) [reference to the German translation in Reinach's original: Hume, *Traktat über die menschliche Natur*; see Reinach, 'Grundlagen' (n 8) 175].

[51] Reinach, 'Foundations' (n 8) 38–42, with references to Theodor Lipps, *Leitfaden der Psychologie* (2nd edn, Wilhelm Engelmann 1906) and Theodor Lipps, *Die ethischen Grundfragen. Zehn Vorträge* (2nd edn, Leopold Voß 1905).

forgotten nineteenth-century moral philosopher Wilhelm Schuppe.[52] In Reinach's reading, Schuppe shifts the emphasis from the inner psychic state of the promisor to the social utility of binding contracts as the basis of legally secured property rights. Thus, for Schuppe, it is neither the mere will nor the intention to be bound which makes the contractual promise binding, but rather the expediency of a legal regime which regards contracts and declarations of will as binding: 'The so-called binding force of a contract consists in nothing other than the importance of the legal order which insists on irrevocability.'[53] Yet again, this begs the question as to how the promisee's reliance on the promise can justify its binding power without already presupposing the binding power of promise itself. Reinach's critique of Schuppe's argument rightly points to this lacuna at the heart of Schuppe's position, which circles around will, declaration of will and the supposed binding power of contract founded on social utility without addressing the very core of the performative promise itself. How can Schuppe, Reinach asks, avoid the difficulties of justifying the unconditional and exclusive bond of contract where there is, in the concrete case, no reliance on its binding power and thus no damage, or, conversely, where there is reliance and damage done, but to third parties alien to the contract? 'In taking his stand on the fact that precisely the promisee relies on the promise, Schuppe presupposes what he wants to explain: the obligation of the promise.'[54]

It is easy to see that all these theories have survived under different guises up to the present day. 'Promise as reliance' is as much a staple of today's debate on the binding power of the promise as is its moral or conventional justification.[55] In these debates, Reinach's argument that all these approaches face comparable difficulties when asked to provide further reasons for the binding power of the promise beyond the nature of promising itself would still be valid and merits a rediscovery. The upshot of Reinach's argument is that *none* of the additional criteria proposed by any of the three theories or their present-day equivalents carries enough weight to prove their point. Rather, all of them end up begging the question or make use of circular reasoning.[56] It is exactly here where Wittgenstein's spade hits bedrock and is turned back. The promise is binding *because* it is a promise, or more precisely, because the performative social act of promising can only be thought of as binding. If it were otherwise, talk of promising would be meaningless. Thus, Reinach's phenomenology of promising as a performative social act provides the best possible *irreducible* interpretation of the emergence of the obligation from the promise under the condition that promising exists as a performative social practice at all. In fact,

[52] Reinach, 'Foundations' (n 8) 42–46, with reference to Wilhelm Schuppe, *Grundzüge der Ethik und Rechtsphilosophie* (Wilhelm Koebner 1881).

[53] Reinach, 'Foundations' (n 8) 42.

[54] ibid 44.

[55] For references, see supra nn 2 and 4.

[56] This argument has much in common with Moore's 'open question argument'. See GE Moore, *Principia Ethica* (Cambridge University Press 1903) 17.

understanding promising is all about *reduction* of unnecessary theoretical effort – even to the extent that Reinach disclaims proposing a theory at all:

> Strictly speaking we are not proposing any theory of promising. For we are only putting forth the simple thesis that promising as such produces claim and obligation. One can try, and we have in fact tried, to bring out the intelligibility of this thesis by analysis and clarification. To try to explain it would be just like trying to explain the proposition, 1 x 1 = 1. It is a fear of what is directly given (*Angst vor der Gegebenheit*), a strange reluctance or incapacity to look the ultimate data in the face and to recognize them as such which has driven unphenomenological philosophies, in this as in so many more fundamental problems, to untenable and ultimately to extravagant constructions.[57]

One final point remains to be made. As already discussed, 'promising' is a performative verb. Etymologically, 'promising' is derived from the old French '*promesse*' and ultimately from the Latin '*promittere*', meaning to send or to put forth, to let go forward or to say beforehand, which is related, inter alia, to mission, admit, commit or permit.[58] The Latin root of the English verb 'promise' already conveys some of the meaning of actively putting forth or sending out something from the promisor in the direction of the promisee. What is not captured in the English etymology, however, is the specific performativity encapsulated in the original German verb: '*Versprechen*' is derived from '*sprechen*', that is, to speak, which literally states that the promise is something that the speaker does to the addressee with words.[59] A direct translation of '*versprechen*' into English is not possible; a close approximation would be something like 'forspeak' or 'forespeak'.[60] Much like the prefix '*ver-*' itself, the verb '*versprechen*' is ambivalent and can mean either 'to promise' or, in its reflexive form, 'to misspeak'. Used as a prefix before a verb root, '*ver-*' dialectically emphasises both its binding, communicating and, at the same time, misleading or confusing aspects. As to the further etymology, '*sprechen*' is not only directly related to the English 'to speak' but also to many ancient Indo-European verbs indicating or imitating sound.[61] This etymology characterises '*versprechen*' as the prototype of a performative verb referring to the activity of speaking to another person with the consequence of bringing future consequences into being by the mere utterance of words.

57 Reinach, 'Foundations' (n 8) 46.

58 See headword 'promise', in *Wiktionary: The Free Dictionary* (April 2024); URL: https://en.wiktionary.org/wiki/promise.

59 Reinach, 'Grundlagen' (n 8) 147–189 and passim.

60 See headword 'forspeak' (Scottish archaic for 'bewitch'), in *Collins Dictionary* (April 2024); URL: www.collinsdictionary.com/de/worterbuch/englisch/forspeak; headword 'forspeak', in *Wiktionary: The Free Dictionary* (April 2024); URL: https://en.wiktionary.org/wiki/forspeak.

61 See headword 'Versprechung', in *Digitales Wörterbuch der deutschen Sprache* (April 2024); URL: www.dwds.de/wb/etymwb/Versprechung.

Indeed, more insight might be gleaned from the study of etymology here, even if one does not believe in linguistic universals.[62] In what follows, I argue that the original German etymology of 'promising' (*versprechen*) as opposed to 'owning' (*gehören*) may teach today's readers of Reinach – regardless of their language – something important about the roots of the doctrinal divides between promising and owning, obligation and property, as well as relative and absolute rights. As I argue in the subsequent part, '*versprechen*' and '*gehören*' have correlative performative functions in Reinach's private law theory that are expressed in their etymologies. While '*versprechen*' is the basis of promise, obligation and relative right, '*gehören*' is the source of owning, property and absolute rights. Moreover, both '*versprechen*' and '*gehören*' refer to the spoken language as the core of their respective performative functions in strikingly complementary ways. Whereas '*versprechen*' is a derivative of the German equivalent of 'speaking', '*gehören*' expresses a similar relation to the equivalent of 'hearing' (*hören*).[63] Just like 'speaking' and 'hearing', the conceptual pairs promise and ownership, obligation and property, and relative and absolute right all share the same performative oppositional structure and act as social correlatives in Reinach's theory: hearing means not speaking; however, there is no hearing without speaking and no speaking without hearing. Reinach must have been aware of this striking etymological correlation. Indeed, no strong reading of Reinach's phenomenology of performative legal language will be able to avoid noticing its significance as a phenomenologically meaningful a priori of the German legal language – thus leading the comparative theorist to search for homologous or, perhaps even more interestingly, for characteristically different linguistic and etymological relations in other languages which might reveal deeper insights about the basic structures of legal relations.

1.4 OWNING AND HEARING (*GE-HÖREN*)

As just argued, the second performative verb that defines the foundations of private law for Reinach is '*gehören*', a derivative of the German '*hören*', which literally means 'to hear'. Translated as 'owning' or 'belonging', this verb provides the performative basis of Reinach's theory of property. Much like '*ver-sprechen*', '*ge-hören*' is constructed through an extension of the root verb '*hören*' with the prefix '*ge*', indicating direction or consequence. Moreover, and even more importantly, the root '*hören*' also appears in German words explicitly linked to performative social acts involving subordination, such as '*hörig*' (subordinate, subservient), '*Hörigkeit*'

[62] This horizon of inquiry cannot be pursued further here. See generally Cliff Goddard, 'The Search for the Shared Semantic Core of All Languages', in Cliff Goddard and Anna Wierzbicka (eds), *Meaning and Universal Grammar. Theory and Empirical Findings* vol 1 (John Benjamins 2002).

[63] Reinach, 'Grundlagen' (n 8) 193–204 and passim.

(subordination, subservience) or '*Höriger*' (serf).[64] Again, these phenomenologically significant semantic relations have no equivalent in the English translations of '*gehören*' as 'owning', 'ownership' or 'property'. The closest approximation of what Reinach does with these performative verbs – picturing the subordinate object of property as 'hearing' and 'obeying' the command of the owner – is probably 'to belong'.[65] Yet, 'belonging' also misses the specific semantic juxtaposition of 'speaking' in '*versprechen*' and 'hearing' in '*gehören*' as referring to two opposite, yet mutually correlative performance functions of spoken language. It should be added that there is a specific socially performative side not only to speaking but also to hearing. Not unlike speaking, hearing necessarily expresses itself through an other-directed social act of attentiveness in the direction of the speaker. There is, thus, good reason to look for a specific linguistic performativity not only in the law of obligations but also in property law, and to imagine it as a narrative of submission to the owner's power – submission of both the object owned and other persons bound to respect the owner's rights.[66]

Read along those lines, what Reinach has to say about the fundamentals of absolute rights, rights over things, the indivisibility of property, as well as the distinction between legal right and legal power is on par with his theory of promising. First of all, Reinach establishes a sharp distinction between absolute rights and rights over things. Though this distinction may come as somewhat of a surprise to modern property theorists, it not only mirrors classical Roman law but also highlights a fundamental semantic distinction when thinking about the structure of rights. A right over a thing (*dingliches Recht*) is a right that establishes an immediate legal relationship between a person and a thing. By contrast, in the usual definition, the absoluteness of a right expresses neither its direct reference to an object nor the scope of its protection, but rather the universality of the claim rights attached to it.[67] In contrast to relative rights, absolute rights are usually described as giving rise to rights of action vis-à-vis *any* third party.[68] In modern property thinking, the absoluteness and the *in rem* character of a right are often confused because both categories coincide – property rights are, incidentally, both the most important category of

[64] See headword 'hörig', in *Digitales Wörterbuch der deutschen Sprache* (April 2024); URL: www.dwds.de/wb/etymwb/hörig.

[65] See headword 'belonging', in *Wiktionary: The Free Dictionary* (April 2024); URL: https://en.wiktionary.org/wiki/belonging.

[66] This argument has much in common with Carol Rose's reading of property as a narrative of persuasion; see Carol M Rose, *Property and Persuasion. Essays on the History, Theory, and Rhetoric of Ownership* (Routledge 1995). See also Bart J Wilson, 'The Primacy of Property: Or, the Subordination of Property Rights' (2023) 19 J Inst Econ 251, 252: 'Property – like grooming, tool-making, and story-telling – is a custom socially taught and learned each generation anew.'

[67] See, e.g., §§ 823, 985, 1004 BGB.

[68] See, e.g., Jürgen F Baur and Rolf Stürner, *Sachenrecht* § 2 n 2 (18th edn, CH Beck 2009) 618. On the distinction between absolute rights and rights over things, see Marietta Auer, *Der privatrechtliche Diskurs der Moderne* (Mohr Siebeck 2014) 94–100.

rights over things as well as universally protected absolute rights.[69] Reinach, however, not only teaches us to keep both categories strictly separate even where they coincide but also rejects outright the usual definition of absolute rights and offers a much more radical view of absoluteness:

> The absoluteness of rights and obligations means the *absence* of every relation to a partner (*jeglicher Gegnerschaft*), and not its *universality*, that is, not the fact that the so-called absolute rights and obligations exist over against *all* persons in contrast to the obligatory rights and obligations, which are tied to a *single* person. [...] Even if this were so, it would not mean that absolute rights *are* nothing but universal rights against all persons, but only that they have such rights *as a consequence*. The very relationship which is here in question presupposes that there are absolute rights, that is, rights without any partner at all.[70]

This is a masterful piece of conceptual clarification by way of an almost Kantian transcendental proof of necessary conditions of the existence of absolute rights. If one assumes that there are absolute rights, they cannot exhaust themselves in mere relative rights. Thus, they cannot be identical with the sum of their own protection through relative rights, nor is there any other way of reducing them to a relationship between persons. Since all relative rights are, by definition, relationships between persons, it follows that absolute rights are only possible if they are conceptualised as the *absence* of any relationship with another person. Reinach thus has to transcend the conventional understanding of 'right' in order to salvage the social apriority of absolute rights. Put differently, he rejects any deduction of subcategories of rights from the mere conceptual umbrella of 'right' and thereby avoids a common formalist fallacy.[71] For Reinach, absolute rights have nothing in common with relative rights; their corona of claim rights directed against any potential violator is just a secondary layer of technical relativity detached from the essential anti-relativity of the absolute right:

> [T]he claim is by its nature something preliminary, something aiming at fulfillment, whereas the absolute right is something definitive, something resting in itself. The claim is in need of fulfillment; the absolute right over one's own action is not

[69] The background against which this coincidence takes place is the demise of the Roman system of actions, where the distinction between *actio in rem* and *actio in personam* was procedurally meaningful: While the former allowed the plaintiff immediate access to the disputed object, the latter referred the plaintiff to personal action against the defendant without being able to access the object itself. Hence the modern debate on the meaning of the dualism between *rights in rem* and *rights in personam*. See supra n 7 for further references.

[70] Reinach, 'Foundations' (n 8) 52.

[71] It is striking that Hohfeld, in his famous analysis of 'jural relations', follows a similar aim, but often comes to a conclusion opposite to that of Reinach, for example, on the 'bundle theory' and the status of *rights in rem*. See Wesley N Hohfeld, 'Some Fundamental Legal Conceptions as Applied in Judicial Reasoning' (1913) 23 Yale LJ 16; Hohfeld (n 7). On Reinach and Hohfeld, see Olivier Massin, 'The Ontology of Rights: Reconciling Reinach and Hohfeld', in this volume, Chapter 8.

even capable of fulfillment at all. It can indeed be *exercised* by the holder of the right himself, but it does not call for such exercise in the sense in which a claim calls for fulfillment.[72]

Let us take this one step further. If a right is relative as opposed to absolute, someone has to *speak*, namely, by making a promise. But absolute rights are not about *speaking*; they are about *hearing*. Under the reading proposed here, the question why an absolute right cannot denote a relation to a person has a phenomenologically valid answer. Such a person would have to *hear absolutely* and *not speak*. But persons are not in the world only to hear. Only things, the mute servants of civilisation, allow for a phenomenology of social acts wherein they figure as mere passive objects. In the same vein, Reinach conceptualises rights over things (*Sachenrechte*) as '[e]verything one can "deal" with, everything "usable" in the broadest sense of the word [. . .]: apples, houses, oxygen, but also a unit of electricity or warmth'.[73] According to Reinach, they *immediately* relate to things in that they 'present themselves as a *dealing* (*Verfahren*) with things'.[74] The *immediate* relation to the object embodied in the right equals the social practice of absolute domination. Seen this way, rights over things also qualify as 'rights that refer to one's own action'[75] – namely, to the absolute power the owner wields over the object, which, in turn, is literally bound to 'hear' and obey his commands and dealings. In fact, Reinach explicitly says so with respect to property as the most important and most powerful subclass of rights over things: 'It lies in the essence of the owning that the owner has the right to deal in any way he likes with the thing which belongs to him.'[76]

Note that this does not imply that the positive law cannot regulate the property relationship in manifold ways which indeed curtail the freedom of the owner to deal with his property at will. Again, it would be a mistake to confuse absoluteness with limitlessness. What Reinach is proposing is only that an a priori – that is, argumentatively irreducible, basal understanding of property requires reading it as the *social act* of *owning*, understood as the *immediate absolute relation of power between the owner and the object owned*. Specifically, this means that property is (1) not a right, but a *relation* between the owner and the object; (2) an *act*, which consists in the perpetual realisation of absolute domination of the owner over the object; (3) a *social act*, defined by its other-directness toward other persons beside the owner; (4) a *performative act* in the specific linguistic sense that the owner's absolute domination requires the object's absolute submission and thus implies an etymological performativity associated with 'hearing' or a similar performative verb. It should be

72 Reinach, 'Foundations' (n 8) 58.
73 ibid 53.
74 ibid.
75 ibid 66.
76 ibid 55.

noted that because of (4), the other-directedness of the property relation (3) does *not* require the *actual* presence of other persons beside the owner as long as property exists as a *social* relation at all, that is, as a relation inseparable from the apriority of human society and its performative practices. Thus, even Robinson Crusoe, alone on his island, can be an owner as long as his being on the island alone is conceptualised against the background of the civilisation he has left behind. In other words, property is a basal legal relationship as soon as there is a civilisation able to express an intersubjective mine and thine, even where there is no law to govern it:

> The relation between person and thing which is called owning or property is an ultimate, irreducible relation which cannot be further resolved into elements. It can come to being even where there is no positive law. When Robinson Crusoe produces for himself all kinds of things on his island, these things belong to him.[77]

From all of this, it follows that the 'bundle theory' cannot provide a basal explanation of property because it mistakes the auxiliary claim rights stemming from the basal social relation between the owner and the object – that is, the absolute right – for this basal relation itself.[78] In Reinach's reading, understanding the social function of property means looking beyond the legal construction of the owner's protection to the performative phenomenology embodied in the property relation as such.[79] As a corollary, this property relation is indivisible – a point which Reinach argues at great length using the example of restricted rights to things.[80] Under the German Civil Code, restricted rights to things such as liens can arguably be construed as partitions of the comprehensive property right with the consequence that the lienholder acquires a limited absolute right, while the diminished remainder of the property right stays with the owner.[81] Reinach makes it clear that this reading is fallacious and that such partitions have no effect on the integrity of the residual property relation:

> We of course reject the usual formulation that property is the *sum* or the *unity* of all rights over the thing. [. . .] If property were a sum or unity of rights, it would be

[77] ibid 56.

[78] On the 'bundle theory', see supra nn 5–6 and accompanying text.

[79] This insight might be of particular interest to property theorists whose focus is shifting away from the protection of the individual owner in the direction of the social function of property regimes. For a recent statement of this position, see Anna di Robilant, *The Making of Modern Property. Reinventing Roman Law in Europe and Its Peripheries, 1789–1950* (Cambridge University Press 2023) 322–326.

[80] Reinach, 'Foundations' (n 8) 58–66. He formulates two further a priori laws for liens that are only partially consistent with the German Civil Code; ibid 62–63: (1) the lien is an auxiliary right, that is, if the claim is extinguished, it is not possible for the lien to stay in existence, (2) a lien on one's own property is impossible.

[81] On this debate ('*Eigentumssplittertheorie*' versus '*Vervielfältigungstheorie*'), see Volker Jänich, *Geistiges Eigentum – Eine Komplementärerscheinung zum Sacheigentum?* (Mohr Siebeck 2002) 241; Auer (n 68) 97.

reduced by the alienation of one of those rights, and it would be eliminated by the alienation of the totality of all rights, for a sum necessarily disappears with the disappearance of all of its parts. [...] We have definitely to hold fast to the thesis that property is itself no right over a thing but rather a *relation* (*Verhältnis*) to the thing, a relation in which all rights over it are grounded. This relation *remains completely intact even if all those rights have been granted to other persons*. [...] One sometimes speaks of divided property. Now nothing is clearer than that *property* itself, the relation of belonging, cannot be divided, just as little as the relation of identity or of similarity. Only if one lets property *consist in* the rights over the thing – in reality these rights are *grounded in* property – can one want to divide it up by dividing up the rights. The rights grounded in owning can of course be divided among ever so many persons; it is also possible to resolve them into ever so many rights by breaking up their content. But it is evident that a division of the *owning itself* is impossible.[82]

One further step remains to be taken. If, as Reinach suggests, it is more apt to describe property and other absolute rights not as rights but as performative social powers of the rightsholder over himself and the objects within his dominion, what is the relationship between rights, powers and possible further subclasses of jural relations?[83] Besides relative rights and absolute powers, Reinach describes yet another class of legal powers denoting the potential of the power holder to effect immediate consequences in the legal sphere. Such legal powers or *abilities* – the terminology is not entirely unequivocal – are distinct from both classes of rights in that their holder can bring about immediate legal effects by transferring, eliminating or modifying both absolute and relative rights:

As we know, rights can refer to one's own action (these are absolute rights) as well as to the action of another (these are relative rights, or claims). We distinguish as sharply as possible from both of them a legal power or capacity (*Können*), which only refers to one's own action. A power reveals itself in the fact that the action to which it refers, produces an immediate effect in the world of right (*rechtliche Wirkung*), for example, produces, modifies, or eliminates claims and obligations. By contrast, it is *not* intrinsic to a right, not even to an absolute one referring to one's own action, to have immediate effects in the world of rights; one has only to consider all the absolute rights over things. It is only through the concept of a legal ability that we are able to understand the origin of absolute rights and obligations, and their passing from one person to another.[84]

In other words, Reinach seems to ascribe a priori power to the German model of transferring rights through the construction of a separate, abstract act of disposition detached from the underlying relation of obligation (non-causa principle;

[82] Reinach, 'Foundations' (n 8) 56.
[83] On the relationship between Reinach and Hohfeld, see supra n 71.
[84] Reinach, 'Foundations' (n 8) 66.

Trennungsprinzip; Abstraktionsprinzip).[85] Under German law, a property transaction demands not one but two legal relationships. The obligatory contract – say, a sales contract – does not in itself transfer the property right in the object sold. For the transfer of property, the owner has to convey the property right to the buyer in a separate, abstract transaction detached from the sales contract.[86] This is usually done implicitly by handing over the object sold while concluding the obligatory contract. Yet, although both agreements often coincide in practice, they are legally independent from one another. The only content of the property transaction is the abstract transferal of the property right, which is made explicit through the transfer of possession of the object sold. But why is it useful to distinguish between the obligatory contract, from which the claim to the object arises, and the property transaction itself? Reinach's response states that this separation emphasises the necessary logical step between the promise to transfer property and its actual effectuation. The in-between step is the *ability* of the owner to transfer the right he has promised: 'The presence of a specific power (*Können*) to transfer, or a *right* to transfer which implies this ability, is required.'[87] Conversely (and leaving aside the positive rules of good faith purchase[88]), the transferor can only transfer a right he actually has. Thus, it should come as no surprise that the brocard '*nemo dat*' constitutes yet another facet of Reinach's a priori: 'The principle, *nemo plus iuris transferre potest quam ipse habet*, expresses of course an apriori truth.'[89]

Again, note that this a priori recognition of the abstraction principle of German property law does not commit Reinach to the uniform construction of both obligatory contracts and abstract transactions under the German Civil Code via matching declarations of intention. On the contrary, as already discussed above, Reinach argues that this constructive principle is conceptually mistaken because it obscures the performativity of the incompatible social acts of promising and owning, including the independent performative forms of transferring, granting, revoking and waiving:

> We have already objected to the dogma of 'declarations of intention' through which relations of right are supposed to come about. Its untenability in every respect has become clear. It may be that promising, aiming as it does at a later action of the

[85] On the significance of these principles, see Yun-chien Chang, *Property Law. Comparative, Empirical, and Economic Analyses* (Cambridge University Press 2023) 104–105; Jürgen F Baur and Rolf Stürner § 5 n 42 (n 68) 56.

[86] §§ 873, 929 BGB; see also Chang (n 85) 104. This construction is also discussed by Reinach as an example of the constructive freedom of the positive law; see Reinach, 'Foundations' (n 8) 119.

[87] Reinach, 'Foundations' (n 8) 67.

[88] §§ 892 ff, 932 ff BGB; see Chang (n 85) 259–288.

[89] ibid 68. On the English equivalent *nemo dat* (*nemo dat quod non habet*), see, e.g., Skelwith (Leisure) Ltd v Armstrong [2015] EWHC 2830 (Ch); [2016] Ch 345 per Newey J, at 54; see also Chang (n 85) 262–263; Andrew S Gold and Henry E Smith, 'Legal Concepts as a Deep Structure of the Law: Reinach's A Priori in Action', in this volume, Chapter 5.

> promisor and presupposing the intention to perform this action, could be confused with the expression of this intention. But there is no intention to perform a later action in the case of transferring and granting, of revoking and waiving. How should it be possible to speak here of a declaration of intention in the strict sense?[90]

Finally, there is yet another consequence that follows from Reinach's embrace of the abstraction principle between promise and power. Reinach insists that the same analytical divide involving the obligatory contract and the abstract disposition over a right also applies with regard to the construction of agency. Again, the German Civil Code provides the blueprint for this two-layered construction by distinguishing between the 'internal' and 'external' relationships created by agency: the mandate contract between the principal and the agent, on the one hand, and the actual exercise of the agent's power, on the other.[91] In line with this differentiation, Reinach argues that the distinction between mandate and representative power must be yet another element belonging to the a priori of private law. Again, while both relations may coincide, they are nevertheless independent from one another, resulting in, for example, the possibility of an *ultra vires* use of the agent's power. The resulting parallel between property and agency is yet another highlight in the garland of Reinach's structural 'must-haves' of private law:

> [T]he obligation to perform a social act with immediate effects in the world of right does not necessarily include any legal power directed to the same content. And: the obligation not to perform a social act with immediate effects in the world of right does not eliminate or restrict a legal power directed to the same content.[92]

1.5 ENACTING AND GIVING VOICE (*BE-STIMMEN*)

In all this, one question has yet to be answered. If Reinach is right about the apriority of principles like the irrelevance of the acceptance for the binding power of a promise, the categorical difference between absolute and relative rights, the indivisibility of property or the precedence of *nemo dat* over the rules of bona fide acquisition, how does he address the challenge of the existing positive law? In Reinach's own words, 'how can one put forward apriori laws which claim absolute validity, when any positive law can stand in the most flagrant contradiction to them?'[93] And, to push this even further, how can Reinach's legal a priori become

[90] Reinach, 'Foundations' (n 8) 69; see also supra Section 1.3 at n 37 and accompanying text.

[91] §§ 164 ff BGB. On the separation between the internal and external agency relation, see, e.g., Werner Flume, *Allgemeiner Teil des Bürgerlichen Rechts* vol 2, § 501 (4th edn, Springer 1992) 839–845.

[92] Reinach, 'Foundations' (n 8) 88–89; emphasis omitted. Reinach treats agency in § 7 of his treatise, directly following his treatment of property.

[93] ibid 103.

relevant at all in a world of widely dominant positive law which, for apparently good reasons, has long ago accepted legal positivism as the leading legal theory?

In answering his own question, Reinach is in no way reluctant to sacrifice his edifice of a priori building blocks of private law to the supervening normative power of the legislator. He emphasises that the legislator may not only be free but indeed often obliged to depart from the a priori foundations of law if social expediency demands their reversal. In such cases, it is not only moral value but virtually 'everything that can take on the character of value' that provides a good reason to overrule the legal a priori through legislative *enactment*:

> It is the function of the enactment either to destroy the relations of right which arise according to apriori laws, or to generate out of its own power relations of right which are apriori excluded. The enacting person will very often have reason to exercise this fullness of legal power. [...] Not only moral value in the strict sense, but also the useful, the pleasant, the practical and the like, that is, everything which can take on the character of value, can also take on, in virtue of its value, the character of being such that it ought to be. This objective ought-to-be which lacks existence acquires it here through its enactment.'[94]

The question of how Reinach can accommodate both the idea of a legal a priori and the facility of the deviating fiat of the positive law in his theory thus has a clear answer. It points once more to Reinach's phenomenology of performative legal language. If the legislator is free to reverse at will the performative acts that constitute the a priori of legal meaning, this can only be accomplished through yet another performative social act, namely, through an enactment, which is derived from Reinach's third basic performative verb 'enacting'. And again, the original German etymology of Reinach's term '*bestimmen*'[95] adds even more phenomenological persuasion to the idea that Reinach is building his entire edifice of the legal a priori on performative verbs that explicitly refer to the human voice, speaking and hearing as basic features of social communication and thus the basis of sound (!) legal acts. For '*bestimmen*' is etymologically related not only to '*Stimme*' (voice) but also to a host of normative concepts indicating consistency, harmony or justification, such as '*stimmen*' (to tune, to be correct), '*Stimmung*' (mood, tune) or '*Stimmigkeit*' (consistency).[96] Moreover, '*be-stimmen*' offers yet another example of a performative verb composed of affixing a prefix to a root verb – a combination resulting in a striking ambivalence between designating or calling out the voiced object, on the one hand, and lending or giving voice to the named object, on the other. This amounts to a theory of positive law in which the legislator both designates the

[94] ibid 111–112.

[95] '*Bestimmungen*'; '*Bestimmungssätze*'; see Reinach, 'Grundlagen' (n 8) 238–251.

[96] See headwords 'bestimmen' and 'Stimme', in *Digitales Wörterbuch der deutschen Sprache* (April 2024); URL: www.dwds.de/wb/etymwb/bestimmen; www.dwds.de/wb/etymwb/Stimme.

desired legislative goal in the positive enactment and gives voice to it as a binding legal commandment.

Yet, despite the seemingly perfect tripartite correlation between 'promising', 'owning' and 'enacting', Reinach's treatment of 'enacting' also shows the limits of the explanatory power of his phenomenology of legal language. Reinach does not simply identify 'enacting' with 'commanding', nor does he perceive both concepts as on a par with each other regarding their performative power. While Reinach is quick to categorise 'enacting' as a social act, he takes pains to distinguish 'enacting' from 'commanding' by emphasising the de-personalised character of 'enacting', which, in his view, rather surprisingly does not qualify as an *other-directed* social act in the strict sense:

> There are neither commands nor enactments which unfold purely within the person; they always address themselves to others, and the need of being heard is intrinsic to them. But whereas commanding is at the same time necessarily an other-directed social act, the act of enacting is not. By its very nature every command presupposes a person or group of persons who are commanded, just as with the act of promising or of granting. But enacting does not have this necessary relation to another person, just as little as do acts like waiving or revoking. Although these acts are addressed to other persons in being performed, their substance (*Gehalt*) lacks any personal moment (*personales Moment*). Whereas I *always* promise to or command *a person*, I simply waive a claim or simply enact that something should be in a certain way.[97]

In other words, we are faced with a dilemma within Reinach's theory. If all legal meaning is based on performative social acts, then the fabric of positive law cannot be an exception. Its substance must also be based on performative legal language, namely, on an enactment. And yet, this precisely means giving up on Reinach's claim that there is a legal a priori *beyond* the positive law. If the phenomenology of positive law shows the *same* performative substance as the legal a priori, then there is, ultimately, no way to distinguish the legal a priori from the positive law designed to replace it. Yet, Reinach shies away from this consequence by introducing even more complexity on the level of the positive law. One enactment, he argues, is not enough to constitute legal meaning. Indeed, thinking 'in terms of an arbitrator'[98] will lead the legal theorist to the result that no enactment can become the basis of normative commands without further normative conditions, which – while Reinach does not elaborate them in any detail – amount to a theory of the social foundation of the state as built on an edifice of performative acts *beyond* promising:

> The enactment has to be preceded by another social act, in particular an act which is addressed to the enacting person by those for whom the enactment is supposed to

[97] Reinach, 'Foundations' (n 8) 105.
[98] ibid 110.

> be efficacious. The power of producing through enactments legal effects has first to be conferred by these persons. Here too the act of promising proves to be insufficient.[99]

But doesn't this prove that legal positivism, which puts all the theoretical emphasis on the state and state-enacted positive law, was on the right track all along? Put differently, what remains of Reinach's a priori in a world wherein, even according to his own theory, the a priori laws of promising and owning are widely overruled by an edifice of legislative enactments? Doesn't this imply the superior explanatory power of, for instance, Hans Kelsen's *Pure Theory of Law*, which holds that only positive law is law and defines the legitimate scope of legal scholarship?[100] Yet, reading Reinach shows why this is not a sound conclusion. The primary merit of his theory is, again, not to add but to *take away* additional metaphysical effort from legal theory where none is needed, even if it comes at the cost of renouncing the possibility of a general theory of law. Reinach *relieves* contract theory from the interminable search for further justifications for the binding nature of contract. Likewise, he *relieves* property theory from the riddle of the dissolution of modern property into a mere bundle of relative rights. And, finally, he offers a theory of positive law that allows *combining* legal positivism with the fruitfulness of phenomenological inquiries into the performative nature of different legal languages and legal cultures.

1.6 CONCLUSION: AGAINST ONTOLOGISM

This chapter aimed to reconstruct Reinach's theory of performative legal language against the dual background of modern language philosophy and German private law. I argued that Reinach uses a triad of performative verbs – 'promising', 'owning' and 'enacting' – to explain the core institutions of private law, that is, contract and property, including the doctrinalisation of these institutions through positive law. I conclude that what Reinach has to offer today's legal theorists shows all the hallmarks of good philosophy. He poses questions until no further justification can be given, and he refrains from metaphysical speculation beyond that point. The strength of Reinach's theory results from its non-commitment to any of the following three systems of tenets (which does not exclude that it is theoretically compatible with all of them): (1) legal positivist claims about what the law *is*, (2) moral and natural law claims as to what the law *ought to be*, as well as (3) legal realist claims as to what the social reality of the law is or ought to be. In other words, Reinach avoids the Ought without essentialising the Is. This is what makes his theory modern, or, indeed, timeless.

99 ibid.

100 Hans Kelsen, *Pure Theory of Law* (M Knight trans, University of California Press 1967).

Is such a slim theoretical setup persuasive as a legal epistemology? Reinach's answer would be to refuse, once again, offering philosophical answers where none can be given. Perhaps the most important lesson to be gleaned from Reinach is that a theorist's metaphysics, even where it cannot be avoided, should not play an *indispensable* role in his theoretical framework when it cannot be questioned further. In other words, even if a metaphysical grounding of ontology and epistemology is ultimately unavoidable – which Reinach would probably concede – one should be ready to bracket it whenever necessary, lest one commit the fallacy of *ontologism*:

> Though we cannot doubt the freedom which an enactment has with respect to the laws of being, and though a *right* enactment often has to deviate from that which is, for the sake of that which ought to be, we nevertheless often find a certain *lack of freedom* on the part of enacting persons, a tendency to cling to that which is, even when it ought rather not to be, an inability or unwillingness to give being, in virtue of one's own efficacious enactment, to that what ought to be, and to replace with this that which prima facie exists. This phenomenon belongs to the sphere of what one is used to calling 'formalism' in the positive law. In order to distinguish it from various other phenomena which better deserve this name, we propose to speak of 'ontologism'.[101]

Reinach's phenomenology of performative legal language not only highlights the manifold ontological, linguistic and social facets of the foundations of private law, but it also provides, on many levels, a powerful antidote to all kinds of legal formalism and doctrinalism. Reinach's ontology is an ontology to end all ontologisms.

BIBLIOGRAPHY

Auer M, *Der privatrechtliche Diskurs der Moderne* (Mohr Siebeck 2014)

'A Genealogy of Private Law Epistemologies', in T Kuntz and PB Miller (eds), *Methodology in Private Law Theory: Between New Private Law and Rechtsdogmatik* 3–24 (Oxford University Press 2024)

Austin JL, *How to Do Things with Words* (JO Urmson and M Sbisà eds, 2nd edn, Harvard University Press 1975)

Baltzer-Jaray K, 'Phenomenological Jurisprudence: A Reinterpretation of Reinach's Jahrbuch Essay', in JE Hackett and JA Simmons (eds), *Phenomenology for the Twenty-First Century* 117–137 (Palgrave Macmillan 2016)

'Bogged Down in Ontologism and Realism: The Phenomenology of Adolf Reinach', in RKB Parker (ed), *The Idealism-Realism Debate among Edmund Husserl's Early Followers and Critics* 151–171 (Springer 2021)

Baur JF and Stürner R, *Sachenrecht* (18th edn, CH Beck 2009)

Birmingham RL, 'Breach of Contract, Damage Measures, and Economic Efficiency' (1970) 24 Rutgers L Rev 273–292

[101] Reinach, 'Foundations' (n 8) 124.

Brown JM, 'Reinach on Representative Acts', in K Mulligan (ed), *Speech Act and Sachverhalt. Reinach and the Foundations of Realist Phenomenology* 119–131 (Kluwer 1987)

Burkhard A, *Soziale Akte, Sprechakte und Textillokutionen. A. Reinachs Rechtsphilosophie und die moderne Linguistik* (Max Niemeyer 1986)

Bydlinski F, *Privatautonomie und objektive Grundlagen des verpflichtenden Rechtsgeschäftes* (Springer 1967)

Canaris CW, *Die Vertrauenshaftung im deutschen Privatrecht* (CH Beck 1971)

'Wandlungen des Schuldvertragsrechts – Tendenzen zu seiner "Materialisierung"' (2000) 200 Archiv für die civilistische Praxis 273–364

Chang Y, *Property Law. Comparative, Empirical, and Economic Analyses* (Cambridge University Press 2023)

Collins Dictionary (April 2024); URL: www.collinsdictionary.com

Corbin AL, 'Jural Relations and Their Classification' (1921) 30 Yale LJ 226–238

'The Effect of Options on Consideration' (1925) 34 Yale LJ 571–590

Crosby JF, 'Adolf Reinach's Discovery of the Social Acts' (1983) Aletheia III 143–194

'Speech Act Theory and Phenomenology', in JF Crosby (ed), *Adolf Reinach, The Apriori Foundations of the Civil Law; Along with the Lecture, 'Concerning Phenomenology'* 167–191 (Ontos 2012)

Di Robilant A, *The Making of Modern Property. Reinventing Roman Law in Europe and its Peripheries, 1789–1950* (Cambridge University Press 2023)

Digitales Wörterbuch der deutschen Sprache (April 2024); URL: www.dwds.de

Duxbury N, 'The Legal Philosophy of Adolf Reinach' (1991) 77 ARSP 314–347 and 466–492

Flume W, *Allgemeiner Teil des Bürgerlichen Rechts* vol 2 (4th edn, Springer 1992)

Fried C, *Contract as Promise. A Theory of Contractual Obligation* (2nd edn, Oxford University Press 2015)

Fuller LL, 'Consideration and Form' (1941) 41 Colum L Rev 799–824

Funke A, *Allgemeine Rechtslehre als juristische Strukturtheorie* (Mohr Siebeck 2004)

Gardies JL, 'Adolf Reinach and the Analytic Foundations of Social Acts', in K Mulligan (ed), *Speech Act and Sachverhalt. Reinach and the Foundations of Realist Phenomenology* 107–117 (Kluwer 1987)

Goddard C, 'The Search for the Shared Semantic Core of All Languages', in C Goddard and A Wierzbicka (eds), *Meaning and Universal Grammar. Theory and Empirical Findings*, vol 1, 5–41 (John Benjamins 2002)

Hoffmann K, 'Reinach and Searle on Promising: A Comparison', in K Mulligan (ed), *Speech Act and Sachverhalt. Reinach and the Foundations of Realist Phenomenology* 91–106 (Kluwer 1987)

Hohfeld WN, 'Some Fundamental Legal Conceptions as Applied in Judicial Reasoning' (1913) 23 Yale LJ 16–59

'Fundamental Legal Conceptions as Applied in Judicial Reasoning' (1917) 26 Yale LJ 710–770

Hume D, *A Treatise of Human Nature: Being an Attempt to Introduce the Experimental Method of Reasoning into Moral Subjects* (John Noon 1739/40)

Husserl E, *Formal and Transcendental Logic* (D Cairns trans, Martinus Nijhoff 1969)

Logische Untersuchungen (E Holenstein ed, Martinus Nijhoff 1975)

Jänich V, *Geistiges Eigentum – Eine Komplementärerscheinung zum Sacheigentum?* (Mohr Siebeck 2002)

Kelsen H, *Pure Theory of Law* (M Knight trans, University of California Press 1967)

Kocourek A, 'Rights in Rem' (1920) 68 U Penn L Rev 322–336

'Polarized and Unpolarized Legal Relations' (1921) 9 Kentucky LJ 131–138
Kronman AT, 'A New Champion for the Will Theory' (1981) 91 Yale LJ 404–423
Larenz K, *Methodenlehre der Rechtswissenschaft* (6th edn, Springer 1991)
Lipps T, *Die ethischen Grundfragen. Zehn Vorträge* (2nd edn, Leopold Voß 1905)
Leitfaden der Psychologie (2nd edn, Wilhelm Engelmann 1906)
Markovits D and Schwartz A, 'The Myth of Efficient Breach: New Defenses of the Expectation Interest' (2011) 97 Va L Rev 1939–2008
Merrill TW and Smith HE, 'What Happened to Property in Law and Economics?' (2001) 111 Yale LJ 357–398
Moore GE, *Principia Ethica* (Cambridge University Press 1903)
Mulligan K, 'Promisings and Other Social Acts: Their Constituents and Structure', in K Mulligan (ed), *Speech Act and Sachverhalt. Reinach and the Foundations of Realist Phenomenology* 29–90 (Kluwer 1987)
Paulson SL, 'Demystifying Reinach's Legal Theory', in K Mulligan (ed), *Speech Act and Sachverhalt. Reinach and the Foundations of Realist Phenomenology* 133–154 (Kluwer 1987)
Penner JE, 'The Bundle of Rights Picture of Property' (1996) 43 UCLA L Rev 711–820
Reinach A, 'The Apriori Foundations of the Civil Law' (John F Crosby tr, 1983) 3 Aletheia 1–142, reprinted in Adolf Reinach, *The Apriori Foundations of the Civil Law; Along with the Lecture 'Concerning Phenomenology'* (John F Crosby ed, Ontos Verlag 2012), originally published as Adolf Reinach, 'Die apriorischen Grundlagen des bürgerlichen Rechtes' in 1(2) *Jahrbuch für Philosophie und phänomenologische Forschung* (Max Niemeyer 1913) 685–847
'Die Apriorischen Grundlagen des bürgerlichen Rechtes', in K Schuhmann and B Smith (eds), *Adolf Reinach. Sämtliche Werke. Textkritische Ausgabe in 2 Bänden* vol 1, 141–278 (Philosophia 1989)
'Über Phänomenologie' (1914), in K Schuhmann and B Smith (eds), *Adolf Reinach. Sämtliche Werke. Textkritische Ausgabe in 2 Bänden* vol 1, 531–550 (Philosophia 1989)
Rose CM, *Property and Persuasion. Essays on the History, Theory, and Rhetoric of Ownership* (Routledge 1995)
Schuhmann K and Smith B, 'Adolf Reinach: An Intellectual Biography', in K Mulligan (ed), *Speech Act and Sachverhalt. Reinach and the Foundations of Realist Phenomenology* 3–27 (Kluwer 1987)
(eds), *Adolf Reinach. Sämtliche Werke. Textkritische Ausgabe in 2 Bänden* (Philosophia 1989)
Schuppe W, *Grundzüge der Ethik und Rechtsphilosophie* (Wilhelm Koebner 1881)
Searle JR, *Speech Acts. An Essay in the Philosophy of Language* (Cambridge University Press 1969)
Singer JW, 'Property as the Law of Democracy' (2014) 63 Duke LJ 1287–1335
Smith B, 'On the Cognition of States of Affairs', in K Mulligan (ed), *Speech Act and Sachverhalt. Reinach and the Foundations of Realist Phenomenology* 189–225 (Kluwer 1987)
Smith HE, 'Property as the Law of Things' (2012) 125 Harvard L Rev 1691–1726
Steinbock AJ, 'Back to the Things Themselves' (1997) 20 Human Studies 127–135
Wiktionary: The Free Dictionary (April 2024); URL: https://en.wiktionary.org
Wilson BJ, 'The Primacy of Property; Or, the Subordination of Property Rights' (2023) 19 J Inst Econ 251–267
Wittgenstein L, *Philosophical Investigations* (GEM Anscombe, PMS Hacker and J Schulte trans, PMS Hacker and J Schulte eds, 4th edn, Wiley-Blackwell 2009)

2

Darwin's Reinach

*James Toomey**

2.1 INTRODUCTION

Adolf Reinach believed three controversial things – that basic legal concepts exist outside of the law; that their existence is conceptually independent of moral obligation; and that their existence entails nothing about positive law.[1] The juxtaposition of these beliefs is almost unheard of in jurisprudence. Those who argue for the extralegal reality of legal concepts tend to think they are inherently ethical, with entailments for both law and moral behavior.[2] And those who are skeptical that the law draws upon external concepts rather than constructs its own tend also to be skeptical of morality – or at least morality beyond ontologically parsimonious utilitarianism.[3]

In his idiosyncratic position, however, Reinach is joined by today's theorists drawing on evolutionary psychology and cognitive science in an account of legal concepts.[4] Like Reinach, these theorists believe that basic legal concepts have a genuine life outside of the law, as universal features of a human mind shaped by

* Associate Professor of Law, University of Iowa College of Law. Thanks to the conference audience at the Max Planck Institute in Frankfurt, the other contributors to this volume, in particular the insights of my co-editors Marietta Auer, Paul Miller, and Henry Smith, and the research assistance of Brooke Wood. Thanks also to Olivier Massin and Kimberly Baltzer-Jaray, my guides in Reinach.

[1] See Section 2.2.

[2] Scott Hershovitz, 'The End of Jurisprudence' (2015) 124 Yale LJ 1160; Steven Schaus, 'A Simple Model of Torts and Moral Wrongs' (2022) 97 Notre Dame L Rev 1029; Ian McLeod, *Legal Theory* (6th edn, Red Globe Press 2012) 18; Michael S Moore, 'Moral Reality Revisited' (1992) 90 Michigan L Rev 2424, 2425.

[3] Joseph William Singer, 'The Player and the Cards: Nihilism and Legal Theory' (1984) 94 Yale LJ 1; Richard Posner, *Economic Analysis of Law* (7th edn, Aspen 2007); Felix S Cohen, 'Transcendental Nonsense and the Functional Approach' (1935) 35 Columbia L Rev 809.

[4] Owen D Jones and Timothy H Goldsmith, 'Law and Behavioral Biology' (2005) 105 Columbia L Rev 405; Bart J Wilson, *The Property Species: Mind, Yours, and the Human Mind* (Oxford University Press 2020).

natural selection.[5] They too don't think the existence of these concepts entails moral conclusions.[6] And, just like Reinach, evolutionary theorists tend to argue that the positive law can vary as it likes from basic concepts of human cognition and whatever morality may be or demand.[7]

And yet Reinach himself could not have been clearer that his claims *were not* to be associated with the inchoate psychology of his day.[8] He insists that the kind of reality he ascribes to legal concepts *is not* about human psychology – 'claims and obligations arise in the angels, devils, and gods – as long as they can really promise and can really hear promises.'[9] Fair enough – Reinach's theory is *different* from cognitive theories – it holds legal concepts to be metaphysical truths for all conceivable intelligence, not evolved partially contingent human universals. But since we *are* theorizing about law by and for human beings, you might wonder what is really at stake in this distinction.[10]

This chapter explains why – in intellectual context – Reinach took such pains to distinguish his account of the *a priori* realism of legal concepts from what might facially be thought of as close psychological equivalents. And I argue that, notwithstanding Reinach's commitment to the distinction, it is perhaps not as essential to his legal theory as he believed. In other words, it may be possible to accept the insights of Reinach's conclusions without fully subscribing to his metaphysics – if you happen to find evolutionary theory, cognitive science, or some similar account more plausible (though these fields are, of course, controversial in their own right).[11]

For Reinach personally, the question of whether legal concepts 'really' exist or are 'just' psychological characteristics was one front in a broader dispute preoccupying German-language philosophy of his time – the firestorm over so-called 'psychologism'; or whether (primarily) logical and mathematical principles are True-with-a-capital-T or generalizations about human thought. For Reinach, the ontological status of legal concepts was a case study in a broader account of ontology and epistemology.

But in fighting this broader battle, Reinach appears to have overestimated how much the outcome of the *Psychologismus-Streit* matters for legal theory. This is so for two reasons. First, the difference between metaphysical and

[5] Wilson (n 4) 19.

[6] Steven Pinker, *The Blank Slate: The Modern Denial of Human Nature* (Penguin 2002) 151.

[7] Jones and Goldsmith (n 4) 484.

[8] Adolf Reinach, 'The Apriori Foundations of the Civil Law' (John F Crosby tr, 1983) 3 Aletheia 1, 72, reprinted in Adolf Reinach, *The Apriori Foundations of the Civil Law Along with the Lecture 'Concerning Phenomenology'* (John F Crosby ed, Ontos Verlag 2012), originally published as Adolf Reinach, 'Die apriorischen Grundlagen des bürgerlichen Rechtes' 1(2) *Jahrbuch für Philosophie und phänomenologische Forschung* (Max Niemeyer 1913) 685–847.

[9] ibid 47.

[10] James Toomey, 'Property's Boundaries' (2023) 109 Virginia L Rev 131, 160.

[11] Linda Gannon, 'A Critique of Evolutionary Psychology' (2010) 4 Psychology, Evolution and Gender 173; Steven Rose and Hilary Rose, *Alas Poor Darwin: Arguments Against Evolutionary Psychology* (Crown 2001).

evolutionary-cognitive theories of legal concepts is narrower than Reinach and his progenitors seem to have appreciated. Taking *natural selection* as the mechanism by which psychological proclivities arise means that there *is* a necessary relationship between psychology and ontology. It's not necessarily correspondence, true, but neither is it *arbitrary* or wholly contingent.

Moreover, the arguments Reinach's progenitors made for the metaphysical reality of logical and mathematical concepts are less persuasive as applied to Reinach's legal concepts.[12] Where logic and math appear to apply to reality generally, law is for Reinach (at least at present, so far as we know), a peculiarly human phenomenon. Distinguishing between psychology and ontology is particularly difficult, maybe impossible, in that context. And in the end, Reinach and his allies stipulate rather than purport to prove the metaphysical reality of the concepts they discuss. In logic and math, this stipulation might be necessary – Reinach's progenitors sought to make claims not merely *about* our logical concepts, but about how we *ought* to think with them. But writing in law, Reinach is different. Reinach *doesn't* derive conclusions about how the positive law ought to be from the ontological existence of his concepts.

This chapter proceeds in five parts. First, I summarize Reinach's legal philosophy, with its three idiosyncratic commitments. Next, I relate these views to theories of legal concepts grounded in evolutionary psychology – noting that, although Reinach predeceased scientific and theoretical developments that have made these theories more plausible, he took a crude sketch of what such theories might look like as a foil. In Section 2.4, I relate Reinach's legal theory to his place in the psychologism dispute, while in Section 2.5 I argue that he overestimated the difference between his account and evolutionary theories. Finally, I argue that arguments in favor of metaphysical reality in other contexts of the psychologism dispute – logic and math in particular – hold less force as applied to Reinach's legal concepts.

2.2 REINACH'S THREE COMMITMENTS

In *The A Priori Foundations of the Civil Law*, Reinach sketches three contestable positions about the nature of legal concepts, morality, law, and the relationship between these domains. First, he argues that legal concepts – such as promise, claim, and ownership – have a real existence outside of the law. Second, he argues that these concepts are distinct from morality – according to Reinach, an immoral promise, like any other, generates an obligation but, ethically, one ought not comply with it. And neither of these domains, for Reinach, has any necessary implications for the positive law, which he apparently took to be a matter of descriptive social fact.

The central thesis of the *Foundations* is that basic legal concepts really exist, independent of their recognition or creation in positive law. 'We shall show that the

[12] Reinach, 'Foundations' (n 8) 45.

structures which one has generally called specifically legal have a being of their own just as much as numbers, trees, or houses, that this being is independent of its being grasped by men, that it is in particular independent of all positive law.... We really do find what one has emphatically denied: the positive law *finds* the legal concepts which enter into it; *in absolutely no way does it produce them.*'[13]

Thus, Reinach believes that we can engage in *a priori* conceptual reasoning about such ideas as 'promise' and 'ownership' without invoking or referencing the positive law at all.[14] And indeed, his efforts at reasoning in this vein make up most of the *Foundations* – he argues, for example, that it inheres in the nature of a promise to create an obligation in the promisor;[15] and that '[i]t lies in the essence of owning that the owner has the absolute right to deal in any way he likes with the thing which belongs to him.'[16]

As for *how* these concepts exist, Reinach was a metaphysical realist.[17] He argued that social acts like promises, and relations like ownership, have a distinctive mode of existence, as states-of-affairs.[18] These states-of-affairs exist (technically, 'obtain') for Reinach in a real, mind-independent way – constituents of the universe just as the physical facts that constitute them in particular instances.[19] Because general, fundamental, and abstract, states-of-affairs are, on Reinach's account, governed by *a priori* laws to be grasped by insight – accessible to intelligence, in principle independent of any experience.[20] So, for example, Reinach holds that property is a state-of-affairs.[21] Given certain sets of physical and relational facts, an instance of property may obtain.[22] But any intelligence can reason to some truths about property – including the sets of facts that would qualify and which would not – without experience of any particular instance of property, because property itself is a fundamental constituent of the universe.[23] Or so goes Reinach's account.

This central thesis of the *Foundations* is its most controversial. Indeed, even at the time he wrote, Reinach was well aware that he was arguing against the jurisprudential grain – noting that there was 'general agreement' that 'all legal propositions and concepts are *creations* of the lawmaking factors,' but that his inquiry would 'really . . .

[13] Reinach, 'Foundations' (n 8) 4.
[14] ibid 5.
[15] ibid 46.
[16] ibid 55.
[17] Kimberly Baltzer-Jaray, 'Bogged Down in Ontologism and Realism' in Rodney KB Parker (ed), *The Idealism-Realism Debate among Edmund Husserl's Early Followers and Critics* (Springer Cham 2021) 151, 161–162.
[18] Adolf Reinach, 'Concerning Phenomenology' (Dallas Willard tr), in John Crosby (ed), *The Apriori Foundation of the Civil Law: Along with the Lecture Concerning Phenomenology* (De Gruyter 2013) 145, 158.
[19] ibid 146–147.
[20] Reinach, 'Foundations' (n 8) 6.
[21] ibid 70–74.
[22] ibid.
[23] ibid.

find what one has so emphatically denied.'[24] And the century in legal philosophy since Reinach has not been kind to metaphysical realism about legal concepts, with Critical Theory and Law and Economics carrying forward Legal Realism's nominalism about legal concepts to the present.[25]

But while Reinach held these basic legal concepts to exist, he maintained that their existence is conceptually independent of how morally we ought to interact with them.[26] A promise, as a matter of its essential character, generates an obligation, but it might be an obligation morally wrong to fulfill.[27] In this insistence that basic legal concepts are morally inert, Reinach departs from most fellow travelers in legal conceptualism. Consider Scott Hershovitz, who, with Reinach and *contra* nominalism, accepts the extralegal reality of promises.[28] But for Hershovitz, promise is an irreducibly normative concept, and its boundaries are coterminous with its moral implications – an immoral promise simply isn't a promise at all, and gives rise to no obligation.[29]

Finally, Reinach refused to infer anything about the necessary characteristics of positive law from either the concepts on which it draws or (apparently) morality – Reinach was a positivist about positive law. For example, analyzing the positive law's concept of causality in his doctoral thesis, Reinach insisted that the question is not whether the law's causal theory is 'correct' as a moral or even philosophical matter.[30] The task instead is to investigate the *positive law*'s theory of causality – with no necessary connection to the philosophically correct account.[31] Thus, Reinach insisted that, although states-of-affairs like promise and obligation exist outside of the law and are governed by essential, descriptive laws, '[t]he positive law can incorporate them into its sphere, it can also deviate from them.'[32] A 'jurist,' he argued 'need not establish what the law should mean according to logical or ethical or other norms, but rather what it in fact means.'[33]

Reinach's theory of the positive law is perhaps his least controversial commitment. His view is one recognizable, still popular position in debates about the nature of positive law – broadly within the 'positivist' umbrella.[34] But when this view is coupled

[24] Reinach, 'Foundations' (n 8) 4.
[25] See n 3.
[26] Reinach, 'Foundations' (n 8) 45.
[27] ibid.
[28] Hershovitz (n 2) 1180.
[29] ibid; John Gardner, *From Personal Life to Private Law* (Oxford University Press 2018) 12.
[30] Adolf Reinach, 'On the Concept of Causality in the Criminal Law' (2009) 1 Libertarian Papers 1, 40 (Berit Brogaard, tr).
[31] ibid.
[32] Reinach, 'Foundations' (n 8) 6.
[33] Reinach, 'Causality' (n 30) 40.
[34] Jules L Coleman, 'The Architecture of Jurisprudence' (2011) 121 Yale LJ, 5; Scott J Shapiro, 'The Hart-Dworkin Debate: A Short Guide for the Perplexed' in Arthur Ripstein (ed), *Ronald Dworkin* (Cambridge University Press 2007) 22.

with his insistence on the extralegal reality of legal concepts, as well as their morally inert character, we can see Reinach as the singular legal philosopher he was.

2.3 EVOLUTIONARY LEGAL CONCEPTUALISM'S THREE COMMITMENTS

In 1859, Charles Darwin published *The Origin of Species*, arguing that natural selection explains the diversity and complexity of biology.[35] Darwin argued that organisms vary in random but heritable ways as to traits that correlate with reproductive success.[36] Assuming that, in our resource-constrained world, in each generation more organisms are born than can live to reproductive maturity, over time traits beneficial for survival will proliferate, and deleterious mutations will die without reproducing – explaining the gradual evolution of complexity, in diverse forms.[37]

'Evolutionary psychology' argues that natural selection has shaped our minds as much as our other organs.[38] So it holds that many basic mechanisms and proclivities of the human mind, both conscious and unconscious, are biological adaptations governed by natural selection and heritably encoded in our genes; heuristics that helped our ancestors better survive in their environment than did their competitors, operationalized in each of us by genetic inheritance.[39]

Methodologically, evolutionary psychology and cognitive science often take the cross-cultural universality of a given psychological fact as *prima facie* evidence of its genetic basis.[40] It is then a question of evolutionary theory whether such a trait could have arisen by natural selection – whether it could have contributed to the individual reproductive success of those with it, even if in complex and indirect ways.[41] And it is ultimately an empirical matter whether in fact the traits in question developed

35 Charles Darwin, *The Origin of Species* (First Signet 2003).

36 ibid.

37 ibid 507.

38 John Tooby and Leda Cosmides, 'Conceptual Foundations of Evolutionary Psychology' in David M Buss (ed), *The Handbook of Evolutionary Psychology* (Wiley 2021) 5, 5.

39 ibid.

40 Livia Beccacece and others, 'Human Genomics and the Biocultural Origin of Music' (2021) 22 International J Molecular Sciences 5397, 5398; David M Buss, *Evolutionary Psychology* (5th edn, Pearson 2011); Daniel L Schacter, Daniel T Gilbert, and Daniel M Wegner, *Psychology* (5th edn, Worth 2007) 26–27; RR McCrae and PT Costa Jr., 'Personality Trait Structure as a Human Universal' (1997) 52 American Psychologist 509, 509.

41 There is a great deal of theoretical dispute about the comparative role of traditional natural selection in this process as compared to the related mechanisms of sexual selection, Richard O Prum, *The Evolution of Beauty: How Darwin's Forgotten Theory of Mate Choice Shapes the Animal World – And Us* (Doubleday 2017), contingency, Stephen J Gould and Richard C Lewontin, 'The Spandrels of San Marco and the Panglossian Paradigm: A Critique of the Adaptationist Programme' (1979) 205 Proceedings of the Royal Society B 581, and whether so-called 'group selection' is ever possible, Egbert Giles Leigh Jr, 'The Group Selection Controversy' (2009) 23 J Evolutionary Biology 6. The details of these disputes aside,

in the hypothesized way – for which evidence of a direct genetic basis is strong evidence.[42] Theorists have applied these methods to argue that a wide range of complex psychological universals – from language to the moralized emotion of disgust and separation anxiety – are genetically mediated products of natural selection.[43]

Legal theorists drawing on evolutionary psychology have argued that many basic legal concepts could similarly be evolved, genetically grounded features of human cognition.[44] For example, the basic concept of ownership that organizes property law appears to be universal,[45] and could plausibly have evolved as an adaptation to ensure access to and dominion over resources.[46] Similar observations have been made, for instance, with respect to other basic legal concepts like promise.[47]

Just like Reinach, these evolutionary psychologists and the legal theorists who follow them hold that basic legal concepts have a real existence outside of the law. Granted, these theorists *ground* the existence of these concepts in a different way – citing evolution and a modular mind. But their conclusions are importantly similar – legal concepts (at least the most basic ones on which both Reinach and evolutionary theorists focus) are not nominalistic legal constructions designed for normative purposes; they are real concepts that exist outside of any legal system and can be analyzed descriptively.

Moreover, perhaps even more emphatically than Reinach, theorists in evolutionary psychology refuse to infer anything moral from the innate existence of concepts in our psychology. The 'naturalistic fallacy' is an oft-repeated dogma – to state a fact

evolutionary psychology holds that psychological traits arose by whatever mechanisms in fact contributed to our evolution.

42 Alessandra Mozzi and others, 'The Evolutionary History of Genes Involved in Spoken and Written Language: Beyond FOXP2' (2016) 6 Scientific Rep 22157, 22157; Faraneh Vargha-Khadem and others, 'FOXP2 and the Neuroanatomy of Speech and Language' (2005) 6 Nature Rev Neuroscience 131, 131.

43 ibid; James M Sherlock and others, 'The Quantitative Genetics of Disgust Sensitivity' (2016) 16 Emotion 43, 43; L Sloman, P Gilbert, and G Hasey, 'Evolved Mechanisms in Depression: The Role and Interaction of Attachment and Social Rank in Depression' (2003) 74 J Affective Disorders 107, 107.

44 Jones and Goldsmith, (n 4); Carlton J Patrick, 'The Long-Term Promise of Evolutionary Psychology for the Law' (2016) 48 Arizona State LJ 995; Owen D Jones and Robert Kurzban, 'Intuitions of Punishment' (2010) 77 U Chicago L Rev 1633.

45 Wilson (n 4) 3; Pascal Boyer, 'How Natural Selection Shapes Conceptual Structure: Human Intuitions and Concepts of Ownership' in Eric Margolis and Stephen Laurence (eds), *The Conceptual Mind: New Directions in the Study of Concepts* (MIT 2015) 185, 186; Julia W Van der Vondervoort, Paul Meinz, and Ori Friedman, 'Children's Judgments About Ownership Rights and Body Rights: Evidence for a Common Basis' (2017) 155 J Experimental Child Psychology 1, 2.

46 Wilson (n 4) 17; Miyashita Haruki, 'On a Trade-Off in the Evolution of Ownership' (2018) 38 Economics Bulletin 1257.

47 Leda Cosmides and John Tooby, 'Evolutionary Psychology and the Generation of Culture, Part II: Case Study: A Computational Theory of Social Exchange' (1989) 10 Ethology and Sociobiology 51.

about our psychology is not to imply anything about ethics.[48] So the innate existence of, say, the concept of 'family' doesn't suggest anything about its moral significance; and it might be that we intuitively understand that the social act of promise gives rise to a 'binding' 'obligation,' but that these intuitions are morally wrong.

Finally, like Reinach, evolutionary theories of legal concepts tend to travel with a positivistic conception of the positive law. Owen Jones and Timothy Goldsmith, for example, argue that the positive law can in principle do whatever it wants, and often that it ought to – pursuing policy goals orthogonal or contrary to the basic concepts evolution has given us.[49] For Jones and Goldsmith (and other theorists in this vein) the positive law is presumed a historical artifact fully determined by social fact – not a concept with any necessary connection to facts about human psychology or morality.[50]

In short, although they ground the existence of legal concepts in different places, and draw on different evidence, evolutionary theorists and Reinach see these concepts and their relation to morality and positive law in similar ways – they agree that legal concepts exist outside the law; they agree these concepts can plausibly be the subject of determinate, descriptive reasoning; and they agree that these concepts have no necessary connection to either moral duty or positive law.

Today's evolutionary psychology, on which contemporary theorists draw, of course, did not exist in Reinach's time. Indeed, the origin of modern evolutionary psychology is often attributed to Edward O. Wilson's *Sociobiology* in 1975,[51] and today's work draws on universal grammar in linguistics in the 1960s,[52] the 'Modern Synthesis' of Darwinian natural selection with Mendelian inheritance of the 1950s and 1960s,[53] the development of game theory in the 1950s,[54] and Fisher's work on sexual selection in the 1930s.[55] Indeed, Darwinian evolution writ large has become vastly more plausible since Reinach's death if for no other reason than the 1953 discovery of DNA as the physical mechanism of inheritance – a famous handwave by Darwin himself.[56]

[48] Pinker, 'Blank Slate' (n 6) 151; David Sloan Wilson, Eric Dietrich, and Anne B Clark, 'On the Inappropriate Use of the Naturalistic Fallacy in Evolutionary Psychology' (2003) 18 Biology and Philosophy 669; Neil Levy, 'Evolutionary Psychology, Human Universals, and the Standard Social Science Model' (2004) 19 Biology and Philosophy 459.

[49] Jones and Goldsmith (n 4) 432–435.

[50] ibid 431–433.

[51] Edward O Wilson, *Sociobiology: The New Synthesis* (Harvard University Press 1975).

[52] Noam Chomsky, *Aspects of the Theory of Syntax* (MIT 1965).

[53] Nicholas H Barton, 'The "New Synthesis"' (2022) 119 Proceedings of the National Academy of Sciences e2122147119.

[54] John von Neumann and Oskar Morgenstern, *Theory of Games and Economic Behavior* (Princeton University Press 1944).

[55] M Anderson and LW Simmons, 'Sexual Selection and Mate Choice' (2006) 21 Trends in Ecology and Evolution 296.

[56] James D Watson and Francis H Crick, 'Molecular Structure of Nucleic Acids: A Structure for Deoxyribose Nucleic Acid' (1953) 171 Nature 737.

That being said, though less plausible, less sophisticated, and less empirically grounded, Reinach encountered and engaged with a basic sketch of the idea. After all, in *Origin*, Darwin himself suggested that '[p]sychology will be securely based on [a new] foundation . . . that of the necessary acquirement of each mental power and capacity by gradation.'[57] Perhaps most prominently in Reinach's lifetime, the American Pragmatists – especially William James – drew on Darwin's theory in suggesting that human psychological 'instincts' might have evolved.[58] Reinach was familiar with this work, having written an obituary for James after his 1910 death.[59] And Reinach's mentor Husserl spent a chapter in his *Prolegomena* responding to the quasi-evolutionary logical theories of Ernst Mach and Richard Avenarius.[60]

Thus, when Reinach insisted that his theory is *not* psychological – 'independent of human knowledge, independent of the organization of human nature'[61] – and *not* an evolutionary account of human cognition – 'not only for our world but for any conceivable world'[62] – it was *not* out of ignorance of what a theory of legal concepts grounded in evolutionary psychology could look like. Granted, and importantly (about which more below),[63] the proto-evolutionary psychology in vogue at the time – that of the Pragmatists – was substantively quite different from today's in its theory of mind. James, Mach, and Avenarius happened to be empiricists about concepts – from their perspective, the human mind and its capacity for subjective experience may have evolved, but our conceptual schema emerge from experience and social linguistic partitioning, not genetics.[64] Today, evolutionary psychologists overwhelmingly posit a modular, computational mind ready built with innate concepts.[65] Still, it is not as though the basic idea were not out there in Reinach's time.

To understand Reinach's efforts to distinguish his theory from psychological ones – notwithstanding their superficial compatibility – then, we have to go deeper and take seriously what was at stake for him in grounding legal concepts in metaphysics rather than an evolutionary account of human psychology.

57 Darwin (n 35) 506.

58 William James, *Principles of Psychology* (originally published 1890, Harvard University Press 1981) 274–285; Susan Haack, 'The Pragmatist Tradition: Lessons for Legal Theorists' (2018) 95 Washington U L Rev 1049, 1055, n 38.

59 Adolf Reinach, 'William James and Pragmatism' in Barry Smith (tr and ed), *Speech Act and Sachverhalt* (Springer 1987) 291.

60 Edmund Husserl, *Logical Investigations, Vol. I* (JN Findlay tr, Routledge 2001) 123.

61 Reinach (n 8) 139.

62 ibid 138.

63 Infra, nn 113–115 and accompanying text.

64 James, 'Principles' (n 58) 274–285; William James, *Essays in Radical Empiricism* (Harvard University Press 1912); infra nn 113–115 and accompanying text.

65 Steven Pinker, *How the Mind Works* (Norton 1997); Daniel C Dennett, *Consciousness Explained* (Back Bay 1992); Henry Plotkin, *Evolution in Mind: An Introduction to Evolutionary Psychology* (Harvard University Press 2000).

2.4 REINACH, LEGAL CONCEPTS, AND THE *PSYCHOLOGISMUS-STREIT*

The proto-evolutionary psychology of the *belle époque* was missing many important theoretical and empirical pieces. But it was wildly fashionable – a 'psychologically obsessed age.'[66] And in the increasingly naturalist intellectual climate after Darwin, psychology aspired to be descriptive and empirical. During this period, foundational psychologists like Sigmund Freud, William James, Wilhelm Wundt, and Reinach's PhD advisor Theodor Lipps hoped to ground a new science of mind-as-brain in empirical study, seeking laws of human thought as universal and empirical as the laws of physics.[67]

One intellectual movement during this time was an effort to situate intuitions about logic and mathematics in psychology – to argue that they were laws of human thought, not truths of our universe.[68] It was against this view that Gottlob Frege inveighed when he launched the *Psychologismus-Streit* in 1884. In his *Foundations of Arithmetic* and a series of works that followed, Frege argued against what he called 'psychologism' about math in particular, arguing that mathematical and logical rules are *a priori*, nonempirically true.[69] And thus was joined the *Psychologismus-Streit* that dominated German-language philosophy until the War.[70]

Frege's arguments against psychologism were suggestive and question-begging rather than dispositive – math, for example, is the most exact of all sciences; psychology perhaps the least.[71] Psychologism conflates 'true' with 'taken-to-be-true';[72] (but isn't that the point?). Perhaps most powerfully, Frege argued that psychologism assumes or leads to solipsism – if numbers are just subject-specific ideas, how could we communicate?[73] '[A] hitherto unknown kind of madness.'[74] But, regardless of their validity, Frege's arguments against psychologism were enough to convince that other titan of *fin-de-siècle* German philosophy, and one importantly closer to Reinach – Edmund Husserl.[75]

66 Husserl (n 60) 64.

67 James, 'Principles' (n 58); Wilhelm Wundt, 'On Psychological Methods' (1883) 1 *Philosophische Studien* 1; Sigmund Freud, *The Interpretation of Dreams* (Basic 2010).

68 John Stuart Mill, *A System of Logic, Ratiocinative and Inductive* (first published in 1843; Cambridge University Press 2011); Benno Erdmann, *Logik, Logische Elementarlehre* (Max Niemeyer 1892).

69 Gottlob Frege, 'The Foundations of Arithmetic' in Michael Beaney (ed and tr), *The Frege Reader* (Blackwell 1997) 84; Gottlob Frege, 'Grundgesetze der Arithmetik, Volume I' in Michael Beaney (ed and tr), *The Frege Reader* (Blackwell 1997) 194; Gottlob Frege, 'Book Review of Husserl 1891' (1894) 103 *Zeitschrift für Philosophie und philosophische Kritik* 313.

70 Martin Kusch, 'Psychologism' in Edward N Zalta (ed), *The Stanford Encyclopedia of Philosophy* (online 2020).

71 Frege, 'Foundations' (n 69) 87.

72 Frege, 'Grundgesetze' (n 69) 202.

73 ibid 206.

74 ibid 203.

75 There is some historical dispute as to whether it really was Frege's criticism that dissuaded Husserl from psychologism (and indeed whether Husserl had ever really endorsed

Arguing against psychologism – and grounding his new method of phenomenology as an alternative – became one of Husserl's primary pre-War projects – 'Husserl's *Prolegomena* has long been regarded as the pre-eminent statement of logical anti-psychologism.'[76] Husserl's arguments on this score were largely of the same flavor as Frege's – logical rules are more determinate than psychological rules, logical rules are phenomenologically *a priori*, etc.[77] And they are vulnerable to the same charges of circularity – presuming the reality of strict laws of logic when that is what the dispute is about.[78] But Husserl argued perhaps most forcefully against psychologism as entailing relativism. Psychologism, he says, amounts to 'species relativism' or 'anthropologism' – the hypothesis that principles of logic could be true *for us* but different for some other species.[79] 'Absurd,' says Husserl.[80]

While this controversy was kicking into gear, Reinach was a graduate student under Theodor Lipps, who was rather a bogeyman to Husserl for suggesting that 'logic is a psychological discipline.'[81] With his fellow students, Reinach read Husserl, found himself convinced, and decamped to Göttingen where he took a position as Husserl's assistant and 'worked closely with Husserl in the preparation of the second edition of the *Logical Investigations*.'[82] Reinach's break with Lipps and his affiliation with Husserl, then, was largely the result of the latter's convincing him that the psychologism of the former was in error.[83]

With this intellectual context, Reinach's efforts to distance himself from a psychological quasi-realism of legal concepts is hardly puzzling. The *Psychologismus-Streit* was a general debate over the relationship between metaphysics and psychology that he had very much joined – so was persuaded by the anti-pyschologist side to uproot his life and help fight Husserl's war against his old mentor. And transcripts of Reinach's seminars show that he 'was perhaps the only philosopher in Germany at

psychologism), but regardless it was after Frege that Husserl took up the mantle of anti-psychologism. Martin Kusch, *Psychologism: A Case Study in the Sociology of Philosophical Knowledge* (Routledge 1995) 12–13.

76 Robert Hanna, 'Husserl's Prolegomena and the Truth in Psychologism' (1993) 53 Philosophy Phenomenological Res 251, 252.

77 Husserl (n 60) 46–55.

78 Paul Natorp, 'On the Question of Logical Method in Relation to Edmund Husserl's Prolegomena to Pure Logic' in JN Mohanty (ed), *Readings on Edmund Husserl's Logical Investigations* (Springer 1977) 55, 57.

79 Husserl (n 60) 78–79.

80 ibid.

81 Quoted in Dale Jacquette, *Philosophy, Psychology, and Psychologism: Critical and Historical Readings on the Psychological Turn in Philosophy* (Springer 2006) 88, 89.

82 John F Crosby, 'A Brief Biography of Adolf Reinach' in John F Crosby (ed), *The Apriori Foundations of the Civil Law: Along with the Lecture 'Concerning Phenomenology'* (De Gruyter 2013) viii.

83 Florian Gödel, 'An Introduction to Moritz Geiger's Psychological Contribution on Empathy' (2015) 8 Dialogues in Philosophy, Mental and Neuro Sciences 161.

this time lecturing on the work of Frege.'[84] The question of whether the basic structures of our reason reflect timeless, *a priori*, metaphysically real truths or psychological facts was among the primary intellectual occupations of Reinach's life.

Through this lens, Reinach's metaphysical realism about legal concepts was another front in the war over psychologism – in law rather than logic or mathematics. Reinach insisted that truths about legal concepts – for example, that a claim dissolves once waived – have the same ontological status as the law of noncontradiction or $1 + 1 = 2$; that they were essentially, mind-independently true.[85] Indeed, throughout *Foundations*, Reinach analogizes reasoning about the essence of legal concepts to the philosophy of mathematics – '[i]n immersing ourselves in the essence of these entities ... we grasp connections in a manner analogous to the way in which we know when we immerse ourselves in the nature of numbers and geometrical forms';[86] 'there are eternal laws governing these legal entities and structures, laws which are independent of our grasp of them, just as are the laws of mathematics.'[87]

Moreover, in trying to show that legal concepts have the same kind of reality as mathematical concepts, part of Reinach's project was to show the *breadth* of the *a priori* – its usefulness and applicability not just to the suite of basic mathematical and logical principles long considered *a priori* in any event. Indeed, as far as Reinach was concerned, Husserl's arguments against logical psychologism were not merely effective against *logical* psychologism, but in fact convincingly demonstrated the existence of a vast range of really existent *a priori* states-of-affairs that philosophy had long failed to appreciate.[88]

We can reason about certain legal concepts in the same way that we can reason about numbers, Reinach is saying in *Foundations*, and the same arguments against psychologism apply – we have discovered the realm of the 'pure essential laws of right.'[89] And this legal case study, then, might help us see that the realm of the *a priori* 'extends absolutely everywhere' – 'one of the most important things in philosophy, and if one thinks it through completely, one of the most important things in the world.'[90] Perhaps Reinach's deepest personal philosophical commitment.

[84] Karl Schuhmann and Barry Smith, 'Adolf Reinach: An Intellectual Biography' in Kevin Mulligan (ed), *Speech Act and Sachverhalt: Reinach and the Foundations of Realist Phenomenology* (Springer 1987).

[85] Kimberly Baltzer-Jaray, 'Phenomenological Jurisprudence: A Reinterpretation of Adolf Reinach's Jarhrbuch Essay' in JA Simmons and JE Hackett (eds), *Phenomenology for the Twenty-First Century* (Palgrave Macmillan 2016) 118, 118.

[86] Reinach, 'Foundations' (n 8) 4.

[87] ibid 6.

[88] Reinach, 'Concerning Phenomenology' (n 18) 15; Barry Smith, 'On the Austrianness of Austrian Economics' (1990) 4 *Critical Review* 212.

[89] Reinach, 'Foundations' (n 8) 139.

[90] Reinach, 'Concerning Phenomenology' (n 18) 156.

2.5 NATURAL SELECTION AND ONTOLOGY

But *we* are not Adolf Reinach, and with presumably less personal investment in Husserl's vindication, it is fair to wonder whether indeed the sharp distinction he drew between phenomenological and psychological accounts of law amounts to all that much for legal theory. I argue that for at least two interrelated reasons legal theorists need not be as preoccupied as Reinach with the ontological status of concepts, at least between evolutionary theories and his own phenomenological realism. First, the difference between *evolutionary* psychological accounts and metaphysical realism is less wide than Reinach, Husserl, and Frege appear to have realized. Second, closely considered, Husserl's and Frege's arguments against psychologism are substantially more persuasive in their own fields of logic and mathematics than they are in law.

Recall one of Husserl's strongest arguments against psychologism – it entails the possibility of 'species relativism'; of the law of noncontradiction's being true as a matter of human psychology but false for some intelligent alien species.[91] In other words, psychologism suggests *ontologically arbitrary* variation across different species' 'laws of thought.' From this perspective, it is an argument against psychologism to point out that it doesn't appear that such variation exists – we *haven't* encountered species that seem to behave as though they have radically different understandings of the basic fabric of the universe than our own.

And consider Reinach:

> Apriori connections find application … in the events of nature. If these connections are conceived of as thought-laws, then the question of how this is possible arises. How does it happen that nature complies with the laws of our thought? Are we to assume here an enigmatic pre-established harmony? … The reason why nature should accommodate itself to the laws of our thinking is not susceptible to insight.[92]

If the principles of logic, mathematics, and private law are just laws of thought, the argument goes, what *keeps* them from being *arbitrary*? And as an actual empirical matter, it doesn't look like they are – the basic ways in which we think *do* seem to largely track reality. If we have one rock and another, we really do have two; we have yet to encounter in the macro world circumstances under which the proposition 'there is now a hungry lion at the cave entrance' is both true and false at the same time.

This is an entirely fair argument against psychologism *per se* – strongly suggestive if not logically dispositive. As against the suggestion that our concepts are rules of thought *full stop*, it is fair to wonder why they wouldn't vary arbitrarily as across individuals, species, or between individuals and the world around them. But it is *not*

[91] Husserl (n 60) 78–79.

[92] Reinach, 'Concerning Phenomenology' (n 18) 159.

a particularly powerful argument against *evolutionary* psychologism. Indeed, if we assume that it is *natural selection* that has given rise to innate psychological concepts – as opposed to, say, random brain development or Humean empiricism – psychologism and metaphysical realism look, from a practical, emergent perspective, much more similar.

Say what you will about natural selection, but it *is not arbitrary*. Indeed, it is thoroughly dependent on and necessarily reflects ontology. From this perspective, basic legal concepts might be both metaphysical truths and laws of thought; or they may only be laws of thought, but which approximate in some nonarbitrary way whatever the truths of metaphysics are.

We can start with the observation that the kind of cognitive concepts and processes at issue – from, say, the law of noncontradiction to intuitions about the nature of 'promise' – are highly energy intensive. For starters, they require a brain, and a fairly complex one – and all of the energy and long and vulnerable childhood that requires.[93] Beyond that minimum, each additional complex informational faculty – like the capacity for language – requires further energy; more calories to sustain neurons rather than, say, physical defenses or the ability to fly.[94] Granting the premises of evolutionary psychology, we can assume that, unless these concepts were fitness enhancing in some way, we presumably would not have them – ancestors who had evolved them would have been outcompeted by organisms with more efficient energy allocation.[95] 'According to evolutionary biology, the structural complexity of a given [trait] can provide evidence that the [trait] is an adaptation, even if nothing is known about [its] causal role.'[96]

So how might concepts like noncontradiction or the relationship between claim and waiver be fitness enhancing? Well, one *obvious* answer is because the *universe really is governed by these laws*.[97] Suppose that we actually do live in a universe in which the law of noncontradiction is true – that it genuinely cannot be that a

93 Michael A Hofman, 'Evolution of the Human Brain: When Bigger Is Better' (2014) 8 Frontiers in Neuroscience 1; Stephen C Cunnane, Laurence S Harbige, and Michael A Crawford, 'The Importance of Energy and Nutrient Supply in Human Brain Evolution' (1993) 9 Nutrition and Health 219; Ana Navarrete, Carel P van Schaik, and Karin Isler, 'Energetics and the Evolution of Human Brain Size' (2011) 480 Nature 91.

94 Chet C Sherwood and others, 'Evolution of Increased Glia-Neuron Ratios in the Human Frontal Cortex' (2006) 103 Proceedings of the National Academy of Sciences 13606.

95 Matt Ridley, *The Red Queen: Sex and the Evolution of Human Nature* (2nd edn, Harper 1993); Steven Pinker and Paul Bloom, 'Natural Language and Natural Selection' (1990) 13 Behavioral Brain Sciences 707, 709.

96 Shaun Nichols and Todd Grantham, 'Adaptive Complexity and Phenomenal Consciousness' (2000) 67 Philosophy Science 648, 648.

97 James Toomey, 'Evolutionary Anamnesis' (2022) 37 Biology and Philosophy 55, 56; S Lehar, 'Gestalt Isomorphism and the Primacy of Subjective Conscious Experience: A Gestalt Bubble Model' (2003) 26 Behavioral Brain Sciences 375; WS Geisler and RL Diehl, 'A Bayesian Approach to the Evolution of Perceptual and Cognitive Systems' (2003) 27 Cognitive Science 379.

proposition is both true and false at the same time. An embedded cognitive shortcut to that effect would be fitness enhancing. Indeed, it is strictly fitter than its alternatives. If we know 'there is now a hungry lion outside of the cave,' we know to wait, because it simply cannot be that there is *not* a lion outside the cave. This is less energy intensive than some kind of freewheeling general intelligence that must deduce noncontradiction *ex nihilo*, and is much safer than not understanding noncontradiction at all. If 1 + 1 really does = 2, and knowing that has any implications for reproductive success, it is at least marginally fitness enhancing to understand that innately.

The same could be true of the concepts of private law – maybe we've evolved to intuitively understand that promise gives rise to obligation *because that really is true* – just as Reinach believes. You might wonder how such a thing is possible, how it could be that the concept of 'promise' actually exists in a universe that has been around, as far as we know, for billions of years before the first promising entity. Which is, of course, entirely fair. But I don't know *how* or *why* the law of noncontradiction might exist either; or math or the laws of physics or any of the truths that we may have been the first to understand but apparently long preexisted us.[98]

Granted, some philosophers have argued that although this line of reasoning might work for descriptive constituents of the universe, it could not account for the evolution of true moral intuitions or evaluative attitudes.[99] But even if this is right,[100] recall that for Reinach these basic legal concepts *are* descriptive – they exist in the same way that logic and math do, and are conceptually independent of our moral intuitions about them and the nature of moral reality.[101] If you reject that, your disagreement with Reinach goes deeper than the concepts' *mode* of existence, to the *nature* of the thing – a defensible view, but no response to an evolutionary grounding of something like *Reinach's* jurisprudence. After all, proponents of this 'Darwinian Debunking' argument are perfectly happy to concede that natural selection can give rise to psychological concepts that *descriptively* reflect ontology,

[98] Martin Heidegger, *An Introduction to Metaphysics* (Ralph Manheim tr, Yale University Press 1959) 6–7; James Ladyman, 'The Foundations of Structuralism and the Metaphysics of Relations' in Anna Marmodoro and David Yates (eds), *The Metaphysics of Relations* (Oxford University Press 2015) 177, 179–80.

[99] Sharon Street, 'A Darwinian Dilemma for Realist Theories of Value' (2006) 127 Philosophical Studies 109; Michael Ruse, *Taking Darwin Seriously: A Naturalistic Approach to Philosophy* (2nd edn, Prometheus 1986).

[100] And it is hardly without controversy. William J Fitzpatrick, 'Why There is No Darwinian Dilemma for Ethical Realism' in Michael Bergmann and Patrick Kain (eds), *Challenges to Moral and Religious Belief: Disagreement and Evolution* (Oxford University Press 2014) 237; Knut Olav Skarsaune, 'Darwin and Moral Realism: Survival of the Iffiest' (2011) 152 Philosophical Studies 229; David Enoch, 'The Epistemological Challenge to Metanormative Realism: How Best to Understand It, and How to Cope with It' (2010) 148 Philosophical Studies 413.

[101] Section 2.2.

and argue rather against inferring moral obligation from that, entirely consistent with Reinach's picture.[102]

In any event, if this all is right – and we've evolved basic legal concepts as a matter of innate psychology because they really exist – Reinach's theory of the realism of concepts and a kind of evolutionary psychologism could be effectively coterminous. The concepts would exist *both* as an ontological matter – as Reinach would have it – *and* as a matter of innate psychology – as the evolutionary psychologists would have it. And indeed, the latter would be true *because of* the former.

Of course, there are other possibilities – natural selection hardly demands that our innate concepts are a one-to-one map of ontology (and obviously they are not – there is a vast range of electromagnetic radiation we are incapable of seeing, and our intuitions of motion are relative to the earth's surface, and so on). But although natural selection does not compel a relationship of correspondence between ontology and innate psychology, it does entail *some relationship* – no options of which are *arbitrary* in the way Reinach, Husserl, and Frege were really worried about.

Suppose that in fact all that exists is a sea of particles. And even suppose *arguendo* that quantum mechanics is right that in the end these particles behave according to probability, not law – a particle actually can be in two places at once; the cat can be both dead and alive.[103] How might the law of noncontradiction as a cognitive heuristic be fitness enhancing in such a universe? Presumably it could only have evolved if it at least roughly reflected ontology *as relevant to us* – a kind of innate nominalism.[104] So long as a law of noncontradiction sufficiently approximates the reality within which the intelligence has to operate, an innate noncontradiction principle could evolve.

There is, indeed, suggestive evidence that this is precisely the relationship between evolved minds and the universe in which they exist. For example, our lay, intuitive physics much more closely approximates the Newtonian mechanics of the world we must navigate than the underlying quantum structure that might really constitute the universe.[105] But while it is fitness enhancing to intuitively grasp how to evade falling objects, our ability to mate evidently almost never turns on the off chance that all our electrons are in the wrong place or whatever. Intuitive, quasi-Newtonian mechanics *is* a pretty good approximation of how objects behave in macro space.[106] Nominalists of all kinds recognize that categories can be efficient mechanisms to bundle, use, and exchange pertinent information, even if those

[102] Street (n 99) 112–113.

[103] David J Griffiths and Darrell F Schroeter, *Introduction to Quantum Mechanics* (3rd edn, Cambridge University Press 2018).

[104] Toomey, 'Evolutionary Anamnesis' (n 97) 55–56.

[105] James R Kubricht, Keith J Holyoak, and Hongjing Lu, 'Intuitive Physics: Current Research and Controversies' (2017) 21 Trends in Cognitive Sciences 749.

[106] HC Corben and Philip Stehle, *Classical Mechanics* (2nd edn, Dover 1994).

categories don't themselves exist metaphysically and are fuzzy at the margins.[107] This account might be equally applicable to the anterior level of natural selection rather than posterior social or linguistic construction.

The important point is that, while this kind of innate nominalism does not faithfully replicate the deep structure of reality, it is hardly *arbitrary*. It only works if it packages reality in ways that *really are useful*. And that is nothing but a question of ontology. The objects that reflect light at 700 nm really are physically more similar to those that reflect light at 701 nm than those that reflect at 400 nm – and innate psychology does not draw a line between 700 and 701, but somewhere between 400 and 700 most languages will demarcate something like 'blue' from something like 'red.'[108] Even if our evolved concepts are rough approximations of reality, then, or nominalistic but useful categories that do not really exist, they necessarily bear some relationship to metaphysical reality.[109]

Husserl, at least, appears to have been willing to accept all this. After a hundred pages of polemic against psychologism, he is more favorable in his treatment of the 'attempt to provide a *biological* basis for logical intuitions,' conceding that '[s]urvival requires a certain adaption to external nature . . . the capacity to judge things more or less rightly, to foresee the course of events, to assess causal consequences, etc.,' and that '[i]f the natural origin of the machinery which economizes thought is not to remain a miracle, . . . we shall have to . . . show . . . how a procedure which has had such success could and must have issued spontaneously out of purely natural causes.'[110]

But Husserl rejected this hypothesis for failing to 'consider how mental processes preserve truth.'[111] The problem was that Husserl did not see how natural selection might give rise to a computational, conceptual mind of the sort he envisioned.[112] And his foils in quasi-evolutionary theories of mind – Ernst Mach and Richard Avenarius – were hardly any help, being associationists about thought and radical empiricists about concepts.[113] But it is *today's* evolutionary theorists who are perhaps

107 Henry E Smith, 'On the Economy of Concepts in Property' (2012) 160 U Penn L Rev 2097.

108 Ara Norenzayan and Steven J Heine, 'Psychological Universals: What Are They and How Can We Know?' (2005) 131 Psychological Bulletin 763, 764; DH Sliney, 'What Is Light? The Visible Spectrum and Beyond' (2016) 30 Eye 222, 225–226; CL Hardin, 'A Spectral Reflectance Doth Not a Color Make' (2003) 100 J Philosophy 191, 196–199.

109 An obligatory caveat – evolutionary psychologists frequently emphasize that our cognitive faculties presumptively evolved to solve survival problems in the so-called Environment of Evolutionary Adaptedness (some 2.6 million to 12,000 years ago) and that they may therefore be out of step with the structure of contemporary society. But we're talking about metaphysics and the basic structure of the universe here, which presumably has not changed radically since then, and if it had, I imagine we would be, to put it mildly, feeling the selection pressure.

110 Husserl (n 60) 123, 128.

111 Jesse D Lopes, 'Phenomenology as Proto-Computationalism: Do the Prolegomena Indicate a Computational Reading of the Logical Investigations?' (2023) 39 Husserl Studies 47, 60.

112 ibid.

113 Iulian D Toader, 'Talking Past Each Other: Mach and Husserl on Thought Economy' in F Stadler (ed), *Ernest Mach – Life, Work, Influence* (Springer Cham 2019) 213, 217; Colin McGinn, 'Mach & Husserl' (1972) 3 J British Society Phenomenology 146, 148;

the *strongest* exponents of a modular, computational theory of mind – who argue that in fact natural selection is the best explanation for a computational mind; that evolutionary psychology has defeated associationism and vindicated something more like an innate *a priori*.[114] If Husserl had *this* evolutionary theory of mind available, perhaps he would have been more receptive.[115]

In short, if we accept that indeed it is *because of* natural selection that we have certain 'laws of thought,' we *must* accept certain ontological claims.[116] With this perspective on the interaction between natural selection and metaphysics, it isn't surprising that we don't observe species behaving as though they had radically different ontological perspectives than us – they would have had to have evolved in radically different metaphysical conditions. Nor is it surprising that our concepts map reality as we perceive it. Of course they do, that is how natural selection works. If they didn't (radically, regularly, etc.) we would die and organisms with more useful concepts would flourish in our stead.

In the end, of course, Husserl and Reinach are right that metaphysical realism is a *different* commitment than evolutionary psychologism. These theories *could be* coterminous, but there is obviously daylight between them. Natural selection is not a perfect designer. We have vestigial organs.[117] Most agree that at least some traits are spandrels – byproducts of the evolution of some other adaptation.[118] And some argue that sexual selection *can* result in the development of arbitrary expensive traits.[119] But all that is controversial, and natural selection remains a brutal constraint – when vestigial organs become too energy intensive, or spandrels too far from the purposes for which they were adaptive, or mating rituals too over-the-top, organisms will start dying before reproducing.

So, yes, while Reinach was right that his theory is different from one grounded in evolutionary psychology, he was wrong about *how* different, and in what sense. We might have evolved concepts that do not 'really' exist. They might mis-map reality, and it's possible that an intelligent species of angels with a different evolutionary history might have slightly different ones. But they are not *arbitrary* and *cannot possibly be too far off*. From this perspective, then, evolutionary theories of legal concepts look much closer to Reinach's.

Milič Čapek, 'Ernst Mach's Biological Theory of Knowledge' (1968) 18 Synthese 171; Paul Pojman, Ernst Mach's Biological Theory of Knowledge (Dissertation, Department of History and Philosophy of Science, Indiana University, 15 June 2000).

114 Zenon W Pylyshyn, *Computation and Cognition: Toward a Foundation for Cognitive Science* (MIT 1986); Konrad Lorenz, 'Kant's Doctrine of the A Priori in the Light of Contemporary Biology' in Michael Ruse (ed), *Philosophy after Darwin* (Princeton University Press 2010) 231.

115 Husserl (n 60) 129–30.

116 I am indebted to my former colleague John Humbach for this point.

117 Biswanath Mukhopadhyay and others, 'Spectrum of Human Tails: A Report of Six Cases' (2012) 17 J Indian Association Pediatric Surgeons 23.

118 Gould and Lewontin (n 41) 581.

119 Prum (n 41).

2.6 REINACH'S LEGAL ANTI-PSYCHOLOGISM

In short, Reinach – and his mentors against psychologism – appear to have overestimated the differences between evolutionary accounts of concepts and metaphysical ones. But it is still worth taking seriously these thinkers' affirmative arguments for metaphysical realism. After all, if Reinach or his intellectual progenitors had managed to *demonstrate* the metaphysical realism of legal concepts, or show some reason that metaphysical reality, and only metaphysical reality, could do the necessary work, whether evolutionary accounts overlap significantly might be beside the point. Reinach himself did not spend all that much time making affirmative arguments for metaphysical realism – rather, he largely assumed it was right; psychologism wrong. Presumably he thought the work had already been done – that Husserl and Frege had won. From this perspective, it seems fair to attribute to Reinach Husserl and Frege's arguments against psychologism. The problem for Reinach is that those arguments are much stronger in mathematics and logic than in private law.

To analyze whether any of Reinach, Husserl, and Frege have given us substantial affirmative reason to accept that metaphysical realism, and not evolutionary accounts of human psychology, is the mode of existence of basic concepts they are talking about, let us take their beliefs about psychologism (whether in logic, math, or law) as making the following two claims –

(1) there exist, metaphysically, certain basic concepts (of logic, math, or law) (a metaphysical claim);

(2) about which insight or intuition can reveal essential truths (an epistemic one).[120]

And what we are trying to figure out is whether any of these thinkers have given us a basis on which to reject –

(1a) the relevant concepts exist as features of human psychology

as a substitute for (1).

What *are* the arguments, then, for (1)? Most of them, as already alluded to, are hardly slam dunks. Frege and Husserl say that logical and mathematical laws cannot be derived from psychological laws because psychological laws are vague where logic is precise – but why not? Surely clarity can sometimes emerge on less-predictable forms – as Newtonian from quantum mechanics. They say that logic by its nature is True-out-there and psychologism requires it to be true in some relativistic sense, but this begs the question. It is circular to *assume* the necessity of Truth-out-there when that is precisely what the dispute is about – the psychologistic camp simply denies that logic, or anything, *is* True-out-there, or denies the

[120] Section 2.2.

possibility that we could know.[121] These sorts of arguments aren't going to cut it – if this were all we had to insist on (1) over (1a), I wouldn't bet the farm.[122]

One stronger argument, already discussed in Section 2.5, is inductive – (2) is true, which suggests something like (1) must be.[123] This is how Reinach proceeds, his clearest argument for (1) in the *Foundations* is that he is *showing* it by *doing* (2) – '[w]e shall *show* that the structures which one has generally called specifically legal have a being of their own . . . .'[124] And for Frege and Husserl, we *can* after all do math and use logic; it must have some kind of existence.

This argument is fair, as far as it goes. It is inductive, and not logically conclusive.[125] But, as discussed, it *is* obviously on to something. Natural selection depends on ontology, and our evolved concepts necessarily bear some nonarbitrary relationship to metaphysics. Indeed, if (1) *is* true, (1a) likely would be as well, *because* of (1). And if (1a) is true, *something like* (1) must be. But if we are trying to show (1) *over* (1a) where they come apart – if we are trying to show that some concept exists metaphysically as opposed to *just* as a matter of human psychology, or both – this inductive approach is much more persuasive for Frege and Husserl in math and logic than it is in law.

This is because law and the social acts that, on Reinach's account, constitute it, are different from math and logic in precisely the relevant respect – even if legal concepts exist as a matter of metaphysics, at least at present truths about them are only accessible to, and visible among, human beings. That makes it *impossible* to inductively distinguish between (1) and (1a) – Reinach's phenomenology can do (2), which can show that something like (1a) must be true, and maybe (1a) is because of (1), but maybe it is because of something *like* (1), and maybe it is not (for example, it might be the result of sexual selection).[126]

Consider the grounds on which Frege and Husserl can suggest (1). They can start by doing (2) themselves – reasoning, apparently *a priori*, to apparently true conclusions. But they might be crazy. So, like Socrates in the *Meno*, they can find random people and do (2) together.[127] But those people might be crazy. So, they talk to everyone, and together everyone does (2). (1) is looking more and more likely. But *everyone* might be crazy. That is just another way of saying that (1a), or some

[121] E Pivcevic, *Husserl and Phenomenology* (Routledge 1970) 38–40; GJ Massey, 'Some Reflections on Psychologism' in T Seebohm, D Føllesdal, and J Mohanty (eds), *Phenomenology and the Formal Sciences* (Springer 1991) 186.

[122] GP Baker and PMS Hacker, 'Frege's Anti-Psychologism' in MA Notturno (ed), *Perspectives on Psychologism* (Brill 1989) 74; Massey (n 121) 183; D Føllesdal, *Husserl und Frege: Ein Beitrag zur Beleuchtung der Entstehung der phänomenologischen Philosophie* (H Aschehoug and Co 1958).

[123] See Section 2.5.

[124] Reinach (n 8) 4 (emphasis added).

[125] Bertrand Russell, *Human Knowledge: Its Scope and Limits* (George Allen and Unwin 1948) 450.

[126] Prum (n 41).

[127] Plato, 'Meno' (WKC Guthrie tr) in Edith Hamilton and Huntington Carnes (eds), *Plato: The Collected Dialogues* (Princeton University Press 1961) 353–384.

psychologism less correlated with ontology than an evolutionary account, might be true, and could account for our ability to collectively (2).

But Frege and Husserl *can* do more than merely (2) with all human beings – they can look at the structure of the world around them. They can see, as we saw above, that animals appear to cogitate according to similar logical rules to the ones they have relied on at (2). Of course that doesn't *prove* (1), rather than convergent evolution (which might well be *because of* (1), but could be for other reasons)[128] but it is something. And Frege and Husserl can go even further, and point out that it appears that the conclusions we reach while (2)ing *are* true about everything – that the world *does* behave according to our *a priori* logical structure, and our *a priori* mathematical conclusions account for innumerable phenomena.[129]

Reinach cannot do this. Social acts don't happen without social entities.[130] And, for Reinach, human beings are the only entities of which we are currently aware that can participate in or reason about legal concepts. '[A]nimals too can be bearers of experience, but never of claims or obligations.'[131] He *claims* that his conclusions apply to angels, gods, and devils, but, as empirical verification of this might be the best way to inductively distinguish between something more like (1) and something more like (1a), forgive me for waiting.[132]

Finally, this brings us to what seems to be the crux of the issue for Frege and Husserl. It is not really an argument at all. It is a stipulation. Frege, for example, admits that '[t]here appears such a world of difference between me and the psychological logicians that there is no prospect of influencing them through my book.'[133] But he inveighs –

> When will an end be put to this once and for all! Everything is eventually dragged into the realm of psychology; the boundary between the objective and the subjective disappears more and more, and even actual objects are treated psychologically as ideas. . . . Thus everything leads to idealism and with perfect logical consistency into solipsism.[134]

'*If we want to emerge from the subjective at all*, then we must *conceive* of knowledge as an activity that does not create what is known but grasps what already exists.'[135]

And Husserl – 'I . . . find myself at a point which I have either to recognize as the Archimedean point from which the world of doubt and unreason may be levered on its hinges, or which I may sacrifice at the peril of sacrificing all reason and

[128] See Section 2.5.
[129] Reinach, 'Concerning Phenomenology' (n 18) 159.
[130] Reinach, 'Foundations' (n 8) 11.
[131] ibid.
[132] ibid 47.
[133] Frege, 'Grundgesetze' (n 69) 207.
[134] ibid 205–206.
[135] ibid 206 (emphasis added).

knowledge';[136] 'One cannot persuade the subjectivist any more than one can the open sceptic, a man simply lacking the ability to see that laws ... have their roots in the mere meaning of truth ... must [embrace a position] count[ed] as the purest nonsense.'[137]

In other words, Frege and Husserl hold that (1) *must* be true. *Must* (1) be true, though? Of course not, not literally; not logically.[138] Hence the stipulation, and its insistence. It *could*, 'in principle,' be that there are some species for which the concept of equality 'exists' and those it does not. The universe *could be* fundamentally disordered; I *could* be a brain-in-a-vat – 'a dream about being a person.'[139] It's not possible for a concept like equality to exist or not exist *metaphysically* across species, and, *if* the law of noncontradiction is metaphysically true, then it couldn't be true and false for different species,[140] but that takes us right back to the circularity. Confining ourselves to strict possibility, we face the specter of an incoherent, disordered, meaningless universe that has only to this point appeared to each of us coherent and ordered and contemplative of meaning. We always have; we always will.[141]

Frege and Husserl's 'must,' in '(1) *must* be true,' then, is not the 'must' of logical entailment. It is, rather, a certain kind of 'must *if*' – (1) must be true *if anything matters*. Granted, (1) might not be true. But perhaps then it'd be time to throw in the towel – at least for their project, presumably for projects, period. Why is this? Stipulating the metaphysical existence of one's concepts of investigation hardly seems demanded by conceptual analysis as such. The language philosophers of the mid-century, for instance (to whom Reinach bears a striking resemblance)[142] were perfectly happy to parse the conceptual structure of speech while disclaiming any views on its metaphysical correspondence.[143] Plenty of people, also like Reinach, analyze the descriptive entailments of legal concepts without stipulating anything like (1), and certainly without the high melodrama of Frege and Husserl on the point.[144]

But this kind of ontologically detached analysis is not a possibility for Frege and Husserl, precisely because of *what they are analyzing*. The difference is that a language or legal philosopher need not tell us anything about how we *ought* to

[136] Husserl (n 60) 94.
[137] ibid 78.
[138] Hanna (n 76) 270–274.
[139] Nic Pizzolatto, 'The Locked Room,' *True Detective* (HBO January 16, 2014).
[140] Husserl (n 60) 78–79.
[141] Robert Nozick, *Philosophical Investigations* (Harvard University Press 1981) 201.
[142] Marietta Auer, 'Promising, Owning, Enacting: Adolf Reinach's Phenomenology of Legal Speech Acts' (Chapter 1, this volume).
[143] JL Austin, *How to Do Things with Words* (JO Urmson and Marina Sibsà, eds Harvard University Press 1975) 164.
[144] Bill Watson, 'The Decline of Natural Law and the Rise of Exclusive Positivism' (2022) 75 SMU Law Review Forum 174.

interact with a social concept they are analyzing – we might be better off without it at all, and still learn something useful from the project. But in theorizing about the foundations of logic and mathematics, Frege and Husserl are hoping to tell us how we *ought to think* – in formal logic and, well, *everywhere*.

It is, after all, implicit in their project that we ought to be persuaded by *their* logic; on the presumption that we ought to think logically. As Husserl puts it, '[t]his being bound is not meant psychologically in the sense of a thought-compulsion, but in the ideal sense of a norm: whoever judges differently, judges quite wrongly.'[145] Without some theory of how we ought to think – what *counts as thinking*, what we ought to recognize as thinking and accord appropriate respect – we *do* confront radical skepticism or solipsism. Frege and Husserl are, in other words, deriving *normative* claims about how we *ought* to think from their descriptive claims about the ontological foundations of logic and mathematics.

For deriving oughts about thought, we need (1), not (1a). If we stipulate (1), we take it that there is a genuine logical structure of truth in the universe. For this fact to ground an ought, all we now need is perhaps the most unobjectionable epistemic norm of all time – (n) *we ought to think truly*. That is, we ought to think according to what is actually true; we do something normatively objectionable when we think incorrectly. If we accept (n), and (1) is true, we get an ought about logic. We can follow, and be persuaded by, Husserl and Frege's emergent analysis of logical and mathematical concepts. Indeed, we can hear each other out in all contexts, without worrying about that defiant rejoinder of the radical skeptic – 'That all sounds right. But even if it is, why should I care?' *That* is what Frege and Husserl stipulate (1) (and (n), more implicitly) against.

(1a) simply does not have the same normative force. You might wonder why this is. After all, even with (1), we face the tried-and-true difficulty of deriving an ought from an is.[146] Indeed, we had to stipulate that we ought to think truly. Why couldn't we rather stipulate (n_a) – we ought to think according to our evolved cognitive proclivities – rather than (n)?

All I can say here is that (n_a) is plainly false, and (n) plainly true. If we have evolved to think a certain way, but doing so is incorrect, and does not track reality, and is wrong, we *ought not think that way*. I take this to be uncontroversial, at least outside of the kind of nihilist circles that so agitate Husserl and Frege. As Husserl puts it, '[t]he constitution of a species is a fact: from a fact it is only possible to derive other facts.'[147] Today's evolutionary psychologists, famously, agree.[148] (n_a) is precisely the species relativism of Husserl's worries; adjacent to perhaps even more nihilistic (n_b) – we *ought* to think however we *do* (individually; Frege's solipsism). Either of

[145] Husserl (n 60) 93.
[146] David Hume, *A Treatise of Human Nature* (John Noon 1739) 335.
[147] ibid 80.
[148] See n 48.

these is a straightforward rejection of the possibility of meaning, of standing to demand that some other's thinking track the same reality as mine. Husserl and Frege are *right*, then, on their own terms, about the domain in which they are writing. In logic, at least, and probably math, if we are to have a theory about how we ought to think and speak, we must accept (1) (or something like it)[149] over (1a).

But what does this all have to do with *jurisprudence*? Maybe nothing, and that's the point. Reinach's own peculiar, descriptive approach to thinking about legal concepts lets us avoid this whole mess. Because Reinach, *unlike Husserl*, does *not* ground normative claims in the existence of the legal concepts he is analyzing.[150] In other words, where Husserl makes claims about how we ought to think, grounded in claims about, metaphysically, how things are, Reinach makes claims about how things, metaphysically, are (there exist these basic legal concepts) but *does not* draw from this claims about how the positive law ought to be. The positive law, he insists, *unlike Husserlian logical thinking*, is normatively free to vary from the *a priori*, and sometimes ought to.[151] Reinach *sets aside* questions about what we ought to do with the concepts he describes.

So insofar as all Reinach is doing, ultimately, is describing his concepts, he loses Husserl's reasons for insisting on (1) over (1a). As already emphasized, (1) and (1a) are similar for many purposes. If one's project is merely to *describe* specified concepts, they might be identical. But they differ in normative force. (n) is banal. (1) plus (n) is a straightforward foundation for epistemic normativity; maybe necessary for normativity writ large. (n_a), by contrast, is facially preposterous, and (1a) plus (n_a) flirts with nihilism. In other words (1) and (1a) might be quite similar, but *n and n_a are not.* If Husserl wants to write about how we *ought* to think and speak and communicate with one another, *he* needs (1). But Reinach's project is different on its own terms. By setting aside the normative implications of the legal concepts he analyzes, Reinach doesn't need (n) over (n_a). He doesn't need any kind of n at all. And if he doesn't need (n_a) over (n), he doesn't need (1a) over (1), either.

In short, it is true that the ontological status of concepts might matter normatively. Frege and Husserl recognize this, and to the extent they want to derive claims about how we ought to think in math or logic, their concepts might have to exist ontologically rather than psychologically. But Reinach is different. His analysis is descriptive, not normative. It illuminates the positive law, rather than tells us how it ought to be. And for *that* project, (1) and (1a) are more closely equivalent. If evolutionary psychology (or any other theory), offers an alternative, relevantly equivalent mode of existence for legal concepts – namely, holds them to exist in a descriptive way that has no necessary connection to either morality or the positive

149 See Section 2.5. Concluding that we ought to think according to the certain mathematical entities does not *demand* Platonism about them, but it does demand that they bear some sort of genuine, nonarbitrary relationship to ontology.

150 See Section 2.2.

151 ibid.

law, accessible to human intuition, as both metaphysics and evolutionary psychology do – it seems that Reinach has no real grounds to reject it.

2.7 CONCLUSION

In insisting that the basic concepts of private law exist outside of their legal construction, but that this fact has no conceptual implications for moral obligations or positive law, Adolf Reinach may be a nearly unique figure in the history of legal philosophy. Perhaps closest to his perspective are those contemporary theorists who have applied evolutionary psychology to a theory of legal concepts – and who agree that basic concepts really do exist in some sense outside of legal construction, but that positive law is free to deviate from them, and often ought to. On its face, it is something of a puzzle, then, that Reinach makes so clear that he is not one of them – prepared to stake everything on his claims being ontological, not psychological.

As a matter of Reinach's personal intellectual history, this commitment makes perfect sense – he saw it as one exemplary application of perhaps the most important philosophical position of his life, a commitment to a thick, epistemically accessible fundamental ontology, shared and hashed out by the leading figures of pre-War German philosophy.

But the *Psychologismus-Streit* ended with the outbreak of actual war in 1914. And post-War philosophers have largely found the stakes of whether the laws and concepts of logic and mathematics are metaphysically real or 'laws of thought' lower than did Frege, early Husserl, and Reinach. I've argued that this is particularly so in jurisprudence. Indeed, the difference between evolutionary theories of legal concepts and metaphysical ones is smaller than Reinach appears to have assumed, and Husserl's and Frege's arguments are more convincing in their own domains than in Reinach's. In short, whatever Reinach himself would have to say (and as several contributions to this volume have argued on different grounds)[152] his insights remain relevant even for many of those who might struggle with his metaphysics.

BIBLIOGRAPHY

Anderson M and LW Simmons, 'Sexual Selection and Mate Choice' (2006) 21 Trends Ecology and Evolution 296

Auer M, 'Promising, Owning, Enacting: Adolf Reinach's Phenomenology of Legal Speech Acts' (Chapter 1, this volume)

Austin JL, *How to Do Things with Words* (JO Urmson and Marina Sibsà, eds Harvard University Press 1975)

[152] Auer (Chapter 1, this volume); Andrew S Gold and Henry E Smith, 'Legal Concepts as a Deep Structure of the Law: Reinach's A Priori in Action' (Chapter 5, this volume).

Baker GP and PMS Hacker, 'Frege's Anti-psychologism' in MA Notturno (ed), *Perspectives on Psychologism* (Brill 1989) 74

Baltzer-Jaray K, 'Bogged Down in Ontologism and Realism' in RKB Parker (ed), *The Idealism-Realism Debate among Edmund Husserl's Early Followers and Critics* (Springer Cham 2021) 151

'Phenomenological Jurisprudence: A Reinterpretation of Adolf Reinach's Jarhrbuch Essay' in JA Simmons and JE Hackett (eds), *Phenomenology for the Twenty-First Century* (Palgrave Macmillan 2016) 118

Barton NH, 'The "New Synthesis"' (2022) 119 Proceedings of the National Academy of Sciences e2122147119

Beccacece L, P Abondio, E Cilli, D Restani, and D Luiselli, 'Human Genomics and the Biocultural Origin of Music' (2021) 22 International J Molecular Sciences 5397, 5398

Boyer P, 'How Natural Selection Shapes Conceptual Structure: Human Intuitions and Concepts of Ownership' in E Margolis and S Laurence (eds), *The Conceptual Mind: New Directions in the Study of Concepts* (MIT 2015) 185

Buss DM, *Evolutionary Psychology* (5th edn, Pearson 2011)

Čapek M, 'Ernst Mach's Biological Theory of Knowledge' (1968) 18 Synthese 171

Chomsky N, *Aspects of the Theory of Syntax* (MIT 1965)

Chow DCK, 'Trashing Nihilism' (1990) 65 Tulane Law Review 221

Cohen FS, 'Transcendental Nonsense and the Functional Approach' (1935) 35 Columbia L Rev 809

Coleman JL, 'The Architecture of Jurisprudence' (2011) 121 Yale LJ 5

Corben HC and P Stehle, *Classical Mechanics* (2nd edn, Dover 1994)

Cosmides L and J Tooby, 'Evolutionary Psychology and the Generation of Culture, Part II: Case Study: A Computational Theory of Social Exchange' (1989) 10 Ethology and Sociobiology 51

Crosby JF, 'A Brief Biography of Adolf Reinach' in JF Crosby (ed), *The Apriori Foundations of the Civil Law: Along with the Lecture 'Concerning Phenomenology'* (De Gruyter 2012) viii

Cunnane SC, LS Harbige and MA Crawford, 'The Importance of Energy and Nutrient Supply in Human Brain Evolution' (1993) 9 Nutrition and Health 219

Darwin C, *The Origin of Species* (First Signet 2003)

Dennett DC, *Darwin's Dangerous Idea: Evolution and the Meanings of Life* (Penguin 1996)

Consciousness Explained (Back Bay 1992)

Dworkin R, *Taking Rights Seriously* (Harvard University Press 1978)

Enoch D, 'The Epistemological Challenge to Metanormative Realism: How Best to Understand It, and How to Cope with It' (2010) 148 Philosophical Studies 413

Erdmann B, *Logik, Logische Elementarlehre* (Max Niemeyer 1892)

Finnis J, *Natural Law and Natural Rights* (2nd edn, Oxford University Press 2011)

Fitzpatrick WJ, 'Why There Is No Darwinian Dilemma for Ethical Realism' in M Bergmann and P Kain (eds), *Challenges to Moral and Religious Belief: Disagreement and Evolution* (Oxford University Press 2014) 237

Føllesdal D, *Husserl und Frege: Ein Beitrag zur Beleuchtung der Entstehung der phänomenologischen Philosophie* (H Aschehoug und Co 1958)

Frege G, 'The Foundations of Arithmetic', in M Beaney (ed and tr), *The Frege Reader* (Blackwell 1997)

'Grundgesetze der Arithmetik, Volume I' in M Beaney (ed and tr), *The Frege Reader* (Blackwell 1997) 194

'Book Review of Husserl 1891' (1894) 103 *Zeitschrift für Philosophie und philosophische Kritik* 313

Freud S, *The Interpretation of Dreams* (Basic 2010)
Gannon G, 'A Critique of Evolutionary Psychology' (2010) 4 Psychology, Evolution and Gender 173
Gardner J, *From Personal Life to Private Law* (Oxford University Press 2018)
Geisler WS and RL Diehl, 'A Bayesian Approach to the Evolution of Perceptual and Cognitive Systems' (2003) 27 Cognitive Science 379
Gödel F, 'An Introduction to Moritz Geiger's Psychological Contribution on Empathy' (2015) 8 Dialogues Philosophy, Mental Neuro Sciences 161
Gold AS and HE Smith, 'Legal Concepts as a Deep Structure of Law: Reinach's A Priori in Action' (Chapter 5, this volume)
Gould SJ and RC Lewontin, 'The Spandrels of San Marco and the Panglossian Paradigm: A Critique of the Adaptationist Programme' (1979) 205 Proceedings of the Royal Society Biology 581
Griffiths DJ and DF Schroeter, *Introduction to Quantum Mechanics* (3rd edn, Cambridge University Press 2018)
Haack S, 'The Pragmatist Tradition: Lessons for Legal Theorists' (2018) 95 Washington U L Rev 1049
Hanna R, 'Husserl's Prolegomena and the Truth in Psychologism' (1993) 53 Philosophy Phenomenological Res 251
Hardin CL, 'A Spectral Reflectance Doth Not a Color Make' (2003) 100 J Philosophy 191
Haruki M, 'On a Trade-Off in the Evolution of Ownership' (2018) 38 Economics Bulletin 1257
Heidegger M, *An Introduction to Metaphysics* 6–7 (R Manheim tr, Yale University Press 1959)
Hershovitz S, 'The End of Jurisprudence' (2015) 124 Yale LJ 1160
Hofman MA, 'Evolution of the Human Brain: When Bigger Is Better' (2014) 8 Frontiers Neuroscience 1
Hume D, *A Treatise of Human Nature* (John Noon 1739)
Husserl E, *Logical Investigations, Vol. I* (JN Findlay tr, Routledge 2001)
Jacquette D, *Philosophy, Psychology, and Psychologism: Critical and Historical Readings on the Psychological Turn in Philosophy* (Springer 2006)
James W, *Principles of Psychology* (originally published 1890, Harvard University Press 1981)
Essays in Radical Empiricism (Harvard University Press 1912)
Jones OD and R Kurzban, 'Intuitions of Punishment' (2010) 77 U Chicago L Rev 1633
Jones OD and TH Goldsmith, 'Law and Behavioral Biology' (2005) 105 Columbia L Rev 405
Kubricht JR, KJ Holyoak, and H Lu, 'Intuitive Physics: Current Research and Controversies' (2017) 21 Trends Cognitive Sciences 749
Kusch M, 'Psychologism' in EN Zalta (ed), *The Stanford Encyclopedia of Philosophy* (online 2020)
Psychologism: A Case Study in the Sociology of Philosophical Knowledge (Routledge 1995)
Ladyman J, 'The Foundations of Structuralism and the Metaphysics of Relations' in A Marmodoro and D Yates (eds), *The Metaphysics of Relations* 177, 179–180 (Oxford University Press 2015)
Lehar S, 'Gestalt Isomorphism and the Primacy of Subjective Conscious Experience: A Gestalt Bubble Model' (2003) 26 Behavioral Brain Sciences 375
Leigh Jr EG, 'The Group Selection Controversy' (2009) 23 J Evolutionary Biology 6
Levy N, 'Evolutionary Psychology, Human Universals, and the Standard Social Science Model' (2004) 19 Biology and Philosophy 459
Lopes JD, 'Phenomenology as Proto-Computationalism: Do the Prolegomena Indicate a Computational Reading of the Logical Investigations?' (2023) 39 Husserl Studies 47

Lorenz K, 'Kant's Doctrine of the A Priori in the Light of Contemporary Biology' in M Ruse (ed), *Philosophy after Darwin* (Princeton University Press 2010) 231
Massey GJ, 'Some Reflections on Psychologism' in T Seebohm, D Føllesdal, and J Mohanty (eds), *Phenomenology and the Formal Sciences* (Springer 1991) 183
McCrae RR and PT Costa Jr., 'Personality Trait Structure as a Human Universal' (1997) 52 American Psychologist 509, 509
McGinn C, 'Mach & Husserl' (1972) 3 J British Society Phenomenology 146
McLeod I, *Legal Theory* (6th edn, Red Globe Press 2012)
Mill JS, A *System of Logic, Ratiocinative and Inductive* (first published in 1843; Cambridge University Press 2011)
Moore MS, 'Moral Reality Revisited' (1992) 90 Michigan L Rev 2424
'The Interpretive Turn in Modern Theory: A Turn for the Worse?' (1989) 40 Stanford L Rev 871
'Metaphysics, Epistemology, and Legal Theory' (1987) 60 Southern California L Rev 453
Mozzi A, D Forni, M Clerici, U Pozzoli, S Mascheretti, FR Guerini, S Riva, N Bresolin, R Cagliani, and M Sironi, 'The Evolutionary History of Genes Involved in Spoken and Written Language: Beyond FOXP2' (2016) 6 Scientific Rep 22157, 22157
Mukhopadhyay B, RM Shukla, M Mukhopadhyay, KC Mandal, P Haldar, and A Benare, 'Spectrum of Human Tails: A Report of Six Cases' (2012) 17 J Indian Association Pediatric Surgeons 23
Natorp, P, 'On the Question of Logical Method in Relation to Edmund Husserl's Prolegomena to Pure Logic' in JN Mohanty (ed), *Readings on Edmund Husserl's Logical Investigations* (Springer 1977)
Navarrete A, CP van Schaik and K Isler, 'Energetics and the Evolution of Human Brain Size' (2011) 480 Nature 91
Neumann JV and O Morgenstern, *Theory of Games and Economic Behavior* (Princeton University Press 1944)
Nichols S and T Grantham, 'Adaptive Complexity and Phenomenal Consciousness' (2000) 67 Philosophy Science 648
Norenzayan A and SJ Heine, 'Psychological Universals: What Are They and How Can We Know?' (2005) 131 Psychological Bulletin 763
Nozick R, *Philosophical Explanations* (Harvard University Press 1981)
Patrick CJ, 'The Long-Term Promise of Evolutionary Psychology for the Law' (2016) 48 Arizona State LJ 995
Pinker S, *The Blank Slate: The Modern Denial of Human Nature* (Penguin 2002)
How the Mind Works (Norton 1997)
Pinker S and P Bloom, 'Natural Language and Natural Selection' (1990) 13 Behavioral Brain Sciences 707
Pivcevic E, *Husserl and Phenomenology* (Routledge 1970)
Pizzolatto N, 'The Locked Room,' True Detective (HBO January 16, 2014)
Plotkin H, *Evolution in Mind: An Introduction to Evolutionary Psychology* (Harvard University Press 2000)
Pojman P, Ernst Mach's Biological Theory of Knowledge (Dissertation, Department of History and Philosophy of Science, Indiana University, June 15, 2000)
Posner R, *Economic Analysis of Law* (7th edn, Aspen 2007)
Prum RO, *The Evolution of Beauty: How Darwin's Forgotten Theory of Mate Choice Shapes the Animal World – And Us* (Doubleday 2017)
Putnam P, 'Realism and Reason' (1977) 50 *Proceedings of the American Philosophical Association* 483

Pylyshyn ZW, *Computation and Cognition: Toward a Foundation for Cognitive Science* (MIT 1986)

Reinach A, 'Concerning Phenomenology' (D Willard tr) in JF Crosby (ed), *The Apriori Foundations of the Civil Law: Along with the Lecture 'Concerning Phenomenology'* (Ontos Verlag 2012) 145

'On the Concept of Causality in the Criminal Law' (B Brogaard, tr) (2009) 1 Libertarian Papers 1

'William James and Pragmatism' in B Smith (tr and ed), *Speech Act and Sachverhalt* (Springer 1987) 291

'The Apriori Foundations of the Civil Law' (John F Crosby tr, 1983) 3 Aletheia 1–142, reprinted in Adolf Reinach, *The Apriori Foundations of the Civil Law: Along with the Lecture 'Concerning Phenomenology'* (John F Crosby ed, Ontos Verlag 2012), originally published as Adolf Reinach, Die apriorischen Grundlagen des bürgerlichen Rechtes, 1 (2) *Jahrbuch für Philosophie und phänomenologische Forschung* (Max Niemeyer 1913), 685–847

Ridley M, *The Red Queen: Sex and the Evolution of Human Nature* (2nd edn, Harper 1993)

Rose S and H Rose, *Alas Poor Darwin: Arguments against Evolutionary Psychology* (Crown 2001)

Ruse M, *Taking Darwin Seriously: A Naturalistic Approach to Philosophy* (2nd edn, Prometheus 1986)

Russell B, *Human Knowledge: Its Scope and Limits* (George Allen and Unwin 1948)

Schacter DL, DT Gilbert, and DM Wegner, *Psychology* (5th edn, Worth 2007)

Schaus S, 'A Simple Model of Torts and Moral Wrongs' (2022) 97 Notre Dame L Rev 1029

Schuhman K and B Smith, 'Adolf Reinach: An Intellectual Biography' in K Mulligan (ed), *Speech Act and Sachverhalt: Reinach and the Foundations of Realist Phenomenology* (Springer 1987)

Shafer-Landau R, 'The Possibility of Metaethics' (2010) 90 Boston U L Rev 479

Shapiro SJ, 'The Hart-Dworkin Debate: A Short Guide for the Perplexed' in A Ripstein (ed), *Ronald Dworkin* (Cambridge University Press 2007)

Sherlock JM, BP Zietsch, JM Tybur, and P Jern, 'The Quantitative Genetics of Disgust Sensitivity' (2016) 16 Emotion 43

Sherwood CC, CD Stimpson, MA Raghanti, DE Wildman, M Uddin, LI Grossman, M Goodman, JC Redmond, CJ Bonar, JM Erwin, and P Hof, 'Evolution of Increased Glia-Neuron Ratios in the Human Frontal Cortex' (2006) 103 Proceedings of the National Academy of Sciences 13606

Singer JW, 'The Player and the Cards: Nihilism and Legal Theory' (1984) 94 Yale LJ 1

Skarsaune KO, 'Darwin and Moral Realism: Survival of the Iffiest' (2011) 152 Philosophical Studies 229

Sliney DH, 'What Is Light? The Visible Spectrum and Beyond' (2016) 30 Eye 222

Sloman L, P Gilbert, and G Hasey, 'Evolved Mechanisms in Depression: The Role and Interaction of Attachment and Social Rank in Depression' (2003) 74 J Affective Disorders 107

Smith B, 'On the Austrianness of Austrian Economics' (1990) 4 Critical Review 212

Smith HE, 'On the Economy of Concepts in Property' (2012) 160 U Penn L Rev 2097

Street S, 'A Darwinian Dilemma for Realist Theories of Value' (2006) 127 Philosophical Studies 109

Toader ID, 'Talking Past Each Other: Mach and Husserl on Thought Economy' in F Stadler (ed), *Ernest Mach: Life, Work, Influence* (Springer Cham 2019) 213.

Tooby J and L Cosmides, 'Conceptual Foundations of Evolutionary Psychology' in DM Buss (ed), *The Handbook of Evolutionary Psychology* (Wiley 2021) 5
Toomey J, 'Property's Boundaries' (2023) 109 Virginia L Rev 131
'Evolutionary Anamnesis' (2022) 37 Biology and Philosophy 55
Van de Vondervoort JW, P Meinz, and O Friedman, 'Children's Judgments about Ownership Rights and Body Rights: Evidence for a Common Basis' (2017) 155 J Experimental Child Psychology 1
Vargha-Khadem F, DG Gadian, A Copp, and M Mishkin, 'FOXP2 and the Neuroanatomy of Speech and Language' (2005) 6 Nature Rev Neuroscience 131
Watson B, 'The Decline of Natural Law and the Rise of Exclusive Positivism' (2022) 75 SMU Law Review Form 174
Watson JD and FH Crick, 'Molecular Structure of Nucleic Acids: A Structure for Deoxyribose Nucleic Acid' (1953) 171 Nature 737
Wilson BJ, *The Property Species: Mind, Yours, and the Human Mind* (Oxford University Press 2020)
Wilson DS, E Dietrich, and AB Clark, 'On the Inappropriate Use of the Naturalistic Fallacy in Evolutionary Psychology' (2003) 18 Biology & Philosophy 669
Wilson EO, *Sociobiology: The New Synthesis* (Harvard University Press 1975)
Wundt W, 'On Psychological Methods' (1883) 1 *Philosophische Studien* 1

3

Is There a Legal A Priori?

On Necessary, Essential, and Non-positive Propositions in Reinach's Theory

Lorenz Kaehler

3.1 THE QUEST FOR A LEGAL A PRIORI

Among Reinach's most central claims is the thesis that there is a legal a priori that constitutes the foundation of private law. It supposedly does not rest on experience but on the essence of legal phenomena. Therefore, a priori legal propositions are in his view independent of any particular legal system.

The chapter subjects this claim to a critical appraisal. Reinach challenges both positivist theories, which ground law solely in social acts without acknowledging a priori legal propositions, as well as those natural law theories according to which moral principles are part of the law. For Reinach excluded not only empirical propositions but also morality from the a priori foundations of law.[1] This shows that the frequently maintained opposition between positivism and natural law theories is incomplete. Reinach's theory, at least, challenges both.

Reinach uses a noteworthy example to show the a priori: the extinction of an obligation with fulfilment.[2] He acknowledges that positive law can differ from such a priori propositions.[3] Thus, it would be consistent with his theory if, for instance, in times of need, the legislature mandated that certain obligations, like wage payments, should not disappear upon fulfilment but rather might have to be partially fulfilled again at a later point in time. According to his theory, such a case would not disprove the thesis of an a priori extinction upon fulfilment, as it pertains to positive law rather than a priori propositions.

1 Adolf Reinach, 'The Apriori Foundations of the Civil Law' (John F Crosby tr, 1983) 3 Aletheia 1, reprinted in Adolf Reinach, *The Apriori Foundations of the Civil Law Along with the Lecture 'Concerning Phenomenology'* (John F Crosby ed, Ontos Verlag 2012), originally published as Adolf Reinach, Die apriorischen Grundlagen des bürgerlichen Rechtes, 1(2) *Jahrbuch für Philosophie und phänomenologische Forschung* (Max Niemeyer 1913), 685–847. Cited in parallel with the German Edition [hereinafter GE]: Adolf Reinach, *Die apriorischen Grundlagen des bürgerlichen Rechtes* (Max Niemeyer 1913) 129.

2 ibid 32; [GE] 39.

3 ibid 103; [GE] 118.

This example of fulfilment is intriguing because, on the one hand, it seems indeed to be natural that obligations are extinguished through fulfilment: but, on the other, this extinction is not inherent in the concept of fulfilment itself. The latter only entails that what has been promised has been done. This raises the question of precisely why one can assume the extinction through fulfilment. How do we know this? Reinach's answer in such cases seems to be that we can discern an a priori essence of this phenomenon.[4]

But even if one grants that an extinction with fulfilment is self-evident,[5] it does not follow from this that it is a priori. This would presuppose that all obvious or self-evident propositions are a priori. For this purpose, one must demonstrate that no proposition derived from experience shares this characteristic. This seems to be an impossible task if one considers propositions such as 'Legal norms are usually not completely implemented'. They seem quite plausible but still rest in part on empirical observations and are therefore not a priori. Hence, there seems to be no easy way to conclude from the fact that something is obvious to the fact that it is a priori.

Furthermore, it is not clear that propositions that rest on the essence of legal phenomena are indeed fundamental for law, as suggested by Reinach. It is at least theoretically possible to assume without contradiction that the law lacks a priori foundations but still contains a priori legal propositions which may concern only non-fundamental questions.

Reinach's theory thus poses numerous challenges and raises a plethora of problems. Its core claim about the existence of a priori legal propositions is far from self-evident, considering the historical evolution of law and the diversity of legal systems. This chapter seeks to explore this claim. It looks at the main candidates for a priori legal propositions and discusses whether there are convincing reasons to assume their a priori character. If it turns out, as will be argued, that this is not the case, this does not completely disprove the existence of a legal a priori. There still may exist a priori legal propositions that have another basis. However, their scope is severely limited if the primary examples for such propositions turn out to rest in part on experience.

At the outset, some terminological clarifications seem appropriate. Legal propositions are in the following understood as true statements that could be made about law without implying their fundamental character. They regularly are – but need not be part of the positive law. A proposition about a certain object is a priori if one can justify its correctness without appeal to experience.[6] Its apriority can but does

[4] ibid 32; [GE] 39.

[5] ibid 130–31; [GE] 153–54.

[6] cf Bruce Russel, 'A Priori Justification and Knowledge', *The Stanford Encyclopedia of Philosophy* (Summer edn., 2020), https://plato.stanford.edu/entries/apriori/ accessed 28 October 2023.

not need to be due to certain properties of this object but might also have to do with properties of the recognizing subject.

The definition of an a priori via justifiability remains neutral towards the question whether and how one forms a belief about a proposition.[7] It is thus independent of whether anybody came to know it and, if so, how they managed to do so. In this regard, one may or may not share Reinach's position that one does not gain a priori insights through experience.[8] It is sufficient for the apriority that one can justify it without appealing to empirical evidence, even though this very evidence might be in fact necessary to become convinced of it. For instance, children might initially come to understand the correctness of a calculation only by counting with their fingers and remembering the result. However, this experience is not necessary to justify the correctness of a calculation. Similarly, one might only be able to grasp a proposition about a legal a priori if one is familiar with at least one positive legal system. Nevertheless, this does not prove that such a proposition is a posteriori, that is, that its justification rests on empirical observations. It might be the case that it is just human incapacity to discern the correctness of this proposition without knowing a particular legal system. Whether there is a legal a priori is thus an epistemic matter of justifying a proposition, not a cognitive one about belief formation.

To define an a priori proposition by its justifiability[9] without empirical evidence does not mean that a priori propositions are unrelated to those that rest on experience. Instead, it allows propositions derived from experience to support or refute a priori propositions, provided that the latter have independent justification to qualify as a priori. For instance, an a priori claim that no legal system can possibly contain a certain norm, say about timeless rights, could be refuted by providing an example of a legal system in which such rights exist. Nevertheless, the lack of such examples does not prove the claim's correctness. For this, one needs a priori reasons.

Finally, apriority is to be distinguished from revisability.[10] While a sentence might be revisable due to the possibility of it being proven wrong through further investigation, it can still be considered a priori. For instance, mathematical hypotheses are open to revision because one could have made an error in calculation, yet they do not rely on empirical evidence and are hence not a posteriori. Similarly, even if one were to convincingly reject all Reinach's a priori legal claims, it would not necessarily negate the possibility that there are a priori legal propositions. Reinach could have made a mistake in his examples, without being wrong about the underlying thesis concerning the existence of a legal a priori.

Unfortunately, Reinach hardly substantiates his concept of apriority. Although the a priori is the central concept of his thesis, he assumes that he does not need to deal

7 Laurence Bonjour, *In Defense of Pure Reason* (Cambridge University Press 1998) 10.
8 Adolf Reinach, 'Über Phänomenologie' in Karl Schuhmann and Barry Smith (eds.), *Sämtliche Werke*, vol. II (Philosophia 1989) 543.
9 cf Russel (n 6).
10 Bonjour (n 7) 73, 113.

with 'the problem-laden theory of the apriori'[11]– thereby acknowledging its precarious character. Instead, he describes the a priori in various ways. In this respect, his remark is central that 'every state of affairs which is in the sense explained general and necessary is in our terminology apriori'.[12] But this leaves open whether necessity is the defining property of apriority or just its consequence. In the former case, a proposition is a priori in virtue of containing a necessary claim. Contrary to that, in the latter case the apriority is defined differently, for example by being justifiable without experience, and can nevertheless hold with necessity because only a posteriori insights might be contingently true.

Reinach's cited description of the a priori has led some commentators to conclude that his concept of apriority relates not to cognition but to states of affairs and thus to ontology.[13] Reinach himself previously stressed that the necessity of the a priori pertains to the necessity of being and not of thinking.[14] However, the alternative of thinking or being is misleading. If the a priori relates to the justifiability of propositions, it neither concerns the act of thinking, as justifiability does not presuppose a conscious act, nor does it merely address how states of affairs are independent of us, as these acts alone do not determine what could count as a justification for us. Instead, the presence or absence of a priori justifiability of a proposition relates to what we should reasonably think under certain circumstances. This might very well be based in part on the properties of the state of affairs to which it refers. In this regard, one is indeed dealing with a 'material a priori'. But in addition, one also deals with epistemic justifications for beings like us. Hence, the a priori concerns the justifiability of propositions about states of affairs and not just states of affairs themselves simpliciter. Thus, the a priori pertains both to being and thinking, which shows that the alternative is misleading.

The definition of the a priori as what one can justify without appeal to experience contradicts, at first glance, Reinach's claim that 'what is *primarily* a priori is neither sentences nor the judgment nor the act of knowledge, but rather the "posited", judged, or known state of affairs'.[15] However, the use of the term 'primarily' suggests that apriority does not only pertain to states of affairs, but also ('secondarily') to judgements and perceptions. The latter aspect aligns with the Kantian usage of the term 'a priori', which formed the backdrop of much philosophical debate in the early twentieth century and, probably, also for Reinach.[16] According to this

[11] Reinach, *The Apriori Foundations of the Civil Law* (n 1) 48; Reinach, *Die apriorischen Grundlagen des bürgerlichen Rechtes* (n 1) 5.

[12] ibid 5; [GE] 5.

[13] James M Dubois, *Judgement and Sachverhalt* (Kluwer 1995) 80, 94; Sophie Loidolt, *Einführung in die Rechtsphänomenologie* (Mohr Siebeck 2010) 79.

[14] Reinach, *Über Phänomenologie* (n 8) 544.

[15] Reinach, *The Apriori Foundations of the Civil Law* (n 1) 48; Reinach, *Die apriorischen Grundlagen des bürgerlichen Rechtes* (n 1) 5 (emphasis added).

[16] Erwin Riezler, 'Apriorisches im Recht' (1923/24) 17(3) Archiv für Rechts- und Wirtschaftsphilo sophie 264.

perspective, the a priori is not derived from experience but rather holds absolutely,[17] which is an epistemic and not an ontological claim. In this vein, Reinach maintains that a priori insights are, without any exception, capable of being based on irrefutable evidence and not gained through experience.[18] This shows once more that the necessity of an a priori proposition might not be its defining feature but its consequence.

Reinach's theory can thus neither be confined to ontology nor to epistemology.[19] Accordingly, he emphasizes that a priori propositions do not stem from positive law,[20] are self-evident,[21] or follow from an intuition of essences.[22] This mixes ontological claims (e.g., about lacking positivity), epistemic claims (e.g., about what is self-evident) and cognitive claims (e.g., about the role of intuitions).

When one attempts to defend Reinach's thesis, several candidates of legal propositions come into sight that possibly are a priori. These are, following Reinach, necessary propositions (3.2) and essential propositions (3.3). Moreover, and independent of his views, non-positive legal propositions could in general be a priori, as they do not rest on propositions from positive law that can only be known a posteriori (3.4). If none of these candidates turn out to be a priori, the question becomes whether self-evident propositions, which were crucial for Reinach, still hold significance. Therefore, the chapter will conclude with the question of whether one can explain the phenomenon of self-evident legal propositions differently. I will argue that non-positive legal reasons provide for such an answer (3.5).

In this discussion, the chapter pursues a systematic approach to examine the plausibility of a legal a priori. It is thus not primarily concerned with an exegesis of Reinach's text or with anchoring it in the phenomenological tradition, although such considerations might explain the boldness of his claims. Instead, the focus is on the persuasiveness of actual and possible arguments supporting his thesis of apriority. Thus, insights from current debates can play a role, without anachronistically accusing Reinach of ignoring them. For it might very well be the case that Reinach's thesis of apriority is correct while his arguments for it are wanting. In order to assess his thesis, it is thus not sufficient to examine his own arguments. In addition, it is necessary to examine arguments Reinach himself did not use but which could, possibly, make his thesis of a legal a priori more plausible. By engaging in this way with later insights, Reinach's work is treated with greater respect than if

[17] Immanuel Kant, *Kritik der reinen Vernunft in Kants Werke* vol. III (2nd edn, Walter de Gruyter 1968) B28.

[18] Reinach, *Über Phänomenologie* (n 8) 543, 546.

[19] Dubois, *Judgement and Sachverhalt* (n 11) 107.

[20] Reinach, *The Apriori Foundations of the Civil Law* (n 1) 4; Reinach, *Die apriorischen Grundlagen des bürgerlichen Rechtes* (n 1) 4.

[21] ibid 5, 78, 103; [GE] ibid 5, 93, 118.

[22] ibid 5; [GE] ibid 5.

one were to confine oneself to its interpretation. Only in this way does his claim to have made timeless observations have a chance to become plausible.

3.2 NECESSARY PROPOSITIONS

The primary source of a priori legal propositions in Reinach's theory are necessary statements.[23] According to him, the a priori is characterized by a necessity of being (and not of thinking).[24] As already mentioned, he thus associates apriority and necessity by calling every state of affairs that 'is general and necessary'[25] a priori, although his comments also encompass epistemic notions.[26] Regardless of Reinach's stance, it appears, at least initially, to be a defining characteristic of a priori propositions that they remain unaffected by contingent circumstances and can thus not be contingently true. If true, they must be true by necessity. In contrast, a posteriori propositions hinge on such circumstances and therefore lack necessity.

For example, it is a question of positive law whether an obligation due for fulfilment becomes time-barred after three years. This depends on empirically contingent decisions of the legislator, which are not a priori given. In contrast, the proposition that an obligation generally is extinguished with fulfilment seems to be necessary. At least, no circumstances are discernible on whose correctness it depends.

However, from the fact that the content of positive law is both non-necessary and a posteriori one cannot draw the converse conclusion that legally necessary propositions are a priori. As Saul Kripke[27] in particular has demonstrated, there can be necessary propositions whose correctness is not established a priori, but only follow from experience. He gives the example, already discussed in antiquity, that the morning star is the evening star, even if this can only be established by astronomical investigation and thus a posteriori.[28] For the name morning star is a rigid denominator whose reference does not change once an object carries it and applies thus with necessity.

One can transfer this argument to law. For here, too, proper names serve as rigid denominators. Then only experience can show that they refer to the same object. For example, the fact that the German Basic Law and the current German constitution are identical does not follow from these concepts alone. According to its disputed original intention, the Basic Law could also be a mere provisional

[23] Reinach, *The Apriori Foundations of the Civil Law* (n 1) 45; Reinach, *Die apriorischen Grundlagen des bürgerlichen Rechtes* (n 1) 55.

[24] Reinach, *Über Phänomenologie* (n 8) 544.

[25] Reinach, *The Apriori Foundations of the Civil Law* (n 1) 5; Reinach, *Die apriorischen Grundlagen des bürgerlichen Rechtes* (n 1) 5.

[26] ibid.

[27] Saul Kripke, *Naming and Necessity* (Harvard University Press 1980) 140.

[28] ibid 104.

law – which is arguably no constitution.[29] In order to establish the identity of the Basic Law with the German constitution, one must therefore examine whether both terms refer to the same law. This is now the case, since, according to Article 146, the Basic Law is no longer merely provisional. For this reason, the Basic Law is also referred to as the German Constitution. One is therefore dealing with different names for the same law. It is true that these names could have been different. But once they were chosen, they necessarily refer to the same object.

This example shows that, contrary to Reinach's assumption, one cannot in general identify the necessity of a proposition with its apriority. Rather, there can be necessary legal propositions that are not a priori. The fact that one has to distinguish between apriority and necessity is not surprising; both deal with different issues. Whether something can only be known through experience is not the same question as whether something is necessarily the case.

This is of particular importance when one deals not with logical but with normative necessity.[30] For example, a prohibition might rest on overwhelming legal or moral reasons that require it and that depend nevertheless in part on empirical considerations. In this case the prohibition is not a priori but still holds with (normative) necessity. Once all factual premises are known, it is even difficult to imagine that a normative conclusion does not follow with necessity, although it might be controversial, for there is no contingent fact that could make it only contingently true. This shows again that one can deal with propositions that are necessary and nevertheless uncertain. If their uncertainty can only be overcome with the help of empirical evidence, they cannot be a priori.

For instance, one might consider the proposition of deontological logic according to which a norm cannot simultaneously provide for a valid prohibition and a valid commandment of the same act A to be a priori plausible. In contrast, the necessity of normative evaluations might go back in part to empirical observations. Contradictory behaviour may be considered against good faith, if there is insufficient time within which others can adjust to the change. Whether something constitutes contradictory behaviour can therefore only be established with the help of evaluations of the period in which the change occurs. Nevertheless, the reasons for such an evaluation might be so strong that it is – despite its lack of apriority – normatively necessary.

Consider as an illustration the following case: It may be impermissible in a legal system on grounds of contradictoriness to initially release a photo for the press, but then to object to its use shortly before publication, while such an objection may be permissible after several years. So, it is not only contradictory to simultaneously

[29] cf Matthias Herdegen, 'Art. 146' in G Dürig, R Herzog, and R Scholz (eds), *Grundgesetz-Kommentar* (100st supp, Beck 2023) 13-8.

[30] Immanuel Kant, 'Die Metaphysik der Sitten' in *Kants Werke* vol. VI (Walter de Gruyter 1968) 222.

allow and prohibit a certain action, but also to undertake both acts consecutively within a short time. The point at which behaviour becomes contradictory, and thus impermissible, may depend on empirical circumstances, such as whether an article or a print is usually prepared in a certain time. Thus, even the question of which acts are prohibited as contradictory, which seems like a good candidate for a priori legal propositions, does not, despite its normative necessity, rest entirely on a priori reasons. Therefore, the mere fact that overriding reasons necessitate a certain legal solution does not demonstrate that this solution is a priori. This may, but need not, be the case.

Note that this argument does not hinge on the distinction between an analytic and a synthetic a priori.[31] If this distinction breaks down, as Quine[32] has argued, nothing would change within it. Whether one can gain a priori insight by analysing a certain concept or whether one can synthesize different concepts into an a priori is independent of the distinction between (metaphysical) necessity and (epistemic) apriority.

Reinach's identification of a priori and necessary propositions therefore seems to be rash. If one wants to prove a priori legal propositions, it requires more than just a reference to their necessity. However, it does not follow from this that there are no a priori legal propositions. They just do not follow from necessity alone.

3.3 ESSENTIAL PROPOSITIONS

For Reinach the existence of a priori legal propositions goes hand in hand with the assumption that there is an essence of legal concepts.[33] In this perspective, it does not depend on the particular legal system what an a priori obligation or an a priori contract is. Rather, the concept is supposedly fixed from the outset, although the legal system can deviate from it.[34] Concepts hence supposedly rest on essences, which are free from accidental circumstances that one can know only a posteriori. What lies in the essence of a thing shall be a priori. Conversely, what is a priori shall lie in the essence of a thing.

Against such a perspective, the accusation often associated with so-called conceptual jurisprudence of drawing legal conclusions from the concept or essence of a thing does not apply. For Reinach[35] repeatedly and explicitly refuses to draw consequences for positive law from the essence of legal concepts and negatively refers to the temptation to do so as 'ontologism'. Consequently, he leaves

[31] Kant, *Kritik der reinen Vernunft* (n 17) B19.

[32] Willard Van Orman Quine, *From a Logical Point of View* (2nd edn, Harvard University Press 1980) 37.

[33] Reinach, *The Apriori Foundations of the Civil Law* (n 1) 5; Reinach, *Die apriorischen Grundlagen des bürgerlichen Rechtes* (n 1) 5.

[34] ibid 6; [GE] ibid 6.

[35] ibid 124; [GE] ibid 145.

unrestricted room for positive law to establish divergent concepts and norms according to expediency. When it comes to the capacity of the legislator, Reinach[36] is a positivist, even though he wants to develop a profoundly non-positivist ontology of law.

In this way, Reinach tries to immunize the essence of legal concepts from the accusation that positive law foresees something else. In his theory, no a priori concept can fail for the reason that actual legal systems contain other forms of it. However, the question then becomes whether by shielding the fundamental concepts of private law from any positive law, Reinach has not thrown the baby out with the bathwater. What exactly is the essence of a legal concept if it is independent of *any* positive law so that no example of positive law can refute it? Such counter-examples are usually a good means to test the essence of entities, as they encompass those characteristics the absence of which would mean dealing with a different kind of entity.[37] If, for example, one considers that one can sit on a chair to be one of its essential properties, then any chair on which one cannot sit would serve as a counter-example. Accordingly, if a property is essential for a legal concept, there should not be a single case to which this concept applies but in which the property is missing. Therefore, it would be natural to look at positive law for such examples in order to test whether a certain legal property is indeed essential for a certain concept.

Reinach excludes such a refutation in principle. He grants the legislator the freedom not only to use a different legal name for a certain phenomenon, but also the freedom to determine the same legal concept differently.[38] Consequently, one cannot, according to his theory, find any counter-example in positive law against a priori concepts. It is therefore unclear on which basis one can establish or refute a priori concepts. For example, it is compatible with his theory that the legislature provides for non-consensual contracts. But how can one be certain that one is then still dealing with contracts and not with another kind of legal entity which the legislature merely calls 'contracts'? By opening up unlimited possibilities for positive law to deviate from a priori law, Reinach makes it doubtful how legal concepts could have any essence, as this by definition excludes deviations from it.

Likewise, the central question of how to determine the essence of a legal concept or entity remains open. Reinach defends himself against the accusation that a priori essence is something 'dark and mystical', but then adopts the phenomenological terminology to 'approach the things themselves unburdened with preconceptions'.[39] How is that supposed to be possible for law? How can one approach an a

36 cf ibid 7; [GE] ibid 8.

37 Teresa Robertson Ishii and Philip Atkins, 'Essential vs. Accidental Properties', *The Stanford Encyclopedia of Philosophy* (Spring edn, 2023) https://plato.stanford.edu/entries/essential-accidental/ accessed 28 October 2023.

38 Reinach, *The Apriori Foundations of the Civil Law* (n 1) 103; Reinach, *Die apriorischen Grundlagen des bürgerlichen Rechtes* (n 1) 118.

39 ibid 5; [GE] ibid 6.

priori right? After all, legal concepts are not like a house or a chair that one could physically approach.

Moreover, it is already unclear what evidence should support such an 'unclouded view'. Unlike material objects such as houses and chairs, of which one has an immediate sensory perception, law deals with ontologically ideal entities, which are frequently referred to as abstract objects.[40] There cannot be a sensual perception of them. Hence, there is not even a sensual experience which one could take as a starting point in order to approach the essence of a legal phenomenon. For material objects such as chairs, one might try to determine what is essential by looking at many different specimens. In this way, one might determine, for example, that the colour of a chair does not belong to its essence, while there must necessarily be a surface intended for sitting on. However, precisely this starting point, which one can grasp by the senses, is missing in the case of non-empirical entities such as law.

One might examine different legal systems in a corresponding manner in order to establish an essence of legal concepts or institutions, as has occasionally been attempted in comparative law projects that search for a 'common core'.[41] In this way, one could, for example, examine the concept of contract in ten legal systems in order to establish its essence. Yet this approach is opposite to Reinach's,[42] because thereby one would only establish empirical commonalities in particular legal systems. There is no guarantee that these legal systems do not jointly deviate from the essence of an a priori concept. How, then, is one to arrive at a conclusion about such concepts if neither sensual perception nor familiarity with particular legal systems can help? How does thinking alone allow one to establish a legal concept?

One could attempt an analogy to mathematical propositions, since there is no sensory perception of them either, and one can also not derive them from particular calculations or other singular acts. As a priori propositions, the validity of which becomes clear merely by thinking, they could, possibly, serve as a model for a priori propositions in law. However, there is the difficulty that mathematical proofs result from axioms,[43] which are set and not a priori recognized. The proofs are thus subject to certain assumptions and in this respect only apply hypothetically.[44]

Contrary to this, a priori legal propositions should apply unconditionally and not only contain hypothetical statements about what results when certain legal norms are valid. For instance, according to Reinach, the proposition that an obligation is

40 José L Falguera, Concha Martínez-Vidal and Gideon Rosen, 'Abstract Objects' in *The Stanford Encyclopedia of Philosophy* (Summer edn, 2022) https://plato.stanford.edu/entries/abstract-objects/ accessed 28 October 2023.

41 Mauro Bussani and Ugo Mattei, *The Common Core of European Private Law* (Kluwer 2002).

42 Reinach, *The Apriori Foundations of the Civil Law* (n 1) 133; Reinach, *Die apriorischen Grundlagen des bürgerlichen Rechtes* (n 1) 156; Riezler (n 16) 268.

43 cf Penelope Maddy, *Defending the Axioms: On the Philosophical Foundations of Set Theory* (Oxford University Press 2011) 1.

44 Reinach, *The Apriori Foundations of the Civil Law* (n 1) 108–9; Reinach, *Die apriorischen Grundlagen des bürgerlichen Rechtes* (n 1) 125.

extinguished by fulfilment should hold unconditionally and not depend upon the validity of certain positive norms. Mathematical propositions thus differ from legal propositions and hardly make a legal a priori plausible.

Reinach often refers to the fact that certain legal propositions are immediately obvious and self-evident, whereby he seems to rely on human intuition.[45] In doing so, he picks up on a real phenomenon, namely that certain legal concepts and their interrelationships are plausible regardless of a particular legal system. The fact that an obligation is extinguished by fulfilment is intuitively obvious without one having to examine a particular legal system. The problem with this claim is not simply that one uses intuitions for the analysis of propositions.[46] Rather, the problem is the claim of 'the intuitive grasping of them in an immediate insight'[47] and that there is 'absolute evidence'[48] for them.[49] For this suggests, against common experience, that one could not make mistakes about one's legal intuitions concerning a priori propositions of law. What seems obvious at first glance might turn out to be wrong, so that it is questionable how absolute the evidence is on which Reinach relies.

Moreover, his underlying assumption that what is immediately insightful must be a priori is problematic. The source of human intuition is not necessarily accessible to the thinker himself, so that one can hardly know with certainty whether an immediate insight is a priori or a posteriori. Having an intuition does not mean knowing where it comes from. At best, further investigation can reveal this. One might simply deal with common sense, in which all kinds of insights, from experience and other sources, play a role. For example, if one considers it immediately plausible that an obligation will be extinguished through fulfilment, one's own experiences with fulfilled obligations could play a role for this insight. It is in general by no means certain that an intuition is based only on a priori insights and not also – or even exclusively[50] – on empirical experience. In view of the fact that one deals with legal norms in many ways in everyday life and that this, possibly, has an impact on one's intuition about law, it cannot be ruled out that these experiences impact one's intuitions about it.

Reinach's claim that one can grasp the essence of legal concepts through intuition is therefore in tension with his claim that these concepts are a priori. The more one relies on intuition, the less one can be sure of gaining a priori insights, because one can then all the less exclude that one's experiences play a role for one's

45 ibid 5–6, 131–32; ibid 18, 154; Reinach, *Über Phänomenologie* (n 8) 535.

46 See the defence of Kripke (n 27) 42.

47 Reinach, *The Apriori Foundations of the Civil Law* (n 1) 131; Reinach, *Die apriorischen Grundlagen des bürgerlichen Rechtes* (n 1) 154.

48 ibid 132; [GE] ibid 154.

49 cf Edmund Husserl, *Ideen zu einer reinen Phänomenologie und phänomenologischen Philosophie* (Niemeyer 2002) 82, 86.

50 David Hume, A *Treatise of Human Nature*, DF Norton and MJ Norton (eds) (Oxford University Press 2000) SB xviii.

judgements. If, on the other hand, one only accepts propositions and concepts that are a priori, one must be prepared to exclude many of one's intuitions because of their a posteriori nature. The danger in this case is that one must limit oneself to a few a priori statements of deontological logic, such as that a legal norm may not demand A and at the same time non-A. Then the more interesting legal questions, such as the consequences of the fulfilment of an obligation, remain out of sight.

The observation that language often, if not exclusively, shapes concepts supports this conclusion that intuitions are not a promising method for identifying a priori legal concepts. The fact that a contract presupposes the participation of at least two persons may simply be due to the fact that certain languages foresee such a concept. It is a long way from this fact to establishing that there is a concept of a contract independent of all languages that has certain essential properties. This requires bold conceptual claims about what is valid beyond any language.

If one refrains from making a judgement about such language-independent concepts, one can only determine what is essential according to the concept established in a particular language. As mentioned, essential properties of an entity are characterized by the fact that they cannot be absent without the entity falling under another concept. If one determines by intuition what is essential to a concept, one is possibly only stating a property of the concept that is established in a certain language, not a property that must also exist independently of any language. When Reinach refers to the intuition that certain statements about legal concepts are immediately obvious, this alone therefore does not prove the existence of a priori legal propositions. Possibly, his analysis only brings to light which properties of a concept are essential in a certain language.

The necessary characteristics of a legal concept within a certain language do not have to follow from a specific positive legal system, although its influence on language is indisputable, because legal concepts often differ in meaning from their everyday usage. Accordingly, determinations about what is essential for a concept can follow from the setup of a language without an anchor in positive law. This shows that legal concepts might occur in legal propositions whose correctness does not depend on a particular legal system.

For instance, according to the concept of a contract in many languages, it is part of its essence that at least two persons agree about it. If this is not the case, one is not dealing with a contract at all, but with another type of norm, such as a statute or an order. Other characteristics of a contract, on the other hand, are accidental, because they could be absent. For example, the fact that at least one party in a contract must pay money is an accidental property because, as in the case of exchange, there are also contracts in which neither side has to do that. The mere fact that such a distinction between essential and non-essential properties of a contract is plausible does not prove that this distinction applies per se and not only to a specific language. Its conceptualization might be contingent and thus, according to Reinach, an empirical question that eludes a priori regularities.

Once again, this suggests that Reinach may draw rash conclusions regarding the apriority of non-positive legal propositions, insofar as he relies on their obvious plausibility. Not only does it remain unclear how one can determine the essence of legal concepts and entities if neither perception through the senses nor experience with positive law is to play a role, but acquaintance with a particular language might also influence one's intuition about legal phenomena. If this is the case, the relevant propositions are not a priori.

3.4 NON-POSITIVE PROPOSITIONS

At first glance, one can infer a legal a priori from those propositions which, on the one hand, do not follow from positive law, but which, on the other, may nevertheless play a role in a legal argument. These non-positive propositions are able to support a statement about law without being traceable back to a social fact such as a legislative or judicial decision. In the absence of such a positive basis, they seem to be fixed for all legal systems and thus, at first glance, a priori.

The already mentioned proposition that an obligation is extinguished by fulfilment would be an example of such a non-positive proposition if one could justify it without referring to a legislative decision or another social fact. One might argue that the purpose of the fulfilment of an obligation is not only that the creditor receives what has been promised, but also that the debtor discharges his debt. If the obligation were not extinguished, he would have no reason to fulfil it. Moreover, the creditor would receive more than he was promised or to which he is entitled by law if the obligation were to persist after fulfilment.

These arguments do not rely on positive law, but nevertheless contain reasons that one could use in a legal argument. Does it follow from this that they are a priori, and can one thereby rescue Reinach's thesis that there is a legal a priori although Reinach himself did not use such an argument? That would only be the case if all propositions that are not based solely on positive law must be a priori. Then one could conclude from the lack of positivity that a legal proposition is a priori. However, this conclusion appears doubtful. As the following discussion shall show, there are other types of non-positive and nevertheless non-a priori legal propositions.

3.4.1 *Presupposed Legal Propositions*

First, a non-positive legal proposition can gain its correctness by the fact that propositions of positive law presuppose it without establishing it explicitly or implicitly. In this case, one needs additional non-positive reasons for the justification of the presupposed proposition. It is then partly based on positive law, partly on non-positive reasons.

To take Reinach's already mentioned example: If a statute provides for an obligation without determining its extinction through fulfilment, this extinction is nevertheless plausible. Otherwise, as explained, the fulfilment would make no sense – which is ultimately an argument about what is a reasonable outcome of positive law. This shows in general that not all correct statements about law that do not exclusively rest on positive law have to be based on an a priori insight. Rather, they can also find their justification in considerations about what would be reasonable in the context of a specific positive law. In this case, one is dealing with a combination of positive law and non-positive arguments about how to reasonably construct it.

Thus, non-positive legal propositions that are 'self-evident' do not have to be independent of all positive law but can also result from an interplay of it with assumptions about how to construct it reasonably. That Reinach has not addressed these combined propositions is probably because he only distinguishes positive law from a priori propositions. In this vein, even the slightest positive element would disturb the purity[51] of the a priori law. This leaves no room for propositions that arise from a combination of positive law and non-positive arguments.

Such combined propositions are, possibly, a part of the law. In the interpretation of legal concepts and norms one frequently finds references to what is reasonable, although the explicit reference to reason might be avoided. The openness of many concepts used in law requires an interpretation that can only be justified if it is built on such reasons. They impact, among others, propositions about what a norm presupposes. Therefore, such propositions cannot be traced back entirely to positive norms or to assumptions about what is reasonable. Instead, they require a combination of both. The fact that a legal proposition is not based solely on positive law does thus not show that it is a priori.

One might object that reasonable assumptions about what is presupposed by positive law are themselves based on reason and are therefore a priori. One could form hypothetical a priori propositions that foresee further legal consequences under the condition that certain norms are positive law.[52] The apriority of these hypothetical propositions would not be refuted by their reference to positive law. For a distinction exists between the a priori condition that a certain positive norm exists and this norm itself. In the example discussed, the conditional proposition that an obligation is extinguished as a result of fulfilment *if* a legal system provides for this fulfilment must be distinguished from the unconditional norm that an obligation is extinguished by fulfilment. The occurrence of the condition depends on positive law, but not the proposition containing this condition. The proposition might thus be a priori despite its reference to positive law. Because of this dependency on the positive law prevailing in a particular legal system, one might call it, borrowing a term from Putnam,[53] a contextual a priori.

[51] ibid 6; [GE] ibid 7.

[52] cf ibid 113–14; [GE] ibid 131.

[53] Hilary Putnam, *Realism and Reason* (Cambridge University Press 1983) 99.

Yet, such an explanation does not prove that propositions presupposed by positive law are indeed a priori. For if they are based on a combination of a priori reasons and positive law, they belong to neither of them. They are valid only because one can combine both sources. Therefore, they are not identical with a priori propositions that foresee a condition. There is a difference between dealing with hypothetical statements about possible positive law and dealing with unconditional statements about it. If one wants to know what the law is, it is not enough to rely on hypothetical statements.

For example, the statement that an obligation is extinguished with fulfilment differs from the proposition that an obligation is extinguished with fulfilment *if* the legal system orders its fulfilment without determining its extinction. In the latter case, one is not dealing with an unconditional statement about law, but with a hypothetical proposition about what the law would be if positive law contained certain norms. Such hypothetical legal propositions do not necessarily form the independent a priori legal order that Reinach has in mind. Their application remains dependent on positive law. If a proposition has only a hypothetical character, it is therefore unclear in which sense one can ascribe a legal character to it, because it is always subject to the proviso that positive law contains certain norms. Whether the proposition accurately reflects the legal situation can therefore only be said with a posteriori knowledge of positive law.

Legal propositions presupposed by a legal system, which are not subject to any condition, are therefore not to be confused with hypothetical legal propositions. Although the former contain true statements about the law, they cannot be traced back entirely to positive norms. Nevertheless, they are not a priori, because they go back in part to positive law, the content of which can only be ascertained through experience. The mere fact that a true legal proposition does not exclusively rest on positive law alone is therefore insufficient to prove its a priori character.

3.4.2 *Morally Based Legal Propositions*

Concluding the priority of a legal proposition from its lack of positivity might nevertheless become plausible if one looks at propositions that are wholly or partly based on moral reasons. One cannot arguably trace back these reasons to social facts such as decisions of the legislature or the courts. Therefore, such reasons do not rest on experience, at least in this respect,[54] and are to that extent not a posteriori. This suggests their apriority. Reinach does not use these sorts of propositions to prove the existence of a legal a priori. On the contrary, he distinguishes a priori propositions

[54] Non-naturalistic theories would deny a dependency upon natural facts as well; see David Enoch, 'Non-naturalistic Realism in Metaethics' in Tristram McPherson and David Plunkett (eds), *The Routledge Handbook of Metaethics* (Routledge 2018) 29.

about the essence of things from considerations of expediency and morality.[55] However, he offers no justification for this exclusion. Perhaps, then, Reinach just took the wrong reasons for a right thesis, and it is worth investigating whether there are a priori legal propositions that rest on moral reasons and can prove his thesis.

For instance, a legal decision may hinge on the fact that a particular behaviour is contradictory, unreasonable, or against good faith. Such reasons are moral because, first, they serve to prescribe rather than describe behaviour, and second, they are not at the discretion of the individual but are – in Kantian[56] terms – categorical and thus not subject to the condition that a certain legal norm applies. Whether such arguments are generally considered to be moral or the name 'morality' is instead confined to a more limited set of socially established rules is immaterial to this characterization.

Courts often refer to moral reasons in this broad sense. Their opinions contain more than just references to legislative decisions and other social facts. Instead, they often provide reasons for what seems to be a just arrangement of interests. For example, it may be argued that it would be unacceptable if the person who has already fulfilled an obligation had to fulfil it again. This is because he would have to pay twice for something that he receives only once. The argumentative force of such a reason does not depend upon whether there is any legislative decision and nevertheless concerns the question of how one shall act. It is thus moral in the described broad sense. Another moral reason against renewed fulfilment is that it would unjustly enrich the person who would receive more than he paid for.

All this does not mean that any moral reason may occur in legal arguments. On the contrary, the law might use only a certain kind of moral reasons, for instance those that are minimal in nature and therefore obvious to almost everyone.[57] What is decisive here is rather that, in contrast to Reinach's view,[58] one can use moral reasons in legal arguments at all. Their argumentative force is based on the fact that they are justifiable and not that one can trace them back to a legislative decision or another social fact. How precisely their usage is to be explained is very controversial. In part, they are attributed to the reference of positive law to morality,[59] in part to the authorization of judges to fill gaps,[60] in part they might be explained by the role

[55] Reinach, *The Apriori Foundations of the Civil Law* (n 1) 95–96, 111; Reinach, *Die apriorischen Grundlagen des bürgerlichen Rechtes* (n 1) 114, 128.

[56] Kant, *Die Metaphysik der Sitten* (n 30) 222.

[57] Lorenz Kaehler, 'The Minimal Morality of Private Law' in Thilo Kuntz and Paul B Miller (eds), *Methodology in Private Law Theory* (Oxford University Press 2024) 299.

[58] Reinach, *The Apriori Foundations of the Civil Law* (n 1) 95–96, 112; Reinach, *Die apriorischen Grundlagen des bürgerlichen Rechtes* (n 1) 114, 129.

[59] Kenneth E Himma, 'Inclusive Legal Positivism' in Jules L Coleman and Scott J Shapiro (eds), *The Oxford Handbook of Jurisprudence and Philosophy of Law* (Oxford University Press 2002) 125, 136.

[60] Hans Kelsen, *Reine Rechtslehre* (2nd edn, Verlag Österreich 1960) 353.

justice plays in the interpretation of law.[61] This controversy can be left aside here, since the relevant question is only whether the occurrence of such reasons allows a conclusion that there is a legal a priori. Since moral reasons are normative in nature and differ thus from descriptions that are obtained from experience, their classification as a posteriori legal propositions seems excluded. At first glance, this suggests an a priori character.

However, the apriority of moral reasons cannot be inferred from their normativity, at least not without further ado. Normative evaluations *can* rest in part on empirical observations of what would be the case if certain actions were carried out. For example, one might argue that, from a moral point of view, the fulfilment of a debt ought to occur during the day in order to not disturb the sleep of the recipient. This proposition is based in part on the empirical observation that human beings need sleep. For beings that are different, no such restriction is necessary. Although this seems trivial, it is important to stress that one is dealing in this case with a moral reason which rests in part on an empirical observation, namely about the biological need of sleep, and can thus not be a priori in total.

Moreover, the belief that a certain moral proposition is correct could rest, at least in part, on empirical observations of how people react to a certain behaviour. For instance, the experience that corporal punishment of children is detrimental to their development could strengthen the belief that such punishments are immoral. Part of the justification for such beliefs is then grounded in a posteriori knowledge about child development. The mere fact that a certain proposition is moral in nature does not, therefore, show that it rests completely on a priori reasons. Morally based legal propositions thus do not prove Reinach's thesis about a legal a priori.

3.4.3 *A Priori Uncertain Legal Propositions*

In order to show that a certain proposition is a priori, one must understand what is and what is not involved in such a claim. For this purpose, one must strictly separate the ontological question of what is the case from the epistemic question of how one can justify what is the case.[62] That a proposition is a priori amounts to the purely epistemic claim that one can justify this proposition without reference to experience.[63] This says nothing about the content of this proposition, in particular whether it is normative in kind. In contrast, characterizing a proposition as normative is a claim about its content.

Moreover, the ontological classification of a proposition as a priori does not imply how it is to be recognized. One cannot rule out that experiences play a role for this. To disprove the role of experiences, it is unhelpful to refer to the distinction between

[61] Ronald Dworkin, *Law's Empire* (Fontana Press 1991) 97.

[62] Kripke (n 27) 36; Bonjour (n 7) 11.

[63] Above n 6.

is and ought, due to which one has to separate normative and descriptive propositions. For this shows only that descriptions derived from empirical facts are insufficient to justify a normative proposition if one wants to avoid a deontological fallacy. This distinction does not determine the way in which one arrives at a normative judgement. Therefore, it is possible for descriptive statements to play a role in the discovery of a normative proposition, even if the latter does not follow from them.

For example, the proposition that night-time delivery is generally against the interests of the addressee and therefore *prima facie* unacceptable can, at least in part, be based on the experience that night-time delivery interrupts sleep. This does not mean that one reduces the judgement on the impermissibility of a night-time delivery to a description of empirical circumstances, but merely that the evaluation on which it is based rests in part on experience. Even the underlying rule that one should not act against the interests of other people and therefore not interrupt their sleep presupposes the empirical assumption that such actions are indeed detrimental for them. At least theoretically, it could be the case that such actions have the opposite effect of furthering the interests of other people in the long run. In this case, such actions would be normatively less questionable. That is why the normativity of moral or legal propositions does not exclude that experiences play a role both in their discovery and their justification.

For this reason, it is, at least in some cases, possible to base legal propositions on both a priori and a posteriori insights. Such a combination can increase the certainty that a proposition is correct. This certainty is especially important for law, which is implemented with coercion. In contrast to philosophical opinions on which no coercive act depends, legal propositions require a comparatively high degree of certainty and cannot be based on uncertain assumptions. If a proposition is a priori, but not sufficiently certain, it requires further justification, possibly based on experience. This experience can, for instance, concern the practical repercussions that a certain norm has.

Even if Reinach's extremely ambitious programme should succeed in exploring a priori 'eternal laws of being',[64] this does therefore not show that one should not also rely on experience to gain certainty about them. Certainty does in general not follow from apriority.[65] This might become clearer by looking at mathematical propositions such as Fermat's last theorem.[66] These can be true a priori and yet be uncertain for most people because they can only be proven by complex proofs.[67] The same holds for legal propositions. Even if they are true a priori, they might be insufficiently

[64] Reinach, *The Apriori Foundations of the Civil Law* (n 1) 98; Reinach, *Die apriorischen Grundlagen des bürgerlichen Rechtes* (n 1) 117.

[65] Kripke (n 27) 39; Ivette Fred-Rivera, *A Historical and Systematic Perspective on A Priori Knowledge and Justification* (Springer 2022) 72, 213.

[66] Kuldeep Singh, *Number Theory* (Oxford University Press 2020) 155.

[67] Reinach, *Über Phänomenologie* (n 8) 546 admits this but insists on the evidence of the insights on which complex proofs are built.

certain to be used in a legal argument, unless supported by a posteriori reasons. It is then not only helpful but also necessary to substantiate them with a posteriori reasons.

For example, the proposition that human dignity is inviolable may be derived from a priori assumptions about rational beings.[68] However, this does not exclude the possibility of using negative historical experiences from systematic violations of human rights to justify this statement. They can at least illustrate why some actions are inherently wrong. History is therefore not immaterial for the discussion of human dignity although this dignity does not rest on it. Thereby it helps to increase the certainty with which one makes arguments about human dignity in a legal context.

Consequently, if a normative reason is justified a priori, this does not show that there cannot be any experience that supports it. In law, as elsewhere,[69] there can be a posteriori reasons for a priori propositions. It might even be the case that moral beliefs in general originate in emotions and social conventions but that would not exclude the existence of a priori reasons that support such beliefs.[70] In the already mentioned case of moral reasons in legal decisions, these a posteriori considerations might be, for example, general observations about basic human needs and physical laws that the legal system has to take into account. If these considerations play a role in law, one is dealing with non-positive propositions that are not a priori because they rest in part on experience.

This shows again that non-positive propositions do not have to be a priori. A different result would be surprising in view of the fact that the two concepts are based on different questions. Positivity in law is about the ontological question of whether there are social facts underlying a norm.[71] Apriority in law, on the other hand, is about the epistemic question of how to justify a legal proposition. There is no strict connection between the two questions. Therefore, the answers to them do not have to go hand in hand. In particular, there might be non-positive propositions that are justifiable only a posteriori. It is one thing to claim that a certain proposition ultimately rests on non-empirical premises and another thing to claim that empirical observations cannot in principle support it.

For this reason, of particular interest are a priori uncertain legal propositions about which one gains certainty only by taking into account empirical evidence. They rest neither totally on social facts nor on a priori reasons. To show the a priori character of a legal proposition, it is hence insufficient to prove its non-positivity. Rather, it can be

68 Immanuel Kant, 'Grundlegung zur Metaphysik der Sitten' in *Kants Werke* vol. IV (Walter de Gruyter 1968) 434.

69 Kripke (n 27) 35.

70 Jonas Olson, 'Error Theory in Metaethics' in Tristram McPherson and David Plunkett (eds), *The Routledge Handbook of Metaethics* (Routledge 2018) 58, 67.

71 E.g., Andrei Marmor, *Philosophy of Law* (Princeton University Press 2014) 35.

non-positive and still not a priori because partially based on empirical evidence. One must strictly distinguish between apriority and non-positivity.

3.5 TOWARDS NON-POSITIVE LEGAL REASONS

It turns out, thus, that neither necessary (3.2), nor essential (3.3), nor non-positive propositions (3.4) prove the existence of a legal a priori. This raises the question of whether Reinach's theory should be dismissed as interesting but ultimately unsustainable. That there are a priori foundations of law is after all not only the title, but also the central thesis of Reinach's treatise.

However, such a conclusion would be premature. For the fact that the apriority of certain phenomena has not been proven does not mean that they are of no interest at all.[72] Maybe, Reinach was just too ambitious to explain them with an a priori, thereby excluding even the slightest empirical evidence. In this respect, it is worth returning to Reinach's starting point. He begins by refuting the claim that all legal propositions and concepts are creations of positive law.[73] Against this backdrop, he undertakes the search for a legal a priori. Rejecting this apriority does not mean, conversely, that all legal concepts and legal propositions are to be understood as positive law. As has already been argued,[74] there are several kinds of plausible propositions about law that do not completely rest on positive law. Presupposed and morally based legal propositions are examples of them. They remain an important part of the law although they neither rest exclusively on positive law nor on a priori insights.

Reinach's opposition to explaining legal phenomena with the help of positive law can therefore possibly be maintained without having to adopt his thesis of a legal a priori. This requires that one must explain the phenomena treated by Reinach without reference to an a priori. Whether or not this is possible cannot be decided across the board, as it requires an analysis of the particular phenomena treated by Reinach, which may be successful for some but not for other phenomena.

It should suffice here to look at the example that an obligation is extinguished through fulfilment. Such a claim becomes plausible if one looks for normative reasons that support it. In this regard reasons are understood in a broad sense as everything that helps to justify a proposition.[75] They are normative if they count in favour of some action or attitude.[76] Such reasons do not have to be independent of experience. For instance, historical insights about the fallibility of governments

[72] For a similar strategy to transfer Reinach's claims about an a priori into a less daring claim about human psychology see Andrew S. Gold & Henry E. Smith, Chapter 5 in this volume.

[73] Reinach, *The Apriori Foundations of the Civil Law* (n 1) 3–4; Reinach, *Die apriorischen Grundlagen des bürgerlichen Rechtes* (n 1) 4.

[74] See Section 3.4.

[75] cf Russel (n 6).

[76] Thomas Scanlon, *Being Realistic about Reasons* (Oxford University Press 2014) 30.

might be part of the reasons that are decisive for the design of the state. It is thus not plausible to assume that all reasons that support non-positive legal propositions are a priori. Reinach's[77] opposite view, possibly, is motivated by the fear that an established morality ('positive morality') can fail and is thus no reliable basis for law. However, his exclusion of all moral reasons from the foundations of law goes too far if it is to cover also those reasons that stand up to critical reflection ('critical morality').[78] These include, in particular, minimal reasons as to which actions should be dismissed as obviously unacceptable.

For example, that an obligation disappears with performance, finds, as seen, its justification in the fact that the debtor would otherwise have no reason to perform, and the creditor would be unjustly enriched if he could demand performance again. The argumentative force of these reasons does not depend on whether there are certain positive norms about performance or extinction of obligations. Such reasons are thus non-positive.

Equally, the fact that an obligation is extinguished by waiver[79] does not have to be attributed to a mystical essence that holds a priori. Rather, one can simply explain this extinction by the fact that the reason for an obligation is to provide a benefit to a particular person and that it is not an end in itself that such an obligation exists. Therefore, if the creditor decides by waiver not to receive the promised benefit, the reason why the obligation exists in the first place ceases to exist. Accordingly, it is reasonable for the law to order the extinction of the obligation in this case. One can understand the reasonableness of this proposition without referring to positive law.

The fact that there are such non-positive reasons for legal propositions does not mean that positive law always follows these reasons. As Reinach[80] emphasized, the legislator is free to determine deviating norms. Indeed, what is reasonable is often disputed. Therefore, the legislator usually determines the law by an authoritative decision, even if it deviates from the non-positive reasons that weigh in favour of another decision. The dependence of private law on legislative determinations should not, however, lead to the conclusion that there are no non-positive legal reasons for private law propositions.

For such reasons to exist, it is by the stated definition merely necessary that there is something independent upon positive law that counts in favour of or against a certain action or state of affairs. If one considers that every action and most states of affairs have an impact on somebody's freedom or autonomy, it is highly unlikely that there is nothing at all that would count for or against them. Therefore, it seems quite plausible that there are in *most* situations such normative reasons. This can

77 Reinach, *The Apriori Foundations of the Civil Law* (n 1) 111; Reinach, *Die apriorischen Grundlagen des bürgerlichen Rechtes* (n 1) 128.

78 HLA Hart, *Law, Liberty, and Morality* (Stanford University Press 1963) 20.

79 Reinach, *The Apriori Foundations of the Civil Law* (n 1) 5, 32–33; Reinach, *Die apriorischen Grundlagen des bürgerlichen Rechtes* (n 1) 5, 40.

80 ibid 5–6; [GE] ibid 6.

also be seen in the fact that the difficulty of legislation and the accompanying discussions are regularly about which reasons are more convincing and hardly ever about the question of whether there is any reason at all for or against a certain proposal. The fact that a concept has a certain content and is related to other concepts is accordingly not necessarily a whim of positive law, but possibly an expression of a conception based on reasons. What is important about these reasons is not only that they do not refer to positive law, but also that their argumentative force is independent of it.

One might still ask whether such reasons are of a purely moral and thus not legal nature. In at least three respects this answer is negative. First, the fact that a reason is of moral nature does not exclude that it also states how the law should be designed and is thus to that extent related to law. This does not mean that propositions justified with the help of such reasons are necessarily valid law, but only that they at least *should be* valid law. In this regard, such reasons differ from those moral reasons that do not justify legal norms, for example because they concern decisions that should be left to the autonomous decision of individuals and thus not be legally required. Thus, unlike considerations that are decisive only for non-legal decisions, non-positive legal reasons are legal insofar as they take seriously the nature of law, that is, its specific characteristics.

Second, these reasons might not lead to a specific conclusion but might just justify why a certain distinction between two concepts or phenomena exists at all and is potentially significant in a legal context. In this case, these reasons do not justify legal norms but rather the concepts that should be applied within them, thereby highlighting the questions that must be resolved by a legal system. These reasons are legal insofar as they indicate the potential concepts and categories that a legal system could utilize. In the already mentioned example of contracts one can provide reasons for why contracts differ from one-sided decisions without thereby prescribing any legal consequence.

All of this does not mean that the law must encompass such distinctions. Instead, it elucidates why such a distinction exists in principle and why it might be relevant. These reasons concerning potential legal concepts are pivotal for legal analysis, although due to the lack of specific legal consequences, they do not constitute norms. Categorizing them strictly as either moral or legal would be misleading, as it would overlook the significance of having a well-developed terminology that can remain neutral regarding the legal consequences for which it might be employed. The categories, distinctions, and concepts that a legal system might use are at least to that extent legal in character, as a potential legal system might reasonably employ them, although this alone does not make them *part of* the positive law. For instance, there are convincing reasons to distinguish between contract and property, although a legal system might not draw this distinction.

Finally, non-positive legal reasons can rely on minimal preconditions, making their use in a legal decision permissible when there is no applicable positive law on point. The propositions justified with their help can then be legally binding as long as the legislature has not ordered otherwise. The fact that an obligation is extinguished by fulfilment, for example, is likely to be based on such minimal reasons. They are legally acceptable as long as positive law does not state otherwise. In contrast, many moral rules do not even have such a subsidiary character, because they are not based on minimal reasons and are thus incapable of justifying legal decisions. In this respect, minimal reasons that justify legal propositions might differ from general moral reasons.

The reference to the minimal character of these reasons shows that one must distinguish between different types of reasons – even among non-positive reasons that speak for or against a certain legal proposition. To treat them sweepingly as legal or moral is a misleading alternative and obscures such differences. The phenomenon emphasized by Reinach, that a number of legal propositions are self-evident, can be explained precisely by the fact that one is dealing with propositions that are justifiable by reasons that demand few preconditions and are thus minimal,[81] although they have no basis in positive law. What appeared to Reinach as self-evident might rest on minimal moral reasons that could and should be demonstrated.

In short, Reinach's objective of uncovering non-positive elements of law remains a worthwhile project, especially when one looks at minimal reasons that underlie legal concepts, distinctions, and rules. First and foremost, these reasons help to explain self-evident legal propositions. In finding and characterizing non-positive reasons for them, one does not have to deny that in many cases it is controversial what these reasons precisely are. What is important at this point is only that such reasons might justify legal propositions in principle. The phenomenon of self-evident legal propositions emphasized by Reinach remains thus crucial, although his explanation with the help of an a priori is too ambitious to be true.

BIBLIOGRAPHY

Bonjour L, *In Defense of Pure Reason: A Rationalist Account of 'A Priori' Justification* (Cambridge University Press 1998)

Bussani M and U Mattei, *The Common Core of European Private Law* (Kluwer 2002)

Dubois JM, *Judgment and Sachverhalt: An Introduction to Adolf Reinach's Phenomenological Research* (Kluwer 1995)

Dworkin R, *Law's Empire* (Fontana Press 1991)

Enoch D, 'Non-naturalistic Realism in Metaethics' in T McPherson and D Plunkett (eds), *The Routledge Handbook of Metaethics* (Routledge 2017) 29

Falguera JL, C Martínez-Vidal and G Rosen (2022) 'Abstract Objects', *The Stanford Encyclopedia of Philosophy*, summer edn., https://plato.stanford.edu/entries/abstract-objects/ accessed 28 October 2023

[81] For an extended version of this argument see Kaehler (n 57).

Fred-Rivera I, *A Historical and Systematic Perspective on A Priori Knowledge and Justification* (Springer 2022)
Hart HLA, *Law, Liberty, and Morality* (Stanford University Press 1963)
Herdegen M 'Art. 146' in G Dürig, R Herzog, and R Scholz (eds), *Grundgesetz-Kommentar* (Beck 2023)
Himma KE, 'Inclusive Legal Positivism' in JL Coleman and SJ Shapiro (eds), *The Oxford Handbook of Jurisprudence and Philosophy of Law* (Oxford University Press 2002)
Hume D, *A Treatise of Human Nature* (DF Norton and MJ Norton, eds, Oxford University Press 2000)
Husserl E, *Ideen zu einer reinen Phänomenologie und phänomenologischen Philosophie* (Niemeyer 2002)
Kaehler L, 'The Minimal Morality of Private Law' in T Kuntz and PB Miller (eds), *Methodology in Private Law Theory* (Oxford University Press 2024), 299–326
Kant I, 'Kritik der reinen Vernunft' in *Kants Werke vol. III* (2nd edn, Walter de Gruyter 1968)
(1968) 'Grundlegung zur Metaphysik der Sitten' in *Kants Werke vol. IV* (Walter de Gruyter 1968)
'Die Metaphysik der Sitten' in *Kants Werke vol. VI.* (Walter de Gruyter 1968)
Kelsen H, *Reine Rechtslehre* (2nd edn Verlag 1960)
Kripke S, *Naming and Necessity* (Harvard University Press 1980)
Loidolt S, *Einführung in die Rechtsphänomenologie* (Mohr Siebeck 2010)
Maddy P, *Defending the Axioms: On the Philosophical Foundations of Set Theory* (Oxford University Press 2011)
Marmor A, *Philosophy of Law* (Princeton University Press 2014)
Olson J, 'Error Theory in Metaethics' in T McPherson and D Plunkett (eds), *The Routledge Handbook of Metaethics* (Routledge 2018), 58–71
Putnam H, *Realism and Reason* (Cambridge University Press 1983)
Quine WVO, *From a Logical Point of View* (2nd edn, Harvard University Press 1980)
Reinach A, 'Über Phänomenologie' in K Schuhmann and B Smith (eds), *Sämtliche Werke vol. II.* (Philosophia 1989)
Reinach, A 'The Apriori Foundations of the Civil Law' (John F Crosby tr, 1983) 3 Aletheia 1–142, reprinted in Adolf Reinach, *The Apriori Foundations of the Civil Law Along with the Lecture 'Concerning Phenomenology'* (John F Crosby ed, Ontos Verlag 2012), originally published as Adolf Reinach, Die apriorischen Grundlagen des bürgerlichen Rechtes, 1(2) *Jahrbuch für Philosophie und phänomenologische Forschung* (Max Niemeyer 1913), 685–847
Riezler E, (1923/24) 'Apriorisches im Recht', Archiv für Rechts- und Wirtschaftsphilosophie 17 No. 3, pp. 264–84
Robertson Ishii T and P Atkins (2023) 'Essential vs. Accidental Properties', *The Stanford Encyclopedia of Philosophy*, spring edn., https://plato.stanford.edu/entries/essential-accidental/ accessed 28 October 2023
Russel B (2020) 'A Priori Justification and Knowledge', *The Stanford Encyclopedia of Philosophy*, summer edn.), https://plato.stanford.edu/entries/apriori/ accessed 28 October 2023
Scanlon T, *Being Realistic about Reasons* (Oxford University Press 2014)
Singh K, *Number Theory* (Oxford University Press 2020)

4

Adolf Reinach, Negation, and Law*

Kimberly Baltzer-Jaray

. . . but I have to pass my exams right away, so I can convey to some law students as quickly as possible that there can be nothing more pitiful on earth than a jurist who is just a jurist.[1]

Adolf Reinach, Letter to Theodor Conrad, 1905.

In much of the body of work devoted to Adolf Reinach, discussion is concentrated on his phenomenological realist ontology – essences, states of affairs, and judgments. Each of these is explored conceptually and with respect to how it interconnects and grounds the others. But very little attention is paid to negation, specifically negative states of affairs and their connection to both positive and negative judgments. Scholars who work on Reinach's theory of judgment tend to focus on the negative judgment of positive states of affairs, to the neglect of the positive judgment of negative states of affairs. Reinach claims that negative states of affairs ontologically subsist and do so on a par with positive states of affairs: taking a rose, for example, its *not-being*-orange subsists

* I dedicate this article to Prof. Dr. Tomasz Bekrycht, who sadly passed away unexpectedly in 2021. In Spring 2018, Tomasz organized at the University of Łódź, Poland, a wonderful law conference titled *Reinach's Phenomenology of Law*. It was a successful event that brought together scholars from across the globe and ignited significant conversations about Reinach's relevance to modern law. Tomasz was an authentically kind and inspired soul – his love for Reinach and legal scholarship, the joy he exuded when bringing people together in conversation, and the genuine excitement he had for sharing the city of Łódź with the conference participants. He was a brilliant legal scholar, talented editor and author, a serious football fan, and a dear friend who had a smile and a laugh that was contagious. We kept in touch after the conference, and his emails were a welcome and much needed dose of sunshine in the early days of Covid-19. He is sorely missed and will never be forgotten. For more about Tomasz, please read the obituary written by his colleague and friend, Marek Zirk-Sadowski: https://czasopisma.uni.lodz.pl/Iuridica/article/download/17266/17300?inline=1

[1] "...mein Examen aber muss ich bald machen, schon damit ich möglichst schnell ein paar juristischen Studenten vortragen kann, dass es kein ärmeres Ding auf Erden geben kann, als einen Juristen, der nur Jurist ist." (Ana 379, C I 1/15) Adolf Reinach's literary estate is housed at the Bavarian State Library in Munich under the shelf mark (Signatur) *Ana* 379. A table of its contents can be found in Eberhard Avé-Lallemant, *Die Nachlässe der Münchener Phänomenologen in der Bayerischen Staatsbibliothek* (Harrassowitz 1975).

just as much and in the same way as its *being*-red, and the rose *being-red* entails that it is *not-being*-orange. This negation does not just occur mentally for us in a disposition (i.e., on the side of consciousness, or subjectively in a judgment) but, Reinach argues, in the world of events and human interaction (i.e., objectively, in the world). This position on negation was contrary to many of his peers and colleagues who saw negative entities as secondary to or derived from positive ones: specifically, his friend and fellow Munich phenomenologist Johannes Daubert and one of his Göttingen students, Roman Ingarden, both took issue with the idea that negative states of affairs subsisted independently and were on a par ontologically with positive states of affairs.

In this chapter, my focus will be on negative states of affairs and their corresponding judgments, and on connecting them with Reinach's jurisprudence – something that has not yet been done in the literature. Reinach was rather unique in both the Munich and Göttingen phenomenological circles because he was a law student in addition to his studies of descriptive psychology and phenomenology; this interdisciplinary education opened his mind to distinctive ways of seeing the world, in all its ways of being and not being. The position I advance here is that because the law frequently turns on what appears to be negative states of affairs, Reinach's legal training may have contributed to his insistence on their very being and their having the same ontological status as positive states of affairs. Laws have application to both action and inaction – criminality can be something done to another or an omission – and this implies a robust inclusion of negative states of affairs. Negative states of affairs have received far too little attention and serious inclusion in his work, and by engaging in this discussion, we have the potential for Reinach to be made whole again – by bridging his early law education with his phenomenological ontology.

4.1 REINACH'S TERMINOLOGY: JUDGMENT AND STATE OF AFFAIRS

States of affairs, essences, and an expanded notion of the *a priori* are the core entities of Reinach's ontology. These interlace with one another, creating the fabric of reality that we come to grasp both epistemically and metaphysically. In this chapter, I will focus exclusively on states of affairs and the judgments they participate with.[2]

Judgment, for Reinach, can be understood as both assertion and conviction. However, for this chapter, the focus will be exclusively on the latter, as it was what he predominantly utilized for his discussion of negation. Convictions are said to

[2] The choice of preposition here – "participate *with*" – is a deliberate one and is intended to reflect the idea that an individual thing or being is not static, but rather is engaged in essential activity, that is in and through which its matter was being informed. This should more clearly capture the sense of Aristotle's Formal Causality and Plato's notion of Participation. My hope is to avoid the confusion or conflation of participation with imitation, which happens when phrasing like "participate *in*" is used – as if the essence preexisted the thing or entity. To subsist or obtain at all, essence must do so *through* participation.

arise from intuitive acts of presenting.[3] Conviction, for Reinach, possesses both a consciousness-side and an objectivity-side: that is, psychical and physical world aspects. Conviction is an act where we adopt a stance toward something, whether that means striving toward it positively or resisting it negatively.

In his essay on negative judgment, Reinach describes six essential characteristics of states of affairs.[4] These are essential marks meant to distinguish states of affairs from propositions and objects, and they are sufficient in the sense that every entity to which any one of them applies would be a state of affairs. For Reinach, this short list is by no means exhaustive, nor does it constitute a definition. States of affairs are:

1. that which is believed or asserted in judgments (34);
2. that which can stand in the relationship of ground and consequent (34–35);
3. that which can take on modalities, such as possibility and necessity (35);
4. that which stands in the relation of logically contradictory positivity and negativity (35–36);
5. that which obtains or does not obtain (as opposed to existing)[5] – and given (4) above, either a positive or a negative state of affairs obtains (36);
6. that which is apprehended or intuitively discerned, not seen or perceived through the senses (37).[6]

States of affairs have a special mode of being that enables them to participate with both real and ideal objects, but they themselves are not real or ideal. By employing words like "obtain," the list of characteristics reiterates that we must not mistakenly regard states of affairs as existing; it is rather the objects to which they stand in

[3] Adolf Reinach, *Sämtliche Werke: Textkritische Ausgabe in 2 Bänden*, Karl Schuhmann and Barry Smith (eds) (Philosophia Verlag 1989), 108. For English translation, see 'On the Theory of Negative Judgment' (1981) Aletheia 9 [hereinafter "Ferrari"]

[4] Reinach (n 3) 114–118. Ferrari (n 3) 34–37.

[5] An important way in which Reinach differentiates objects from states of affairs is to refer differently to their modes of being: physical objects *exist*; states of affairs *obtain* or *subsist*. Reinach (n 3) 118.

[6] I have modified Don Ferrari's translation of characteristic 6. The original German for characteristic 6 reads: "*Indem ich die rote Rose sehe, 'erschaue' ich ihr Rotsein, wird es von mir 'erkannt'. Gegenstände werden gesehen oder geschaut, Sachverhalte dagegen werden erschaut oder erkannt.*" Reinach (1989) 118. Ferrari translates the verb *erschauen* as "observe." I believe this choice does not capture accurately the meaning of the term. The translation of *erkannt* by "apprehended" is acceptable but should be noted that Reinach's notion of apprehending as applied to states of affairs is not the same as that applied to concepts. For example, to apprehend the concept "man" is not the same as to apprehend the state of affairs "being-man." The way intuition apprehends states of affairs differs from the way concepts are apprehended, because in the former what is grasped or discerned are essential connections, but in the latter, it is abstract ideas. Intuition must operate differently when apprehending states of affairs because these are not necessarily static, but rather occur in connection and participation with other entities.

relation that exist.[7] Reinach adds to this point: "As we immerse ourselves into the essence of these entities [*Gebilde*], we intuitively discern [*erschauen*] what holds for them as a matter of strict law; we grasp interconnections analogously to the way we do through immersion into the essence of numbers and geometric entities: the being-thus [*So-Sein*] is here grounded in the essence of that which is thus [*So-Seienden*]."[8] Reinach emphasizes here the type of immaterial subsistence states of affairs have, and that states of affairs and the laws to which they are subject are immutable and strictly necessary. Moreover, states of affairs are independent of any judgment or cognition on our part, and they are subject to strict laws – laws that also obtain independently of our acknowledgment.

In Reinach's all too brief rough notes on ethics from 1906, he describes an additional characteristic of states of affairs. While objects can be valuable and persons are the bearers of moral values, it is states of affairs that are morally just: A and B can be said to be morally valuable, but *that A is B* is just.[9] States of affairs are independent, immaterial, and subsisting in the world and, for Reinach, justice is as well: what is just is not simply and solely in the consciousness of persons but rather at work in the universe.[10] These notes are early indications of where his phenomenological jurisprudence would go in subsequent writings, such as the *a priori* foundations article.[11] Sadly, this additional characteristic of states of affairs is incomplete; it was underdeveloped at the time of Reinach's death and remains rather obscure to this very day, and all too frequently left out of his ontology altogether.

With the fundamental terminology covered, we now turn to negation.

4.2 NEGATIVE JUDGMENT AND NEGATIVE STATES OF AFFAIRS

In "Toward the Theory of Negative Judgment," Reinach advances two significant and controversial claims: purely in terms of their descriptive essence, positive and

7 In a set of rough notes, Reinach writes that states of affairs can be either temporal or atemporal, and it is their content or "matter" that determines this. See Reinach (n 3) 351.

8 ibid 144.

9 ibid 336. Reinach makes use of the old distinction between justice and law, something that is rather difficult to capture precisely in English.

10 For further details, see Kimberly Baltzer-Jaray, 'Phenomenological Jurisprudence: A Reinterpretation of Reinach's Jahrbuch Essay' in J Edward Hackett and J Aaron Simmons (eds), *Phenomenology for the Twenty-First Century* (Palgrave Macmillan 2016), 117–137; and Kimberly Baltzer-Jaray, 'Reinach and Kantorowicz: Justice, Phenomenological Realism and the Free Law Movement' [2020] 90 Folia Iuridica 91.

11 Adolf Reinach, "The Apriori Foundations of the Civil Law" (John F. Crosby tr, 1983) 3 Aletheia 1, reprinted in Adolf Reinach, *The Apriori Foundations of the Civil Law Along with the Lecture 'Concerning Phenomenology'* (John F. Crosby ed, Ontos Verlag 2012), originally published as Adolf Reinach, Die apriorischen Grundlagen des bürgerlichen Rechtes, 1(2) *Jahrbuch für Philosophie und phänomenologische Forschung* (Max Niemeyer 1913), 685–847.

negative convictions stand on an equal footing with respect to each other, and likewise positive and negative states of affairs are of the same order.[12]

A positive conviction, Reinach posits, is an act of turning toward the object, whereas a negative conviction is an act of turning away from it (in disbelief). If a police detective tells me the body on the floor has a gun in their left hand but when I look I find the gun is actually in the right hand, then a negative conviction arises within me – "this person does not have a gun in their left hand!" – and is quickly followed by a positive conviction that "it is in their right hand!." These judgments, while contraries, are both convictions, and refer to the same intentional correlate – that is, the same state of affairs.

Positive convictions arise straightforwardly when "reading off" states of affairs from what is given around us, but negative convictions require a different intellectual attitude and approach. Referring again to the dead body example, when I approach the body expecting to see the gun in the left hand, but sense perception attests to the gun being in their right hand, this situation results in my grasping two conflicting states of affairs (*being*-left hand vs. *being*-right hand), with only one providing direct evidence that can be apprehended. The other state of affairs (*being*-left hand) has "negative evidence," and it is on the basis of this negative evidence that the negative conviction arises. Comparably, the judgment "nine is not less than five" arises through necessary connection with the positive state of affairs that "nine is greater than five"; the negative evidence of the former is bound by strict necessity with the positive evidence of the latter. The relationship between these judgments generates my positive conviction that nine is indeed greater than five.

Reinach distinguishes two types of negative judgments: a negative conviction of a positive state of affairs (the disbelief that A is B; *I don't believe* the gun is in his left hand) and a positive conviction of a negative state of affairs (the belief that A is not B; I believe this person *does not have* the gun in their left hand).[13] He adds that while these two convictions closely resemble one another in their logical content, they are absolutely different judgments with respect to both their consciousness- and objectivity-sides (in the one judgment, the consciousness-side is reflected by belief and the other, by disbelief; the objectivity-side of the one judgment is the gun *being*-left hand and the other is gun *not-being*-left hand). In fact, the positive conviction of a negative state of affairs has often been neglected, confused, or poorly handled by

[12] Reinach (n 3) 110–111. Ferrari (n 3) 30–31.

[13] He also mentions the negative conviction of a negative state of affairs, a double negative judgment, and it also relies on the apprehending of a positive state of affairs. "Just as in the first case [positive conviction of negative state of affairs], here too [negative conviction of a negative state of affairs] this [positive] state of affairs must conflict with the judged state of affairs, but here we have an especially distinctive relationship of conflicting: the two states of affairs are contradictory to each other." Reinach (n 3) 125. Ferrari (n 3) 43 [Translation slightly modified].

logicians because of outdated ideas about what the correlates of affirmative and negative judgments are.[14]

The list of characteristics of states of affairs offered in the previous section provides the foundation for understanding both positive and negative states of affairs. When we consider the third and fourth essential marks of states of affairs – they can take on modalities (i.e., being possible, probable, impossible, improbable, contingent, necessary, etc.), and stand in the relation of logically contradictory positivity and negativity (i.e., either the positive or the negative state of affairs obtains) – we can gain a more comprehensive picture of what negative states of affairs are and encompass, and how negation operates on the objectivity-side of judgment. Given the third mark, impossible objects involve states of affairs (e.g., square circles), as do probable entities (e.g., Schrödinger's cat's existence) and contingent ones (e.g., the trees in my yard). All these modalities *implicitly* contain negation. Negation can obtain with modalities such as probable and contingent because the temporal nature of the states of affairs allows for it. Reinach writes,

> Positive and negative states of affairs are on a par with one another. If a red rose exists somewhere, then any number of (positive and negative) states of affairs are given with the existence of that thing. 'The red rose exists'; 'the rose is red'; 'the red inheres in the rose'; 'the rose is not white,' 'not yellow,' etc. … Just as we can separate (real or ideal) objects from their (real or ideal) existence, and easily recognize that certain objects, like golden mountains or round squares, do not, or even altogether cannot, exist, so we can separate states of affairs from their obtaining, and speak of states of affairs, like the being-gold of mountains or the being-round of squares, which do not, or cannot, obtain.[15]

Only some states of affairs will obtain, and by necessity a manifold of others will not. If the rose is red, then it is not at the same time purple, not yellow, not orange, etc. This implies that any states of affairs essentially connected to the rose, both positive

[14] Reinach (n 3) 110–111. Two such logicians, Windelband and Sigwart, held the view that positive judgments operate as a union and, when true, comprises a binding relationship between the world and mental acts. Contrariwise, they understood negative judgments as divisive or separating – that is, as not a real relationship (or any relation at all) with objects in the world, but only as a subjective mode within consciousness. Negative judgment was conceived as a mental act of rejecting or disbelieving, hence negation being situated strictly on the consciousness-side. The proper objects of judgments – Reinach would insist – are states of affairs, not relations or objects, and only they can be the intentional correlates of a judgment. To claim that the negation aspect of a negative judgment is only a subjective mode is to posit the view that the negative attitude (disbelief, separation, etc.) is a negative relation, and is as such the intentional correlate of the judgment. To maintain that relations are the intentional correlates of judgments – as logicians like Windelband and Sigwart often do – applies only some of the time to positive convictions, since there are indeed states of affairs that function as relations (such as the *being*-similar of A and B), but more often than not there are instances where the state of affairs is not at all a relation (like the *being-red* of the rose). For more on states of affairs and relations, see Reinach (n 3) 121–122 and Ferrari (n 3) 40–41.

[15] Reinach (n 3) 116–117. Ferrari (n 3) 36 [Translation slightly modified].

and negative, must subsist potentially outside of my mind – "lying in wait," as it were, for the "opportunity" to obtain or not obtain.[16]

Briefly, combining the third and fourth essential marks of states of affairs additionally demonstrates that Reinach maintained a notion of pure possibility within his ontology, which is crucial for upholding a theory of material necessity in the world and for defeating any suggestions of necessitarianism.[17] In other words, for Reinach contingency has a relationship with necessity while allowing at the same time for free will and real possibility. For example, the leaves on my maple tree turned red last fall – they did not *have to be* red, they could have been orange or yellow if the weather conditions had been different, but there is no denying the *being-red* of the leaves that obtained. In his last public lecture "Concerning Phenomenology" (1914), Reinach spoke to this point,

> ... we have to do there not with empirically accumulated facts, but with rational [*Verstehbare*] interconnections grounded in the essence of things [*Wesen der Sache*]. To be sure, we encounter here a new sort of essential interconnections – not interconnections of necessity, but rather of possibility. We can understand that the presentation [*Vorstellung*] of an A can lead to the representation [*Vorstellung*] of a B similar to it, not that it must. Indeed, even interconnections of motivation are likewise largely of a kind that, in accordance with essence, involve a can-be-so, not a must-be-so.[18]

4.3 STATES OF AFFAIRS: INFLUENCES AND DEBATES

4.3.1 *Phenomenology*

Discussions featuring states of affairs surrounded Reinach, in both phenomenology and jurisprudence. Johannes Daubert exposed the Munich Circle psychology club to the writings of the Franz Brentano School very early in the twentieth

[16] For more discussion of Reinach's negation in light of his ontology, see my forthcoming contribution "Reinach's Negative States of Affairs and the Role of Essence" in Till Grohmann (ed) *The Phenomenology of Essences* (Routledge).

[17] In his essay "Kant's Interpretation of Hume's Problem" (1911), Reinach describes *material* necessity, the kind of necessity that occurs amongst and belongs to connections between material contents in the world around us. This type of necessity stands in contrast to the *modal* necessity, which is associated with the realm of mathematics and logic. In judgments of material necessity, the necessity involved not only belongs to the material content of the judgment, but also enriches the predicate term. With modal necessity it is the copula that has been unequivocally determined. Material necessity, for Reinach, was inspired by the rich discussion of causality found in the philosophy of David Hume.

[18] Reinach (n 3) 548–549. Here, Reinach is employing *Vorstellung* in a dual sense. His meaning becomes clear when one takes into account the context – psychological association – wherein he is speaking of a presentation of an A that has a connection via association with some mental representation of a *B* that is similar to A. For example, on hearing the word "red" (presentation), what may immediately come to mind (representations) is an apple.

century – that would have included not only Edmund Husserl, but also his teacher, Karl Stumpf, who was a major contributor to the philosophical literature on states of affairs. Stumpf was a student of Hermann Lotze, who also played a significant role in the conception of states of affairs when he referred to them as the special objects of judgment in his *Logic* (1874).[19] Husserl, a student and colleague of Stumpf and an admirer of Lotze, also wrote about states of affairs in some sections of *Logical Investigations*. Alongside these three, Alexius Meinong is another figure to consider as influencing Reinach on negation. In his *On Assumptions* (1902), Meinong investigated both the ontological understanding of negation and entities that were very similar to states of affairs. The locus of negation is first investigated by analyzing how our mind represents negative entities, and then by examining higher order objects. This kind of object, referred to as Objective [*Objektiv*], is the highlight of Meinong's novel theory of objects: (1) there are objects that do not exist and (2) every object that does not exist is constituted in such a way that it can be the subject of true predication.[20] The square circle is an impossible object owing to its evident self-contradiction and therefore does not exist, but that does not prevent me from judging its properties and describing it; "square circles do not exist" – that judgment too has content and can be true. The square circle has what Meinong calls *Sosein*, that is, some type of subsistence or presence that is available for predication, while at the same time being indifferent toward and independent from any relation to existence or non-existence – one can judge an object's *Sosein* apart from its *Sein* or *Nichtsein*.[21] I do not have the space to elucidate all the layers of Meinong's ontology, nor his overall position on negation, but suffice it to say that he winds up in a position of maintaining that negation is situated on the object-side of the objectivity/consciousness divide.[22] What Meinong was attempting with the status of negation is what inspired Reinach – Meinong pushed the boundaries of being/non-being and intentionality more than anyone else at the time – but, it should be noted, that Reinach was not uncritical of Meinong's ontology and footnotes reveal many disagreements.

Reinach's position that the status of negative states of affairs is on a par with that of positive states of affairs and have a footing in both the objectivity- and subjectivity-sides was a position that made him rather unique amongst the Munich and Göttingen phenomenological circles: no one else was exploring negation this way and in the context of states of affairs. It also stirred up considerable debate amongst a

[19] Hermann Lotze, *Logik: Drei Bücher vom Denken, vom Untersuchen und vom Erkennen* (Verlag von S Hirzel 1874).

[20] For further details on Objectives, see Alexius Meinong, *Über Annahmen*, (2nd edn, J. A. Barth 1910) §14 and Alexius Meinong, *On Assumptions* (James Heanue, ed and tr, University of California Press 1983) §14.

[21] Roderick Chisholm, *Realism and the Background of Phenomenology* (The Free Press of Glencoe 1960) 82. This point is also articulated by Ernst Mally in 1903 (published in 1904 in *Gegenstandstheorie*) with his formulation of an Independence Principle.

[22] Meinong (n 20) 198.

few of his closest peers and students: specifically, Daubert and Ingarden took issue with this notion of negation – the former by way of ontology and the latter by way of epistemology and subjectivity. Daubert did not support the notion of negative states of affairs having an objectivity-side; he did not believe negation to be an independently, objectively subsisting entity.[23] He held a view that reality is unified, that is positive and harmonious – there is no negation in the world, but only in the mind.[24] Contrariety, disunity, negation, antithetical phenomena in general, are only possible within the sphere of consciousness, and we come to know them through judgment and acts of meaning.[25] Ingarden took the epistemological differences in our access to negative states of affairs as a sign that they were dependent and could not be on equal footing: because negative states of affairs required a more complicated intellectual process, that is, they could not be directly read off what was given in perception, which indicates that they must be ontologically dependent on positive states of affairs.[26] He writes,

> What distinguishes the negative states of affairs from the positive is that they are characterized by an existential derivativeness, potentially of a higher degree than is the case for positive states of affairs. Insofar as the positive states of affairs in an autonomous object are existentially original, the negative states of affairs that occur in it are derived from them.[27]

Daubert and Ingarden both failed to properly grasp Reinach's ontology of negative states of affairs and his reasons for establishing the status of these entities. Reflecting on "the how or why" these misunderstandings occur suggests that the source may well be Daubert's and Ingarden's lack of jurisprudence education – they cannot see the world as Reinach does or understand how negation is ever-present in our daily lives and in the law.

[23] Daubert's literary estate is housed at the Bavarian State Library in Munich under the shelf mark (Signatur) *Daubertiana*. A table of its contents can be found in Avé-Lallemant 1975.

[24] Daubertiana A I 9/180 (1911–1913). 'A ist nicht non-A'; es ist unmöglich, daß Dasselbe sei und auch nicht sei; das ist (nach Windelband und mit Recht) ein metaphysischer Grundsatz oder ein erkenntnistheoretisches Postulat mit der Meinung: Die Wirklichkeit schließt den Widerspruch von sich aus.'

[25] Karl Schuhmann and Barry Smith, 'Against Idealism: Johannes Daubert vs. Husserl's "Ideas" I' (1985) 38 Review of Metaphysics 782. The authors note that Daubert's argument that reality is positive and unified sparked a series of important investigations of the logic and ontology of the negative judgment by members of the Munich school.

[26] This is just one of several ways that Ingarden misunderstood and misconstrued Reinach's negative states of affairs. For more on this, see Arkadiusz Chrudzimski, 'Negative States of Affairs: Reinach Versus Ingarden' (2012) 16 Symposium 106,; and my forthcoming article "Reinach's Negative States of Affairs and the Role of Essence" in Till Grohmann (ed), *The Phenomenology of Essences* (Routledge).

[27] Roman Ingarden, *Controversy over the Existence of the World II*, (Arthur Szylewicz, tr, Peter Lang 2016) 292. [In the corrected version briefly published by Peter Lang; p. 294 in the original corrupt edition which continues to be sold despite Peter Lang's pledge not to do so.]

4.3.2 *Jurisprudence*

The most significant influence on Reinach's conception of states of affairs, I contend, came from his legal studies. When one surveys the small body of work Reinach produced over roughly a decade before he left to fight in the First World War, it becomes clear that he never truly left jurisprudence behind: he found novel ways of incorporating it into his own phenomenology[28] and in continuing the project Husserl had outlined in *Logical Investigations*. When one surveys Reinach's educational story, it is clear that he desired to pursue phenomenology and jurisprudence in tandem and saw great mutual benefit for both fields from such an approach.

Reinach arrived at the University of Munich for the Winter semester of 1901 at the age of seventeen; his class schedule included political economy, philosophy, psychology, and jurisprudence. During this time, he befriended Hermann Kantorowicz (a major figure in the Free Law movement), and this friendship proved so influential that in 1903 Reinach followed Kantorowicz to Berlin where all his studies focused exclusively on jurisprudence.[29] In the 1903/04 academic year, he returned to Munich and his studies with Theodor Lipps in psychology and philosophy, while preparing at the same time for his doctoral examinations in penal law and history. In December of 1904, he successfully earned his doctorate in philosophy under Lipps with a thesis on the concept of cause in the penal law (published in 1905). By this time, Reinach was immersed in the phenomenology of Husserl, and even took part in the famous "Munich Invasion of Göttingen": several of Lipps' students began shuttling to and from Göttingen to study with Husserl. In the summer of 1906, he returned again to Munich and immersed himself exclusively in law studies, and in the fall of that same year he travelled to Tübingen to further his legal education. During the weeks leading up to his departure for Tübingen, Reinach composed a letter to his best friend and fellow Lipps' classmate, Theodor Conrad, dated October 16, 1906, in which he asked: "Do you now know what a *Sachverhalt* is? The Imperial German Code of Civil Procedure always says *Sachverhältnis*. If you want, I will also send you the section numbers. I know it all by heart."[30]

In Tübingen, he attended courses offered by different theorists, but the lectures on penal law offered by Ernst Beling would have the most significant impact on Reinach's phenomenology of states of affairs and his extraordinary monograph on

[28] Reinach's own phenomenology is a blend of Theodor Lipps' phenomenology and descriptive psychology of the late nineteenth and early twentieth centuries, and Husserl's early realist phenomenology of *Logical Investigations*.

[29] For more on the relationship, see Kimberly Baltzer-Jaray, 'Reinach and Kantorowicz: Justice, Phenomenological Realism and the Free Law Movement' (2020) 90 Folia Iuridica 91.

[30] "Wissen Sie jetzt, was ein Sachverhalt ist? Die Civilprozessordnung des deutschen Reichs sagt immer: Sachverhältnis. Wenn Sie wollen, schreibe ich ihnen auch die Paragraphen. Ich kann alles auswendig." Letter to Conrad, Ana 379, C I 1/19.

the *a priori* foundations of civil law. Reinach wrote the first state examination in law in Tübingen, in the spring of 1907, and returned to Munich afterward to complete his habilitation. Lipps' poor health prevented the work on a theory of judgment from being submitted in Munich, and the Tübingen faculty made it clear they would not accept it; so Reinach turned to Husserl, who was enthusiastic about the manuscript. In spring of 1909, Reinach successfully habilitated at Göttingen[31] and began working closely with Husserl, as an assistant and colleague. Yet, the influence of his legal studies remained strong, with robust presence in his publications and seminar topics – especially those that focused on judgments and states of affairs: in 1911, he transformed part of his habilitation thesis into a work for the *Festschrift* for Lipps, titled "*Zur Theorie des negativen Urteils*" (*The Theory of Negative Judgment*); in 1913, he published "*Die Überlegung; ihre ethische und rechtliche Bedeutung*" (*Deliberation; Its Ethical and Legal Significance*); in 1912, he offered a seminar on the philosophy of civil law that served as preparation for his 1913 contribution to the first volume of *Jahrbuch*, titled "*Die apriorischen Grundlagen des bürgerlichen Rechtes*" (*The A Priori Foundations of Civil Law*); and in the final public lecture delivered in 1914 at the University of Marburg for a Neo-Kantian audience, "*Über Phänomenologie*" (*Concerning Phenomenology*).

As mentioned above, Beling's penal law lectures had the most profound impact on Reinach and his theorizing about states of affairs.[32] These lectures were likely based on Beling's *Die Lehre von Verbrechen* [*Theory of Crime*] volume from 1906, which is, by design, an ontology of criminal actions. In this work, Beling considers different types of criminal actions in relation to each other (including any modifications of these relations); to the agent(s) involved; and to the legal and punishment processes.[33] Schuhmann and Smith emphasize that the "importance for the penal law of the notion of typicality is clear: the punishment for a crime is a function of the *type* of behaviour that is involved. Beling's work can indeed be seen as an attempt to provide an account of the various ways in which rightful or wrongful behaviour can come to be demarcated into delict-types of different sorts."[34] He demarcates primary from secondary delict-types: such as the difference between murder and attempted

[31] Reinach's habilitation work was titled "*Wesen und Systematik des Urteils*" (*Essence and Systematics of the Judgment*). All that remains of this document is a fragment of rough notes; Reinach's wife, Anna, was instructed by him to destroy any incomplete or rough works if he should die at war, and sadly this document was included in the list.

[32] My overview of Beling is sourced exclusively from Karl Schuhmann and Barry Smith, "Adolf Reinach: An Intellectual Biography" in Kevin Mulligan (ed) *Speech Act and Sachverhalt: Reinach and the Foundations of Realist Phenomenology* (Martinus Nijhoff Publishers 1987) 3–27. Beling has sadly become an obscure figure and finding detailed information about his legal theory, in particular that which pertains to his 1906 book *Die Lehre von Verbrechen* [*Theory of Crime*], is no easy or expedient task. While I am utilizing the summary to describe Beling's 1906 work and its influence on Reinach, I intend to steer Schuhmann and Smith's work in a direction they did not take it – specifically, into negative states of affairs.

[33] Schuhmann and Smith (n 32) 11.

[34] ibid 11.

murder, where the former are capable of existing in their own right independently and the latter are dependent formations that require certain corresponding primary delict-types for supplementation. Beling puts forward the position that there is a whole, a unity, that comes to be constituted by different elements of a certain criminal behavior, and this happens by virtue of a *unifying schema*. The example Schuhmann and Smith offer is battery. The chain of actions for battery would be organized around the schema of injuring another, wrongfully bringing oneself into contact with another, etc.[35] For battery to have occurred, this schema must necessarily be realized in certain actions of the offender(s) and certain consequences for the victim(s), and both the actions and consequences must be accompanied by specific mental state(s) of the individuals involved. In other words, every delict-type relies on a unifying schema that is realized in some *objective* event and reflected in some *subjective* act or mental state of the criminal.[36] The schema as a whole has external, objective aspects (actions, consequences, bruises) and internal, subjective aspects (premeditation, deliberation, hate). These two factors together render the delict-type a unified, independent whole. If the schema is absent or only partially fulfilled, then the delict-type may also be doomed, or is, at best, realized in some modified form.[37] Furthermore, the objective and subjective aspects may or may not conform to one another, and that can lead to behavior which falls within various kinds of delict-types.[38] For Beling, the penal law is a catalogue of delict-types with associated schemas and scales of punishment: Only with a valid schema can the legal process establish that an offender is liable and should be punished in this or that way. This constructs the sphere of law as a space constituted by a web of interdependent typical legal formations and extralegal concepts that become relevant only when they enter into relations with any of the typical legal formations.[39]

Schuhmann and Smith point out that Reinach's style and terminology in his civil law monograph takes many cues from Beling, and Reinach mentions penal law explicitly as being one of many legal disciplines having *a priori* foundations. They also provide a list of similarities between Beling and Reinach: (1) Beling's schema corresponds in several ways to Reinach's legal formation [*Rechtsgebilde*], but lacks some of the *a priori* connotations; (2) both men share a doctrine of contextualism in legal theory; (3) both recognize internal/subjective and external/objective dimensions in legal formations; and (4) both acknowledge the significance for legal theory of the dichotomy of standard/typical and derived/modified instances of legal types.[40] It is with Beling's schema, as illustrated here in the third point of similarity, that we can begin to understand why Reinach argued for both positive and negative states of

35 ibid 11.
36 ibid 12.
37 ibid 11–12.
38 ibid 12.
39 ibid 12.
40 ibid 13.

affairs, and that negative states of affairs necessarily have objectivity- and subjectivity-sides of judgment. In the case of an act deemed to be criminal negligence (i.e., a crime of omitting to do something that one has a legal duty to do, or of acting in disregard for the lives of others), negative states of affairs are at the heart of the crime itself and of the offender: there are objective/external aspects – not acting, no forethought of consequences; and there are subjective/internal aspects – a mental state characterized by absence of forethought, care, or sense of duty. If, for example, I were to synthesize an antihistamine medication for distribution, but then learn from lab testing and drug trials that it has a significantly high likelihood of being fatal to people with brown hair, and do not disclose this information and/or remove my dangerous drug from the market, then I am guilty of not acting to warn or protect brown-haired consumers and of failing to show regard for, or behave with a sense of duty toward, people with brown hair. More than likely, Reinach would frame this situation as "Dr. Baltzer-Jaray was clearly negligent in her decision to disregard the lab evidence and drug trials showing fatal reaction for brown-haired individuals" or even, "Dr. Baltzer-Jaray clearly failed to act, regard, or care about consequences of this drug she synthesized and distributed" – both of these judgments are examples of a positive conviction of a negative state of affairs, where the negation functions on both the objectivity- and consciousness-sides.

In Reinach's *a priori* foundations article, the sections on social acts and, in particular, the act of promising are also relevant here. Promising is what he calls an other-directed social act that has both an inner experience – a directed willing – and an external action that results in fulfillment or failure to fulfill.[41] A promise brings forth claims and obligations between the parties involved. Situations where promises can be waived, revoked, or broken and where claims can be violated, all pertain to negative states of affairs. If I promise to bring Reinach some nice tobacco for his birthday and I forget to stop by the shop on my way to his party, I have broken the promise I made – I have failed to fulfill my obligation (I arrive tobacco-less). Reinach would possibly come up with a positive judgment of a negative state of affairs, "You didn't bring me the tobacco you promised!" and I would likely be left to answer in the same mould, "Sorry, I didn't remember to buy it!" A similar circumstance would arise if Reinach waived the promise – "You don't have to buy me tobacco. You're off the hook!"; where the promise has not been consummated but rather no longer holds as an obligation for me to fulfill. It is now a *non*-promise with a negated obligation, and as such involves negative states of affairs.

A version of Beling's schema is fulfilled in these instances, in that there are both external and internal aspects: my inactions are both in the world and in my mind. A schema such as Beling's, one that demonstrates the necessity of both objective and subjective aspects of criminal acts, supports, for Reinach, the necessity for negation to have both objective/external and subjective/internal aspects. Reinach, I suggest,

[41] Reinach (n 3) 165–166.

adopted what he learned from Beling and adapted it to an ontology of states of affairs, in which positive and negative states of affairs subsist on a par.

The law utilizes negative states of affairs often and broadly: negligence, the crime illustrated in the previous paragraph, is far from the only one that involves negative states of affairs. There is nonfeasance, fraud, breach of contract, and "crimes of failure" such as failing to perform, prevent, protect, comply, remain, appear, etc. In these circumstances, the negative states of affairs that obtain properly occur on both the objectivity- and subjectivity-sides: a crime of *not-acting* has consequences in reality (e.g., someone is injured physically) and also a connection to the mindset of the offender regardless of whether the *not-acting* was intentional or accidental (e.g., willing to not act as a choice, no forethought of the obvious consequences of *not-acting*). At the core of the crime of fraud – where one is deceitfully presenting themselves, an item, or a situation in order to gain something unlawfully – are negative states of affairs: the elixir sold at the carnival will *not* cure cancer, *not* regenerate an amputated limb, and it will definitely *not* provide immortality, and the salesperson knows this while pitching exactly the opposite. The elixir is *not* what the label says it is.

Another example of law relying upon negative states of affairs involves the notion of "reasonable doubt." When reasonable doubt is created, the verdict a jury returns resembles a positive conviction of a negative state of affairs ("not guilty: person X did not with certainty murder person Y" or "guilty: person X is not innocent with certainty of the murder of person Y"). Reasonable doubt relies on negative states of affairs – creating reasonable doubt is not just stirring beliefs but is the use of evidence to tell a necessity-connected story that solidifies strong convictions that something is not the case or is not certain.

These examples are merely a selection of instances within law where negative states of affairs are engaged. A survey of the domain of jurisprudence shows that negative states of affairs are all-pervasive, and that serves as a strong indicator of both their necessity and their ontological status on a par with positive ones. Law studies opened the door, for Reinach, to a domain where negative states of affairs are acknowledged and engaged, and phenomenology provided him with a toolbox – a method for insight into, and description of, the being and essence of these entities.

4.4 CONCLUDING REMARKS

Reinach was deeply influenced by his law studies. He never abandoned jurisprudence; in fact, he incorporated what he learned into his realist phenomenology. I contend that because the law frequently turns on what appears to be negative states of affairs, Reinach's legal training may have contributed to his insistence on independent subsistence of negative states of affairs and their having the same ontological status as positive states of affairs; his law studies provide insight into why the pursuit of negative states of affairs is absolutely necessary ontologically. His education in law at Munich, Berlin, and especially at Tübingen with Beling, underpins much of his early, persistent and profound interest in states of affairs and judgments, and in his phenomenological writings on them right up to his final lecture before enlisting in the First World War.

Reinach and the topic of negative states of affairs might seem to some as a rather obscure, philosophical niche and one that lacks relevance to larger issues; however, to consider it such would be gravely mistaken. First and foremost, Reinach's sense of justice seems to harken back to an older sense of justice (*Recht*) and is in the universe as a transcendent harmony and should undergird any written form of law (*Gesetz*). This entails all of us having a connection to and being able to participate with justice, using insight, and an ability to grasp it even if we have never read a law book. On January 1, 1900, the *Bürgerliches Gesetzbuch* (BGB) came into effect in Germany; it was a monolithic, groundbreaking positivist project that interpreted justice as achievable purely through application of the codified law. Reinach was one among many legal scholars at the turn the century who attempted to push back against this shift in the direction of jurisprudence. His *a priori* foundations article, as a whole, stands as a powerful critique of what the lawmakers of the BGB failed to grasp – justice is in the world, the laws we write should reflect this harmony at work. Laws are written and can be changed but justice is an entity we grasp using insight, not create. In this way Reinach connects with legal philosophers like Leibniz, but he leaves the notion of God or any teleology off the table (as a realist phenomenologist, he is only concerned with that which is and not how it came to be). This distinction between justice and law is currently all too relevant and extremely significant.

Reinach, like many early phenomenologists, was critical of positivistic philosophy given its bias for defining knowledge as necessarily linked to existence and sensory evidence. His ontology of states of affairs serves as a refutation of this type of positivism since they are intuitively discerned and not perceived by the senses, subsisting in the world independently, and participate with all kinds of being – real, ideal, possible, and impossible – and they can be positive or negative. He extended this critical position into his jurisprudence theorizing by incorporating ontology to ground legal concepts: positive and negative states of affairs and, most importantly, the conception of an *a priori* foundation that underpins *all* written laws, thus connecting them with a larger, transcendent justice at work in the universe.

We live in a world that remains under the influence of philosophical positivistic thinking, where there is a preference for tangible actions – for sheer deeds rather than inaction or omission. People want to *see* a crime: they want evidence showing directly that an employer discriminated against an employee, not by searching through all the structural ways that a system fails to support diversity and difference and that creates various obstacles for a marginalized individual. Reinach's robust ontology provides a foundation from which we can ground the ethical conclusions we draw. The injustices committed by failing to act or prevent something from happening are very much a part of today's dialogue about complicity in systems of power and privilege. The witness to a violent crime on the street who says and does nothing is often perceived as an unjust person, and their perceived injustice does not stop at the failure to report or stop a crime in progress, but ripples outward in the ways their silence and inactivity supports structures of violence, inequality, inequity, misogyny, racism, colonialism, ableism, etc. Negative states of affairs bring us back to these dialogues, ontologically as well as practically, and allow us to explore negation in meaningful ways as never before and connect them as a ground for our ethical viewpoints. With so much oppression and violence against women and gender equity-seeking groups, Indigenous Peoples, racialized individuals, persons with disabilities, and 2SLGBTQIA+ persons, the issue of what so many of us are not doing or are failing to prevent has become a central issue in our thinking about how to achieve justice.

BIBLIOGRAPHY

Avé-Lallemant, E, *Die Nachlässe der Münchener Phänomenologen in der Bayerischen Staatsbibliothek* (Harrassowitz 1975)

Baltzer-Jaray, K, 'Bogged Down in Ontologism and Realism: The Phenomenology of Adolf Reinach' in Rodney KB Parker (ed) *The Idealism-Realism Debate among Edmund Husserl's Early Followers and Critics*, (Springer 2021)

'Phenomenological Jurisprudence: A Reinterpretation of Reinach's Jahrbuch Essay' in J Edward Hackett and J Aaron Simmons (eds) *Phenomenology for the Twenty-First Century* (Palgrave Macmillan 2016)

'Reinach and Kantorowicz: Justice, Phenomenological Realism and the Free Law Movement" (2020) 90 Folia Iuridica 91 [2020] Ed. Tomasz Bekrycht. *Acta Universitatis Lodziensis Folia Iuridica* (90)

Chisholm, R, 'Alexius Meinong: The Theory of Objects" in Roderick Chisholm (ed) *Realism and the Background of Phenomenology* (The Free Press 1960)

Chrudzimski, A, 'Negative States of Affairs: Reinach Versus Ingarden' (2012) 16 Symposium 106

Husserl, E., *Logical Investigations*. (JN Findlay tr, and Dermot Moran ed, Routledge 2001)

Ingarden, R, *Controversy over the Existence of the World II*. (Arthur Szylewicz tr, Peter Lang 2016)

Jacquette, D, *Alexius Meinong: The Shepherd of Non-being* (Springer 2015)

Meinong, A, *On Assumptions* (James Heanue ed and tr, University of California Press 1983)

Über Annahmen (2nd ed JA Barth 1910)

Parker, R, (ed.,) *The Idealism-Realism Debate Among Edmund Husserl's Early Followers and Critics* (Springer 2021)

Reinach A, 'The Apriori Foundations of the Civil Law' (John F Crosby tr, 1983) 3 Aletheia 1–142, reprinted in Adolf Reinach, *The Apriori Foundations of the Civil Law Along with the Lecture 'Concerning Phenomenology'* (John F Crosby ed, Ontos Verlag 2012), originally published as Adolf Reinach, Die apriorischen Grundlagen des bürgerlichen Rechtes, 1(2) *Jahrbuch für Philosophie und phänomenologische Forschung* (Max Niemeyer 1913), 685–847

'Kant's Interpretation of Hume's Problem' (JN Mohanty tr, 1976) 7 Southwestern J Phil 161

'On the Theory of Negative Judgment' (Don Ferrari tr, 1981) 2 Aletheia 315

Sämtliche Werke: Textkritische Ausgabe in 2 Bänden (Karl Schuhmann and Barry Smith eds, Philosophia Verlag 1989)

Schuhmann, K and B Smith, 'Against Idealism: Johannes Daubert vs. Husserl's "Ideas" I' (1985) 38 Review of Metaphysics 763

'Adolf Reinach: An Intellectual Biography' in Kevin Mulligan (ed) *Speech Act and Sachverhalt: Reinach and the Foundations of Realist Phenomenology* (Martinus Nijhoff Publishers 1987)

PART II

Reinach and Private Law Theory

5

Legal Concepts as a Deep Structure of the Law

Reinach's A Priori in Action

Andrew S. Gold & Henry E. Smith***

5.1 INTRODUCTION

Private law theory increasingly gravitates toward extremes. In area after area and across methodologies, private law is pushed in opposite directions. This polarization takes place along many dimensions. Familiar are the opposition of internal and external perspectives on law, holistic and reductionist methodologies, conceptualism and nominalism, deontology and consequentialism. Often what is left out in this picture are the details of law and its workings, which relate individual behavior and morality to larger questions of justice and societal organization. As a result of privileging the micro or the macro, private law theory has trouble relating these two levels, with a lot of hand waving substituting for a well-grounded account of any kind.

All of which makes an encounter with the legal phenomenology of Adolf Reinach more than a little startling. According to Reinach, a close consideration of our intuitions will provide access to a realm of law made up of real, timeless entities, which he identifies as being synthetic a priori.[1] That is, it is not logical, but neither is it conventional or contingent. Broader than the Kantian a priori, what the a priori was for Reinach is intertwined with the kind of close analysis called for in his

* Professor of Law, University of California, Irvine. Email: agold@law.uci.edu.

** Fessenden Professor of Law, Harvard Law School. Email: hesmith@law.harvard.edu. For helpful comments and discussion, the authors would like to thank Seana Shiffrin and audiences at the Conference on Reinach and the Foundations of Private Law at the Max Planck Institute for Legal History and Legal Theory in Frankfurt and at the UCLA Legal Theory Workshop.

1 Adolf Reinach, 'The Apriori Foundations of the Civil Law' (John F Crosby tr, 1983) 3 Aletheia 1, reprinted in Adolf Reinach, *The Apriori Foundations of the Civil Law along with the Lecture 'Concerning Phenomenology'* (John F Crosby ed, Ontos Verlag 2012), originally published as Adolf Reinach, Die apriorischen Grundlagen des bürgerlichen Rechtes, 1(2) *Jahrbuch für Philosophie und phänomenologische Forschung* (Max Niemeyer 1913) 685–847.

phenomenology. An entry point to the a priori is by way of our considered intuitions about law. The intuition can be direct, or it can be indirectly ferreted out through telltale signs like the naturalness of enactments that accord with the a priori.[2] We will argue that these signposts of the a priori are important for private law theory regardless of the ultimate status of what Reinach sees as a priori.

For Reinach, the a priori or essential in law is not conventional, but it can be superseded by positive enactment when it comes to actual law and legal concepts. Although such enactments can deviate from the a priori, the latter is always there. It not only leaves hints at its presence in terms of ease of enactment, patterns of legal thinking in new contexts, and the like. Reinach also suggests that the a priori has a gravitational pull such that deviations from it would be more common if they only responded to external considerations and did not work against the pull of the a priori.[3]

Most importantly, the a priori is a legal ontology that is presupposed when we deal with law, even when law deviates from this underlying reality. By studying closely the presuppositions of law we can get a sense of its architecture – its deep structure – even if we don't have infallible access to the a priori – or, we will argue, even if it does not have that status. That is, looking for the a priori can put on the table what about law is so robust as to be more than conventional and perhaps so taken for granted that it is not immediately apparent. Sometimes it will be difficult to tell this deep structure apart from certain widespread and psychologically, socially, or economically motivated aspects of law. In the end, one can question whether there is that much difference: one can accept that Reinach's phenomenological procedure gets at something deep about law while entertaining a range of sources for it, ranging from natural law to psychology to overwhelming practical considerations.

This is strong stuff. It grows out of a phenomenological tradition that is quite optimistic about the project of direct analysis of experience. We will not enter into the debates over phenomenology itself, nor will we argue that Reinach's extension of this methodology into law is the solution to the ills of current private law theory. Instead, we will employ the lens of Reinach's a priori and its surprising successes in providing insights into aspects of private law to argue that his philosophy can be the starting point for thinking about how to fill the law-shaped gap in current theorizing.[4] We will show that Reinach's a priori is a good entry point to aspects of law that are deep and robust, whatever their source – natural, psychological, or practical. These aspects of law relate to the social acts between individuals and their 'micro' interactions, and at the same time they organize behavior in a way that allows society to function better or worse. In Reinach's a priori we can be attentive to detail and

2 ibid 131.

3 ibid 5–7.

4 We do not mean to imply that Reinach's framework would not be useful in thinking about public law. Reinach's book was concerned with the civil law, and we are scholars of private law. Many of the social acts involved in public law will be different from those considered here.

venture abstract generalizations, without thereby becoming overly reductionist. By ferreting out the Reinachian a priori in law, we can in the spirit of the New Private Law bring the poles of thinking we began with – the internal and external, holistic and reductionist, conceptualist and nominalist – closer together and ultimately relate the micro in law to the macro of the legal system and society writ large.

This chapter will examine current private law theory through a Reinachian lens. In Section 5.2, we set the stage by pointing out what is missing from a wide variety of approaches to private law across legal systems: how the details of law as a working system relate to the micro and the macro. In Section 5.3, we show how Reinach tackles the law on its own terms and brings out some striking insights about law, especially in the areas of property, the transfer of rights, and representation. Finally, we draw some lessons from Reinach for addressing the micro–macro problem in private law theory and examine the full range of foundational theories that could benefit from an infusion of Reinachian deep structure, whatever its ultimate status.

5.2 PRIVATE LAW THEORY AND ITS DISCONTENTS

Private law is less unified than ever. Along quite a few dimensions, theorists push in wholly opposite directions and wind up standing at odds with one another. First, internal and external perspectives style themselves as opposites.[5] Internal theories seek to understand law from the perspective of a participant, to get at the law's 'self-understanding', during which one is to take what courts say seriously rather than as deception or false consciousness. By contrast, external perspectives analyze the law in light of some extralegal criterion, be it efficiency, distributive fairness, or even deontology. With the rise of Legal Realism in the United States, external perspectives, especially functionalist ones, have become the mainstream there.

Related to but distinct from the internal–external divide are various approaches to reductionism. Functionalist theories of law often seek to explain or justify law in terms of one variable, such as efficiency, welfare, or fairness, and in some versions, like much of law and economics, employ simple models of individual behavior. Internal perspectives run the opposite risk, of replicating the phenomenon they seek to explain or justify. However, reductionism does not track the internal–external divide exactly. Functional theories can be pluralist, responding to multiple values, and internal theories can see in (or read into) law one overriding value. An interesting contrast are old and new institutional approaches to law and economics: the style of the original institutionalists was holistic, with the invocation of society-level variables like culture and power.[6] New institutionalists react to but still

[5] AS Gold, 'Internal and External Perspectives: On the New Private Law Methodology' in AS Gold et al (eds), *The Oxford Handbook of the New Private Law* (Oxford University Press 2020) 3.

[6] See, e.g., JR Commons, *Institutional Economics: Its Place in Political Economy* (Macmillan 1934). For a discussion, see HE Smith, 'The Complex Architecture of Property Rights' in Lee

take as a starting point modern microeconomics with its methodological individualism and (unless modified) rational actor models.[7]

One major arena in which the question of reductionism looms large is the nature of concepts in law. In natural law, legal concepts are taken as robust and not the result of convention. Doctrinalism sees concepts as more or less given and not easily manipulated, and crucially as performing an important role in the law. The caricature of 'deductive' formalism would be an extreme example.[8] At the opposite extreme is a kind of nominalism. Notably, the Legal Realists preferred narrow and shallow concepts that stuck close to 'the facts' and could be altered easily in response to social needs and policy.[9] (Realists wrote casebooks that were organized around industries and social situations – employment contracts, medical contracts, construction contracts – rather than offer and acceptance, consideration, conditions, and the like.[10])

Finally, and again in a somewhat crosscutting fashion, deontologists and consequentialists face off, with the former evaluating law in terms of its inherent rightness or wrongness with the latter more focused on law's consequences. Sometimes this dichotomy closely tracks external and internal, with external theories explaining law in terms of (external) consequences and internal perspectives positing an immanent morality of the law. However, one can be an external deontologist.[11] And consequentialist reasoning has always been a part of judges' reasoning. Nevertheless, in modern theory, deontology and consequentialism stand largely in opposition to each other.

How related these polarizations are presents a large and difficult question and one open to dispute. We can offer no more than some informed speculations on how we got here. Our main focus is the future: what can be done about the systematic – and yawning – lacuna in private law theory? There is an unaddressed yet vitally important gap between the law's micro and macro levels, and, not unrelatedly we think, there is a series of divides between internalists and externalists, holists and reductionists, conceptualists and realists, deontologists and consequentialists. Later we will

Alston, Eric Alston, and Bernardo Mueller (eds), *Handbook on Institutions and Complexity* (Elgar, forthcoming).

7 See, e.g., C Ménard and MM Shirley, *Advanced Introduction to New Institutional Economics* (Elgar 2022).

8 PB Miller, 'The New Formalism in Private Law' (2021) 66 American Journal of Jurisprudence 175.

9 HE Smith, 'On the Economy of Concepts in Property' (2012) University of Pennsylvania Law Review 2097, 2100–06.

10 See HC Havighurst, *A Selection of Contract Cases and Related Quasi-Contract Cases* (Lawyers Co-operative Publishing Company 1934) iii ('Cases are grouped according to subject matter and not according to the doctrines employed'); see generally HE Smith, 'Modularity in Contracts: Boilerplate and Information Flow' (2006) 104 Michigan Law Review 1175, 1217–19.

11 See EJ Weinrib, *The Idea of Private Law* (Harvard University Press 1995) 50–53 (arguing that Charles Fried's *Contract as Promise* uses Kantian morality as an external criterion and fails to capture the intrinsic bipolar structure of law).

argue that legal phenomenology is a good place to start in diagnosing the problem and in evaluating various solutions.

What is the source of this polarization? We can start by recognizing that it was not always so. In earlier times natural law could be used directly to make arguments of obvious relevance at the level of the law itself.[12] Natural law connected private law to larger questions of justice on the one hand and to morality at the individual level on the other. Once very widely accepted, natural law as an underpinning for law receded in the later nineteenth century.[13] The loss of faith in natural law left a vacuum that rendered late nineteenth-century formalism vulnerable: even if it was not as mechanically formal as its detractors claimed, post-natural law mainstream legal thought was rather hollow. It purported to be about the level of law but was not grounded or even tethered to much of anything.

Intellectual histories of law capture this polarization in various ways. Famously, Duncan Kennedy contrasted classical and modern legal thought in terms of individualism and altruism.[14] These broad movements were said to be reflected in individual decisions. However, these decisions were taken more as results than as internally justified, and tellingly, many of Kennedy's examples of altruism in law were equity cases. The more legal-level view of law and equity is suppressed. Nevertheless, it cannot be gainsaid that at the level of legal thought broad tendencies have contended and sometimes contradicted each other. In the civil law too, individualism and community have been a theme among legal commentators.[15] And Marietta Auer has located the necessity of these high-level oppositions – between the social and the individual, and between community and autonomy – in an irreducible conflict within modernism itself.[16]

Private law theorists might seem to be suffering from irreconcilable differences. But before going their separate ways, theorists should take a closer look at Reinach's account of law. If one does so, one discovers connective tissue in law that was hiding in plain sight.

5.3 REINACH'S EXCAVATION OF LAW'S FOUNDATIONS

Reinach's book is entitled 'The Apriori Foundations of the Civil Law', and it is the insights that he provides into the civil law itself that provide a starting point for a new kind of theorizing in private law. Reinach posits an ontology of 'essential' law that is

[12] RH Helmholz, *Natural Law in Court* (Harvard University Press 2015).

[13] See, e.g., S Banner, *The Decline of Natural Law: How American Lawyers Once Used Natural Law and Why They Stopped* (Oxford University Press 2021).

[14] D Kennedy, 'Form and Substance in Private Law Adjudication' (1976) 89 Harvard Law Review 1685, 1695–96.

[15] See, e.g., A di Robilant, *The Making of Modern Property: Reinventing Roman Law in Nineteenth Century Europe and Its Periphery* (Cambridge University Press 2023).

[16] M Auer, *Der privatrechtliche Diskurs der Moderne* (Mohr Siebeck 2014).

universal and foundational in the sense of being presupposed in actual legal systems, even when actual law deviates from the a priori. Before we turn to how this deep structure can inform current private law theory, we take a close look at some examples of Reinach's theory in action. After all, if Reinach's a priori helps bridge the various gaps in private law theory discussed in the previous section, there must be something specific there to play this role.

5.3.1 *Reinach on Property and Transfer*

Property is notoriously contested terrain in the debate over legal concepts. Reinach's treatment of property attempts to sift out the a priori while forthrightly facing some of the difficulties in doing so. In the process, he captures quite a few features of the legal system that have resisted analysis. Most strikingly, his analysis is flexible and intuitive and yet highly integrated.

Reinach posits ownership as a priori and something that is independent of and presupposed by actual property rights. As Olivier Massin argues, this account is not vulnerable to a range of conventionalist objections because it is about the *nature* of ownership, whereas the *existence* of ownership depends on human conventions.[17] As we will see, Reinach's account affords something in between formalism and contextualism, and is well suited to capturing the generative and loosely systematic quality of property.

A good testing ground is the nature of ownership and 'property' itself. From the traditional notion of a right to a thing to the bundle of rights, we can see almost all the dichotomies on display in the various pictures of the structure (or not) of property entitlements.

The bundle of rights itself can be seen in the light of the a priori and positive enactments. For Reinach the relation of owning is between a person and a thing and is 'an ultimate, irreducible relation which cannot be further resolved into elements'.[18] He contrasts this view with what sounds very much like the Realist bundle of sticks: 'We of course reject the usual formulation that property is the *sum* or the *unity* of all rights over the thing. If something is grounded with essential necessity in another, this other can never consist in the thing'.[19]

Reinach points out that if property were a bundle of rights, then transferring one right would diminish the 'belonging' and that if all the rights were alienated there would be no belonging. However, Reinach takes *nuda proprietas* – or bare or abstract ownership without a right of use – very seriously. Reinach notices that his

[17] O Massin, 'The Metaphysics of Ownership: A Reinachian Account' (2017) 27 Axiomathes 577. See also J Toomey, 'Property's Boundaries' (2023) 109 Virginia Law Review 131.

[18] Reinach (n 1) 55. For a recent economic and psychological treatment of property in this spirit, see BJ Wilson, *The Property Species: Mine, Yours, and the Human Mind* (Oxford University Press 2020).

[19] Reinach (n 1) 56.

more indefinite approach to ownership captures the 'residual' character of property. Ownership is bounded but not from within: the actual limits on ownership of a thing are grounded in positive law. Thus, when external bounds are removed, ownership fills the void. If an easement is destroyed or a claim against property is waived, ownership becomes visible in this 'gap'. It might seem that ownership 'springs back to life' when such a restriction on what would otherwise be ownership is removed, but for Reinach ownership was there all along.[20] For Reinach, '[t]his is the essential necessity which underlies the so-called "elasticity" or "residuarity" of property and which can hardly be reasonably considered as an "invention" of the positive law'.[21] Indeed, as we will see with transfer, some of the 'indefiniteness' of property seems to be more of a by-product of our presuppositions about property rather than a conscious choice.

Despite how attenuated they may become in practice, the rights associated with ownership are absolute, not in the sense of being unqualified and not in the sense of being universal. Indeed, exceptionlessness and universality are commonly mistaken for 'absoluteness' and 'in rem' status both in Reinach's day and our own. Instead, an absolute right is one that is not directed at anyone. In this Reinach anticipates the analysis of Albert Kocourek of in rem rights as 'unpolarized'.[22] Kocourek objected to Wesley Hohfeld's analysis of in rem rights as collections of in personam rights ('multital' rights would be a collection of 'unital' or 'paucital' rights).[23] Instead, for Kocourek an in rem right is 'one of which the essential investitive facts do not serve directly to identify the person who owns the incident duty'.[24] A contract right when it is created is directed to a specific person, but a property right avails against people generally; more precisely no duty holder is specifically identified (in an intensional way).[25]

Reinach contrasts ownership with possession, which is much closer to the 'surface' in many ways. As with the bundle of rights, he argues that ownership cannot be simply possession-plus. As for possession itself, Reinach provides a sophisticated account that captures how it straddles the social and legal world. Reinach notes

[20] ibid.

[21] ibid.

[22] A Kocourek, *Jural Relations* (2nd ed., Bobbs-Merrill 1928) 201; see also A Kocourek, 'Polarized and Unpolarized Legal Relations' (1921) 9 Kentucky Law Journal 131, 131.

[23] WN Hohfeld, 'Fundamental Legal Conceptions as Applied in Judicial Reasoning' (1917) 26 Yale Law Journal 710, reprinted in WW Cook (ed), WN *Hohfeld, Fundamental Legal Conceptions as Applied in Judicial Reasoning and Other Legal Essays* (Yale University Press 1923) 65–114.

[24] Kocourek, *Jural Relations* (n 22) 201.

[25] Legal Realists and other nominalists tend to define legal concepts as being equivalent if they have the same extension. (Hence the attempt to replace ownership with a collection of use rights and related entitlements.) However, from a functional point of view, different intensions can have very different implications in terms of information costs. See HE Smith, 'Emergent Property' in J Penner and HE Smith (eds), *Philosophical Foundations of Property Law* (Oxford University Press 2013) 320.

that a natural power over things is totally distinct from a legal power.[26] The latter has to do with waiver, revocation, and the like, and as we will see it features centrally in Reinach's account of transfer. In contrast to a legal power, a natural power involves physical control of a thing and forms the basis for notions of possession. Possession is related to social fact (control) but must be distinguished from a right to the possession and a right to take possession.[27] (Here too he anticipates Kocourek's strong distinction between possession and the right to possess.[28])

Reinach develops his framework of property by examining the domain of transfer. He starts out by noting the *nemo dat* principle (*nemo plus iuris transferre potest quam ipse habet*, 'one cannot transfer better rights than one has oneself'),[29] which Reinach says 'expresses of course an a priori truth'.[30] Why 'of course'? Reinach does not elaborate but extends this idea in two directions: Reinach points out that one cannot transfer rights unless one has the power to transfer and that if one has the power to transfer a right one can transfer that right even if one does not have it oneself. We interpret Reinach as laying out here an essential architecture of transfer that captures the presuppositions and tendencies one can see in the law.

Although Reinach passes quickly over his reasons for taking *nemo dat* as a priori, a closer look reveals how much grist for his mill it offers. To begin with, *nemo dat* has an immediate appeal to the intuition. If A transfers a thing – or more accurately A's rights to a thing – to B and then performs similar acts directed to C, then B has the rights A had and C does not. A had rights to transfer at the time of the transfer to B and had no such rights to give to C. And if one never had the rights, one can likewise not transfer them. This is why the idea of an offer to sell the Brooklyn Bridge is the paradigm of an obvious scam and potential gullibility on the part of the offeree.[31]

The law sometimes deviates from the *nemo dat* principle by positive enactment. If in our example, C does not know that A does not have rights, then C presents a sympathetic claimant. If, further, B could have warned C but did not, then there is a case for allowing C to have better rights than B, *nemo dat* notwithstanding.

[26] Reinach (n 1) 53.

[27] ibid 53–64.

[28] Kocourek, *Jural Relations* (n 22) 361–71. Yun-chien Chang argues that keeping possession close to physical control and distinct from the right to possess captures possession in the civil law. Y Chang, 'The Economy of Concept and Possession' in Y Chang (ed), *Law and Economics of Possession* (Cambridge University Press 2015) 103

[29] An alternate, perhaps better-known formulation in common law jurisdictions is *nemo dat quod non habet* ('one cannot give what one does not have'), *nemo dat* for short. We will refer to the principle as '*nemo dat*'.

[30] Reinach (n 1) 68.

[31] JL Schroeder, 'Is Article 8 Finally Ready This Time? The Radical Reform of Secured Lending on Wall Street' (1994) Columbia Business Law Review 291, 296 n 6. ('[T]he reason we New Yorkers consider the rube who thinks he bought the Brooklyn Bridge as the archetype of gullibility is precisely because the derivation rule is considered to be common knowledge in our society').

Similarly, with entrustment to a merchant: if A entrusts watch seller B with a watch, this creates an appearance of ownership in the merchant. If B wrongfully 'sells' the watch to C, then as between A and C, again C looks like a good candidate for an exception to *nemo dat*. And entrustment is indeed a common exception to *nemo dat* across legal systems in favor of good faith purchasers.[32] Some systems, including the German Civil Code, feature a very wide good faith purchase exception.[33]

Good faith purchase is so compelling in some cases and so useful in many situations, that some see it as having superseded *nemo dat*.[34] Reinach's analysis helps us see why this is wrong. Reinach takes good faith purchaser rules as responsive to considerations that cause a deviation (*Abweichung*) from the a priori.[35] As already mentioned, the mechanism of good faith purchase means that when it does not apply, *nemo dat* applies. This is true of recording acts in real property and the Uniform Commercial Code (where it is captured by the concepts of void and voidable title). If a new situation arose outside these laws (a new resource that is neither real property nor covered by the UCC), it would fall under *nemo dat*. Moreover, it is easier to state the system with *nemo dat* as the base case and the good faith purchase rule as the exception even if good faith purchase applies much of the time. The pattern of exceptions is directed to good faith purchasers, not to anything about *nemo dat*. For *nemo dat*, the law shows what system designers call default hierarchies and linguists call an 'elsewhere' pattern; good faith purchase is specific and *nemo dat* is the encompassing default (a relationship to which we return in Section 5.4).[36] Stating the law as good faith purchasers winning and then having

[32] Unif. Comm. Code § 2-403(2). See generally Y Chang, *Property Law: Comparative, Empirical, and Economic Analyses* (Cambridge University Press 2023) 261–69; S Levmore, 'Variety and Uniformity in the Treatment of the Good-Faith Purchaser' (1987) 16 Journal of Legal Studies 43; A Schwartz and RE Scott, 'Rethinking the Laws of Good Faith Purchase' (2011) 111 Columbia Law Review 1332.

[33] See, e.g., BGB § 932 (good faith purchase in property transfers); ibid § 935 (good faith purchaser wins if good purchased at public auction). See also Kunstsammlungen zu Weimar v. Elicofon, 536 F. Supp. 829, 839 (E.D.N.Y. 1981), aff'd, 678 F.2d 1150 (2d Cir. 1982) (applying *nemo dat* after canvassing many potentially applicable but inapplicable laws including the German law of good faith purchase). England had the market overt rule until recently. Sale of Goods (Amendment) Act 1994, ch. 32; M Smith, 'Valediction to Market Overt' (1997) 41 American Journal of Legal History 225.

[34] Cf B Arruñada, G Zanarone, and NM Garoupa, 'Property Rights in Sequential Exchange' (2019) 35 Journal of Law, Economics and Organization 127, 142–43.

[35] Reinach (n 1) 74, 111.

[36] On default hierarchies, see JH Holland et al, Induction: Processes of Inference, Learning, and Discovery (MIT Press 1989) 18–19. The similar notion in linguistics, sometimes called the 'elsewhere condition' or nested defaults, can be traced back to the ancient Indian grammarian Pāṇini. See, e.g., SR Anderson, *A-Morphous Morphology* (Cambridge University Press 1992) 45, 132; P Kiparsky, '"Elsewhere" in Phonology' in SR Anderson and P Kiparsky (eds), *A Festschrift for Morris Halle* (Holt, Rinehart, and Winston 1973) 93; see also S Pinker, *Words and Rules: The Ingredients of Language* (Basic Books 1999) 13–19. In a fashion parallel to *nemo dat*, a controversy arose in the nineteenth century among Western Indologists about whether the accusative case should be treated as the default case in Vedic Sanskrit, with one of the

an exception for *nemo dat*, or positing two freestanding nonhierarchically arranged rules for *nemo dat* and good faith purchase, would be cumbersome.[37] Very strikingly, virtually all the statutes around the world canvassed in a recent survey by proponents of an expansive approach to good faith purchase show *nemo dat* as the base case.[38]

This foray into good faith purchase illustrates some of the benefits of paying attention to the a priori in Reinach's sense. In the first place, inquiring into the a priori elucidates the relationship of an oft-displaced principle, *nemo dat*, to its exceptions, which makes understanding the system much easier than if one jumped straight into the good faith purchaser issue. Relatedly, some good faith purchase situations at least at their edges are close to equipoise, as where original owners and good faith purchasers are equally innocent and neither is better positioned to prevent the conflict from arising (by, for example, guarding against theft or fraud, or inquiring into the provenance of a good offered for sale).[39]

Interestingly, the history of good faith purchase also reflects a robust underlying status for *nemo dat*. Originally good faith purchase was introduced in equity by use of the 'mere equity' (a mini-interest that is a toehold for an equitable remedy). When B defrauds A into transferring a thing and then transfers to C, A would retain an 'equity' that would travel with the rights to the thing. The equity was a placeholder for an equitable remedy and was in a sense a right to a right: when A sues, A could get a court to compel C to use the power of transfer in A's favor. However, if C were a good faith purchaser for value, the equity would be overcome because C's conscience was not affected by holding the rights. (The good faith purchaser was termed 'equity's darling'.[40]) Here we see equity taking a first attempt at overcoming practical problems with the a priori system being directly reflected in law, as Reinach allows for.

In the common law systems, equity played a role in modulating the effect of what Reinach would call the a priori essential underlying legal stratum.[41] Reinach notes that assignment of rights is much less obvious than one might think from studying current law.[42] Reinach mentions the possibility of A effecting something like a

arguments in favor of such an analysis being that it unified a wide and disparate set of functions of the Vedic accusative. See H Smith, *Restrictiveness in Case Theory* (Cambridge University Press 1996) 39–40; see also Smith (n 9) 2010 and n. 46.

37 Smith (n 9) 2120–24.

38 Schwartz and Scott (n 32) 1378–83. It is not clear that the few countries that they list as not having *nemo dat* as the base case actually do not have *nemo dat* as an unstated base case.

39 Levmore (n 32).

40 See, e.g., A Nair and I Samet, 'What Can "Equity's Darling" Tell Us about Equity?' in D Klimchuk, I Samet, and HE Smith (eds), *Philosophical Foundations of the Law of Equity* (Oxford University Press 2020) 264, 278; HE Smith, 'Equity as Meta-Law' (2021) 130 Yale Law Journal 1050, 1065–66, 1095.

41 As it did with privity, another candidate for Reinach's a priori. Smith (n 40) 1065–66, 1109.

42 Reinach (n 1) 127.

transfer by promising someone that A will exercise the rights at the other's behest.[43] This is exactly what happens with an equitable assignment, which is an earlier version of modern assignment and which can be still found as an alternative to a legal assignment in English law.[44]

Strikingly, Reinach uses his method to open up possibilities that conventional legal theory (if not the law itself) of his time had labelled 'conceptually impossible'. Chiefly, he argues for the possibility, from the point of view of the essential, for rights in rights.[45] He sees this as possible from the a priori point of view because in principle an action can be directed toward rights and an action can be the subject of a right. And he points to waiver as being an action directed to rights, and so the power to waive is in a sense the right to a right. Although the possibility of a right in a right had been aired in civil law scholarship before and was a natural interpretation of various provisions in the Civil Code about liens, it was apparently contested as a matter of theory and according to Reinach often dismissed as a conceptual impossibility.[46] Reinach takes this opportunity to distinguish talk of 'conceptual impossibility of rights over rights' (*begriffliche Unmöglichkeit der Rechte an Rechten*) in the positive law discourse from essential impossibility. He argues that rights in rights are possible a priori and found in certain respects, as in the law of liens. It is notable that in the common law, a leading theory of equitable rights in trust is a right in a right: the beneficiary has a right to the trustee's right and has the ability to require actions by the trustee's use of the powers of title, coming under the heading of fiduciary duties.[47] Indeed, Reinach's analysis suggests the possibility of an 'obligational' theory of trust that is compatible with the civil law, where conventional wisdom holds that civil law notions of ownership as dominium are an insuperable obstacle to recognizing the trust.[48]

43 ibid 126.

44 See B McFarlane and R Stevens, 'What's Special about Equity? Rights about Rights' in D Klimchuk, I Samet, and HE Smith (eds), *Philosophical Foundations of the Law of Equity* (Oxford University Press 2020) 191, 206–08.

45 Reinach (n 1) 63–64.

46 ibid; Reinach, 'Die apriorischen Grundlagen des bürgerlichen Rechtes' (n 1) 758. Presumably the objection to rights in rights is that this sounds like a right in a thing, but things are supposed to be tangible (in keeping with the strict separation of in rem and in personam as implemented in German property law). See GL Gretton, 'Ownership and Its Objects' (2007) 71(4) Rabels Zeitschrift für ausländisches und internationales Privatrecht 802. For an early discussion of rights in rights, see W Schuppe, *Der Begriff des subjektiven Rechts* (Wilhelm Koebner 1887) 204–10.

47 B McFarlane and R Stevens, 'The Nature of Equitable Property' (2010) 4 Journal of Equity 1; see also JB Ames, 'Purchase for Value without Notice' (1887) 1 Harvard Law Review 1, 9–10.

48 See, e.g., P Matthews, 'The Compatibility of the Trust with the Civil Law Notion of Property' in L Smith (ed), *The Worlds of the Trust* (Cambridge University Press 2013); L Smith (ed), *Re-imagining the Trust: Trusts in Civil Law* (Cambridge University Press 2012); L Ho and R Lee (eds), *Trust Law in Asian Civil Law Jurisdictions: A Comparative Analysis* (Cambridge University Press 2013); see also R Helmholz and R Zimmermann (eds), *Itinera Fiduciae: Trust and Treuhand in Historical Perspective* (Duncker & Humblot 1998).

Further, Reinach's analysis of transfer is as the exercise of a power. It is not a simple subtraction of primary rights. For one thing, as noted earlier, Reinach does not analyze ownership as a mere collection of rights. Moreover, for Reinach, 'insofar as owning essentially implies the right to deal in *any and every* way with the thing, the power to transfer the thing into the property of others is contained in this right'.[49] What is the nature of this implication? It is not deduction, because we could imagine prizing apart the right and the power to transfer it, as we saw with good faith purchase and we will see in the next section on representation.[50] Instead, the relation seems to correspond to what Ted Sichelman calls 'tight' bundles in his extension of the Hohfeldian framework.[51] Sichelman gives the example of what he calls a 'common right' which is made up of a privilege and a claim right that protects that privilege. For example, the privilege to use a thing is often coupled with a claim right to prevent access, which protects the privilege. Such a complex relation often travels as a unit, and the connection between its constituents stands on a different footing than a portfolio of use rights, for example.[52]

Perhaps what is most striking about Reinach's excavation of the essential in the domain of rights and transfer is that his propositions hang together. They simultaneously meet criteria of simplicity, generalizability, and coherence. For one thing, the 'residual' character of property along a number of dimensions 'falls out' of the theory rather than needing to be stated. For another, the entire scheme generates subtle and complex results from a loose and yet compact set of natural elements. We return to the significance of the integrity of the a priori in Section 5.4.

5.3.2 *Representation*

Reinach's account of representation is significant both for its extralegal sources and for its nuanced analysis of the relationship itself. It is also significant for what it shows

[49] Reinach (n 1) 70.

[50] Perhaps inspired by the bundle of rights theory, many assume that transfer is a parceling out of 'sticks' from the bundle. Even though Hohfeld did regard ownership as a collection of rights, Hohfeld did distinguish rights from powers. A transfer effects a change in legal rights. What is problematic about the Hohfeldian picture is that because a right is defined by who holds it, a transfer is the extinguishment of one right and its replacement by another. For an argument that a transferee receives the right the transferor had, see J Penner, 'On the Very Idea of Transmissible Rights' in J Penner and HE Smith (eds), *Philosophical Foundations of Property Law* (Oxford University Press 2013) 244.

[51] T Sichelman, 'Very Tight "Bundles of Sticks": Hohfeld's Complex Jural Relations' in S Balganesh, T Sichelman, and HE Smith (eds), *Wesley Hohfeld a Century Later: Edited Work, Select Personal Papers, and Original Commentaries* (Cambridge University Press 2022) 345.

[52] Sichelman draws an analogy to atomic and subatomic physics. ibid 364. See also T Sichelman, 'Quantifying Legal Entropy' (2021) 9 Frontiers in Physics 665054, 4–6. As we will discuss in Section 5.4, these kinds of connections that reconcile a kind of reductionism with practical holism could be one way to think about the phenomena that Reinach takes as a priori.

about how a priori rules may be interconnected, with insights from one a priori rule (e.g., *nemo dat*) offering insights into other a priori rules. Understanding how transfers work helps us to understand how representation works, at least indirectly.

Reinach's starting point is to rule out some of the leading approaches to this topic. Thus, he begins by rejecting the idea that intentions and declarations of intention can adequately explain representation. For example, he notes that in the case of a conveyance effectuated by a representative, the represented party's intention that a conveyance occur is not required. Nor does the representative's intention prove decisive: 'it is incomprehensible how something which obviously does not belong to [the representative] can by him expressing his intention be transferred into the property of a third party'.[53] In this, we see an example of the *nemo dat* principle in action. As a result of these conclusions, Reinach suggests that for the intention-focused theorist, '[t]here remains no alternative but to assume here an artificial institution of the positive law which is called for by all kinds of practical considerations'.[54] And yet, for Reinach, the need for an artificial legal institution is 'fundamentally wrong'.[55]

This is another reminder of Reinach's view that the essential rules of the civil law exist independently of positive law (and, indeed, that they may exist independently of law). One does not need law to find examples of representation worthy of study. On Reinach's view, what is needed 'is no "institution" of the positive law but rather a modification of social acts, which goes far beyond the world of right. For one cannot doubt that there is a requesting, an admonishing, an informing, a thanking, an advising in the name of another'.[56] The law, in other words, discovers the rules involved in representation, rather than coming up with them on its own. In this respect, as in others, Reinach sees the law finding essential rules rather than creating them.

Reinach next rejects the idea that a promise can explain the efficacy of representative actions.[57] A promise could be directed to either the representative or to a third person, he notes, but in neither case would it be sufficient to explain the power the representative has to effectuate, say, a transfer of property. Thus, Jack might promise to Jill that he will do whatever it is that Jill promises to a third party that he will do. Even if a third party then gets a right as a consequence of Jill's making such a

[53] See Reinach (n 1) 82.

[54] See ibid 82.

[55] See ibid 83.

[56] ibid. The existence of such extralegal cases may help explain why fiduciary law is in a position to make use of nonlegal conceptions of loyalty in the context of legal fiduciary relationships. On this concern, see AS Gold, 'The Reasonably Loyal Person' in H Psarras and S Steel (eds), *Private Law and Practical Reason: Essays on John Gardner's Private Law Theory* (Oxford University Press 2023) 330, 341. But cf J Gardner, *Torts and Other Wrongs* (Oxford University Press 2020) 299 (suggesting that the role of trustee may have 'no law-independent existence').

[57] See Reinach (n 1) 86.

promise to that third party, this results not because Jill had the *power* to promise on Jack's behalf. Likewise, if Jack instead made a promise to the third party to do whatever it is that Jill promises he will do, this could mean that Jack is bound to do whatever Jill promised to the third party. But again, such a promise to a third party cannot produce the representative power itself; the effect of a representative power is merely replicated in that case.[58]

Instead, Reinach suggests that the power to modify our own obligations is something that we can grant to others. But what kind of a grant is this? Reinach begins with the premise that the only way that a representative power can be granted is by the represented party. Here, we might again hear echoes of the *nemo dat* principle. Recall the idea that one cannot transfer what one does not already own. We might think that the reason why a representative power can only be transferred by the represented party is that only the represented party has this power to start with. Interestingly, Reinach does not take that path.[59] This granting is not a transfer, he concludes, for the grantor does not give up his or her own powers in granting the representative power. It is, rather, a creative granting that produces a new power in the representative.[60] As he puts it: 'This legal power which is grounded in the person as such can as it were be reproduced in the person of others; this is what gives representative acts their characteristic efficacy'.[61]

The idea that representative power can only be granted by the represented party is apparently based on intuition, although the argument may also be tracking social practices. And, Reinach says little about why, morally speaking, such a creative granting should succeed in producing a representative power in its recipient. Note, however, that Reinach's project is not to show why the synthetic a priori makes moral sense, but rather to successfully capture the features of the a priori. Here, he identifies a social phenomenon of represented parties providing representative powers to third parties, one that exists not only in the law, but also in mundane events like one person offering thanks on behalf of another. Reinach then makes a strong argument that this representative power is not achieved by promises or transfers. The idea that this is a creative granting is then recognized through a process of elimination.

If accepted, this account has important implications for how we theorize fields like agency law. Consider the agency law question posed by Henry Hansmann and Reinier Kraakman:

[58] For Reinach's discussion, see ibid 85–86.

[59] It bears noting, however, that Reinach adopts a *nemo dat*-like principle for grants and not just for transfers. See ibid 68 ('So we can formulate the following new principle of right: no one can grant more legal ability than he has himself').

[60] See ibid 86. The representative can, however, transfer this power once it is granted. See ibid 87. That, in Reinach's view, comes down to what was included by the granting person in his or her act. See ibid.

[61] See ibid 86–87.

> The concept of agency, in which a principal can authorize an agent to bind the principal to contracts with third parties, is crucial to the construction of a nexus of contracts with any appreciable scope, whether the juridical person that is the central node of that nexus is an individual human being, a group of individuals, or an organization. It is interesting to ask whether the legal doctrine of agency is primitive, or whether it would be feasible to construct the functional equivalent of agency using other, more basic elements of contract doctrine.[62]

That question is indeed interesting, and if we take contracts to be promissory at base, then Reinach's view may suggest an answer: agency is primitive.

Reinach's close analysis also highlights less appreciated features of legal representation, some of which are striking. For example, it is very common to think through legal representation in terms of one person acting on behalf of another. Yet, in trying to find the essence of representation, Reinach locates cases that do not involve any social acts by the representative.[63] As he indicates, it is possible to be a passive representative, merely by hearing what a third party says: '[o]ne can hear without intending and even against one's own intention; something can penetrate me from the outside without the least cooperative activity on my part'.[64] In such cases, the mere hearing of social acts may change the legal rights and obligations of the represented party.[65]

The concepts involved in this account are Hohfeldian only in part. There is a legal power that plays a role in the creation of this relation, for, as Reinach elaborates:

> If A confers passive representative power on B, then any given person C has as a result the power to produce legal effects in the person of A through acts in which he addresses himself to B 'for' A. But with regard to the representative, by contrast, we cannot speak of a legal power, since he does not have the possibility of undertaking any action (*Tun*) with effects in the world of right. We will rather speak of an ability which is shown in the fact that as a result of his hearing social acts, the effects of them come about in the represented person.[66]

[62] See H Hansmann and R Kraakman, 'The Essential Role of Organization Law' (2000) 110 Yale Law Journal 387, 406 n 27.

[63] J Penner, 'Understanding the Rules of Attribution in Private Law' in S Bray et al (eds), *Interstitial Private Law* (Oxford University Press 2024).

[64] See Reinach (n 1) 91. For a potential policy-based justification of such rules, see RRW Brooks, 'Knowledge in Fiduciary Relations' in AS Gold and PB Miller (eds), *Philosophical Foundations of Fiduciary Law* (Oxford University Press 2014) 225, 237 (discussing how 'the agency law rule presuming that the principal knows what the agent knows' can 'protect[] third parties from negligent or scheming principals').

[65] Query whether this passive representation has existing nonlegal analogues in the way that active representation does. Granted, for Reinach it is not a problem if there are no such nonlegal analogues. He would allow for a priori rules that are not instantiated in any existing human relation or system. See Reinach (n 1) 139 (noting that on his view, pure essential laws of right are 'independent of human knowledge, independent of the organization of human nature, and above all independent of the factual development of the world').

[66] See ibid 92.

The 'ability' Reinach describes is not a Hohfeldian incident, and its presence gives us a distinctive picture of what it means to represent someone.

The resulting picture of representation is both broader in coverage than the law provides for (covering extralegal cases like invitations and giving thanks), and potentially narrower in important respects. Reinach's recognition of both active and passive representation also suggests types of representation that may differ noticeably from the way representation is commonly formulated by legal theorists. In addition, we see a broader pattern whereby Reinach builds on insights regarding the a priori in one area as a means to figure out the a priori in another area. Understanding what is, and is not, a transfer helps us to understand how representative powers are conferred on representatives.

5.4 REINACH AS A CHALLENGE AND CATALYST

As we saw in the previous section, Reinach's method offers many surprising insights about law. Many of these insights stand whether or not one regards them, as did Reinach, as being essential and timeless – a priori. There is a deeper contribution that Reinach's work offers: it points to the need for a level of law or, rather, some kind of structure supporting the law that has some robustness. This 'deep structure' is needed to bridge the micro and the macro and the various dichotomies that are characteristic of current theorizing about private law.[67] Again, this level is important even if it can be grounded in various ways, some very different from Reinach's a priori.

We adopt the term 'deep structure' with caution. 'Deep' is evocative, and the notion of deep structure in linguistics has led to much confusion. However, what deep structure was in early generative grammar bears some resemblance to the 'essential' or a priori layer that Reinach exposes. Deep structure is a level that is presupposed by all the rules that get us to the surface structure of what we see.[68] Deep structure is distinct from the more readily apparent surface structure, and one of its selling points is how it allows linguistic structures to hang together in a uniquely compelling fashion. Deep structure was also offered as being psychologically real, and in its outlines hardwired. Deep structure has its own architecture that is accessible through analysis of patterns in language. As in the study of law, there is a debate as to how much crosslinguistic variation we need to examine in order to be able to make universal statements, including about the contours of deep structure. In both the legal a priori and deep structure in 1960s linguistics, there are

[67] For clarity, we wish to distinguish a theory, like ours, that focuses on mid-level law from a mid-level theory. Cf JL Coleman, *Risks and Wrongs* (OUP 1992) 8 ('In middle-level theory, the theorist immerses herself in the practice itself and asks if it can be usefully organized in ways that reflect one or more plausible principles'.). Law that bridges the micro and macro-levels of a legal system can be theorized in various ways.

[68] The classic statement is N Chomsky, *Aspects of the Theory of Syntax* (MIT Press 1965).

challenging questions about its status and how it relates to other aspects like meaning.[69] Finally and quite strikingly, Chomsky introduced a level of deep structure in defiance of the then reigning strictures of behaviorism that eschewed 'mental' entities in theorizing. An analogous preference for the concrete is also characteristic of post-Realist theories of law, which are highly skeptical of 'abstract' legal concepts altogether.

We can range the possibilities for the sources of deep structure from the more given to the more constructed.[70]

At the most robust end are various ways of taking deep structure as metaphysically real. Reinach sees it as having a nonphysical but timeless existence. He distinguishes this view from natural law.[71] As Reinach sees it, natural law tries to account for actual law, and as law that is unconditionally valid. Reinach's a priori stands outside the law and is not contradicted by deviations from it in the actual law. At any rate, one source for a robust deep structure of law would be something exogenous and irreducible – metaphysically real.

Moving away from the metaphysical, one could take Reinach's a priori as not really a priori but built into human psychology. There could be various accounts of how it got there, running from the contingent to a robust neo-Kantian view about how we are made up to encounter the world. Interestingly, the kind of evidence for psychological versions of Reinach's a priori might include the kinds of arguments Reinach made. Perhaps at some point we might be able to appeal to neurological evidence as well.

The Reinachian layer might also be a result of social practice, even though it is in some sense abstract. This could be for functional reasons. More abstract concepts might emerge from complex interactions at a more basic level.[72]

Perhaps any Reinachian deep structure might have multiple sources. Another way to think about it is in terms of information and complexity. As we saw with *nemo dat*, stating *nemo dat* with exceptions like good faith purchase is simpler than the other way around. The idea would be that *nemo dat* is formulated in such a way that the

[69] The conflict between adherents of generative semantics and interpretive semantics was one of the fiercest academic battles of all time. RA Harris, *The Linguistics Wars: Chomsky, Lakoff, and the Battle over Deep Structure* (2nd ed, Oxford University Press 2021). This controversy may have some relevance to interpreting Reinach's a priori. Some passages of Reinach's book, including those on liens, may be susceptible of a more 'functionalist' or a more 'autonomous' reading, corresponding respectively to generative versus interpretive semantics. We would argue that the more autonomous reading is more in keeping with Reinach's general approach to the synthetic a priori.

[70] In his discussion of Reinach's theory of ownership, James Toomey notes that one can endorse Reinachian insights on ownership while taking ownership to be metaphysically real, a human cognitive category, or an extralegal social practice. Toomey (n 17) 154–58.

[71] Reinach (n 1) 134–35.

[72] See, e.g., AS Gold and HE Smith, 'Sizing Up Private Law' (2020) 70 University of Toronto Law Journal 489; T Sichelman and HE Smith, 'A Network Model of Legal Relations' (2024) 382 Philosophical Transactions of The Royal Society A 20230153; Smith (n 6).

situations it potentially applies to are a superset of those for good faith purchase. This can be true even if good faith purchase actually applies more often. If *nemo dat* is taken as a more general rule encompassing the domain of good faith purchase in a pattern of general case and exceptions, this formulation may correspond to the shortest description in an agreed-upon metalanguage, making it less complex in an important sense.[73] Perhaps the Reinachian layer generally allows for more compact formulation. Or, corresponding to the 'naturalness' of law that tracks the a priori, we might say that such law contains less information (is less 'surprising', or shows lower 'entropy'); perhaps we might find that law that respects Reinachian presuppositions minimizes legal entropy in a quantifiable way.[74]

Reinach's a priori might relate to complex systems in a variety of ways. If we think of the elements of the a priori, the various concepts and social acts, as standing in relationships to each other, we can see that some are more interconnected than others. One interpretation of Reinach's a priori would deny that it is on some categorically different metaphysical footing. However, the dense interconnection of some elements, ownership and promise for example, suggests that it would be very difficult to alter them.[75] The more systemic the notion, the more robust and the more apparently a priori it will be.[76]

Relatedly, in the vein of the social and practical, one heuristic for deep structure is the impossibility of replicating it by contract. Henry Hansmann and Reinier Kraakman argue that asset partitioning (especially the protection of entity assets from the claims of owner's creditors) cannot be accomplished by contract.[77] They term this the 'essential' role of organization law, and it makes organizational law a kind of property law. Gabriel Rauterberg likewise offers an account of the essential role of agency law in terms of asset partitioning that could not be replicated by

[73] Kolmogorov complexity is a measure of complexity based on the shortest description in an agreed upon language. M Li and P Vitanyi, *An Introduction to Kolmogorov Complexity and Its Applications* (4th edn, Springer 2019).

[74] See Sichelman (n 52). Sichelman discusses the connection between entropy in physics and Claude Shannon's theory of information (in which entropy is a measure of the quantity of information). CE Shannon, 'A Mathematical Theory of Communication (pts. 1 & 2)' (1948) 27 Bell System Technical Journal 379; (1948) 27 Bell System Technical Journal 623, reprinted as CE Shannon and W Weaver, *The Mathematical Theory of Communication* (University of Illinois Press 1949).

[75] For a discussion of how interconnectedness relates to unchangeability in legal systems across the world, see Y Chang and HE Smith, 'Convergence and Divergence in Systems of Property Law: Theoretical and Empirical Analyses' (2019) 92 Southern California Law Review 785.

[76] We can draw an analogy to WVO Quine's denial of a sharp analytic-synthetic distinction, with everything in principle revisable but the more interior and interconnected statements being harder to revise. WVO Quine, 'Two Dogmas of Empiricism' (1951) 60 Philosophical Review 20, reprinted in WVO Quine, *From a Logical Point of View* (Harvard University Press 1953). The analogous idea would be that Reinachian legal concepts and presuppositions could in principle be revised but the more interconnected ones (as in Quine's web) will be practically impossible to revise.

[77] Hansmann and Kraakman (n 62).

contract.[78] What form asset partitioning may take varies, but it may be the case that the concept of asset partitioning and its basic vocabulary are more invariant.

Reinach's a priori also relates to complexity: the a priori responds to the problem of complexity as a method of managing it. Reinachian deep structure points us toward the role of architecture in private law and its practical consequences. For example, consider Carliss Baldwin and Kim Clark's account of how to modularize a complex system:

> For human beings, the only way to manage a complex system or solve a complex problem is to break it up. In the breaking apart, it is best to look for points of natural division, carving 'the Idea … at the joints, as nature directs, not breaking any limb in half as a bad carver might'.[79]

It is an interesting and much-debated question whether nature has 'joints', and it is not obvious that our language can or should carve at those joints if they exist.[80] We take no position on such questions here. Yet the natural breaking point idea is suggestive for present purposes.

One of the most prominent reasons for modularizing a complex system is that it will make complexity more manageable. Such modularity can be achieved by breaking a system apart in a wide range of places, even arbitrary ones. We might nonetheless think that there is value in breaking apart a complex system at those places where users of the system will perceive natural breaking points (whether or not such points exist in nature). If we use a car for an example, we might treat the brake system as a unit rather than the brake plus adjustable seating system. And this idea of what is a 'natural' breaking point may be true for legal systems as well. Why should that be? It is not because modularizing at an apparently 'natural' point of division will necessarily lead to optimal substantive outcomes in the law; nor can we rely on such breaking points to increase simplicity in comparison to other locations. Rather, it is because doing so may lead to greater accessibility. And here we can see an additional way that Reinach's work is useful.

If Reinach is right about the synthetic a priori, the essential rules that apply to legal structures are not merely essential: we also have ready intuitive access to them. Their details may need to be worked out through painstaking thought and research,

78 G Rauterberg, 'The Essential Roles of Agency Law' (2020) 118 Michigan Law Review 609.

79 CY Baldwin and KB Clark, *Design Rules: The Power of Modularity* (MIT Press 2000) 64 (citing Plato, *Phaedrus*, 265D).

80 Compare E Hirsch, *Dividing Reality* (Oxford University Press 1993) 52 ('A belief in reality's joints does not, at least obviously and in itself, entail a belief in any division principle. The latter makes a normative claim about language, which cannot follow, at least obviously, from a metaphysical claim about objective sameness and difference in nature') with T Sider, 'Ontological Realism' in DJ Chalmers, D Manley, and R Wasserman (eds), *Metametaphysics: New Essays on the Foundations of Ontology* (Oxford University Press 2009) 384, 401 ('An ideal inquirer must think of the world in terms of its distinguished structure; she must carve the world at its joints in her thinking and language. Employers of worse languages are worse inquirers').

but their basic implications are easily recognized.[81] And some are basic indeed. Thus, Reinach notes: 'What we understand with evidence is that for instance a claim is extinguished on being fulfilled'.[82] That does not take much legal training or research to figure out. We know it almost immediately, and maybe without being able to say why. Indeed, the legal features that Reinach uncovers are often matters of tacit knowledge,[83] known by lawyers and laypersons alike.[84]

This accessibility shows up repeatedly in Reinach's work. For example, Reinach concludes that the essential rules are not only there to be found by law, but also that they are capable of being 'grasped and intuited' by 'untrained laymen'.[85] In saying this, he doesn't just mean that they are simple; they are also experienced as 'self-evident'.[86] He likewise emphasizes that the legally talented jurist will have a knack for understanding these essential laws. The jurist will have "the sense" for *what is legally relevant*, that is for events of a certain kind which are subject to essential laws, as well as the understanding of these laws'.[87] Furthermore, in application, he thinks people use these essential laws without being fully aware of them.[88] The idea that certain aspects of law come so naturally to trained and untrained alike suggests something valuable that is distinct from what you get with modularity in the abstract. These features are accessible, in addition to being modular.[89]

We have just emphasized the micro level (e.g., how claims are extinguished), but such accessibility may also bear on the relation of the micro to the macro.[90] There is

[81] It might seem strange or even self-contradictory to claim, as Reinach does, that the a priori is at once accessible and that it requires close and careful study to bring out in the open. The difference stems from different modes of accessing the a priori. In employing the a priori in our thinking and in reacting to legal situations, it is supposed to come to us as intuition. But to isolate the a priori and describe it is another matter, requiring, in Reinach's view, the attention of a phenomenologist and the skills of a jurist.

[82] See Reinach (n 1) 138.

[83] For a leading discussion of tacit knowledge, see M Polanyi, *The Tacit Dimension* (University of Chicago Press 2009). For a connection between tacit knowledge and the synthetic a priori as recognized by various Austrian theorists (Reinach included), see B Smith, 'On the Austrianness of Austrian Economics' (1990) 4 Critical Review 212, 224–25.

[84] This is not to deny that some of the purportedly a priori features of private law that Reinach identifies are contestable; in some cases, his idea of what is an essential rule feels more like a statement of the German civil law in a certain time period. Likewise, in some cases the implications of Reinach's a priori rules are only figured out through complex thought processes that the lay person might not find accessible. The point about accessibility nonetheless holds for many of the most basic propositions Reinach endorses, such as the way in which claims are extinguished, or the *nemo dat* principle.

[85] See Reinach (n 1) 131.

[86] ibid.

[87] ibid 130–31.

[88] ibid 135.

[89] How accessibility and modularity relate to each other is an important question. Modular structure can be detected by well-studied algorithms, such that modularity need not be taken as exogenously given. See Sichelman and Smith (n 72).

[90] Note, in this regard, that the Austrian thinkers were also characteristically interested in how the micro and macro interrelate, and in a non-reductive way. See B Smith (n 83) 215. For our thoughts on that problem, see Gold and Smith (n 72).

a suggestion of system effects in Reinach's discussion of how investigating civil law concepts can illuminate concepts within public law. As Reinach argues:

> The same concepts can be formed and the same laws grounded in them are encountered only because there are in all of these spheres of law those legally relevant structures of which we have spoken and above all those social acts with all their modifications, promising and granting, allowing and transferring, waiving and revoking, addressing several persons and addressing one person, performing acts in one's own name and performing them in the name of another, conditional and unconditional acts, etc.[91]

Whether or not these concepts are genuinely a priori, Reinach's idea of accessible rules – rules that are often experienced as self-evident – is illuminating if we want to understand how concepts will operate when we move from one part of the legal system to another.[92] And, notwithstanding the ways that Reinach distances his approach from a psychological one, there is a psychological point to be made here. If the features Reinach describes are accessible in the ways he describes, then we have a reason in favor of using them to help modularize the law. We need not decide if they actually carve at nature's joints in that case; it may be enough if they seem to do so. In all these ways, Reinach's interest in essential law is, despite initial appearances, anything but distant from legal policy debates.

Reinach's a priori has much to offer private law theory. Let us return to the dichotomies with which we opened this chapter. The a priori, whatever its ultimate status, transcends the internal–external divide among theorists. Like the internal perspective it is something – something deep – about law's own self-understanding. And yet it stands outside enacted law and connects to something beyond the law. This may be psychological, or it may be the complex process of navigating the world and solving the problems to which social acts are directed. Or it may be both. In any case, the a priori points to ways of thinking about how the internal and external perspectives are connected.

Likewise for holism and reductionism. Reinach's method is far from reductionist. Indeed, the point is to look closely at what is actually there. And yet what he finds is a rather compact set of interlocking notions presupposed by the law. Here Reinach's project suggests the right kind of reductionism, seeking simple local structures that produce complex and nuanced results at a more systemic level.

Reinach's a priori manages to produce complex results with relatively simple materials, because his a priori also transcends the debates over conceptualism. As we have seen, Reinach is no apologist for existing legal concepts and is unafraid to go against the grain of positive law, even in the face of claims about what is

[91] See Reinach (n 1) 133–34.

[92] On the importance of being able to track what legal concepts will mean across different areas of the law, see J Waldron, '"Transcendental Nonsense" and System in the Law' (2000) 100 Columbia Law Review 16.

conceptually impossible. On the other hand, his philosophy is anything but nominalist. If he is right, his a priori is highly robust. And to the extent that actual legal concepts track the a priori – and there is a gravitational pull in terms of workability and understanding for them to do so – legal concepts partake of this robustness as well.[93]

Finally, Reinach's a priori accommodates a measure of both deontology and consequentialism. We say 'accommodates', because Reinach insists that the a priori is not inherently moral and he distinguishes his approach from natural law in not being a theory directly about actual law. Nevertheless, many of the social acts that interest Reinach have a moral dimension – think promise, release, and the like – and deontologists thus gain a foothold for their own program. Furthermore, as we have seen, part of the appeal, and perhaps the very accessibility, of Reinach's a priori is how it is built into a practical system of social acts and presuppositions that permit us to navigate the world. This is why his a priori is a good candidate for psychology, for functional practicality, and emergence from a complex social system.

By asking questions about law's 'deep structure', one is engaging in the New Private Law. The essence of this movement is to take law seriously but to be open to perspectives that bring out its nature and importance. Especially in bringing internal and external perspectives together and relating the micro to the macro, Reinachian themes will doubtless feature prominently in the New Private law in the future.[94]

5.5 CONCLUSION

Reinach's synthetic a priori offers an approach to private law that cuts through the seemingly intractable debates between those who favor internal and external perspectives, between reductionists and doctrinalists, between deontologists and consequentialists. Much of what he describes looks like a deep structure to the law, presupposed by widely divergent legal theories. To say this is not to say that his approach dissolves all debates, nor is it to endorse phenomenology or Reinach's idea of timeless, essential rules. Rather, his work merits our attention for what it picks out: whether it is a matter of metaphysics, psychology, conventional practices, or functional benefits, the rules he describes are often deep-seated components of legal

[93] In addition to workability and understanding, we might also consider questions of acceptability to legal actors. As Stephen Smith has noted, judges tend to justify their reasoning on the basis of intermediate justifications, rather than comprehensive moral theories. See SA Smith, 'Intermediate and Comprehensive Justifications for Legal Rules' in S Degeling, MJR Crawford, and N Tiverios (eds), *Justifying Private Rights* (Hart 2020) 63; see also PB Miller, 'Juridical Justification of Private Rights' in ibid at 105. Much of what Reinach sees as a priori appears to play a role in these intermediate justifications. If, as Smith argues, courts need to use intermediate justifications in order to render their reasoning more broadly acceptable in a pluralist society, they may also have reason to adopt rules that track Reinach's a priori.

[94] Gold and Smith (n 72).

reasoning. They are robust, accessible, and, in many cases, possessed of considerable gravitational pull.

Thinking through Reinach's applications also offers repeated insights into law and the surrounding social practices that law interacts with. With his analyses of property, transfers, and representation, Reinach explains the structures within private law – and within social practices – in a way that illuminates both. His work is thus a valuable starting point if we want to discern and understand that architecture. Perhaps surprisingly, his work is also a valuable starting point if we want to adjust the law's architecture.[95] Reinach offers provocative and yet very productive new ways to take the law seriously.

BIBLIOGRAPHY

Ames JB, 'Purchase for Value without Notice' (1887) 1 Harvard Law Review 1
Anderson SR, *A-Morphous Morphology* (Cambridge University Press 1992)
Arruñada B, G Zanarone, and NM Garoupa, 'Property Rights in Sequential Exchange' (2019) 35 Journal of Law, Economics and Organization 127
Auer M, *Der privatrechtliche Diskurs der Moderne* (Mohr Siebeck 2014)
Baldwin CY and KB Clark, *Design Rules: The Power of Modularity* (MIT Press 2000)
Banner S, *The Decline of Natural Law: How American Lawyers Once Used Natural Law and Why They Stopped* (Oxford University Press 2021)
Brooks RRW, 'Knowledge in Fiduciary Relations' in AS Gold and PB Miller (eds), *Philosophical Foundations of Fiduciary Law* (Oxford University Press 2014) 225
Chang Y, 'The Economy of Concept and Possession' in Y Chang (ed), *Law and Economics of Possession* (Cambridge University Press 2015) 103
Property Law: Comparative, Empirical, and Economic Analyses (Cambridge University Press 2023)
Chang Y and HE Smith, 'Convergence and Divergence in Systems of Property Law: Theoretical and Empirical Analyses' (2019) 92 Southern California Law Review 785
Chomsky N, *Aspects of the Theory of Syntax* (MIT Press 1965)
Coleman JL, *Risks and Wrongs* (Oxford University Press 1992)
Commons JR, *Institutional Economics: Its Place in Political Economy* (Macmillan 1934)
Di Robilant A, *The Making of Modern Property: Reinventing Roman Law in Nineteenth Century Europe and Its Periphery* (Cambridge University Press 2023)
Gardner J, *Torts and Other Wrongs* (Oxford University Press 2020)
Gold AS, 'Internal and External Perspectives: On the New Private Law Methodology' in AS Gold et al (eds), *The Oxford Handbook of the New Private Law* (Oxford University Press 2020), 3–20
'The Reasonably Loyal Person' in H Psarras and S Steel (eds), *Private Law and Practical Reason: Essays on John Gardner's Private Law Theory* (Oxford University Press 2023) 330
Gold AS and HE Smith, 'Sizing Up Private Law' (2020) 70 University of Toronto Law Journal 489

[95] It is a separate question how one might adjust this architecture while retaining its main features (if so desired). On ways to revise legal concepts and their operation, see AS Gold and HE Smith, 'Managing Legal Concepts: Maintenance, Modulation, Modification' (ms on file with authors).

Gretton, GL, 'Ownership and Its Objects' (2007) 71(4) Rabels Zeitschrift für ausländisches und internationales Privatrecht 802
Hansmann H and R Kraakman, 'The Essential Role of Organization Law' (2000) 110 Yale Law Journal 387
Harris RA, *The Linguistics Wars: Chomsky, Lakoff, and the Battle over Deep Structure* (2nd edn, Oxford University Press 2021)
Havighurst HC, *A Selection of Contract Cases and Related Quasi-Contract Cases* (Lawyers Co-operative Publishing Company 1934)
Helmholz RH, *Natural Law in Court* (Harvard University Press 2015)
Helmholz R and R Zimmermann (eds), *Itinera Fiduciae: Trust and Treuhand in Historical Perspective* (Duncker & Humblot 1998)
Hirsch E, *Dividing Reality* (Oxford University Press 1993)
Ho L and R Lee (eds), *Trust Law in Asian Civil Law Jurisdictions: A Comparative Analysis* (Cambridge University Press 2013)
Hohfeld, WN 'Fundamental Legal Conceptions as Applied in Judicial Reasoning' (1917) 26 *Yale Law Journal* 710, reprinted in WW Cook (ed), *WN Hohfeld, Fundamental Legal Conceptions as Applied in Judicial Reasoning and Other Legal Essays* (Yale University Press 1923) 65
Holland JH et al, *Induction: Processes of Inference, Learning, and Discovery* (MIT Press 1989)
Kennedy D, 'Form and Substance in Private Law Adjudication' (1976) 89 Harvard Law Review 1685
Kiparsky P, '"Elsewhere" in Phonology' in SR Anderson and P Kiparsky (eds), *A Festschrift for Morris Halle* (Holt, Rinehart, and Winston 1973) 93
Kocourek A, 'Polarized and Unpolarized Legal Relations' (1921) 9 Kentucky Law Journal 131
Jural Relations (2nd ed, Bobbs-Merrill 1928)
Levmore S, 'Variety and Uniformity in the Treatment of the Good-Faith Purchaser' (1987) 16 Journal of Legal Studies 43
Li M and P Vitanyi, *An Introduction to Kolmogorov Complexity and Its Applications* (4th edn, Springer 2019)
McFarlane B and R Stevens, 'The Nature of Equitable Property' (2010) 4 Journal of Equity 1
'What's Special about Equity? Rights about Rights' in D Klimchuk, I Samet, and HE Smith (eds), *Philosophical Foundations of the Law of Equity* (Oxford University Press 2020) 191
Massin O, 'The Metaphysics of Ownership: A Reinachian Account' (2017) 27 Axiomathes 577
Matthews P, 'The Compatibility of the Trust with the Civil Law Notion of Property' in L Smith (ed), *The Worlds of the Trust* (Cambridge University Press 2013), 313–339
Ménard C and MM Shirley, *Advanced Introduction to New Institutional Economics* (Elgar 2022)
Miller PB, 'Juridical Justification of Private Rights' in S Degeling, MJR Crawford, and N Tiverios (eds), *Justifying Private Rights* (Hart 2020) 105
'The New Formalism in Private Law' (2021) 66 American Journal of Jurisprudence 175
Nair A and I Samet, 'What Can "Equity's Darling" Tell Us about Equity?' in D Klimchuk, I Samet, and HE Smith (eds), *Philosophical Foundations of the Law of Equity* (Oxford University Press 2020) 264
Penner J, 'On the Very Idea of Transmissible Rights' in J Penner and HE Smith (eds), *Philosophical Foundations of Property Law* (Oxford University Press 2013) 244
'Understanding the Rules of Attribution in Private Law' in S Bray et al (eds), *Interstitial Private Law* (Oxford University Press 2024)
Pinker S, *Words and Rules: The Ingredients of Language* (Basic Books 1999)
Polanyi M, *The Tacit Dimension* (University of Chicago Press 2009)

Quine WVO, 'Two Dogmas of Empiricism' (1951) 60 Philosophical Review 20
Rauterberg G, 'The Essential Roles of Agency Law' (2020) 118 Michigan Law Review 609
Reinach A, 'The Apriori Foundations of the Civil Law' (John F Crosby tr, 1983) 3 Aletheia 1–142, reprinted in Adolf Reinach, *The Apriori Foundations of the Civil Law Along with the Lecture 'Concerning Phenomenology'* (John F Crosby ed, Ontos Verlag 2012), originally published as Adolf Reinach, Die apriorischen Grundlagen des bürgerlichen Rechtes, 1(2) Jahrbuch für Philosophie und phänomenologische Forschung (Max Niemeyer 1913) 685–847
Schroeder JL, 'Is Article 8 Finally Ready This Time? The Radical Reform of Secured Lending on Wall Street' (1994) Columbia Business Law Review 291
Schuppe W, *Der Begriff des subjektiven Rechts* (Wilhelm Koebner 1887)
Schwartz A and RE Scott, 'Rethinking the Laws of Good Faith Purchase' (2011) 111 Columbia Law Review 1332
Shannon CE, A Mathematical Theory of Communication (pts. 1 & 2)' (1948) 27 *Bell System Technical Journal* 379; (1948) 27 *Bell System Technical Journal* 623, reprinted as CE Shannon and W Weaver, *The Mathematical Theory of Communication* (University of Illinois Press 1949)
Sichelman T, 'Quantifying Legal Entropy' (2021) 9 Frontiers in Physics 665054
'Very Tight "Bundles of Sticks": Hohfeld's Complex Jural Relations' in S Balganesh, T Sichelman, and HE Smith (eds), *Wesley Hohfeld a Century Later: Edited Work, Select Personal Papers, and Original Commentaries* 345 (Cambridge University Press 2022)
Sichelman T and HE Smith, 'A Network Model of Legal Relations' (2024) 382 Philosophical Transactions of The Royal Society A 20230153
Sider T, 'Ontological Realism' in DJ Chalmers, D Manley, and R Wasserman (eds), *Metametaphysics: New Essays on the Foundations of Ontology* (Oxford University Press 2009) 384, 401
Smith B, 'On the Austrianness of Austrian Economics' (1990) 4 Critical Review 212
Smith H, *Restrictiveness in Case Theory* (Cambridge University Press 1996)
Smith HE, 'Modularity in Contracts: Boilerplate and Information Flow' (2006) 104 Michigan Law Review 1175
'On the Economy of Concepts in Property' (2012) University of Pennsylvania Law Review 2097
'Emergent Property' in J Penner and HE Smith (eds), *Philosophical Foundations of Property Law* (Oxford University Press 2013) 320
'Equity as Meta-Law' (2021) 130 Yale Law Journal 1050
'The Complex Architecture of Property Rights' in L Alston, E Alston, and B Mueller (eds), *Handbook on Institutions and Complexity* (Elgar, 2025)
Smith L (ed), *Re-imagining the Trust: Trusts in Civil Law* (Cambridge University Press 2012)
Smith M, 'Valediction to Market Overt' (1997) 41 American Journal of Legal History 225
Smith SA, 'Intermediate and Comprehensive Justifications for Legal Rules' in S Degeling, MJR Crawford, and N Tiverios (eds), *Justifying Private Rights* (Hart 2020) 63
Toomey J, 'Property's Boundaries' (2023) 109 Virginia Law Review 131
Waldron J, '"Transcendental Nonsense" and System in the Law' (2000) 100 Columbia Law Review 16
Weinrib EJ, *The Idea of Private Law* (Harvard University Press 1995)
Wilson BJ, *The Property Species: Mine, Yours, and the Human Mind* (Oxford University Press 2020)

6

Private Law beyond the Law

Sandy Steel

In this chapter, I consider the extent to which the concepts recognised in the positive private law are answerable to concepts that exist outside of the law and in what ways the justification of positive private law rests upon its relationship to normative facts that exist independently of it. Reinach prompts reflection on these matters in that he directs his attention to a set of abstract entities (rights, claims etc.), and propositions relating to those entities (*a priori* laws) which, he claims, do not owe their validity to the positive law, but exist in the same way as mathematical objects and truths. In this way, he goes *beyond* the positive law, and in a subtle sense to be explored, considers the positive law answerable to the *a priori* law.

I will argue, in a section on 'Concepts', that performing Reinach's kind of analysis on concepts to which the positive law refers can be illuminating, and normatively fruitful, but carries with it the risk of deflecting attention from the normative issues faced by the positive law – a risk to which Reinach himself is alert. I then consider, in a section on 'Justifications', Reinach's understanding of the normative demands placed on the positive law by *a priori* truths about law, and the normative impact of the positive law. Here I examine his view that there are non-moral obligations to which the law may give effect, and his explanation of how the positive law can alter what people are genuinely required, permitted, or empowered, etc., to do.

6.1 A BRIEF PRIMER ON REINACH

In contemporary theorising about private law, few, if any, theorists describe their enterprise, with Reinach, as a search for the 'a priori foundations' of the domain. This eyebrow-raising category does not appear, for instance, in Stephen Smith's well-known taxonomy of the field.[1] Other, more detailed, treatments of the nature of

[1] See, especially, Stephen Smith, *Contract Theory* (Clarendon 2004), ch 1, which describes historical, interpretive, and normative approaches. See also the contents of Thilo Kuntz and Paul Miller (eds), *Methodology in Private Law Theory: Between New Private Law and Rechtsdogmatik* (Oxford University Press 2024), and Tarunabh Khaitan and Sandy Steel, 'Theorising Areas of Law' (2022) 28 Legal Theory 325. For an influential modern view of

Reinach's inquiry will be found in this book, but it will be useful to have a brief statement of his basic approach.

Reinach aims to identify *a priori* foundations (*Grundlage*) of civil law. What are 'a priori foundations'? It's not *exactly* clear what Reinach intends here.[2] It seems to range from *necessary* truths about the subject matter of the civil law, to *necessary* truths about the *essence* of civil law or the normative entities which it employs and to which it makes reference, to necessary, essential truths about civil law that can be known by intuition and justified independently of experience. Perhaps the last of these three possibilities is the predominant one.

It is in this way knowable and true, Reinach says, that a promissory duty is discharged when performance is rendered, that a promisee has a power to waive the promissory duty, that a promise creates a non-moral obligation to perform it, that a person may acquire rights in their own capacity or in a representative capacity for another, that a promise is only made when the promise is heard by the promisee, that a person who produces an object from unowned materials owns the object, that factual possession is different from a *right* over an object, and so on.[3] These are like mathematical truths (a comparison Reinach makes).[4] This seems to involve their being knowable *a priori* and their existence as abstract objects.[5]

In so far as it focuses on 'legal entities', an *a priori* account aims to understand their 'essence' and the necessary truths concerning these entities – the a priori entailment relations that hold between them.[6] In relation to some of these truths, no more foundational explanation can be given of their validity: 'To try to explain it [why a promise binds] would be just like trying to explain the proposition, 1 x 1 = 1. It is a fear of what is directly given (*Angst vor der Gegebenheit*), a strange reluctance or incapacity to look the ultimate data in the face and to recognize them as such which has driven unphenomenological philosophies, in this as in so many other more fundamental problems, to untenable and ultimately to extravagant constructions.'[7]

philosophy as concerned with identification of *a priori* truths, see Timothy Williamson, *Philosophical Method: A Very Short Introduction* (Oxford University Press 2022).

2 See Lorenz Kaehler's contribution to this volume.

3 Presumably, Reinach is concerned with something like 'a priori truths about the subject matter that *constitutes* private law'. It is a necessary truth about civil law that, if it exists, it exists in a world where 2+2 = 4, but this is not what interests Reinach.

4 Adolf Reinach, 'The Apriori Foundations of the Civil Law' (John F Crosby tr, 1983) 3 Aletheia 1, 46, reprinted in Adolf Reinach, *The Apriori Foundations of the Civil Law Along with the Lecture 'Concerning Phenomenology'* (John F Crosby ed, Ontos Verlag 2012), originally published as Adolf Reinach, Die apriorischen Grundlagen des bürgerlichen Rechtes, 1(2) *Jahrbuch für Philosophie und phänomenologische Forschung* (Max Niemeyer 1913), 685–847.

5 Cf Reinach (n 4), 111: 'We have in this work shown that in addition to the well-known sphere of natural objects, that is, of the physical and the mental, there is a world of its own consisting of entities and structures which are in time, though they do not belong to nature in the usual sense'.

6 Reinach (n 4), 96.

7 Reinach (n 4), 46.

How exactly does one come to know *a priori* truths about the subject matter of civil law? Not by empirical generalisation from past or present civil law systems.[8] Even if every positive system of civil law claims that a non-promisee directly gains rights from a promise, this does not alter the truth of the proposition that promises only directly create rights in the promisee. Instead, *a priori* truths are arrived at through reflection on the subject matter of civil law. By considering whether things could be other than they are, one arrives at the necessary properties of the phenomena; these are 'self-evident'.[9] These properties may then entail further necessary truths, which it is the task of an *a priori* theory to reveal.

Reinach has a subtle account of the relationship between the *a priori* foundations of civil law and the content of any particular positive civil law. It is not the case that the positive law always ought, all things considered, to mirror the content of the *a priori* foundations:

> We of course fully recognize that the positive law makes its enactments in absolute freedom, exclusively with a view to economic necessities and to the given moral convictions and unbounded by the sphere of apriori laws which we have in mind. The positive law can deviate as it likes from the essential necessities which hold for legal entities and structures – though it is of course a problem for itself to make understandable how such deviations are possible.[10]

In the next two sections, we will consider in greater depth Reinach's precise account of the relationship between the positive law and the *a priori*.

6.2 CONCEPTS

Theoretical accounts of private law and its concepts are often classified as 'internal' or 'external'.[11] The former are conventionally described as foregrounding the law's own conceptual self-understanding, the perspective adopted by legal officials in applying and developing the law and being resistant to 'functional' explanations. The latter, often associated with work in the law and economics tradition, are conventionally described as providing explanations and justifications which do not privilege the law's own conceptual self-understanding.

Reinach is not straightforwardly classifiable in either category. On the one hand, he is an 'externalist' in that he seeks to identify *a priori* foundations that may or may not be reflected in the law; even if the positive law wholly departed from such

8 Reinach (n 4), p.133. The history of civil law is not, however, entirely irrelevant to an *a priori* theory. Robustly prevalent features of civil law systems provide some evidence that the feature belongs to the *a priori* foundations. Conversely, the absence of a feature in all positive law systems casts an explanatory burden on the proponent of the view that the feature so belongs.

9 Reinach (n 4), p.96.

10 Reinach (n 4), p.5.

11 See Andrew Gold and Henry Smith, 'Sizing Up Private Law' (2020) 70 UTLJ 489 (arguing that the distinction is exaggerated). See also Khaitan and Steel above n 1.

foundations, the *a priori* law would be unaffected. The views of legal officials are largely irrelevant to the content of the *a priori* law. On the other, he resists 'reductive' explanations of the concepts employed by the law when these overlap with or refer to the *a priori* concepts and laws.

Yet Reinach is ultimately not so different from modern arch-internalists, such as Ernest Weinrib. Weinrib's work moves out from an analysis of the essential structure of private law, which, in this view, is constituted by relational duties that correlate with rights, powers of enforcement vested in right-holders, and remedial rights and duties that aim to ensure or restore a normative equality between the parties. The foundational concepts in this theory do not owe their existence to the positive law and have an existence independent of their construal in the positive law. Whatever judges might say about the matter, for instance, what makes a duty owed to another is whether the duty's mandated conduct is required in order to maintain normative equality between the duty-bearer and another person; the positive law does not alter this. Of course, and this is a major emphasis in such views, the positive law has a normative impact, making determinate the abstract notions built in to abstract right, and rendering innate and acquired right possible and enforceable without wronging others. However, it is still the case that the foundational concepts of innate right, epistemically, causally and ontologically, are not due to the positive law. Indeed, it would seem that these concepts can be known *a priori* in much the way that Reinach claims his laws can be known, albeit that reflection on the positive civil law may guide the way.

Is there a value in pursuing an investigation into *a priori* concepts of the civil law? Here are three possible reasons for doing so. First, if one takes seriously the analogy with mathematical truths, one might say that, just as there can be a value in knowing the abstract truths of mathematics ('there is no highest prime'), there is a value in knowing abstract normative truths ('promises necessarily generate waivable claims'), and understanding the essential properties of abstract normative objects ('commands are inherently addressed to another's conduct), regardless of their recognition in the positive law.

Second, there is plausibly some kind of normative constraint that justifies criticism of legal departures from certain truths that do not owe their existence to law. When a *legal* argument involves a logical circularity, for instance, its objectionability is, fundamentally, a moral one. Consider, as an example, the role of locality in determining whether an interference is unreasonable in the tort of private nuisance. In English law, the position is that interference with another's land not amounting to physical damage will be wrongful only when it is abnormal by reference to the standards of the locality.[12] One problem that arises in the application of this principle is the role of the defendant's own conduct in determining the character of the locality: if the defendant builds a new shopping centre, can they rely

[12] See, for a new emphasis on 'abnormality', *Fearn v Tate Galleries* [2023] UKSC 4.

upon their own conduct to say that the neighbourhood has changed? In *Lawrence v Fen Tigers*, the majority took the view that the interferer's activity (running a speedway stadium) could not be relevant to how one defines the locality *if it amounts to a private nuisance.*[13] This introduces a logical circularity into the law. The defendant's activity is relevant to the characterisation of the locality only if it is not a private nuisance, but to determine whether it is a private nuisance one already needs to have specified whether it is part of the character of the locality.

Fundamentally, what is objectionable about this departure from the demands of logical validity is not its illogic, however, but rather the fact that it makes the law impossible to determine. This is not necessarily to deny that there is a general value in correct (including, logically correct) reasoning. It seems doubtful, however, that failures of reasoning always amount to a breach of a moral obligation. If I believe that I have solved a maths puzzle but in fact my reasoning involves a failure, I breach no duty, even if things go worse (for me). The special moral significance of *judicial* or legal failures of reasoning is the triggering of other moral obligations that apply in that context, including the risk of causing wrongful harm, and the moral values implicated in the Rule of Law. Since it should be possible to have reasonable clarity about one's private rights and duties, rules which make the content of one's rights dependent on circular arguments make this impossible and are objectionable on this ground. The point is not merely that, in the absence of reasonable clarity about the content of primary rights, there is a risk that force will be employed without fair warning, but also, simply, that a person may be held to have violated another's rights in circumstances in which it was impossible to determine in advance whether the conduct amounted a right violation. Nor is the concern exhausted by the failure to provide guidance to legal subjects; circular rules effectively lead to rule by judicial fiat, the rules themselves not pointing in the direction of a particular legal conclusion.[14] Insofar as there any legal *a priori* laws, there may be a similar moral reason to adhere to them on grounds of otherwise making the law unclear or confusing, albeit not simply on the ground that the law does not live up to its *a priori* foundations.

A third reason is simply that identifying the nature of the concepts employed by the law allows for clearer normative disputes – in identifying the essential features of such concepts, one better understands what is at stake in normative disputes. It is true that some, perhaps all, normative disputes can be conducted without a complete conceptual analysis of the concepts in question. For instance, we can

[13] [2014] UKSC 13, [66]. For discussion, see Sandy Steel, 'The Locality Principle in Private Nuisance' (2017) 76 Cambridge Law Journal 145.

[14] This point is missed when the value of the 'rule of law' is reduced only to the value of guidance (in accordance with valuable rules). In *Patel v Mirza* [2016] UKSC 42, [113], introducing a test involving balancing of multiple vague criteria was considered more tolerable in relation to the defence of illegality since would-be criminals need not be able to determine reliably when they will be entitled to rely upon their private law rights in connection with planned criminal activity. More tolerable, perhaps, but there is also the cost of rights-enforcement being made subject less to rules and more to judicial idiosyncrasy.

reasonably engage in normative disputes about outcome luck – whether the causal effects of one's conduct bear upon one's moral assessment – without a complete analysis of the concept of causation. This may be because we know that whatever the necessary and sufficient conditions, or grounding properties, of causation turn out to be, we know that they will always involve a relation between facts or events that may fail to hold due to matters of luck, and the moral puzzle of outcome luck resides in that property. However, sometimes, the concept in question may be open to several possible analyses that need disambiguation in order to make any progress. For instance, consider the question of whether tort liability ought to depend upon the breach of a moral *duty*. The answer to this question may turn on whether one understands duties as exclusionary reasons, as weighty reasons, as all-things-considered requirements, and so on. It may be that tort liability ought to depend upon a breach of a duty in some of these senses but not others.[15]

A clearer articulation of the conceptual structure of the law also sometimes leads to normative insight, or more modestly, suggests a possible normative insight. One example of this in private law is the distinction between primary duties and primary liabilities.[16] A primary duty is a legally recognised or imposed requirement to do or not to do an act, which does not arise from the breach of another requirement. A primary liability is being situated such that another person may alter one's position by the exercise of a power, absent the breach of a duty on one's part. The very fact of making this distinction reminds one of the possibility that, for instance, court-ordered duties to compensate may not always hinge upon the breach of an anterior legal duty. Not all the reasons that support the recognition of being liable to be ordered to pay compensation support primary duty norms. In so far as legal duties state all-things-considered requirements – they tell us what we must do all things considered – then they give us a very particular form of guidance. Yet it is not obvious that duties to compensate should always be made contingent upon the breach of such a primary duty. There are plausibly situations in which a person is permitted to act in a certain way, yet the costs of doing so, if these involve harm to others, are justly theirs. Now, doing the conceptual work of distinguishing between 'primary duties' and 'primary liabilities' does not itself, of course, tell us anything of normative significance, but the distinction may be useful in drawing attention to a possible kind of legal relation that persons might justly be held to be under. Admittedly, it may sometimes, perhaps always, be an inchoate, unarticulated, normative insight that drives the recognition of a conceptual distinction.

Here is another, recent, example, of how analysis of the *nature* of a legal concept – and, arguably, an implicit claim that the concept corresponds to an external abstract

[15] See Leo Boonzaier, 'Gardner on Duties' in Haris Psarras and Sandy Steel (eds), *Private Law and Practical Reason* (Oxford University Press 2022).

[16] On liabilities generally, see Wesley Hohfeld, 'Some Fundamental Legal Conceptions as Applied in Judicial Reasoning' (1913) 23 Yale LJ 16, 44–54.

object, a la Reinach – can prompt a normative claim. Consider the claim made by Robert Stevens and Donal Nolan that a legal wrong happens at a moment in time.[17] Stevens and Nolan effectively propose this, in Reinachian spirit, as a necessary, *a priori*, truth about wrongs. From it, they draw a surprising implication: the conceptual impossibility of having a legal right not to be caused *loss*. There is no point in time, Nolan argues, at which a person is caused to be worse off. Suppose that after one is negligently injured, one meets the love of one's life in hospital, but later this leads to a terrible accident in which one suffers further injuries. It is impossible, Nolan thinks, to say that the initial injury has made one worse off at a particular time, yet if there is a right not to be negligently caused loss, then it must be possible to say at a particular time that one has been made worse off. They infer that one cannot have a right not to be caused loss because the violation of a right must be something that can be determined at a particular time. Nolan employs the conclusion of this argument to argue that (i) the right in negligence is a right not to be caused *damage* (roughly, being put in a negative state at a particular time) through unreasonable risk impositions, and (ii) limitation periods based on *when* a person suffers a *loss* are hopelessly confused. Whatever we think of the merits of this argument,[18] it makes a normative proposal based on a purported *essential* and *a priori* truth about wrongs, and thus about civil law.[19]

Clearly, one can accept that there are benefits in conceptual clarity without following Reinach in believing that some legal concepts correspond or refer to abstract objects that exist independently of the law. There is a value in conceptual clarity about the concepts employed in the positive law, independently of whether they have extra-legal existence. And even when concepts do not owe their existence to the law, such as the concept of causation, a conceptual analysis might seek to capture ordinary understandings without being committed to Reinach's metaphysical claims (even if some modern authors, in their analysis of the nature of duties, rights and wrongs do seem committed to something like this). Still, Reinach reminds of the possibility that a clarifying conceptual analysis need not be tied entirely to the positive law.

Now, two broad reasons for scepticism about Reinach's enterprise. First, while Reinach is surely correct in claiming that certain conceptual distinctions he identifies hold independently of whatever the positive law says – for instance, factual power and ownership are simply different ideas, or the distinction between acquisition on one's behalf and for another – it seems doubtful that one can move, as

[17] Robert Stevens, 'Rights and Other Things' in Donal Nolan and Andrew Robertson (eds), *Rights and Private Law* (Hart Publishing, 2012) 119 and Donal Nolan, 'Rights, Damage, and Loss' (2017) 37 OJLS 255.

[18] An obvious objection is that the argument confuses epistemic uncertainty about what would have happened but for an act, and metaphysical indeterminacy.

[19] The usual example given of a necessary truth that is not *a priori*: 'Water is H_2O'. Nolan and Stevens presumably think that reflection on the nature of wrongs, independently of empirical experience, justifies their view, however. Hence it is a claim about *a priori* truths.

Reinach does, from these conceptual claims to claims that, *ontologically*, the normative entities or relations to which they refer are actually instantiated independently of the positive law.[20] We can accept, as a matter of our deep conceptual architecture, if you like, that there is a distinction between acquisition on one's own behalf and representative acquisition of rights. However, is it the case that anyone can indeed successfully achieve acquisition on behalf of another – make it normatively the case that through their purported exercise of a power, they succeed in conferring a right on the represented – independently of the positive law? It seems to me that whether any of these normative relations or entities are *realised* (other than as a matter of social fact) depends upon – perhaps very abstract – normative argument. There is a gap, in other words, between identifying a set of deep conceptual possibilities, and the claim that those conceptual possibilities are in fact instantiated as a matter of normative reality. Compare the Hohfeldian scheme of jural relations. One can accept the conceptual possibility of claims, privileges, immunities, disabilities, etc, without also accepting that these *in fact* exist. Whether anyone has a genuine claim or immunity depends (at least partly independently of the law or a conventional practice that purports to confer on them) on a normative argument that explains why.

A second reason points to a general difficulty with moving from *a priori* philosophical analysis of a concept and then using this analysis as part of a normative argument about the concepts which the law should recognise. In short, there is a risk, in such an inquiry, in moving illicitly from the claim that such and such represents the *a priori* nature of a concept to the claim that the law ought to reflect that *a priori* nature in its conceptual scheme. Reinach himself is keenly aware of this:

> Just as this theory emphatically distinguishes itself from the positive law and from the application of positive law, and warns against every ontologism which wants to bind the positive law to essential laws of being, so it also has to refuse to be interpreted as right or valid law. Although that which holds apriori is at the same time prima facie something which ought to be, the philosophy of right or valid law considers the apriori laws in the context of the concrete community in which they are realized and in which their ought-character can undergo very various modifications.[21]

Clearly, this allows for a divergence between the *a priori* laws and the justified positive law. It may even resist the idea that there is a *pro tanto* reason for the positive law to reflect the *a priori* law or concept. That seems the correct position: in the contingent circumstances of a particular legal system, recognising the *a priori* position in the positive law may have detrimental consequences that prevent there being even a *pro tanto* reason for legal recognition. Enoch, Fisher and Spectre have

[20] See also Lorenz Kaehler's chapter in this volume.

[21] Reinach (n 4) 136.

recently made a similar point in relation to epistemology and (some) normative theories of the law of evidence. They identify as mistaken 'the attempt, roughly, to do legal epistemology just by doing epistemology, or to treat epistemological considerations (say, about the nature of knowledge or evidence) as decisive, or even just intrinsically relevant, to normative questions in evidence law theory'.[22] The background to their article is a literature in the theory of evidence law which draws extensively upon certain privileged epistemic statuses that a belief might have, as identified by epistemology – it might constitute *knowledge*, or have *warrant* or be produced by a process that is *highly likely to produce knowledge*, etc. – and then argues that the law should track that status. For instance, various objections to the use of purely statistical evidence are put in epistemological terms – one view is that statistical evidence that p cannot generate *knowledge* that p.[23] Enoch and his co-authors argue, somewhat similarly to Reinach's warning above, that, without more, insisting that factfinders' beliefs have certain epistemic status amounts to a kind of epistemological fetishism. In every case, one should ask whether one is willing to trade off the existence of that epistemic status against the other goods which evidence law must secure. For instance, if one insists that factfinders have *knowledge*, and do not act upon purely statistical evidence, one must be willing to accept an increased rate of false convictions or false acquittals. Once we see that insisting upon a certain privileged epistemic status rubs up against the pursuit of other goals, it follows that some *value* must be identified in beliefs having that status which can justify this.

A similar point could be made about another area in which the results of philosophical inquiries seem, sometimes, to be taken to bear directly upon the content of the law: causation.[24] One approach to theoretical questions about how the law should approach causation might be described as 'metaphysics first'. Essentially, one outsources the question to the metaphysicians.[25] Legal norms employing the concept CAUSE should, ideally, track whatever the best metaphysical account of causation is. This approach, unadorned, is subject to a similar objection to that framed by Reinach (and Enoch, Levi and Spectre). Suppose that the best view is that absences (omissions are an example) are not causes, or that absences, in so far as they are causes, are metaphysically importantly different,

[22] David Enoch, Talia Fisher, and Levi Spectre, 'Does Legal Epistemology Rest on a Mistake? On Fetishism, Two-tier System Design, and Conscientious Fact-finding' (2021) 31 Philosophical Issues 85, 85.

[23] See, e.g., Sarah Moss, 'Knowledge and Legal Proof' in T Gendler, J Hawthorne, and J Chung (eds), *Oxford Studies in Epistemology* (vol. 7, Oxford University Press 2022).

[24] Reinach's doctoral dissertation was on causation in the criminal law: Adolf Reinach, 'On the Concept of Causality in the Criminal Law'. Reinach makes the point here that philosophical theories are not a reliable guide to the positive law, but his point is different to that in the text. It is a point about what is relevant to legal interpretation of the positive law.

[25] For this kind of approach, see Michael Moore, *Causation and Responsibility* (Oxford University Press 2009).

causally speaking, from positive states of affairs or events. Even if so, it seems an entirely open question whether this metaphysical fact should have any legal significance. If a person can be morally responsible for omissions and outcomes to which those omissions stand in a certain relation, and such omissions ground moral rights which the law may permissibly enforce, then it is neither here nor there whether the relation in question is properly termed 'causal' by metaphysical lights.

It might be objected that, if the best metaphysical view is that omissions are *not* causes, then the law should not misdescribe reality by purporting to hold people liable on a causal basis for their omissions. Omissions liability should be described by the law as 'non-causal' in nature, similar to a company's vicarious (non-causal) liability for the acts of its employee. After all, it matters that the law accurately describes the reasons for its decisions, independently of the outcomes reached. In response to the objection, two points may be made. First, in deciding what legal rights, duties, liabilities etc. to recognise, one can accept the objection and still deny that metaphysical truths or distinctions have a direct bearing on the ideal content of those rights, duties and liabilities. In designing the ideal laws, the question is essentially: 'What relations to an outcome should give rise to legal liability?' In answering *that question*, it is at best a secondary matter whether the relevant relations are properly described according to the best philosophical theory as 'causal' or not. Second, if there is a reason for the law accurately to describe the metaphysical basis of liability, it is surely easily defeated. Suppose that ordinary thought recognises omissions as causes, contrary to metaphysical reality, and so guidance to legal subjects is considerably better achieved by describing omissions liability in law as 'causal'. In other words, suppose the law is much more readily understandable by legal subjects if this description is used, and the only reason for departing from this description is metaphysical accuracy. In those circumstances, it does seem like a kind of fetishism to insist upon metaphysical accuracy.

Nothing I have said casts doubt on the value of normative theorists of causation in the law engaging in, or with, metaphysical analysis. Understanding the kinds of relation to an outcome that generate moral responsibility (and so, potentially, legal responsibility) in respect of an outcome will require such analysis. If we can better understand the relation that exists between an agent and an outcome when that person is not necessary for the outcome, yet still seems to play a role in its production, we will better be able to identify situations in which a person is potentially morally responsible for the outcome. The only point, with which Reinach would agree, is that one should not assume that a metaphysical distinction tracks a moral, and legally relevant, one.

6.3 JUSTIFICATIONS

It should already be clear that Reinach's project in the *Foundations* is not intended to be a normative one. It does not seek to provide a justification of a system of private law, nor does it contain any specific normative proposal about the content of the positive law. Still, Reinach makes some interesting general observations that bear upon questions of justification, and the relationship between law and normative standards that do not owe their existence to the positive law. These can usefully be grouped into two general themes: (i) the relationship between positive civil law and morality, and (ii) the normative effects of the positive law.

6.3.1 *Moral and Non-moral Demands on the Law*

Reinach draws distinctions between kinds of normative demand, with each having some bearing on what the positive law ought to be. First, there are moral facts that hold regardless of social facts, or empirical facts more generally. These include the fact that a promise normally generates a moral duty to perform the promise.[26]

Second, there are principles, again independent of the positive law which determine 'legal oughts'. Reinach briefly elaborates that 'This [legal] ought is not a purely moral ought, but rather a legal ought (*rechtliches Sollen*); it is an ought which has to do with principles according to which a community of men can be regulated in an objectively valid way'.[27] Perhaps what Reinach has in mind here is something in the vicinity of the distinction between justice or *ius* and other domains of morality, or between 'right' and 'virtue'.

Reinach's remarks on the matter are relatively cursory, so it's not entirely clear what relationship he envisages between morality and *ius* or the 'legal ought'. At times, it seems as if the latter is simply a sub-set of the former (for instance, when he writes that legal oughts are not *purely* moral oughts, suggesting that they are moral, but there is some additional feature of the legal ought). In particular, it is not clear that Reinach would endorse the Kantian view that the 'juridical' (*ius*-related) concerns the set of non-positive principles that properly determine the content of enforceable positive law rights and duties. In the Kantian picture, these principles determine what *rights* persons should have in positive law, and are concerned exclusively with the protection of external, equal, freedom. For instance, Reinach mentions that intimate or consanguineous relationships generate moral 'rights' between the parties to such relationships, and that these rights may be recognised by the positive law;[28] this might be taken to suggest that the grounds of justified legal rights are not exclusively freedom based.

There is a danger of terminological disputes in carving up normative territory between 'ius' and morality, or between the juridical and the purely moral. Everyone ought to agree that there are some obligations whose existence is not grounded in

[26] Reinach (n 4) 14.
[27] Reinach (n 4) 136.
[28] Reinach (n 4) 52.

positive law which ought not to be enforced in the positive law. It doesn't matter a great deal whether we refer to the enforceable set as 'juridical' and the non-enforceable sub-set as 'moral' or consider them to be sub-sets of the more general category of 'moral'. The substantive question is: What normatively explains when and why certain obligations should be recognised and enforced in positive law? The central, distinctive, feature of the Kantian view, for instance, is the substantive claim that positive law enforceability is connected to *freedom-grounded* non-positive rights and duties; duties with a different ground are not enforceable.[29] The interesting question is, then, whether the Kantians are right that the distinction between freedom-based rights and non-freedom-based rights provides a persuasive account of which duties are, by their nature, enforceable and unenforceable, respectively, or whether a more pragmatic account is preferable. Such an account might rest not on the justificatory basis of certain duties, but to the characteristic negative effects of public enforcement.

The third category of 'normativity', for Reinach, as we know, are the non-moral *a priori* laws: facts about legal entities that do not owe their existence to the positive law, such as the fact that a claim is waivable by the claim-holder, which '*prima facie*' ought to be, and which may justly be reflected in the positive law depending on the contingent circumstances.

Reinach explicitly distinguishes the kinds of 'obligation' generated by certain acts, according to *a priori* laws, from *moral* rights and duties. For instance, he describes promises as generating non-moral obligations of performance.[30] What distinguishes the non-moral obligations that correlate with claims from 'moral' duties is (i) their freely assumed character, and (ii) their waivability by the exercise of a power. By contrast, while actions on the part of moral right-holders can *cause* a moral duty to be discharged, such right-holders lack a power directly to make it the case that a duty is not owed by waiver.

It is tempting to read this as simply a taxonomic distinction amongst moral duties with different sources, some moral duties being sourced in a free choice to incur the duty, others not; in today's parlance, some moral duties derive from the exercise of normative powers, others do not. But Reinach is explicit that there are two separate things going on when a promise is made: a non-moral 'obligation' arises *and* there is a moral duty to perform that is grounded in that non-moral obligation. So, the distinction is not simply between different compartments of morality. Nor is the distinction being drawn between 'relational' obligations and 'non-relational' moral

[29] Still, if it is insisted that the juridical is non-moral because it concerns freedom-grounded enforceable rights and duties, this involves a non-standard restriction of the domain of morality. If the idea that duties which, by their nature (perhaps by virtue of the values they serve) are unenforceable are the only moral ones, this, again, involves an unusual restriction of the domain of the moral; duties not intentionally to kill others are then non-moral duties.

[30] Reinach (n 4) 14.

duties: Reinach is, again, clear that there can be relational *moral* duties, though he regards these as being unnoticed in ethics.[31]

Another possibility is that promises create obligations in the sense that the rules of the social institution of promising make it the case that promising involves an obligation – on this Hartian-type view, promises create a distinctive 'ought' relative to a social institution. But, of course, this cannot exactly be Reinach's view either: promises and their direct bindingness are to be explained independently of social, conventional facts; *a priori*. It almost seems as if Reinach wants to say that promises create obligations in a similar way that positive laws create legal obligations, but without these obligations having a social source. Just as an evil law *in a sense* creates a binding obligation (in law), so too a promise to do an immoral act creates a binding obligation according to the in-built normativity of promising. If that's the character of Reinach's view, it fails, however, as a contribution to the debate on why promises are binding. The puzzle that motivates this debate is precisely how one could become *morally* bound to do what one promised to do, without more – how it could be that an agent could change their moral position in the peculiar way by a kind of voluntary commitment. Pointing out that promises create non-social, non-moral obligations by their nature, does not solve or dissolve this puzzle. For every such obligation, it seems one should ask whether it ought to guide one's conduct by reference to other valid norms – be they moral norms or norms of *ius*. Ultimately, the view which makes Reinach's contribution to this debate more interesting, and more consonant with his intention to contribute to the philosophical discussion as to why promises bind, is to construe it as the view that promises *do* create moral obligations, or at least obligations which, by their nature, have some genuine hold on an agent's practical reasoning, but there is no reductive explanation of why this is so.[32]

6.3.2 *The Relationship between the Positive Law and Non-institutional Norms*

For Reinach, the positive law may diverge from the *a priori* position in at least two ways. First, it may justifiably create normative incidents which it is impossible to create *a priori*. The positive law might confer rights on third parties to a promise – for Reinach, promises only generate entitlements in the promisee as a matter of the *a priori* laws.[33] In this case, the third party's right is grounded in the positive law; the right does not arise 'directly' from the promise, but through the mediating ground of the positive law. Another example given is prescriptive acquisition, which, for

[31] Reinach (n 4) 13.
[32] See Olivier Massin and Alessandro Salice's chapter in this volume.
[33] Reinach (n 4) 113.

Reinach, involves a mode of acquisition that is not part of the *a priori* nature of property rights. It is adopted for 'reasons of practicality'.[34]

A similar idea about the relation between the positive law and what lies beyond it is found in Weinrib's work. Weinrib gives the example of the tort duty not to induce a breach of contract. While an agreement, in private right (roughly, the non-positive interpersonal principles that regulate enforceable rights and duties), creates only relational duties between the parties to the agreement, public right may permissibly step in to provide parties with additional assurance that their agreements will not be deliberately thwarted by others.[35] Another is market overt, which confers a limited power to pass good title although the transferor had none.[36]

Second, the positive law might cancel or 'suppress' the normative pre-positive law effect of a transaction. Here Reinach envisages not merely that the positive law does not provide legal protection to an *a priori* claim, with the *a priori* claim continuing to exist. Rather, the positive law *cancels* the usual normative effect of some pre-legal transaction. Again, there is a useful parallel in Weinrib's work. The latter gives the example here of the permission to use another's land in an emergency, when being excluded from the land would result in a much graver interference with the user's right than the interference to the owner. This is how Weinrib analyses the well-known decision in *Vincent v Lake Erie Transportation Co.*[37] In this case, a ship captain fastened *The Reynolds* to the plaintiff's dock, without permission, in order to save the cargo on board from destruction in a storm. Waves and wind thrust the vessel against the dock, damaging it. The court ordered the defendant to pay compensation, despite describing the conduct as morally justified. In Weinrib's view, this rule recognised or established by this decision is an instance of public right justifiably qualifying or 'cancelling', in Reinach's terms, the owner's right to exclude. Private right permits the owner to exclude, but public right qualifies this in order to render rights consistent with one another.[38] However, precisely because private right confers the permission to exclude, public right requires compensation; the duty to compensate reflects the fact that public right is depriving the owner of what is properly theirs as a matter of private right. The possibility of compensation for departures from *a priori* right is not discussed by Reinach, but again this seems potentially consistent with his analysis; in some cases – when the positive law

[34] Reinach (n 4) 74.

[35] Ernest Weinrib, *Reciprocal Justice* (Oxford University Press 2022), ch 4.

[36] Unlike Reinach, Weinrib's view is that public right has distinctive normative constraints – its business is only the modification of private right to ensure that rights form a consistent set and satisfy certain 'publicity' requirements. Precisely what constraints these somewhat loose notions of 'consistency' and 'publicity' involve is not very clear, however. On the face of it, public right substantially enriches the normative austerity of private right, understood as a domain of rights grounded only in considerations of equal freedom.

[37] 124 N.W. 221, 222 (Minn. 1910).

[38] Weinrib (n 35).

requires a person to bear a burden which *a priori* right permits them not to bear, for instance – this plausibly would require compensation.

One normative contribution of the positive law which Reinach does not discuss in any detail is its bringing *determinatio* to the inherently indeterminate content of the *a priori* law. This feature of the positive law has been particularly emphasised in recent Kantian scholarship on private law. It is part of what is meant by Weinrib's claim that the value of private law is to be private law. What is truly meant is that there is a value in the positive law determinately part-constituting the underlying juridical norms. This value is, *pace* Kantians, partly instrumental: it is valuable in so far as it co-ordinates legal subjects' conduct around a determinate version of interpersonal juridical rights. There is plausibly also, *pace* instrumentalists, an intrinsic value in one's being able to enforce one's rights without being at substantial risk of wronging others.[39] Absent a public, authoritative determination of innate right, we are faced with such a risk in so far as we adopt our own interpretation of what each person's innate right requires or permits. An omnilateral determination by a legitimate public authority is needed to resolve this problem. If authoritative *determinatio* is necessary for this to be the case, in virtue of avoiding the problem of 'unilateralism', then there is an intrinsic value in *determinatio* of innate right. Nothing Reinach says seems incompatible with this kind of *determinatio* adding detail to *a priori* principles of right. Indeed, it might be considered *a fortiori* his analysis of third-party rights being conferred by the positive law: if the positive law can confer wholly new entitlements, it must be able to lend determinacy to pre-existing *a priori* entitlements.

6.4 CONCLUSION

No contemporary theorists describe their work as seeking the *a priori* foundations of private law. Yet sometimes it does. Unlike Reinach, contemporary theorists not infrequently seek to identify *normative* truths, rather than essential non-moral laws, that they ultimately seem to consider knowable *a priori*. The basic, appealing, idea underpinning neo-Kantian theories that each person is entitled to stand in an equal relation to each other is not something that is read off the content or structure of legal institutions; it is a normative truth (albeit its content is open to multiple institutional concretisations) that is grasped by reflection on the kind of beings that we are, and obtains regardless of any institutional fact. The boundaries between abstract *a priori* truths about *normative* entities such as duties, rights, powers and so on, and *a priori* moral truths are porous, however, and so the distance between Reinach and contemporary normative theories is not as great as may initially appear. I have suggested that Reinach's attention to the abstract conceptual structure of basic normative ideas referred to in private law can be normatively fruitful, albeit it carries

[39] Arthur Ripstein, *Private Wrongs* (Harvard University Press 2016).

a risk, one Reinach recognises, of imbuing features of concepts with a normative significance that they have not been established to have.

BIBLIOGRAPHY

Boonzaier, L, 'Gardner on Duties' in H Psarras and S Steel (eds), *Private Law and Practical Reason* (Oxford University Press 2022)

Enoch, D, Fisher, T, and Spectre, L, 'Does Legal Epistemology Rest on a Mistake? On Fetishism, Two Tier System Design, and Conscientious Fact-Finding' (2021) 31 Philosophical Issues 85

Gold, A and Smith, H, 'Sizing Up Private Law' (2020) 70 UTLJ 489

Hohfeld, W, 'Some Fundamental Legal Conceptions as Applied in Judicial Reasoning' (1913) 23 Yale LJ 16

Khaitan, T and Steel, S, 'Theorising Areas of Law' (2022) 28 Legal Theory 325

Kuntz, T and Miller, P (eds), *Methodology in Private Law Theory: Between New Private Law and Rechtsdogmatik* (Oxford University Press 2024)

Moore, M, *Causation and Responsibility* (Oxford University Press 2009)

Moss, S, 'Knowledge and Legal Proof' in T Gendler, J Hawthorne, and J Chung (eds), *Oxford Studies in Epistemology* (vol. 7, Oxford University Press, 2022)

Nolan, D, 'Rights, Damage, and Loss' (2017) 37 OJLS 255

Reinach, A, 'The Apriori Foundations of the Civil Law' (John F Crosby tr, 1983) 3 Aletheia 1–142, reprinted in Adolf Reinach, *The Apriori Foundations of the Civil Law Along with the Lecture 'Concerning Phenomenology'* (John F Crosby ed, Ontos Verlag 2012), originally published as Adolf Reinach, Die apriorischen Grundlagen des bürgerlichen Rechtes, 1(2) *Jahrbuch für Philosophie und phänomenologische Forschung* (Max Niemeyer 1913), 685–847

Ripstein, A, *Private Wrongs* (Harvard University Press 2016)

Smith, S, *Contract Theory* (Clarendon 2004)

Steel, S, 'The Locality Principle in Private Nuisance' (2017) 76 Cambridge Law Journal 145

Stevens, R, 'Rights and Other Things' in Donal Nolan and Andrew Robertson (eds), *Rights and Private Law* (Hart Publishing 2012)

Weinrib, E, *Reciprocal Justice* (Oxford University Press 2022)

Williamson, T, *Philosophical Method: A Very Short Introduction* (Oxford University Press 2022)

7

Reinach on Personality and Representation

*Paul B. Miller**

7.1 INTRODUCTION

Adolf Reinach died tragically at a young age, and with his death the world was deprived of a talented philosopher who was revered by his contemporaries. Reinach left us with a significant scholarly legacy that is yet to be properly appreciated, including, prominently, his *A Priori Foundations of the Civil Law*. In *Foundations*, Reinach offers original and insightful perspectives on general jurisprudential questions (e.g., on the nature of law, and the relationship between natural law, positive law, and universal elements of legal form), interlaced with equally illuminating reflections on enduring philosophical questions about private law (e.g., about promissory obligations and the nature of property rights). The insights in *Foundations* reflect the ingenuity of Reinach's theory of social acts (a precursor of the speech act theories of Austin and Searle) as well as Reinach's conviction in his novel method of phenomenological elucidation of a priori truths about law (i.e., about *juridical* social acts).

Reinach's phenomenological method is not Kant's, yet both may be viewed as offering variants on themes common to transcendental idealist thought about law. Reinach, like Kant, believed in the possibility of reasoned discernment of a priori truths about relations of right, and both believed themselves to have identified them. Furthermore, Reinach, like Kant, held that these truths – being a priori – are true universally and independently of contingent features of human experience

* Robert and Marion Short Professor of Law, Associate Dean for International and Graduate Programs, and Director of the Notre Dame Program on Private Law, Notre Dame Law School.
I am grateful for comments from my coeditors – Marietta Auer, Henry Smith, and James Toomey – as well as Andrew Gold, Larissa Katz, and Dennis Klimchuk. I am also grateful for comments from participants in a workshop on Reinach and the Foundations of Private Law hosted by the Max Planck Institute for Legal History and Legal Theory and attendees of the Yale-Toronto Private Law Theory Discussion Group. Email: paul.miller@nd.edu

(including those that influence the development of positive law). Of course, unlike Kant, Reinach recognized that relations of right are not merely *given* as a matter of practical reason but are available to reason through experience insofar as they are *practiced* as social acts (a distinctive subset of normative speech acts). Further, and again departing from Kant, Reinach denied that a priori truths about law are grounded on metaphysical and/or moral truths about human nature and the human condition.[1]

Kant's account in the *Doctrine of Right* of three basic categories of private right (property, contract, and status) is undeniably elegant. But, notwithstanding celebrated efforts to show that it illuminates contemporary private law,[2] the gulf between Kant's transcendental rendering and what is familiar in, and important from, lawyerly experience diminishes its appeal to some. Reading Reinach, by comparison, those interested in philosophical theories that make closer contact with law are rewarded with richly nuanced analysis of a wider array of familiar legal concepts that are undeniably profoundly important to private law, all presented without any attempt to locate them within a constraining transcendental deduction of categories of private right. One finds in *Foundations* bracingly original treatments of notions of personhood, capacity, power, obligation, claim, promise, grant, waiver, revocation, transfer, assignment, command, possession, lien, authorization, representation, and more. Contemporary private law theorists should find in Reinach's analysis of these concepts several profitable points of departure and return, whatever they think about the merits of his method.

As is reflected in other chapters in this volume, Reinach has much to offer even to those working the well-tilled fields of tort, contract, and property theory. This chapter ventures in a different direction, looking for insights from Reinach on two related, under-analyzed, legal concepts found interstitially and transversally, between and across private law's basic categories of private right: concepts of personality and representation.

One cannot understand, much less evaluate, Reinach's account of representation without examining it alongside his treatment of personality and, in turn, one cannot properly evaluate either contribution without coming to terms with his method. Accordingly, my presentation of Reinach's thought will proceed sequentially as follows. Section 7.2 offers a brief summary and critical analysis of Reinach's method, focusing on his claim to offer phenomenological analysis of a priori synthetic truths about law as well as his suggestion that law is constituted by social acts (Reinachian

1 E.g., *pace* Kant, that relations of right are premised on the moral-metaphysical truth that human beings are uniquely capable of self-determination, and that the equal freedom of human beings is the constitutive value that undergirds and shapes terms of right that govern relations of right.

2 Ernest J Weinrib, *The Idea of Private Law* (Harvard University Press 1995); Arthur Ripstein, *Force and Freedom* (Harvard University Press 2009); Arthur Ripstein, *Private Wrongs* (Harvard University Press 2016).

speech acts). Section 7.3 examines Reinach's views on legal personality, highlighting the sense in which persons are pivotal to Reinach's method (phenomenological discernment of a priori synthetic truths) and his objects of analysis (law, manifested behaviorally in juridical social acts). Section 7.4 investigates Reinach's account of representation, noting ways in which it parallels that of Hobbes, subject to Reinach's distinctive emphasis on representation as something performative (i.e., as manifested in successful social acts of representation).[3] Section 7.2 also introduces some concerns about aspects of Reinach's method (the aims and modality of phenomenological discernment of a priori truths about law, *not* his speech act theory of law), and Sections 7.3 and 7.4 show how these concerns are borne out by certain deficiencies in Reinach's analyses of personality and representation. Section 7.5 concludes with thoughts on how contemporary private law theorists might make the most of Reinach's contributions.

7.2 METHOD

The philosophical questions that Reinach pursued, and the interest held by his answers, are attributable in part to his innovative phenomenological method. The method combines elements of phenomenological and transcendental idealist thought in ways that are, to an analytical mind, nonobvious and even awkward.[4] It is phenomenological insofar as it aims at the elucidation of truths disclosed by deliberate and self-conscious attention to experience of the human condition.[5] But it shares in aspects of transcendental idealist thought: the truths meant to be disclosed are a priori and so are believed to have truth-value prior to and independent of experience. In combination, the method appears to involve a breadth and depth of meditative deliberation on experience that permits transcendent discernment (i.e., that enables one to notice and to see through, and hence beyond, what is merely contingent in human experience).

The characteristics of Reinach's method were touched upon by Husserl in his commemoration of Reinach:

> [Reinach's work has attempted] something completely new ... on the basis of pure phenomenology it attempts to develop the idea ... of an apriori theory of right ... Reinach brings to light a whole array of 'apriori' truths which underlies [sic] any real or possible legal code; and these truths, as he shows, are apriori exactly in the sense of the basic axioms of arithmetic and logic, that is, they are truths which are grasped

[3] That is, it is a mode of *acting* for another.

[4] In this, Reinach followed in the footsteps of his mentor, Edmund Husserl. On Husserl, see Dan Zahavi, *Husserl's Legacy: Phenomenology, Metaphysics, and Transcendental Philosophy* (Oxford University Press 2017).

[5] See generally Alessandro Salice and Genki Uemura, 'Social Acts and Communities: Walther between Husserl and Reinach,' in A Calcagno, (ed) *Gerda Walther's Phenomenology of Sociality, Psychology, and Religion* (Springer 2018).

in intellectual insight as being valid without any possible exception, and they are prior to all experience.[6]

Unfortunately, the modalities of thought involved in Reinach's method are exemplified rather than described by him. Thus, his method remains opaque *as a method* (i.e., as a structured way of contemplating and of elucidating what is salient in experience). While one will look in vain for detailed exposition and defense of the phenomenological method, there are occasional suggestive comments in *Foundations*, such as this one:

> Here we do not just stand before a world in which we can observe all kinds of states of affairs; here a different and deeper possibility is available to us. In immersing ourselves in the essence of these entities, we spiritually see what holds for them as a matter of strict law; we grasp connections in a manner analogous to the way in which we know when we immerse ourselves in the nature of numbers and geometrical forms: that a thing is so, is here grounded in the essence of the thing which is so.[7]

In this passage, Reinach nods to the phenomenologist's emphasis on insight gleaned through deliberate attention to experience as well as to the transcendentalist's aim to uncover a priori truths. Also notable is his insistence that there *are* a priori truths about law; axioms that have truth-value every bit as robust as those of mathematics and the natural sciences. This claim is certainly bold, and one might understandably be skeptical about it. But Reinach is alive to reasons for skepticism or, at least, reasons that derive from the view that law is inherently artifactual. Reinach has something to say about that view, and so one should shelve associated doubts for now.

In understanding Reinach's phenomenological method, it is important to notice that it is applicable to different objects of experience. In *Foundations*, it is said to enable elucidation of a priori truths about law. This, in turn, meant, for Reinach, disclosing the sense in which law is constituted by a distinctive set of social acts (speech acts), each of which has formal properties that can be known a priori. One could therefore treat Reinach's phenomenological approach as his *method* and social acts as being amongst its possible *objects*. But I think a better approach – apt in itself and more fitting in its recognition of Reinach's legacy – is to treat Reinach's analysis of social acts as, at once, a subsidiary but severable element of his phenomenological method and an object of inquiry. Reinach is, after all,

[6] Edmund Husserl, 'Obituary for Adolf Reinach,' reprinted in Adolf Reinach, *The Apriori Foundations of the Civil Law* (John F Crosby tr, Ontos Verlag 2012) xiii.

[7] Adolf Reinach, 'The Apriori Foundations of the Civil Law' (John F Crosby tr, 1983) 3 Aletheia 1, 4 reprinted in Adolf Reinach, *The Apriori Foundations of the Civil Law Along with the Lecture 'Concerning Phenomenology'* (John F Crosby ed, Ontos Verlag 2012), originally published as Adolf Reinach, Die apriorischen Grundlagen des bürgerlichen Rechtes, 1(2) *Jahrbuch für Philosophie und phänomenologische Forschung* (Max Niemeyer 1913), 685–847.

responsible for a major innovation in the philosophy of language *and* its extension to the philosophy of law: development of a speech act theory of law. The speech act theory encompasses a distinctive method of examining law as a set of sociolinguistic practices *as well as* the results of same (i.e., analyses of particular speech acts).

Reinach's speech act theory antedated those of J.L. Austin and John Searle, both usually credited as progenitors. In Reinach's terminology, speech acts are 'social acts.' Social acts are 'social' insofar as they are communicative acts directed at others (or at oneself positioned as other, as in social acts of self-evaluation). They involve 'action' insofar as they are directly performatively effective where communicatively successful (e.g., expression of consent is effective *as* consent). Social acts encompass both 'spontaneous acts' (acts initiated by the actor) and 'passive' acts (acts responsive to the spontaneous acts of others). Both kinds of social act encompass 'internal' states (e.g., intentions) and 'external' communicative behavior. Spontaneous social acts are communicatively successful, and hence performatively effective, only where the external communicative behavior is 'heard' via the passive social acts of a listener/ correspondent. And, Reinach emphasizes, they are authentic or 'sincere' only where internal and external dimensions are aligned.[8]

As is true of other speech act theories, Reinach's theory is illuminating on matters of *general jurisprudence* (e.g., the sense in which lawmaking and law enforcement involve social acts, such as enacting and ordering) while also informing *conceptual analysis* aimed at elucidating, and discerning the relationship between, normative concepts and the social behavior, ritualized and spontaneous, that these concepts contemplate, denote, shape, or otherwise structure.

It should be remembered that, for Reinach, social acts constitutive of law (*juridical social acts*) are but a species of social act. That said, they were a species of special interest to Reinach; indeed, seemingly of greater interest than the genus. Reinach would not deny that other normative systems are constituted by social acts. However, he was interested in elucidating a priori truths about juridical social acts, not contingent truths about social acts that figure in positive law, in custom, in conventional morality, or in other constructed normative systems.

Given Reinach's insistence that there are a priori truths to be discovered about law, one should be unsurprised by his insistence upon maintaining analytical distance from conventional morality and positive law. Equally, though, given that law is inherently normative,[9] one might be surprised by Reinach's rendering of the a priori foundations of law as a set of value-neutral existential rather than moral truths. Nevertheless, Reinach also maintains deliberate analytical detachment from

[8] Reinach recognizes that the performance of social acts can involve mistakes and deception, these being two sources of misalignment between the internal and external dimensions of a social act.

[9] That is, the fact that the law claims moral authority, and more specifically, the authority to supply peremptory normative guidance. Joseph Raz, *The Authority of Law* (Oxford University Press 2009).

morality and from the natural law tradition and its aim to show how the law is or ought to be responsive to moral truths about human nature and the human condition. I shall comment briefly on both points of detachment in turn.

Reinach emphasizes that the a priori foundations of law and phenomenological discernment of them ought not to be confused with positive law and positivistic legal analysis, whether the latter takes the form of lawyerly doctrinal or philosophical thought. As he would have it, '[t]he positive law is caught up in constant flux and constant development ... the propositions found in the positive law are quite essentially different from the propositions proper to science.'[10] The a priori foundations of law are taken by Reinach to be *illuminating* of positive law, in that discernment of them might have influenced its development. But, being a priori, they are utterly independent of the positive law and the contingent social and political forces that influence lawmaking. Hence, Reinach suggests that rich experience with positive law can disclose and validate but not disconfirm statements about the a priori foundations of law.[11] Indeed, it should be expected, Reinach says, that the positive law will often diverge from what is given a priori (e.g., positive law's concept of promising may deviate from what is essentially true of promising).[12]

Reinach's reasons for distancing phenomenological discernment of the a priori from positivistic analysis of positive law are also his reasons for rejecting the notion that conventional morality has any bearing upon the essential formal properties of juridical social acts. Whatever the relationships of mutual influence that might link positive law and conventional morality, Reinach treats them as irrelevant to his project. Both concern contingent specification of norms and points of connection between constructed normative systems. One cannot hope to elucidate a priori truths about law by dwelling upon the interaction of what is historically, socially and culturally contingent in constructed normative systems.

One might think that Reinach would be at least open to the idea that the a priori foundations of law (essential formal properties of juridical social acts) evince universal moral truths about human nature and the human condition. But Reinach flatly rejects any association between the a priori foundations of law and natural law.[13] For Reinach, truths about the nature of juridical social acts are a priori and synthetic but

[10] Reinach, *Foundations* (n 7) 2.

[11] As he explains: "the positive law *finds* the legal concepts which enter into it; *in absolutely no way does it produce them*" and, later "[t]hough they make our positive law and positive legal theory possible at all, they enter into them only as transformed and modified." Reinach, *Foundations* (n 7) 4 and 6.

[12] "We of course fully recognize that the positive law makes its enactments in absolute freedom ... unbounded by the sphere of apriori laws which we have in mind. The positive law can deviate as it likes from the essential necessities which hold for legal entities and structures." Reinach, *Foundations* (n 7) 5.

[13] As Husserl emphasized in commenting upon the originality of Reinach's work: "What is utterly original in this essay of Reinach's ... is the idea that we have to distinguish this apriori which belongs properly to the nature of any legal order, from the other apriori which is related to positive law as something normative and as a principle of evaluation: for all law can and must

not moral truths. One might think, nevertheless, that fulsome understanding of juridical social acts demands normative *as well as* formalistic analysis.[14] But Reinach shows little sensitivity on this point. Furthermore, he is clearly diffident about the general normative upshot(s) of the a priori. For example, Reinach treats it as an open question whether and how the a priori should influence the development of positive law. He is seemingly of the view that if a priori truths about law have normative force, it is epistemic and linguistic rather than practical: it governs the true or correct invocation of words (e.g., 'promising,' 'claiming,' and 'enacting') denoting juridical social acts.

If we may now examine the merits of Reinach's method, the results are mixed. It cannot be doubted that he achieved great insight. He offers compelling analyses of many legal concepts that are profoundly important to private law (and to public law as well). For example, his account of representation is arguably rivalled only by that of Hobbes in its sophistication. Any legal theorist interested in conceptual analysis should find engagement with Reinach richly rewarding.

But *how* did Reinach achieve the insights he did? And, where he disclosed important truths about legal concepts, what *kind* of truths are they?

As to the question *how*, I think that most of the fruits of Reinach's labors are attributable to his novel speech act theory of law. It was in recognition that law is constituted partly by social acts that Reinach identified and profitably analyzed the content and conditions requisite to the performative effectiveness of legal notions of *promising*, *granting*, *transferring*, *owning*, *enacting*, *representing*, and so on. He understood that these notions are better understood through a speech act rather than reference theory of meaning (e.g., to understand what promising is, one must understand how it is enacted and what it accomplishes; to understand authorization one must understand acts of authorization and how they beget authority, etc.).

It is difficult to say what additional contribution, if any, is attributable to Reinach's phenomenological method. Reinach is clearer in asserting that there are a priori truths to be discovered phenomenologically about social acts, and in delineating what he takes these truths to be, than he is in explaining how one goes about discovering them. More specifically, it is not clear what the method involves (how it is practiced) and how one could be reasonably confident that one has successfully deployed it (i.e., that one has unearthed a priori truths about law). As noted earlier, Reinach suggests that the method begins with, but entails transcendence of, what is given in human experience. But it is unclear how one could practice contemplation so as to achieve knowledge of transcendent truths about law. And there is a real risk of self-delusion in the aspiration. People are in the habit of developing highly

be subjected to the idea of 'right law' – 'right' from the point of view of morality or of some objective purpose.' Husserl, "Obituary" (n 6) viii.

[14] For instance, the "fact" that promises generate claims and obligations, or that the exercise of powers changes the normative situation of the powerholder and of persons who bear correlative liabilities.

abstract generalizations – synthetic interpretations – based on observation and experience and are prone to the vice of falsely believing them to reflect axiomatic truths. How is one to know that one has in fact achieved transcendent knowledge of truths about law, and not, rather, robust (credible, yet empirically falsifiable) generalizations still very much rooted in experience?

As for the question *what kind* of truths Reinach might have unearthed, it is most probable that they are synthetic a posteriori truths and not, as he believed, synthetic a priori truths. Because the phenomenological method is opaque, one is reluctant to follow Reinach fully through to his conclusion that the formal elements of juridical social acts are true of law a priori. Despite Reinach's insistence upon detachment from positive law and positivistic thought, his analyses of social acts are imbued with insights borne of lawyerly perspectives: the perspectives of those who, like Reinach, are deeply learned in law and versed in the formal technicality of legal semantics and of legal argument. This aperture is at once partial (e.g., not likely to be shared by laypersons) and firmly rooted in experience. Thus, my suggestion that the truths uncovered upon by Reinach are likely a posteriori. Reinach would have doubtless resisted this on the basis that inconsistency in the specification of juridical social acts in positive law is a bar to robust generalization. But these worries are overblown. It is possible to develop robust generalizations from experience of positive law that have truth value (i.e., that may be reasonably believed true, on a synthetic a posteriori basis) without treating every instance of deviation as falsifying the generalization. Rather, it is common – and, I think, perfectly valid – to engage in synthetic interpretation of positive law that aims at rational reconstruction of the formal properties of legal rules and concepts, with the rationality of the reconstruction being a function of its absolute and relative coherence (relative coherence being assessed in terms of the practical point of the rule or concept).

Finally, as intimated earlier, Reinach's insistence upon detachment from knowledge rooted in experience of morality and of positive law put him in the difficult position of claiming to elucidate truths about a normative system and associated normative social practices without being able to ground or otherwise to explain their normativity. The normativity of positive law is often thought to be grounded upon morality as well as the political authority of lawmakers and legal institutions. The normativity of natural law is, in turn, usually thought to be rooted in reasoned appreciation of the objective moral value of the good, the virtuous, and the just. By insisting upon methodological detachment from positive law and morality, Reinach's a priori looms as a phantasm of normativity. Even if one were to allow that it enjoys an epistemic rather than a practical normativity, one worries that that is not the *right sort* of normativity. Juridical social acts are, after all, prescriptive in what they imply of necessity about right conduct (e.g., about the kinds of obligations and claims that promising in fact generates), and not just right ways of thinking (e.g., of forming justified true beliefs about what promising consists in).

7.3 PERSONS

All conceptions of law as a normative system are impliedly premised on a conception of persons (a juristic conception, or set of conceptions, which we may call *legal personality* or *legal personhood*, or *personality* or *personhood*, for short). This is true whether by *law* one means to refer to a priori, natural, or positive law. In positing and in interpreting positive law, lawmakers develop conceptions of persons iteratively, explicitly, and impliedly, for every law necessarily denotes persons as author(s), addressee(s), and/or object(s).

In respect of positive law, the pertinent conception of persons is that which is found in the law as such. In respect of natural law, the conception is at once juristic and moral (and, often, also metaphysical or ontological), with emphasis on the moral status, capacities, and inherent (natural) rights and duties that obtain for human beings generally. As I shall explain, Reinach recognizes that a conception of persons is pivotal to his elucidation of the a priori foundations of law, both in respect of his method and objects of inquiry.[15] However, his treatment of persons is sporadic and unresolved and, by the end of *Foundations* Reinach seemed ambivalent, suggesting that a priori truths about law transcend human experience and the human condition.

Why might Reinach have become ambivalent? And why was his exposition of legal personhood – in marked contrast to his analysis of other legal concepts – sporadic and unresolved? I will suggest that Reinach's ambivalence might have reflected the destabilizing effect of attempting to analyze the concept through his preferred methods. Reinach's speech act theory presupposes personhood but cannot illuminate it, other than indirectly (i.e., insofar as social acts reveal aspects of human nature and the human condition). And his phenomenological method, aimed at elucidation of a priori truths, was believed by him to entail detachment from normative judgments of the sort that imbue positive and natural law alike. Reinach, like so many other jurisprudes of his time and ours, had a real facility with analysis of the legal concepts that delineate jural relations but grave difficulty devising a nonnormative concept of personhood. That is because personhood is, at once, pivotal to our concept of law and ineluctably normative.

But we should begin with the positives, for there are some. Reinach's comments on persons are suggestive. And he is, I think, to be commended for addressing the topic, especially in view of a long-dominant tendency to ignore it.

In a prefatory way, we ought to begin with this tendency of avoidance, for I suspect it has origins in common with the reasons for Reinach's ambivalence. The tendency is especially prominent for jurisprudes in the positivist tradition who are committed to a concept of law rooted in social facts and responsive to what is

[15] Neil Duxbury, 'The Apriori and the Legal,' (1990) 21 Rechtstheorie 297, 301 ("For Reinach, our entire understanding of the *a priori* domain is premised on a specific ontology of the person.").

familiar in our social landscapes (e.g., the relationship between legal and other social rules, and the links between legal and other social practices). Avoidance of talk of persons and personhood by positivists is, in one sense, unsurprising if, as I have claimed, the concept is inherently normative and so exerts pressures on one's commitments to positivism. But it is remarkable given positivists' points of emphasis (on social facts and social practices) and characteristic claims about the concept of law (e.g., that law is a system of peremptory normative guidance traceable to persons or institutions with recognized authority to govern). These points of emphasis and these claims direct attention to what is normatively salient about, and for, persons, viewed in social context. Social facts about law are, after all, facts about persons living in communities that feature legal systems; social rules are authored by persons and they figure in constructed normative systems (systems of social rules); social rules (including legal rules) are addressed to persons and are typically about and involve characterization of persons; and social practices, insofar as they might be shaped by legal and other social rules, are defined by and constituted through the interaction of persons. Positivists' relative neglect of legal personhood is thus glaring, even if it is also predictable.

Reinach is, as I have said, ambivalent about, not neglectful of, legal personhood. And in comparing his approach to that of positivists it bears repeating that Reinach rejects any association with positivists' interest in developing a concept of law that privileges experience with systems of positive law. That said, Reinach's views seem perfectly compatible with certain precepts held in common by many positivists *and* natural lawyers; namely that law is meant to supply practically authoritative normative guidance to persons; that law guides by treating *and* by characterizing persons as amongst its authors, addressees, and objects; that individuals enact generic legal personhood through normative economies of behavior in which law is one currency (alongside others, consisting in norms derived from other sources); and that individuals prove capable of authoring and of being addressed by law through linguistic expression rooted in and reflective of a common human capacity for practical reason.

I think that Reinach was willing to allow (as positivists generally have not) that personhood is pivotal to law in that he recognized, however dimly, a similar set of precepts as underlying his thesis that law is constituted by juridical social acts (enactments, declarations, orders, justifications, promises, waivers, offers, acceptances, hearings, statements, replies, rejoinders, objections, and so on). Reinachian social acts are modalities of normative speech acts through which law is discerned, articulated, and its guidance realized in the context of social practices that exemplify a legal-normative economy (i.e., practices that are intelligible as evincing a legal form of social order).

Reinach seemed to recognize that a conception of persons and, in turn, a juristic notion of personhood, is presupposed by his method and objects of philosophical interest. The phenomenological method presupposes a practitioner: a self-conscious intelligent being possessed of capacities for practical reason and language. And, again, social acts are acts of persons – focally: individual human beings or natural persons – with the same capacities.

Where positivists sidestep, Reinach backs uneasily into the concept of legal personhood, refusing to ignore it even as he was indecisive about it. Reinach's views on persons and legal personhood must be gleaned from scattered references, each of which indicates something different about what it is to be a legal person.[16]

Reinach sometimes treats *legal persons as bearers of entitlements and burdens*, distinguishing persons from things. Whereas things (property) can be the subject matter of claims and obligations, they cannot be *bearers*. To be a legal person is, then, at least in part to be rationally fit or eligible to bear claims and obligations.[17] In turn, Reinach says, claims and obligations are unintelligible absent reference to a person: 'Claim and obligation presuppose universally and necessarily some bearer (*Träger*), some person to whom the claims and obligations belong.'[18]

Elsewhere, Reinach construes *legal persons as agents*, focusing upon a capacity for self-determination. Persons are agents who are or who become self-determining by engaging in juridical social acts, these being 'experiences which not only belong to a self but in which the self *shows itself as active (tätig).*'[19] The capacity for self-determination and hence this facet of legal personhood is construed as inherently social, just as social acts are social. Both contemplate *interpersonal* encounter. Commenting on social acts, Reinach explains that 'in distinction to other spontaneous acts ...[a social act] presupposes in addition to a performing subject a second subject to whom the act of the first subject is directed in a very definite way.'[20] Later, Reinach evocatively suggests that social acts are those 'which, by the one who performs them and *in the performance itself*, are as it were cast towards another person in order to fasten themselves in his soul.'[21] Reinach does not describe legal agency, but he evidently takes it to encompass legal capacities ('abilities' to engage in various particular juridical social acts).[22] His most extensive comments

16 Those whom Reinach influenced had rather more to say about personhood, although many of them – including Edith Stein and Max Scheler – developed disparate views. See Kevin Mulligan, 'Persons and Acts – Collective and Social. From Ontology to Politics,' in Alessandro Salice and Hans Bernard Schmid (eds) *The Phenomenological Approach to Social Reality* (Springer 2016).

17 "That a thing belongs to me is a thoroughly 'natural' relation which is no more artificially produced than is the relation of similarity or of spatial proximity ... There is a bearer of the relation and a 'borne' object. The first can necessarily only be a person and the second only a thing." Reinach, *Foundations* (n 7) 54.

18 ibid 11. See also, ibid, at 12: "Claim and obligation necessarily involve a bearer and a content" and at 102 "only persons can be the holders of rights and obligations."

19 ibid 18 (original emphasis).

20 ibid 19.

21 ibid 20.

22 "It is only through the concept of a legal ability that we are able to understand absolute rights and obligations, and their passing from one person to another." ibid 66.

connecting agency and associated concepts (capacity and power) with legal personality are as follows:

> Social acts such as granting or transferring and the like cannot possibly function as the ultimate source of legal power, for these acts … are themselves always made possible by legal power, and this more basic power must have some other source if we are to avoid a fallacious *regressus in infinitum. Such an ultimate source is in fact present in the person as such* … This gives evidence of a legal power which cannot be derived from any other legal ability but which has as its ultimate origin the person as such. We speak here of the fundamental legal capacity or power of the person … *Insofar as it is grounded in the nature of the person as such, it is inseparable from the person; it forms the ultimate foundation for the possibility of legal-social relationships.*[23]

At yet another juncture Reinach treats *persons as bearers of legal statuses* and of *status-mediated inalienable claims and obligations.* Persons are, viewed from this aspect of personhood, bearers of certain claims and obligations that are absolute, which Reinach suggests indicates something (it is not clear what) definitive and decisive about legal personhood and an individual's enjoyment of same. Being absolute and vested (rather than provisional and/or conditional), claims and obligations mediated by statuses cannot be assigned, granted, waived or otherwise treated as fungible. Illustrating this point, Reinach emphasizes family statuses: 'Let us also recall the *Persönlichkeitsrechte* of the civil law … let us just think of the duties of spouses to each other, and their duties toward their children. None of these rights and duties can be transferred. Whatever is grounded in the person as such or in certain relationships between or among persons, cannot be separated from this ground.'[24]

Reinach's comments on persons and legal personhood are mostly lawyerly. However, an exception is found where he links personhood with self-consciousness and, more specifically, self-aware *experiencing* of juridical social acts as normative. In distinguishing persons from other beings capable of *experience* (e.g., animals), Reinach says: '[b]eing grounded in a supporting subject is something which our legal entities have in common with *experiences* (*Erlebnisse*) of all kinds, for these too always presuppose a subject whose experiences they are. But this class of possible bearers is here much broader; animals too can be the bearers of experiences but never of claims and obligations. Here it is persons who by an essential law are presupposed as bearer.'[25] Put otherwise, persons are beings who have and can reflect insightfully and productively upon an experience of normativity that belongs properly to law. Hence, Reinach's insistence that only human beings are 'persons' a priori, with the implication that artificial persons (e.g., corporations) enjoy

23 ibid 81 (second and third emphasis supplied).

24 ibid 81.

25 ibid 11.

personality only by 'fiction' of positive law.[26] As he puts it: 'It is an essential law that only persons can be holders of rights and obligations. *That a given being is a person is a fact which can never be produced by an efficacious enactment.* When therefore the law recognizes rights and duties in foundations or even in certain estates, we can only be dealing with a fiction in virtue of which such a thing is treated 'as if' it were a person.'[27]

Finally, in tallying Reinach's views, we come to some surprising sentences at the end of *Foundations*. There, despite having acknowledged that persons and legal personhood are pivotal to his project, Reinach seems to deny that any of part of it – the phenomenology, the elucidation of a priori truths about social acts, the extension of both to law – depends in any way on insights about persons, and so, in turn, about human nature and the human condition. A priori truths about law, Reinach now urges, transcend everything that is given in experience, including the qualities of being human and modes of experiencing normativity that are uniquely available to us in virtue of our humanity:

> We can no longer be led astray by the idea that the essential laws of right, even if they do not depend on men for their validity, nevertheless refer exclusively to men. It is true that we only know of social acts performed by men, only of rights and obligations held by men. But the essential laws which we understand with certainty are not grounded in the fact that these men or some men or other perform the acts and hold the rights and obligations, but are rather grounded in the essence of the acts and in the essence of relations of right, no matter when and where they are realized. They hold not only for our world but for any conceivable world.[28]

This surprise turn, being inconsistent with Reinach's other comments on persons and legal personhood, might be dismissed as aberrational. It *is* an aberration. But it deserves attention because it is telling of wider and deeper problems with Reinach's method and with the analyses he provides of personality and representation.

Let me introduce three problems with Reinach's account of personality, some of which reflect limitations of his method and, specifically, his ambition to discover a

[26] ibid 124. Reinach treats the personification of foundations and other legal institutions as an example of how lawmakers can achieve by mere "enactment" a state of affairs that diverges from what is true (here, of persons) a priori, noting that "there are … undoubtedly *deviations (Abweichungen)* of the enactments from essentially given relations of right." ibid at 104 (original emphasis). For discussion of corporate personality and representation relative to the function of the corporate form in enabling cooperation for common (corporate) purposes, see Paul B Miller, 'Corporate Personality, Purpose, and Liability,' in Elizabeth Pollman and Robert Thompson (eds) *Research Handbook on Corporate Purpose and Personhood* (Elgar 2021).

[27] Reinach, Foundations (n 7) 128 (emphasis supplied). Reinach considers but equivocates on the question whether, as a matter of social ontology independent of positive law, corporations, states and other groups might be persons or have social-ontological indicia of personhood, and hence in that sense might be "real" persons, whatever their juridical status a priori and/or as a matter of positive law. Ibid at 129.

[28] ibid 138.

priori truths about law, the truth-value of which obtains independently of considerations of morality and of positive law.

The first problem, already noted, is that Reinach does not give us a cohesive account of the a priori essentials of legal personality. Given Reinach's predominant tendency to view persons and personhood as central to his project, it is striking that his thoughts are unresolved. As Neil Duxbury has noted, this is a significant lacuna in Reinach's thought.[29] One does not find in *Foundations* a single clear paragraph or page in which he explains the essentials of personhood, what it is about persons that enable us to appreciate a priori truths about law and other things, and/or how the formal properties of legal personhood prefigure and are manifested in the social acts of actual persons. Reinach does usefully highlight important facets of legal personhood: agency, the bearing of claims and obligations, and the bearing of statuses, these being features prominent in positive law.[30] However, Reinach does not even gesture at the relationship between these facets of legal personhood, much less does he show that they are jointly constitutive of personhood viewed a priori.

The second problem is that some of Reinach's characterizations of persons and legal personhood – offered as a priori truths – defy the strictures of his phenomenological method, being best construed as either (a) a posteriori synthetic truths (or statements that are plausibly true) about received conceptions of persons in broader culture and of legal persons as characterized in positive law; (b) *sub silentio* moral judgments about features of human nature and/or of the human condition that are pertinent to law; and/or (c) both (a) and (b). Each of these alternatives is a plausible candidate for assessing Reinach's claim that persons are distinguished from non-persons (including animals and things) insofar as the former but not the latter are proper bearers of claims, obligations, and statuses. The same holds for Reinach's claim that agency and self-determination are essential to legal personhood (on which, see also his assertion that persons have an absolute 'moral entitlement' to personal development[31]). And consider Reinach's suggestion that self-conscious experience of normativity is essential to personhood. If this capacity is linked to our ability to discern what is true a priori about law, and so to understand and to

[29] Neil Duxbury, 'The Legal Philosophy of Adolf Reinach (II),' (1991) 77 Archiv für Rechts-und Sozialphilosophie 466, 466–467 ("Reinach's position [is] . . . that the law can only come about due to the fundamental capacities of the person . . . [and so it is] remarkable that Reinach attributes so little discussion to the fundamental capacity of the person.").

[30] Paul B Miller, 'The Concept of Personality in Private Law,' in Samuel L Bray, John CP Goldberg, Paul B Miller, and Henry E. Smith, (eds) *Interstitial Private Law* (Oxford University Press 2024).

[31] Reinach, *Foundations* (n 7) 13, where Reinach notes that certain absolute moral obligations and claims, such as "the right to develop one's personality . . . have [their] ground in the person as such . . . [and] can never be grounded in arbitrary acts" such as spontaneous juridical social acts through which persons can generate and transfer legal obligations with the implication that "it is impossible for a person to transfer to another his moral entitlement to free personal development." This is because one "cannot abolish by an arbitrary act what is grounded in the nature of a person or in the relation of one person to others."

participate in *its* pure normativity, self-conscious discernment of the a priori must be dissociable from self-aware participation in other normative systems (e.g., of positive law, conventional morality, or true morality). But this begs questions of comprehensibility. What is this experience of a pure, transcendent normativity like? Reinach does not say. And perhaps he does not say because knowledge of a genuine practical normativity that is utterly detached from morality is unavailable to us.

The third and final problem is the incoherence introduced by Reinach's concluding comments to the effect that the a priori foundations of law are true independently of truths about persons and are valid 'not only for our world for any conceivable world.' One way of coping with indecision is minimization of the significance of a matter for decision. So, if persons and legal personality proved a conundrum for Reinach, one can understand his caving in to impulse in suggesting that his project is unaffected by his inability to come to terms with the notions. But the dodge is glaring because Reinach had already articulated powerful reasons for thinking it to be of central importance to his work. Briefly, again: (a) the phenomenological method implies the existence of self-conscious beings – persons – who are aware of and can access and reflect productively on social experience of normativity; (b) social acts are acts of persons, and moreover, reflect distinctively human capacities (practical reason and language); and (c) juridical social acts are, ipso facto, also acts of persons.

By suggesting that 'men' (human beings) are immaterial to the a priori foundations of law, Reinach introduces a host of difficult and unanswered questions. For instance: in what sense is law intelligible absent reference to the focal exemplar of a person – a human being – and of legal personhood? And, supposing that law might be intelligible for nonhuman beings or entities, what analogues of human nature and the human condition must be true of such a being or entity for something like law to be intelligible as a mode of order? Further: why should we suppose that nonhuman beings in '*any* conceivable world' would have need of or use for law?

The destabilizing effect of these questions for Reinach's project may be best appreciated through reflection on a hypothetical. Imagine, at opposite ends of a spectrum, beings who have bodies like ours but have hive minds (i.e., collective consciousness, motivations, intentions, and other cognitions) and beings whose minds are like ours but whose bodies are protected by an impenetrable carapace, both in environments in which resources essential to meeting needs and desires are plentiful. Would these beings experience and know of what Reinach deems to be the a priori essentials of promising? What need would the hive-minded have for promising? For them, solidarity and, in turn, cooperation and coordination, are instinctive. What impulse would drive the carapace-embodied to promising, lacking need-based motivation to promise or the sense of risk latent in interpersonal dependence and vulnerability consequent upon transactions that we, soft-bodied, beings often experience? What need would either species have for private ownership, given an abundance of goods and the impulse of the hive-minded to put the needs of the hive first, alongside the impulse of the carapace-embodied to delight in opportunistic satiation, free of the worst sort of credible threats of violent dispossession? The point is not that these beings would have *no* need for laws, nor even that their laws would be completely unlike ours (they might still benefit from laws somewhat like ours that facilitate cooperation or coordination). The point is that Reinach's concluding assertion that his account of the a priori foundations of law hold for nonhuman beings and for all possible worlds is dubious. When one strips important features of human nature and the human condition away from the concepts of 'person' and 'law,' it is not clear what, if anything, is left for common signification by these terms.

7.4 REPRESENTATION

If Reinach's analysis of persons reveals limits of his phenomenological method, his analysis of representation shows those limits, too, while also exemplifying the methodological promise held by his speech act theory of law. Where Reinach hesitatingly and sporadically expressed views on persons and legal personhood, he was comparatively (and characteristically) direct and confident on representation. Indeed, his account is rivalled only by Hobbes' in the way in which it illuminates the nature of the specifically *legal* form (as contrasted with social and political forms) of representation.

Reinach begins by critically examining a positivistic view of representation as an artificial mode of social action: one foreign to extralegal social experience,[32] being something conjured and regulated by positive law. The positivistic view does not claim, implausibly, that we have no extralegal concept(s) of representation. Rather, the thought is that the positive law leads with its artifice, shaping downstream social practices and beliefs. Through increasing familiarity with mechanisms of representation in public law (e.g., via laws creating and regulating public offices) and in private law (e.g., via laws enabling private administration of persons, property, and institutions) we have come to develop rough analogues of legal representation in extralegal spheres of social life (i.e., in informal social practices of speaking or acting for others).

Reinach recognizes the intuitive appeal of the positivistic view but rejects it as 'fundamentally wrong.'[33] Representation is, he maintains, a distinctive kind of juridical social act cognizable a priori.[34] By implication, the essential formal properties of representation have nothing to do with positive law; one can understand

[32] Reinach, *Foundations* (n 7) 81–84. "On this view we really do have here an institution which exists 'by the grace of the positive law'." ibid 82.

[33] ibid 83.

[34] ibid 25: noting first the wider genus of which representation is a species, namely, acts by proxy: "[there is a] difference between those social acts which are performed by their subject and those which are performed by a proxy. There is such a thing as commanding, informing,

them without canvassing the various mechanisms of representation found in or made available by private or public law. Indeed, Reinach suggests, experience of 'acting on behalf of another' is a commonplace in extralegal settings in which people speak up for, attend to the interests of, assert claims for, answer for, or otherwise put themselves in the position of another.

Before analyzing representation, Reinach carefully distinguishes it from other modes of conduct in which one is deliberately responsive to the ends or interests of another, all falling under a wide genus of social action undertaken 'on behalf of another.' Amongst other things, he distinguishes representation from mandate, command, commission, and advisement. Each of the latter kinds of social act involves 'action on behalf of another,' in the sense of deliberate responsiveness to the ends or interests of another, but none involves representation in the sense governed by its essential formal properties.

In comparing representation with adjacent varieties of juridical social action, Reinach insightfully suggests that they have in common the engagement of a capacity for attentiveness to others consisting in 'inner experiences' of sympathetic attunement. Attunement, Reinach emphasizes, is *not* merely a matter of deciphering and/or being motivated to act according to another's intentions. Rather, it involves 'feeling oneself sympathetically into the experiencing of another.'[35] Sympathetic attunement, so understood, encompasses sharing in the perspective of another with respect to their views, plans (including intentions), feelings, interests, prospects for flourishing, and so on. Importantly, it *does not* imply endorsement, acceptance, or personal identification otherwise with another's experience (these being distortions of sympathy: a substitution of *appraisal* for *understanding* another's experience).

On representation specifically, Reinach notes that, like all social acts, it encompasses 'internal' and 'external' dimensions. *Authentic* social acts reflect continuity between the 'internal experience' of the act by the actor and 'external experience' of it by others. *Inauthentic* social acts are those in which the internal experience is discontinuous with the external experience (e.g., reflecting mistake or deception). For example, one whose behavior bears outward indicia of representative action will be a *false* representative if their internal experience is one of self-concern (e.g., one poses as a representative in order to evade liability) rather than sympathetic attunement.[36] Here, too, Reinach breaks ground, anticipating later work distinguishing *vires* and *fides* in representative action. He suggests, plausibly, that although improperly motivated representation might be effective (lawful), it is *inauthentic as*

requesting 'in the name of another' ... the proxy performs the act quite personally, but in such a way that the act is presented as ultimately proceeding from another person."

35 ibid 84.

36 For discussion of Reinach on the internal and external dimensions of representation, see James M Brown, 'Reinach on Representative Acts,' in Kevin Mulligan, (ed) *Speech Act and Sachverhalt: Reinach and the Foundations of Realist Phenomenology* (Kluwer 1987) 126–128.

representation precisely in virtue of a discontinuity between internal and external dimensions of ostensibly representative behavior.

Somewhat less innovative is Reinach's characterization of representation as such. Here, one finds plentiful echoes of Hobbes' thought. Reinach observes that representation entails the performance of the very juridical social acts that individuals usually and presumptively undertake personally. Representation modifies attribution of the legal consequences, but not the legal nature, of juridical social acts. Just as we can *directly* shape the normative landscape within which we are positioned vis-à-vis others by personally performing juridical social acts (e.g., by promising, claiming, exercising a power, or waiving a right) so too can we do so *indirectly* through representatives who bear our person. It is thus that representation is correctly understood in terms of capacities ('abilities,' in Reinachian lingo) and powers. Representatives personate others by acting upon their normative capacities and powers. Furthermore, Reinach emphasizes, representation can be effective absent the represented person having specific knowledge, much less settled intentions, in respect of particular juridical social acts performed on their behalf by a representative.[37] Representatives wield standing authority: an authority that is prior to and that transcends representative performance of discrete juridical social acts.

Further on authority: Reinach recognizes that one cannot fully comprehend representation by focusing on the position and behavior of representatives alone. Representation is premised on bilateral or multilateral relationships that bind representatives and persons represented. Legal representation implies the legal authority to act for others, which in turn means that it is premised on *constating juridical social acts*. Reinach considers and rightly dismisses the notion that the pertinent act is *transferring* or *promising*. Transferring effectuates alienation of resources and alienable entitlements, while promising effectuates personal undertakings; neither can explain the third-party effects that are essential to representation (the representative's authority to exercise entitlements and to incur burdens for represented person(s) vis-à-vis others). The pertinent constating act is, instead, *granting*.[38] Representation arises when represented persons *grant* to representatives the authority to act on their behalf, with the implication that juridical social acts subsequently performed by representatives will be attributed to represented persons as having been *authorized* by them.[39]

[37] In representation "an extraordinary thing happens: rights and obligations arise, change, and come to an end in the person of the other without him having even to suspect it himself." Reinach, *Foundations* (n 7) 85.

[38] "The problem of efficacy of representation comes down to this: how can a person acquire such a power? There is only one person who can grant it, namely the person in whom the legal effects are supposed to come about. Whoever can by his acts produce and modify rights and obligations in his own person, can perform an act which grants this power to others. This act is of course not a transferring – the one who performs this act does not forfeit his power in the least – but rather a purely creative granting." ibid 86.

[39] "Two things are set up by this act: a legal power (*Können*) and something which we would better designate as a legal ability (*Fähigkeit*)." ibid 92.

Reinach has rather less to say about representation 'in action,' perhaps because he (correctly) believes that juridical social acts undertaken representatively are usually formally identical to those undertaken personally. However, one finds fresh insight in Reinach's distinction between active and passive dimensions of representation, tracking a broader distinction between active and passive social acts. Certain juridical social acts (e.g., promising, claiming, waiving) are *active* in that they involve the deliberate exercise of a legal capacity in ways that are *patently* performative. Others – especially *responsive* juridical social acts (e.g., receipt, acknowledgement, acceptance, acquiescence) – tend to be passive or *less patently* performative. Reinach innovates in observing that both are important modalities of representation.[40]

With the essentials of his account of representation now in view, we may take stock. As noted, Reinach's is one the most compelling accounts ever provided of the nature of *legal* representation. His account echoes that of Hobbes in its rendition of the nature of representation,[41] but this is to his credit: Hobbes and Reinach landed at the same place from divergent glide paths, giving additional reason for confidence that we've arrived with them at something approximating the truth about what representation consists of. Furthermore, there is much that is original in Reinach's analysis. His speech act theoretical method enabled him to surface facets of representation that others miss, including (a) the 'internal experience' of representation via sympathetic attunement and the expectation of continuity between it and the more familiar 'external experience' of representation through observation of juridical social acts; (b) the distinction and relationship between *constating* juridical social acts *establishing* representation (authorizing acts) and *performative* juridical social acts *of* representation (representing acts); and (c) in respect of the latter, the distinction and relationship between active and passive social acts undertaken by representatives.

Despite being mostly convincing, Reinach's analysis does have a few flaws. I will highlight three.

The first is that Reinach's account is likely not what it purports to be. That is, it is not an elucidation of a priori truths about representation. As noted in Section 7.2, Reinach has not given us a convincing reason to think his phenomenological method results in statements about law that have *this sort* of truth-value. That is partly because the method is poorly described, and also because, unlike laws of science and of mathematics, the a priori status of truths about the formal properties of social acts does not reveal itself to us, even upon prolonged reflection. But one

[40] ibid 91: "We distinguish between the performance of [juridical social] acts and their being heard by the addressee, which is what alone gives rise to the effect of the act. Here, too, there is such a thing as representation."

[41] For more on Hobbes' views on representation and how they illuminate contemporary law and practice of fiduciary administration, see Paul B Miller, 'Fiduciary Representation,' in Evan J Criddle et al, (eds) *Fiduciary Government* (Cambridge University Press 2018).

ought not to despair over this. If one can be contented with apprehension of a posteriori synthetic truths about law – robust generalizations informed by experience of positive law – one will find good reason for appreciation of Reinach's analysis of representation.

The second flaw is really an entire set of problems that Reinach's account of representation inherits from his analysis of personality. As Reinach recognizes, representation involves *personation*: legal representatives bear the legal person(s) of those whom they are authorized to represent. Representation is therefore unintelligible absent reference to persons and social acts, the latter being a form of communicative behavior for which human beings are by our nature uniquely fit. Defects in one's views on persons and legal personality may be expected to have ripple effects for one's account of legal representation. And so it proves for Reinach. I will note just a few issues. First, because Reinach does not provide a coherent account of the essential formal properties of legal personhood, it is unclear whether and how the various facets of personhood that he mentions are manifested in the social acts through which representation is established (constating acts) and made effective (representing acts). Second, Reinach's evocative suggestion that the 'internal experience' of representation involves sympathetic attunement requires an account of the moral capacities of human beings such as might support the claims (a) that persons are capable of sympathetic attunement; and (b) that authentic representation entails such attunement. Reinach here runs aground, again, as a result of his deliberate refusal to comment on the distinctive moral status, anthropology, and psychology of human beings. Third, we can perhaps now better appreciate the absurdity in Reinach's concluding suggestion that persons and personhood are immaterial to a priori truths about juridical social acts. Reinach's references to sympathetic attunement imply the existence of beings with a capacity for same, much as his wider theory of social acts implies other capacities (notably, of language and practical reason) that are distinctively human. Reinach's ambivalence on persons destabilizes the entire edifice of his theory of social acts.

Fourth and finally, because Reinach was so preoccupied with phenomenological elucidation of a priori truths about *law* that transcend experience, Reinach failed adequately to consider points of similarity and difference between legal representation and adjacent modes of relating to others through sympathetic attunement. In this, his work is out of step with more recent studies – including Pitkin's celebrated work[42] – that emphasize semantic and phenomenological variation in relationships of 'representation' (relationships in which a person or group is said to represent, or to be representative of, other persons or groups). Reinach asserts that representation in the narrower sense of interest to him is familiar from extralegal experience. Everyday life, he says, supplies examples of situations in which one claims standing to speak or to act for another. But given his narrow and lofty

[42] Hanna Pitkin, *The Concept of Representation* (University of California Press 1972).

gaze – his aim, again, for *transcendent* truths about *law* – Reinach does not consider that some of these situations might involve representation in a materially different sense, or modes of care and concern for others that do not involve representation in any sense. In some, the experience of attunement and assertion of standing to speak or act for another is *spontaneous* and *unilateral*. That is, the 'representative' *presumes* to speak for, advocate on behalf of, defend, or otherwise align themselves with another. In others, there is a more innocent (less officious) identification with another that involves attunement and responsive behavior (acts of care and concern). It is, of course, fine for Reinach to focus on distinctively *legal* representation, but given that his phenomenological method compels a finer attention to experience, his exposition would have been more plausible had he contemplated different varieties of representation and forms of behavior reflecting sympathetic attunement.

7.5 CONCLUSION

My assessment of Reinach's contributions is mixed. Praise for his speech act theoretical method is leavened by criticism of his phenomenological method (especially his central claim to have disclosed a priori synthetic truths about the nature of law). Likewise, I have suggested that Reinach's largely convincing speech act theoretical rendition of representation is marred by his irresolution on persons and personhood. While most work of legal theory can be faulted for ignoring ontological, moral, and juridical questions about persons and personhood, Reinach's work surprises, excites, and disappoints, especially because puzzles about persons and personhood go to the very core of what is original and insightful in *Foundations*.

Reinach surprises in forthrightly recognizing the centrality of persons and legal personhood to his project (its methods and aims). He recognizes that law is not *merely* a construct of reason (a set of artifacts, to be equated with institutions and their workings, and especially the generation and interpretation of legal texts); it is also – and more primordially – a system of norms that implicate normative *practices* constituted in and through normative *performances* (social acts). He recognizes, too, that these practices, these performances, these acts (and, one might add, the workings of institutions and the communication of, and about, law through authoritative text) are the practices, performances, and acts of *persons* (i.e., of intelligent linguistic beings possessed of a capacity for practical reason manifested in law). With these insights foremost in mind, one might initially be struck with excitement upon reading Reinach's first comments on persons and personhood, imagining, perhaps, that promised 'truths' about the 'foundations' of law will include insights about how law is, at once, *possible* and *necessary* for persons, given other, more fundamental, truths about human nature and the human condition. These truths might disclose what law *is* partly by disclosing what it is *for* (i.e., how law is practically intelligible relative to its practical point or purpose(s)).

If one were to judge him harshly, one would say that Reinach disappoints on most of these expectations. He does not provide a cohesive account of persons and legal personhood, and is averse to questions about how legal rules and concepts are or ought to be rooted in normatively significant facts about human nature and the human condition. Reinach believed, mistakenly, but sincerely, that truths about law – including, presumably, about the law's concept of a person – are normatively neutral (i.e., that they imply nothing about the moral status of persons or about what human beings have reason to value in and beyond the reliance we place on law as a source of authoritative normative guidance). While Reinach alights upon various facets of legal personhood that are important to a sound positivistic rendering of the notion, he has nothing to say about the more profound questions noted above (e.g., about how law is possible and necessary for persons, or what law is *for*). A harsh critic might say that the return on investment in Reinach consists mainly in the interest held by speech act theoretical analyses of law *and* in productive deployment of that method in the analysis of particular legal concepts (e.g., promising, enacting, granting, representing, and so on).

But one should not judge Reinach harshly. Viewed charitably, he may be credited with marshalling phenomenological methods so as to humanize law: to put lived experience at the center of our understanding of law and appreciation of the proper aims of legal theory. In turn, Reinach may be credited with profound insights about the nature of law that were won only through recognition that law is constituted through speech acts (social acts). Further, while his thinking on persons and personhood remained indefinite, Reinach clearly realized that phenomenological insights about law and other modes of social action are the insights of persons gleaned through human experience, and, in turn, that posited law is a construct dependent upon an apt marshalling of distinctively human capacities in ways responsive to our common humanity.

BIBLIOGRAPHY

Brown, JM, 'Reinach on Representative Acts,' in K Mulligan (ed) *Speech Act and Sachverhalt: Reinach and the Foundations of Realist Phenomenology* (Kluwer 1987)

Duxbury, N, 'The Apriori and the Legal,' (1990) 21 Rechtstheorie 297

'The Legal Philosophy of Adolf Reinach (II),' (1991) 77 Archiv für Rechtsund Sozialphilosophie 466

Husserl, E, 'Obituary for Adolf Reinach,' reprinted in Adolf Reinach, *The Apriori Foundations of the Civil Law* (John F. Crosby tr, Ontos Verlag 2012)

Miller, PB, 'Fiduciary Representation,' in EJ Criddle et al (eds) *Fiduciary Government* (Cambridge University Press 2018)

'Corporate Personality, Purpose, and Liability,' in E Pollman and R Thompson (eds) *Research Handbook on Corporate Purpose and Personhood* (Elgar 2021)

'The Concept of Personality in Private Law,' in SL Bray, JCP Goldberg PB Miller and HE Smith (eds) *Interstitial Private Law* (Oxford University Press 2024) 179

Mulligan, K, 'Persons and Acts: Collective and Social. From Ontology to Politics,' in A Salice and HB Schmid (eds) *The Phenomenological Approach to Social Reality* (Springer 2016)

Pitkin, HF, *The Concept of Representation* (University of California Press 1972)

Raz, J, *The Authority of Law* (Oxford University Press 2009)

Reinach, A, 'The Apriori Foundations of the Civil Law' (John F Crosby tr, 1983) 3 Aletheia 1–142, reprinted in Adolf Reinach, *The Apriori Foundations of the Civil Law Along with the Lecture 'Concerning Phenomenology'* (John F Crosby ed, Ontos Verlag 2012), originally published as Adolf Reinach, Die apriorischen Grundlagen des bürgerlichen Rechtes, 1(2) *Jahrbuch für Philosophie und phänomenologische Forschung* (Max Niemeyer 1913), 685–847

Ripstein, A, *Force and Freedom* (Harvard University Press 2009)

Private Wrongs (Harvard University Press 2016)

Salice, A and Uemura, G, 'Social Acts and Communities: Walther between Husserl and Reinach,' in A Calcagno (ed) *Gerda Walther's Phenomenology of Sociality, Psychology, and Religion* (Springer 2018)

Weinrib, EJ, *The Idea of Private Law* (Harvard University Press 1995)

Zahavi, D, *Husserl's Legacy: Phenomenology, Metaphysics, and Transcendental Philosophy* (Oxford University Press 2017)

8

The Ontology of Liberties

Reconciling Reinach and Hohfeld

Olivier Massin

The year 1913 saw the publication of two foundational works of legal theory: Hohfeld's 'Some Fundamental Legal Conceptions as Applied in Judicial Reasoning'[1] and Reinach's *A Priori Foundations of Civil Law*.[2] Hohfeld's paper, introducing his famous taxonomy of rights, proved to be more influential than Reinach's.[3] While Reinach's text has been praised for his pioneering elucidation of social acts (promising, commanding, granting, transferring, allowing, enacting), his thorough accounts of moral and nonmoral rights and obligations, of ownership and of legal representation have all been largely overlooked. This is unfortunate: Reinach's *Foundations* contains a myriad of insights, some of which reveal and permit correction of deficiencies in Hohfeld's taxonomy of rights. In this chapter, I focus on what is arguably the most basic disagreement between Hohfeld's and Reinach's ontologies of rights. The disagreement concerns the kind of rights that Hohfeld calls 'liberties' and Reinach calls 'absolute rights'. Reinach and Hohfeld both argue that the category of right should be divided between claim rights (for instance, claims that ensue from promises) and liberty rights (for instance, freedom of trade). Both characterize claim rights in a very similar manner, emphasizing that claims are necessarily correlated with an obligation of a counterparty. But they disagree on the topic of liberties. Hohfeld assumes from the outset that all rights are relations and maintains consequently that all liberties have correlatives. He calls these correlatives 'no-rights', for lack of a better term. Reinach, for his part,

[1] Wesley Newcomb Hohfeld, 'Some Fundamental Legal Conceptions as Applied in Judicial Reasoning' (1913) 23 Yale Law Journal 16.

[2] Adolf Reinach, 'The Apriori Foundations of the Civil Law' (John F Crosby tr, 1983) 3 Aletheia 1, reprinted in Adolf Reinach, *The Apriori Foundations of the Civil Law Along with the Lecture 'Concerning Phenomenology'* (John F Crosby ed, Ontos Verlag 2012), originally published as Adolf Reinach, Die apriorischen Grundlagen des bürgerlichen Rechtes, 1(2) *Jahrbuch für Philosophie und phänomenologische Forschung* (Max Niemeyer 1913), 685–847.

[3] That text was followed in 1917 by a second text with nearly the same title: Wesley Newcomb Hohfeld, 'Fundamental Legal Conceptions as Applied in Judicial Reasoning' (1917) 26 Yale Law Journal 710.

maintains that in contrast to claims, liberties essentially lack correlatives and counterparties, which is why he calls them 'absolute rights'.

Who is right? Do liberties have or lack correlatives? I argue that both Reinach and Hohfeld overgeneralized an initially correct insight: Reinach is right, *pace* Hohfeld, that some liberties are absolute, but wrong that all are. Hohfeld is right, *pace* Reinach, that some liberties have no-rights as correlatives, but wrong that all liberties have such correlatives. The argument will be developed as follows. After having stressed some striking similarities between Reinach's and Hohfeld's ontologies of rights in Section 8.1, I characterize in Section 8.2 the notion of legal correlatives in terms of converse relations. Section 8.3 explains why duties of noninterference cannot be the legal correlative of liberties, a point on which Reinach and Hohfeld agree. I next present in Section 8.4 Hohfeld's proposal according to which the correlative of liberties are no-rights, and defend it against three objections. Section 8.5 argues, this time against Hohfeld, that some liberties, in particular property rights, lack counterparties. Reinach's proposal according to which liberties have no correlatives is presented in Section 8.6 and criticized in Section 8.7. Finally, in Section 8.8, I propose an encompassing ontology of rights which welcomes both relative and absolute liberties.

8.1 REINACH AND HOHFELD: SIMILARITIES

Before delving into the main disagreement between Hohfeld and Reinach, it is worth emphasizing some striking commonalities between their two projects. Both consider the legal practices and scholarship of their time to be riddled with confusion. As a result, they both set out to clarify key legal concepts by drawing overlooked distinctions. In doing so, they engage in research from an a priori perspective: both are optimistic that a priori legal reasoning can help disentangle important conflations and discover fundamental distinctions between legal entities. Admittedly, Reinach is more of a committed a priori essentialist than Hohfeld is. Reinach thinks that legal phenomena have essences that can be grasped a priori. Reinach's famous claim that 'Positive law finds the legal concepts which enter into it; *in absolutely no way does it produce them*'[4] finds no counterpart in Hohfeld, who has little patience for metaphysical inquiries.[5] The idea of prelegal rights is not just absent from Hohfeld's approach, but appears to be excluded by his assumption that all jural relations 'take their significance' from positive law.[6]

Yet, Hohfeld also uses essentialist expressions. Hohfeld's repeated claims that legal discussions of his times 'are not founded on a sufficiently comprehensive and discriminating analysis of jural relations in general', and that we should strive for 'clear understanding' of these, presuppose that the relevant understanding is provided

4 Reinach (n 2) 4.
5 Hohfeld (n 1) 20, 44.
6 Hohfeld (n 3) 721.

not by positive law alone, but that some other source of legal knowledge lies beyond positive law. Remarkably, both Reinach and Hohfeld are skeptical of reductive analyses or definitions. They thus both adopt a primitivist approach. In this approach, basic legal entities cannot be reduced to nonlegal entities. This does not mean, however, that nothing can be said about them. Both believe that instead of analyzing into components, one can explain them by bringing out their various relationships with other legal and nonlegal entities. Thus, Hohfeld maintains that rights cannot be strictly speaking defined: they are *sui generis* legal relations. The elucidation of these phenomena is not a matter of defining them, but rather of showing the various relationships that they have with other phenomena:

> The strictly fundamental legal relations are, after all, *sui generis*; and thus it is that attempts at formal definition are always unsatisfactory, if not altogether useless. Accordingly, the most promising line of procedure seems to consist in exhibiting all of the various relations in a scheme of "opposites" and "correlatives", and then proceeding to exemplify their individual scope and application in concrete cases.[7]

Reinach, likewise, maintains that rights cannot be defined and are instead best understood in terms of essential connections between them:

> It is a sign of a philosophically misshapen mind to demand definitions where none are possible or have any value. [. . .] With regard to owning, [. . .] it is not possible to penetrate into it by listing certain immanent elements of it, for we have to do here with something ultimate, with something which is not composed out of other things. It is, as Descartes rightly remarks, "perhaps one of the main errors which one can commit in the sciences to try to define what can only be seen through itself". [. . .] And so we decline to attempt a definition of rights and of obligations.[8]

In this respect, Reinach and Hohfeld both adopt a descriptive approach to the ontology of rights, as contrasted with a reductive one (such as the will theory or interest theory of rights).[9]

The affinities between Reinach and Hohfeld are both substantive and methodological. In their typologies of law, Hohfeld and Reinach often independently arrive at exactly the same distinctions. For example, each emphasizes a distinction between legal phenomena and the nonlegal phenomena that determine legal phenomena. Reinach emphasizes that promises and other social acts are not themselves legal but natural phenomena which nevertheless, by their very nature, ground or generate different kinds of rights.[10] Likewise, Hohfeld insists on the

7 Hohfeld (n 1) 30.

8 Reinach (n 2) 65.

9 Kathrin Koslicki and Olivier Massin, 'A Plea for Descriptive Social Ontology' (2023) 202 Synthese 59.

10 Reinach (n 2) 13, 81 even uses the fact that some rights can arise from free acts – promises, transfer, orders . . . – to distinguish nonmoral rights from moral ones; the former only can be modified by free acts.

existence of operative facts which 'under the general legal rules that are applicable, suffice to change legal relations, that is, either to create a new relation, or to extinguish an old one, or to perform both of these functions simultaneously'.[11] Relatedly, both insist on the distinction between possession and ownership.[12] However, they disagree on the nature of ownership. For Hohfeld, ownership is a legal phenomenon, a bundle of rights. For Reinach, by contrast, ownership is not a bundle of rights itself, but rather the basis of property rights.[13] Additionally, both Reinach and Hohfeld elaborate the distinction between physical and legal power.[14] Both define legal power as the power to modify the realm or rights:

REINACH: A [legal] power reveals itself in the fact that the action to which it refers, produces an immediate effect in the world of right *(rechtliche Wirkung)*, for example, produces, modifies, or eliminates claims and obligations.[15]

HOHFELD: A change in a given legal relation may result (1) from some superadded fact or group of facts not under the volitional control of a human being (or human beings); or (2) from some superadded fact or group of facts which are under the volitional control of one or more human beings. As regards the second class of cases, the person (or persons) whose volitional control is paramount may be said to have the (legal) power to effect the particular change of legal relations that is involved in the problem.[16]

Reinach and Hohfeld also both distinguish between legal powers and what Hohfeld calls liabilities and Reinach calls (admittedly less systematically) legal abilities (*Fähigkeiten*),[17] that is, the capacities of having one's rights impacted by the social acts of other persons. Finally, and crucially for this chapter, both stress the distinction between claim rights and liberty rights. Moreover, both characterize the correlative of claim rights in the very same way, as we shall see. But liberty rights are also the chief locus of divergence between their ontologies of rights.

8.2 THE NOTION OF LEGAL CORRELATIVES

Both Reinach and Hohfeld propose to divide rights into claims and liberties (which Reinach calls 'absolute rights'). Thus, Hohfeld argues that *liberties* (which he also calls *privileges*) should be distinguished from *claims* or *rights* in the strict sense. Reinach draws the very same distinction between claims and absolute rights.

[11] Hohfeld (n 1) 25.
[12] Hohfeld (n 1) 721.
[13] Reinach's position on this matter is presented and defended by Olivier Massin, 'The Metaphysics of Ownership: A Reinachian Account' (2017) 27 Axiomathes 577.
[14] Reinach (n 2) 53. Hohfeld (n 1) 52.
[15] Reinach (n 2) 66.
[16] Hohfeld (n 1) 44.
[17] Reinach (n 2) 92.

A common example of a claim, for each of them, is a promissory or contractual claim. For instance, if Eve promises Bob to come to dinner, Bob has the right to have Eve come to dinner. A typical example of a liberty, for each of them, is a property right. For example, because Eve owns her bike, she has the liberty to use it as she wishes. Other liberties include freedom of speech, trade, movement, and religion. Firstly, let us focus on claims. Reinach and Hohfeld agree that claims have correlatives, which are relative duties or obligations. For example, if Paul is entitled to Julie buying him a beer, then Julie has a correlative obligation to buy him a beer. Similarly, if Margaret has a claim against Bob that he washes her car, then Bob has a correlative obligation to wash her car. Reinach offers a description of the various elements of claims and relative duties that helps us capture their relation:

(i) All claims and correlative duties have a *holder*: they are claims and duties of someone.
(ii) All claims and correlative duties have a *counterparty*, *addressee*, or *destinee*: they are held against/relative to/towards/versus/vis-à-vis somebody distinct from their holder.
(iii) All claims and correlative duties have a *deontic force:* namely, they are either claims or duties.
(iv) All claims and correlative duties have *contents* (Hohfeld also speaks of 'tenor'): they are claims or duties to do something or to get something done.

On the whole, claims and correlative duties are of the form:

1. X has a claim against Y to the effect that Y Fs.
2. Y has a duty towards X to the effect that Y Fs.

Where 'X' and 'Y' stand for the parties, and 'Fs' stands for Y's action (e.g., 'X sings'). The relation between claims and obligations provides a paradigmatic and uncontroversial example of 'correlativity'. But how exactly should we understand the relation of legal correlativity in general? That question is crucial for our present purposes. To determine whether liberties have correlatives or not, one needs to be clear about the nature of correlativity.

Reinach stresses that correlative claims and obligations have the very same content (here: that Y Fs).[18] Accordingly, a first proposal here is that legal correlatives must have the same content (a point which Kramer rightly rehearses in a recent paper).[19] Second, both Reinach and Hohfeld stress that sentences 1. and 2. are related as a matter of necessity. Reinach maintains that it is *essentially* impossible to have the one without having the other (they start and cease to exist at exactly the

[18] Reinach (n 2) 12.
[19] Matthew Kramer, 'On No-Rights and No Rights' (2019) 64 The American Journal of Jurisprudence 213.

same time); Hohfeld makes an even stronger claim as he maintains that 1. and 2. are *logically* equivalent.[20] Strictly speaking, however, 1. does not logically entail 2., nor the reverse. My proposal is that correlativity should be understood in terms of converse relations. Every relation has a converse. The converse of X *is over* Y is Y *is under* X. Likewise, the converse of X *has a claim against* Y *(to the effect that* Y *Fs)* is Y *has a duty towards* X *(to the effect that* Y *Fs)*.[21] On top of clarifying the otherwise elusive notion of correlativity, understanding legal correlatives in terms of converse relations presents three advantages.

First, it helps us make sense of Hohfeld's idea that legal correlatives logically imply each other. Though strictly speaking, legal correlatives are not logically equivalent (Y *has a duty towards* X does not logically follow from X *has a claim against* Y), one can understand the temptation of describing them as logically connected once one thinks about them in terms of converse relations. As plausibly argued by Williamson,[22] converse relations are identical. That is, if 'R' stands for a relation and 'R^C' stands for its converse, *xRy* (e.g., Bob is shorter than Eve) and $y\ R^C\ x$ (e.g., Eve is taller than Bob) express one and the same fact in two different ways.

Second, the proposal that legal correlatives are converse relations helps us understand why rights without counterparties also lack correlatives: rights without counterparties are monadic, and monadic predicates lack converses.

Third, an understanding of legal correlatives in terms of converse relations explains why some correlatives may lack proper denominations in ordinary language. While English and other languages provide lexical (e.g., taller/smaller) and syntactic (passive voice) ways of expressing converse relations, not all relational predicates have converses. Thus, dyadic predicates such as 'being biased against', 'being infatuated with', 'being conscious of', 'being at the disposal of', 'having a reservation against' lack converses. The only way to express their converses is to use periphrases, such as 'being the object of the infatuation of' or to introduce new terms (e.g., 'Let us now say that when x is infatuated with y, y "fatuates" x'). 'Having a liberty right relative to' is arguably a predicate of this sort, which is why Hohfeld has to introduce the neologism 'no-right' to express its converse.

8.3 CORRELATIVES OF LIBERTIES ARE NOT DUTIES OF NONINTERFERENCE

We are now able to address the question raised by Hohfeld: what are the logical correlatives of liberties? One natural proposal is that the correlative of Bob's freedom

[20] Hohfeld (n 1) 36.

[21] Substantially the same point is pressed by Davis Lyons, 'The Correlativity of Rights and Duties' (1970) 4 Noûs 45. Consequently, it is possible to build a logic of claims and relative obligations, by retaining only one of these as our primitive, and by introducing the other thanks to a definition from the first, as proposed by Stig Kanger and Helle Kanger, 'Rights and Parliamentarism' (1966) 32 Theoria 85.

[22] Timothy Williamson, 'Converse Relations' (1985) 94 The Philosophical Review 249.

to F is everyone else's duty not to interfere with Bob's F-ing. This proposal is rightly rejected by Hohfeld, albeit for two reasons that are not quite convincing. After presenting them, I shall advance two more straightforward reasons to reject the view that duties of noninterference are correlatives of liberties.

Hohfeld's first argument is that there could be liberties without duties of noninterference, for positive law may not recognize such obligations.[23] For example, it is conceivable that Eve has the freedom to use her bicycle, while Bob has no duty not to interfere with Eve's use of her bicycle. Hence, Hohfeld concludes, duties of noninterference cannot be correlatives of liberties. But this argument is wanting. Admittedly, in such cases there are no correlative duties recognized by positive law. Nevertheless, it could be argued that there is a prelegal duty of noninterference. In order for this argument to be convincing, it must be assumed that there are no prelegal or natural rights. This is a debated assumption, and it would be best to avoid relying on it.

Hohfeld's second argument does not rely on such an assumption. Suppose Eve allows Bob to use her bicycle, saying to him: 'You can use it if you like, but I'm not obliged to let you use it: if I'm the first on it, too bad for you.' In such a case, Hohfeld argues, Bob is free to use Eve's bike, but Eve is under no obligation to let Bob use her bike. Thus, Bob's freedom is not correlated with any duty of noninterference, legal or prelegal. However, proponents of the view that duties of noninterference are correlative with liberties are unlikely to be convinced. They might reply that sentences like 'You can use it if you like, but I don't commit to letting you use it' (or Hohfeld's 'Eat the salad if you can; you have our license to do so, but we don't commit to not interfering with you.') are problematic: if you let someone use something, you thereby commit, or so they claim, not to interfere with his use of the thing.

Can we find more compelling reasons to reject the view that duties of noninterference are correlatives of liberties? Why is A's liberty to F not equivalent to other people's duties not to interfere with A's F-ing? There is one reason to reject the left-to-right entailment, and two reasons to reject the right-to-left entailment.

The reason to reject the left-to-right entailment is that the content of duties of noninterference includes a notion of interference absent from the content of the corresponding liberty. This is problematic because, as we saw, legal correlatives must have the same content (otherwise, they cannot be converses of each other).

On the other hand, there are at least two reasons for rejecting the implication from duties of noninterference to liberties. First, the correlative of duties of noninterference (assuming such duties are relative) are not duties but claims. Consider Mary's duty not to interfere with Bob's singing. The correlative of this duty is not Bob's freedom to sing, but Bob's claim not to be prevented from singing by Mary (by the correlativity of claims and relative duties). Second, Mary's duty not to prevent

[23] Hohfeld (n 1) 36–7.

Bob from singing does not entail Bob's freedom to sing, because we may be prohibited (morally, legally, positively) from interfering with someone's action even if that person has no freedom to act in that way. Suppose I walk on the grass when it is forbidden to do so. The fact that you see me breaking this rule does not give you the license to prevent me from walking on the grass. So, the duty not to interfere with someone's action does not automatically entail that the person has the right (liberty) to act as he does.

To sum up, duties of noninterference are not logical correlatives of liberties because (i) the notion of interference is absent from the content of liberties; (ii) the correlatives of duties of noninterference are claims, not liberties; and (iii) everyone's duty not to interfere with my action does not entail my liberty to take that action. One might turn to a looser notion of correlativity to claim that duties of noninterference are correlatives of liberties in a broader sense. Thus, Thomson argues that genuine liberties (which she distinguishes from mere privileges) must have duties of noninterference as correlatives.[24] But if we stick to Hohfeld's original program of mapping 'logical' correlatives, such a proposal must be rejected.

What, then, is the relation between liberties and duties of noninterference, if they are not correlatives? One possibility, touched upon by Hohfeld and made explicit by Reinach is this: Bob's liberty to sing partly *explains* or *grounds* Bob's claim not to be prevented from singing. It is partly because Bob has the liberty to sing that Mary has the duty not to prevent Bob from singing. Reinach develops the proposal as follows:

> one could also say – although we are not ready to venture such an assertion – that the subject of absolute rights [i.e. liberties] has a claim on all persons to respect his rights and not to violate them. Even if this were so, it would not mean that absolute rights *are* nothing but universal rights against all persons, but only that they have such rights *as a consequence*.[25]

According to this proposal, the relation between Bob's liberty to sing and Mary's duty not to prevent Bob from singing is explanatory, and therefore asymmetrical, as opposed to the symmetrical relation between logical correlatives.

8.4 HOHFELD: CORRELATIVES OF LIBERTIES ARE NO-CLAIMS

So far, Hohfeld and Reinach agree: duties of noninterference are not correlatives of liberties (in the strict, logical sense of legal correlatives). Hohfeld however, maintains that logical correlatives of Bob's liberty to sing are the 'no-rights' of third parties that Bob does not sing (a proposal that Reinach would reject). The term 'right' is meant here in the sense of a claim: a 'no-right' is indeed a 'no-claim'. So, if Bob has the liberty to sing, relative to Mary, Mary does not have the claim that Bob does not

[24] Judith Jarvis Thomson, The Realm of Rights (Harvard University Press 1990) 53.

[25] Reinach (n 2) 52.

sing, relative to Bob. Generalizing Hohfeld's proposal, we get the following pairs of correlatives:

3. X has a liberty relative to Y to the effect that X Fs.
4. Y has a no-claim relative to X to the effect that X does not F.

Three objections to Hohfeld's notion of 'no-rights' can be raised. Since I shall argue that *some* liberties have no-rights as correlatives, I need to answer them.

(Bad) *Objection 1: ad hocery*. Faced with the problem of finding correlatives for liberties, Hohfeld forges a neologism. This seems *ad hoc*. But note that Hohfeld readily concedes that 'no-right' is a term of art. The reason why Hohfeld is justifiably nonplussed becomes clear once correlatives are understood in terms of converse relations: as noted above we should not expect all converse relations to be readily expressible in ordinary language. Every relation has a converse, but not every converse has a morpheme in ordinary language. 'Having a liberty relative to' is one relation of this sort.

(Bad) *Objection 2: reifying a negation*. 'No-right' is a negation, indicating merely the absence of a right.[26] Contrast correlative claims and duties: one party has a claim, and the counterparty a duty, such that there is clearly something – some normative position – that each party has relative to the other. But in the present case, one party has a liberty while the other, instead, lacks a claim. If some person lacks something (here, the normative position of holding a right), ascribing to her possession of a negative entity ('no-right') seems awkward. Lacking a hat is not having a no-hat; by parity, lacking a claim should not be equated with having a no-claim. The answer to this objection is quite straightforward once legal correlatives are conceived in terms of converse relations. Indeed, if, as proposed above, converse relations represent no addition of being, the sentences 'Bob has the liberty to sing relative to Eve' and 'Eve has a no-claim that Bob does not sing' express one and the same relational fact in two different ways. Despite the 'no claim' nominalization it contains, the second sentence does not quantify over an absence of claim, but over the presence of a liberty. It just describes that liberty from the point of view of its counterparty, while the first sentence describes it from the point of view of its holder.

(Bad) *Objection 3: violation of the requirement of same content*. Recall that one central feature of legal correlatives is that they have identical contents. The correlative of Mary's claim (that Bob sings) is Bob's duty (that Bob sings). This same content requirement is crucial to understanding the logical equivalence between legal correlatives. The violation of this requirement was one of the reasons for rejecting the view that duties of noninterference are correlatives of liberties. However, so the third (bad) objection goes, the view that no-rights are correlatives

[26] See Heidi Hurd and Michael Moore, 'The Hohfeldian Analysis of Rights' (2018) 63 American Journal of Jurisprudence 307.

of liberties also violates the same content requirement: the correlative of Bob's liberty (that Bob sings) is Mary's no-right (that Bob does *not* sing). One content is the negation of the other. To answer that important worry, I suggest a slight modification of Hohfeld's original proposal. Instead of saying that no-claims are the correlatives of liberties, we should say that the correlative liberties are *no-claim that not* (or better: *no-claim-that-not*). That is, the correlative of Bob's liberty (that Bob sings), would be Mary's no-claim that is it not the case (that Bob sings). To satisfy the same content requirement, we have moved the negation outside the content of the correlative, so as to make it a constituent of the correlative itself. Thus, instead of having the two following correlatives, as per Hohfeld's original proposal:

5. X has a liberty relative to Y to the effect that (X Fs).
6. Y has a no-claim relative to X to the effect that (X does not F).

We now have two pairs with the same content:

7. X has a liberty relative to Y to the effect that (X Fs).
8. Y has, relative to X, a no-claim-that-not (X Fs).

This satisfies the same content requirement while preserving Hohfeld's original insight. One might object that putting the negation on the side of the deontic connective rather than in its content is spurious. But such a move is far from unprecedented. It is endorsed, for instance, by those who think, following Reinach, that *disbelieving that p* and *believing that not p*, though logically equivalent, are distinct.[27] Likewise, closer to our topic, it is endorsed by those who think that *being obligatory that not p* and it *being impermissible that p* are equivalent, but nonetheless distinct.

Kramer has recently argued along similar lines that legal correlatives must have the same content.[28] How does the present proposal relate to his? According to Kramer, the correlative of *X's liberty to enter the land* is '*Y's no-right concerning X's entering the land*'. But how exactly should this formulation be understood? Kramer insists that it should not be understood to mean that Y has no right that X does not enter the land. How is it to be read, then? In particular, what has happened to the negation in the rejected formulation? Has it been dropped altogether? Or has it been moved within the 'no-right' connective?[29] In the first case, it is hard to see how there

[27] Adolf Reinach, 'On the Theory of Negative Judgment' in Barry Smith (ed and tr) *Parts and Moments. Studies in Logic and Formal Ontology* (Philosophia Verlag 1982) 333; originally published as Zur Theorie des negativen Urteils, *Munchener Philosophische Abhandlungen*, Festschrift for T Lipps, A Pfander (ed) (Barth, 1911) 196–254.

[28] Kramer (n 19).

[29] A similar concern is expressed by Andrew Halpin, 'No-Right and Its Correlative' (2020) 65 The American Journal of Jurisprudence 147.

can be a necessary equivalence between no-rights and liberties: Bob's liberty to dance, relative to Eve is not equivalent to Eve's no-right that Bob dances, relative to Bob. In the second case, Kramer's proposal and the present one are indeed one and the same. Let us assume that it is so.

Even so, there remains one point of divergence between Kramer's picture and the present one. Kramer maintains that liberties and duties are not contradictories but 'duals' because they do not have the same content. Bob's liberty to dance is opposed to Bob's duty not to dance: the content of the one is the negation of the content of the other. I would like to suggest, following an early suggestion by Mullock,[30] that once the idea of moving the negation from the content to the connective is taken on board, it is easy to apply the same content requirement to the whole Hohfeldian table (which Kramer rejects), in order to get a clearer picture of the logical relations between legal connectives:

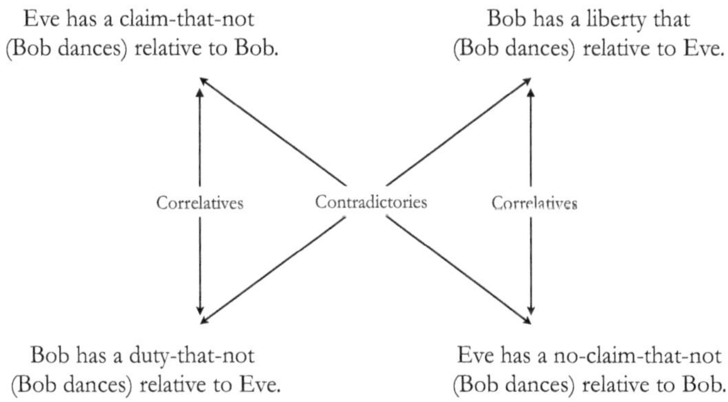

By neutralizing variations in content, such a picture, I submit, better captures the logical relations between the legal concepts themselves. Admittedly, we then get unusual expressions for legal concepts: 'duty-that-not', 'claim-that-not', and 'no-claim-that-not'. But note that *Bob's having a duty-that-not (Bob dances)* amounts to *Bob's having a prohibition that (Bob dances)*. In other words, we usually allow a distinction between positive duties and negative duties (i.e., prohibitions). This is not a content-based distinction: the same content can be obligatory or impermissible. The proposal is to extend this distinction to claims (so that positive claims must be distinguished from negative claims, or claims-that-not), but also to no-claims and liberties. Thus, with liberties-that-not, we get the following square:

30 Philip Mullock, 'The Hohfeldian No-Right: A Logical Analysis' (1970) 56 Archives for Philosophy of Law and Social Philosophy 265.

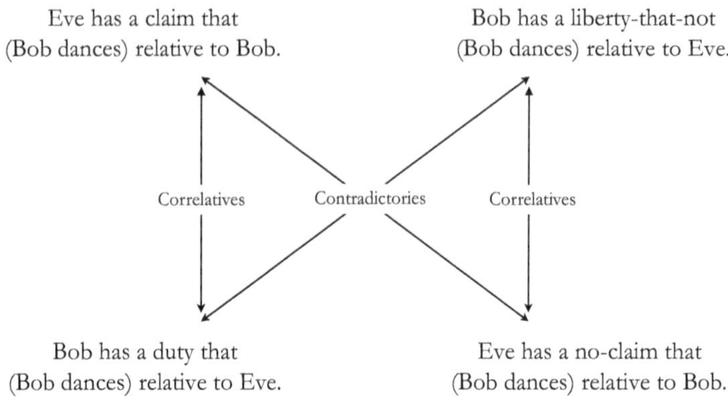

To be clear, none of this is meant to preclude the view that negative legal connectives can be reduced to positive connectives with negative contents, for example, that the *liberty-to-not pay*, can be reduced to the *liberty not to pay*; or that the *prohibition to sing* (i.e., the *duty-to-not sing*) can be reduced to the *duty not to sing*, just as, according to some, *disbelieving that p* amounts to *believing that not p*. But the point is that these are *reductions*, and that, insofar as we are interested in *describing* the logical connections between legal connectives, we should eschew any reductionist commitments.

In conclusion, Hohfeld's view that 'no-claims' are correlatives of relative liberties, once interpreted in the light of the proposal that liberties and no-claims are converse relations, turns out to be neither ad hoc, nor committed to reifying absences, nor incompatible with the idea that legal correlatives must have the same content. I conclude that Hohfeld's proposal is coherent.

8.5 OBJECTIONS TO HOHFELD: PROPERTY RIGHTS

Why, then, should we not accept Hohfeld's amended proposal that every liberty is correlated with a no-claim-that-not? The (Reinachian) view I will defend in this section is that property rights have no counterparties (and hence no correlatives). Such a possibility has been largely overlooked. Even those legal scholars who rightly emphasize the qualitative distinction between rights *in personam* and rights *in rem* (which include, first and foremost, property rights) take it for granted that both kinds of rights have counterparties.[31] Here are three objections to the view that all freedoms have counterparties.

[31] See in particular James E Penner, *The Idea of Property in Law* (Oxford University Press 1997); Thomas W Merrill and Henry E Smith, 'What Happened to Property in Law and Economics?' (2001) 111 Yale Law Journal 357; Thomas W Merrill and Henry E Smith 'The Property/Contract Interface' (2001) 101 Columbia Law Review 773.

Objection 1: from number of property rights. The liberty rights that attend owning something (whether such rights are grounded in ownership, as per Reinach, or constitutive of ownership, as per Hohfeld) are, under Hohfeld's proposal, liberties that are relative to every other person, *ceteris paribus*. If Bob owns a car, he has, *ceteris paribus*, the liberty to use it as he sees fit, and that liberty is relative to Eve, Max, you, me, and every other person. (The *ceteris paribus* clause is needed, for Bob may have, for instance, promised to Eve not to use his car.) As a result, we all have a no-claim that Bob does not use his car as he wants. Let us now ask what happens to Bob's liberty to use his car when other persons come into being or pass away. There are two equally unappealing options.

The first option, arguably endorsed by Hohfeld, is to claim that Bob has as many liberties as there are other persons: one liberty to use his car for each counterparty.[32] This implies that when Eve dies, Bob loses one such liberty. To make the situation more vivid, suppose Bob knows nothing at all about Eve, who lives in another region. How could Eve's dying be relevant to Bob's right(s) to use his car? Suppose, likewise, that a new person is born, whom Bob will never meet. This would mean that Bob gains a new right to use his car. Again, this seems odd: it does not seem appropriate to suggest that Bob gains or loses liberties to use his car with every variation in human population.

According to the second option, Bob has just a single liberty to use his car, but that this liberty is relative to all other persons in the world (or in the legal system at stake), independently of any variation in the number of those other persons. This need not be read as entailing the liberty relation has as many places as they are counterparties (i.e., that liberty is sometimes dyadic, sometimes triadic, sometimes n-adic, according to the number of counterparties); more plausibly, the liberty could be seen as a constantly dyadic relation between its holder, on the one hand, and the plurality of its counterparties, on the other hand. That proposal, contrary to the previous one, does not imply that when the population increases, Bob's liberties to use his car increase proportionately. But it does imply that when a population increases, Bob's single liberty to use his car in a way becomes greater. But this is implausible. On this view, Robinson on his island would not be free at all to use a tool he built until the arrival of Friday. When Friday arrives, Robinson would gain the liberty to use that tool, although that liberty would be of the lowest possible level – Friday being but one person. Robinson would have a greater degree of liberty to use the tool when returning to a populous England. This all sounds rather counterintuitive: Robinson, Reinach would have it, has always been free to use his

[32] Hohfeld (n 3) 740 endorses this option when it comes to claims directed at several persons. Such claims, he maintains, should be understood as several claims, rather than as one single claim held against many persons. So, he would arguably endorse this same option when it comes to liberties.

tools; changes in his social environment have never altered his freedom (although they have certainly affected the likelihood of his freedom being interfered with).

Objection 2: from the transfer of property rights. To introduce the second objection let us briefly return to claim rights. Eve promises Bob that she will eat. As a result, Bob has a claim right against Eve that she eats. Now, Bob cannot unilaterally transfer that claim to Ralf: to transfer the claim, he needs Eve's consent. This is because Bob's claim is relative to Eve: both must consent to change it. Now consider Bob's liberty right to use his car. That right, on Hohfeld's proposal, is relative to all other persons who, correspondingly, have no-claims that Bob refrain from the use of his car. Suppose now that Bob decides to transfer his right to use his car to Eve, by lending his car to her for one week. As a result, Eve has the liberty right to use Bob's car for one week. Eve's newly gained liberty right is, according to Hohfeld's proposal, correlated to all other persons' no-claims that Eve does not use Bob's car. Hence the no-claims of all the other persons have been changed from no-claims that Bob refrains from the use of his car, to no-claims that Eve refrains from the use of Bob's car. Shouldn't all these people have a say on Bob's transfer? After all, this transfer affects their deontic status. If the addressees of claim rights have to give their consent to the holder's transfer of these rights, why mustn't the addressees of liberty rights consent to the holder's transfer of such rights as well? That consequence of the view that all liberty rights are relative rights, and therefore have correlatives, is very odd: surely, we are not violating any obligation when we lend our bike to a friend without asking for the authorization of everyone. One possible answer is that claims require the consent of third parties, but liberties do not. But such an answer seems ad hoc: why should it be the case that claims relative to Bob should require Bob's consent to be transferred, but not liberties relative to Bob? It is hard to think of any relevant difference between the two cases that would justify such an asymmetry. Such a difference would perhaps appeal to the fact that Bob tends to be more prejudiced in the first case than in the second, but it is far from obvious that this has to be the case in general.

Objection 3: from absolute obligations. The third objection does not appeal to property rights but challenges the idea that the absence of counterparties' claims implies the party's liberty (which should be the case, since correlatives are equivalent). Consider for simplicity a world with only two people, Bob and Ida. Can we conclude from the fact that Ida does not have a claim to the effect that Bob does not sing, that Bob has the liberty to sing? Not necessarily. For this to hold, one must assume that absolute obligations – obligations lacking any counterparty, that is, obligations which are not obligations *to* someone – are impossible. But that assumption is quite controversial.[33] Bob may be under some absolute duty not to sing. For

[33] Absolute obligations are defended, among others, by Reinach (n 2); Joel Feinberg, 'Duties, Rights, and Claims' (1966) 3 American Philosophical Quarterly 137; Margaret Gilbert, Rights and Demands: A Foundational Inquiry (Oxford University Press 2018); David Lyons, 'Rights,

this objection to work, it is enough to show that absolute obligations are possible, since no-claims are meant to entail liberties in all possible cases. Hohfeld, therefore, must deny the possibility of absolute obligations. But doing so undermines the appeal of his proposal.

Consider general duties not to kill, not to damage works of art or not to destroy landscapes in the absence of strong countervailing reasons. To many, such duties are not only possible, but also actual. One answer would be that we owe it to the person not to kill him or her; that we owe it to the landscape not to destroy it. But, as Reinach 'emphatically stresses', we should not confuse the addressee of the content of a duty with the addressee of that duty (if there is one).[34] Hence his assertion that such duties are not directed to persons. The proponent of the view that all duties are relative certainly has several maneuvers at his disposal to counter this claim. He can argue, for example, that we owe it to actual or potential beneficiaries of the landscape (which may include future humans) not to destroy it; that we owe it to the artist (who may be dead) not to destroy his work; that we owe it to any other human or to God not to kill any human, etc. The present argument, however, is not premised on the idea that there are absolute duties; it only makes the weaker claim that, since absolute duties make sense, they should not be made impossible by our taxonomy of rights. Yet they are made impossible by Hohfeld's view that liberties and no-claims are equivalent.

These problems disappear if one agrees that some liberties, such as property rights, are absolute instead of relative, as Reinach argues. So, let us now turn to his account.

8.6 REINACH: LIBERTIES HAVE NO CORRELATIVES

So far, we have argued that duties of noninterference cannot be the correlative of liberties, and that in some cases at least, no-rights are not correlatives of liberties either. What then are the correlatives of liberties? Reinach maintains that there are none: liberties are absolute rights, by which he means that liberties lack any correlative. Hohfeld assumes from the outset that all rights are relations between two parties: the holder of the right and a counterparty. Such an assumption is rejected by Reinach, who stresses that both rights and obligations come in two types, relative and absolute:

> Claim and obligation necessarily involve a bearer and a content. The direction against another person, by contrast, is not necessarily connected with them.

Claimants, and Beneficiaries' (1969) 6 American Philosophical Quarterly 173; Gopal Sreenivasan, 'Duties and Their Direction' (2010) 120 Ethics 465; Thomson (n 24) 61–4; Siegfried Van Duffel, 'The Nature of Rights Debate Rests On a Mistake' (2012) 93 Pacific Philosophical Quarterly 104.

[34] Reinach (n 2) 76. An analogous claim is made by Hohfeld (n 3) 721–22 about rights, when he urges not to conflate rights *in rem* with right against things.

> There is indeed the a priori law that every obligation which exists over against another implies a corresponding claim of this other, and every relative claim implies a relative obligation. But this relativity of claim and obligation is nothing necessary; there are absolute obligations and absolute claims, or better, absolute rights.[35]

Reinach's absolute rights correspond to Hohfeld's liberties. An *absolute* right (or obligation), Reinach stresses, is not a *universal* right (or obligation), in the sense of a right (or obligation) relative to every other person. To have the absolute right to F does not mean to have the right to F relative to everybody. Quite the contrary, absolute rights (and obligations) are absolute in the sense of having one bearer but lacking any opposite party (*Gegnerschaft*):

> The absoluteness of rights and obligations means the *absence* of every relation to a partner, and not its *universality*, that is, not the fact that the so-called absolute rights and obligations exist over against *all* persons in contrast to the obligatory rights and obligations, which are tied to a *single* person.[36]

Because absolute rights lack counterparties, they lack correlatives: the claim that Eve has against Bob is equivalent to a duty of Bob towards Eve; but Eve's absolute right to F, because it is not a relation to another person, cannot be equivalent to a deontic property of someone else. The core essential feature of absolute rights, Reinach maintains,[37] is their reference to one's own action. Relative rights, by contrast, always refer to another's action. One can have the freedom to express one's opinion, but one cannot have the freedom that somebody else express his opinion. By contrast, relative rights never bear on one's own action (that would be 'contradictory' according to Reinach):[38]

> absolute rights, which also presuppose only one person, their bearer, but do not need any second person over against whom they would exist. But obligations and rights do differ in an essential point: whereas obligations by their very nature refer only to one's own action, and this whether they are relative or absolute, we have to distinguish two different cases with regard to rights. Relative rights can only refer to the action of another, absolute rights, by contrast, always refer to one's own action. Rights which, though they are over one's own action, exist only over against some person seem to us just as impossible as rights to (claims on) the action of another which do not exist over against this other.[39]

35 Reinach (n 2) 12.
36 ibid 52.
37 ibid 12, 51, 58, 66.
38 ibid 120.
39 ibid 13.

That absolute rights always refer to the actions of their holders allows Reinach to distinguish between at least three kinds of absolute rights. The first are the rights over things or property rights, which are the rights to use things. All rights over things arise ultimately, Reinach contends, from ownership.[40] The second kind of absolute rights are the rights to perform certain actions which do not consist in using things: these are actions such as moving, expressing one's opinion, or the moral right 'of the free development of one's personality'.[41] These absolute rights are not grounded in a relation of ownership, but in the person as such. The third kind of absolute rights mentioned by Reinach are rights over rights, that is, the right to perform actions which modify rights. These come in two sub-kinds:[42] the rights over one's own rights, such as the right to waive one's claims, and the right over somebody else's right, such as the right to revoke another's right.

> Just as we have learned that rights over things are absolute rights to some action of mine directed to the things, so we have to see that rights over rights are rights to some action of mine directed to rights.[43]

Note that the way Reinach describes rights over rights is strikingly close from the way he characterizes legal powers a few pages later.[44] One question is whether he intends to draw a distinction, and another is whether he could draw it in a convincing way. There is reason for doubt on both questions. What would distinguish them is unclear: both have content directed to the action of their holder which produces an immediate effect in the world of rights, both are absolute.[45] Reinach writes, besides 'This *power or right* to transfer is a *power or right* over one's own right' (italics mine).[46] If Reinach indeed equates powers with (absolute) rights over rights, then a further divergence between Reinach's and Hohfeld's typologies of rights appears. While Hohfeld sees legal powers as a new kind of legal phenomenon on top of claims and liberties, Reinach equates legal powers with a sub-kind of liberties.[47] I shall not explore this important difference further here.

[40] ibid 56.
[41] ibid 81.
[42] ibid 63.
[43] ibid 64.
[44] ibid 66. See Section 8.1.
[45] ibid 55.
[46] ibid 67.
[47] Albert Kocourek ('The Hohfeld System of Fundamental Legal Concepts' (1920) 15 Illinois Law Review 24) notes that Hohfeld sometimes confuses liberties with powers and suggests that the two might in fact overlap.

Reinach's typology of rights can be represented thus:[48]

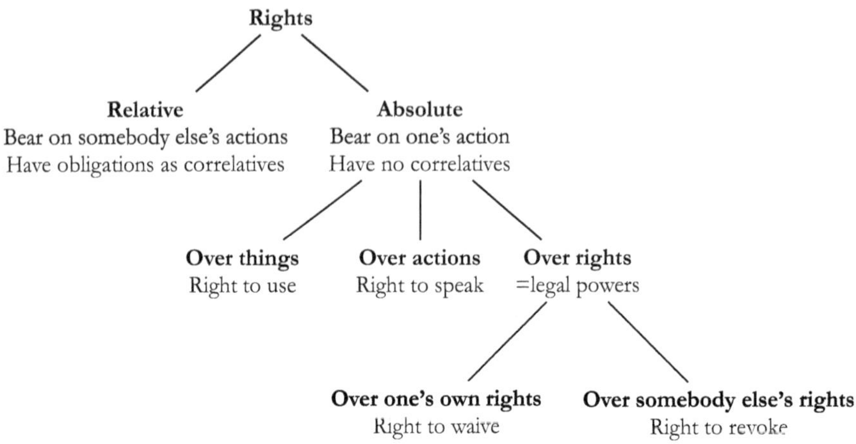

We have mentioned so far three essential differences, according to Reinach, between relative rights (that is, claims) and absolute rights (that is, liberties):

(1) Relative rights are directed towards another person, whereas absolute rights are not.
(2) Relative rights have correlatives, whereas absolute rights have no correlatives.
(3) Relative rights concern the action of another person, whereas absolute rights concern one's own action.

Reinach advances six other, related, essential differences between claims and absolute rights:

(1) While a claim can be *fulfilled* an absolute right can only be *exercised*. It is impossible to exercise a claim, or to fulfill an absolute right.
(2) Relatedly, a claim is awaiting or 'aiming at' its fulfillment, while an absolute right 'is something definite, something resting in itself'.[49] This may be compared to active and passive dispositions: active dispositions, such as the force exerted by a magnet, tend to bring about their effect unless prevented from doing so; passive dispositions, such as the fragility of a piece of glass, remain latent unless triggered.
(3) While a claim, in virtue of its nature, ceases to exist when fulfilled,[50] an absolute right typically survives its exercise.

[48] I here ignore the distinction between moral and nonmoral rights; Reinach's more complete ontology of rights is presented in Massin (n 13).
[49] Reinach (n 2) 58.
[50] ibid 14, 32.

(4) While any claim may be waived,[51] absolute rights can only be waived in special cases. The owner of a thing, for instance, cannot waive his right to use it. He may at best transfer or grant that right to another person or transfer his ownership altogether. One may, however, waive one's absolute right to use the things owned by another person (when that person lends them to us for instance).

(5) Relatedly, while claims cease to exist when they are waived, waiving one's right to use a thing owned by another person does not destroy that absolute right, but returns it to the owner.[52]

(6) While absolute rights can sometimes be transferred by their holder without further condition (the owner of a thing may lend it, that is, transfer or grant the right to use to another person),[53] claims can only be transferred with the agreement of a counterparty.[54] If Eve has as a claim against Bob to the effect that Bob sing, Eve cannot transfer that claim to Dan without Bob's consent.

These nine essential differences between absolute and relative rights, according to Reinach, are recapped in the following table:

	Relative rights (claims)	**Absolute rights (liberties)**
Content	Bear on the action of another	Bear on one's action
Parties	Have opposing parties	Lack opposing parties
Correlatives	Have relative obligations as correlatives	Lack correlatives
Satisfaction	Are fulfilled	Are exercised
Dynamics	Tend towards their fulfillment	Rest until they are exercised
Duration	Cease to exist when fulfilled	Continue to exist while being exercised
Waiving (1)	Essentially can be waived	Sometimes cannot be waived
Waiving (2)	Cease to exist when waived	Do not cease to exist when waived
Transferring	Can only be transferred with the consent of the counterparty	Can be transferred without any consent of the counterparty

[51] ibid 33.
[52] ibid 56, 70, 75.
[53] ibid 66–7.
[54] ibid 75–80.

Reinach does not just provide an alternative to Hohfeld's account of liberties. He also explains why we are tempted to mistakenly believe that liberties are directed towards others.

First, absolute rights may have their source in another person.[55] Thus the owner of a thing may grant to another person the absolute right to use that thing.[56] Bob may grant to Mary the right to use his bike. In such a case, the right (liberty) which Mary gets is not relative to Bob.[57] Likewise, the social act of allowing somebody to do something results, Reinach contends, in that person having the absolute right to do it.[58] The destinee of the act gets that right thanks to the author of the act, but his right is not directed to the author.

Second, as pointed out above, the fact that absolute rights may refer to another person in their content does not mean that they are directed towards that person. The right to make promises to other people (by contrast to rights generated by promises themselves) is not directed towards anybody.

Third, absolute rights and relative rights may be related in different ways (by essential or positive laws) which may lead to confusion. Thus, if an absolute right is related to a relative right, it is easy to confuse the third party of the relative right with a supposed third party of the absolute right. A first example stems from cases in which the positive law provides for a claim of compensation when an absolute right is violated.[59] In such cases, it is the compensatory claim that is directed, not the underlying absolute right. A second example is the right of lien. A lien is an absolute right on a thing that is used to secure a claim.[60] If Eve does not fulfill Bob's claim by not giving his money back, Bob becomes entitled to use Eve's car (an absolute right). Bob's claim is directed, but the absolute right it secures is not directed. In the first example, a violation of an absolute right gives rise to a claim; in the second example, an absolute right secures a claim. In none of these examples is the absolute right a directed right, although it is easy to mistake the direction of the claim for a direction of the connected absolute right.

8.7 OBJECTIONS TO REINACH: ALLOWING

For all its acuity, Reinach's account of absolute rights overlooks the distinction between absolute and relative liberties. By maintaining that all liberties are relative,

55 ibid 52.
56 ibid 119.
57 Couldn't we answer that in such a case, Mary is granted a claim to use Bob's bike? No, answers Reinach (n 2) 120 for claims are essentially related to the action of another; claims to one's own action are contradictory; at best, Mary may have the claim *not to be prevented by others* from using Bob's bike.
58 ibid 120.
59 ibid 52.
60 ibid 59.

Hohfeld, we saw, cannot properly accommodate absolute liberties that arise from ownership. Analogously, I shall now argue, by maintaining that all liberties are absolute, Reinach encounters difficulties when it comes to social acts such as allowing, which arguably give rise to relative liberties.

Let us first get clear on the social act of allowing. Reinach maintains that allowing is a distinct kind of social act that not only needs to be heard by another person, but that is also addressed to another person, in virtue of which that other person gains the absolute liberty to perform a certain kind of action.[61] This characterization, I believe, is nearly correct: its only flaw is to assume that the liberty given to the addressee is absolute. Here are two objections that show that the liberties generated by that act of allowing are relative.

First objection: allowing and transferring. Max is the owner of a piece of land and hence has, *ceteris paribus*, the liberty right to use that land. The right to use what is ours, Reinach correctly argues (*pace* Hohfeld), is absolute. Suppose that Max allows Eve to use his land. As a result, Eve also has the liberty right to use the land. Max's and Eve's liberties are numerically distinct, because though they have the same content, they have different holders. But these liberties also appear to be distinct in kind: while Max is entitled, tout court, to use the land, Eve is entitled to use the land only relative to Max.

One way to bring out this distinction is to consider the conditions under which liberties can be transferred. As Reinach points out, Max, the owner of the land, can transfer the right to use that land without third-party consent, while Eve, who has been granted that right by Max, cannot do the same: she needs Max's green light to do so. Why? On Reinach's view, the nature of these liberties is *ex hypothesi* the same and hence cannot explain the difference. We must refer instead to the origin of the liberties: while Max's liberty to use his land stems from his ownership of the land, Eve's liberty to use Max's land stems from Max having allowed her to do so. But it is unclear why a right's history should make any difference to how it now 'behaves'. Under the present proposal, by contrast, there is no need to investigate the genesis of liberties to understand why some are transferable and others not. This difference in transferability is due to an essential difference between these liberties: absolute

[61] ibid 120. Reinach is not quite explicit about this, but there are strong Reinachian reasons for considering allowing someone to do something as a kind of granting of an absolute right to someone. Indeed, Reinach (n 2) 68 distinguishes between the transfer of rights, where the transferred right is lost by the transferor, and the granting of rights, where the granted right is not lost by the granter, either because he never had the right in the first place, or because he retains the right. This, I think, helps to clarify the distinction between lending something to someone and allowing someone to use something. If Max lends his land to Eve for a while, Max transfers the right to use his land to Eve for that time, and thereby loses that right for a while. On the other hand, if Max allows Eve to use his land for a while, then Max can keep his right to use it for that time as well, so two people can use Max's land at the same time.

liberties can be transferred without the consent of third parties (because they have none), whereas relative liberties require the consent of their third parties in order to be transferred.

Second objection: allowing and forbidding. Ann's father has allowed her to go to the party, but Ann's mother has forbidden her to do so. The straightforward thing to say, in such cases, is that Ann has the liberty, *relative to her father*, to go to the party, while she has the interdiction, *relative to her mother*, to do so. This answer is, of course, not open to Reinach. How else could he treat cases like this? He seems to have two equally unappealing options.

First, Reinach could maintain that Ann at once has an absolute liberty to go to the party and an absolute obligation not to go to the party. Contradictory rights and obligation are not a problem *per se* for Reinach: he allows for incompatible *pro tanto* rights and duties. However, this case is special because the liberty and interdiction are directly and completely contradictory: they have contradictory contents, and the same holder. But they also have the same counterparty if they are absolute (none, *ex hypothesi*), and are of the same kind: nonmoral obligations and rights stemming from similar social acts (allowing and forbidding). It is one thing to maintain that contradictory rights are possible so long as they are of different kinds or have different counterparties. It is quite another to maintain that one can be at once entitled and forbidden, absolutely and in the very same sense, to perform the same action at the same time. Under the standard hypothesis, having the permission to F is logically equivalent to not having the obligation to non-F.[62] If so, the present proposal leads to a contradiction.

The second option is to maintain that Ann has the absolute liberty to go to the party, but the obligation *relative to her mother*, not to go to the party. This is likely the strategy Reinach would adopt. The reasons for this are twofold. First, he maintains that allowing generates absolute obligation.[63] Second, while he never explicitly considers the act of forbidding, he considers in detail the close act of commanding (*forbidding to F*, one may think, is equivalent and perhaps identical to *commanding not to F*). Reinach maintains that like promising, commanding essentially generates relative claims and obligations.[64] Third, this strategy presents the advantage of putting the former worry of contradiction to rest, for Ann now has an

[62] Like the equivalence between relations and their converses, that relation is not quite logical, but still is arguably analytic. It belongs to what McNamara and Van de Putte call the 'traditional definitional scheme' (Paul McNamara and Frederik Van De Putte, 'Deontic Logic', *The Stanford Encyclopedia of Philosophy*, Edward N Zalta and Uri Nodelman (eds) available at https://plato.stanford.edu/archives/fall2022/entries/logic-deontic/).

[63] Reinach (n 2) 120.

[64] ibid 24. The obvious difference between commanding and ordering being that promising generates a relative obligation in the promisor, while commanding generates a relative obligation in the commandee.

absolute liberty conflicting with a relative obligation, this being a noncontradictory form of deontic conflict.

However, this strategy comes at a high cost. It assumes that the social act of allowing generates absolute liberties, while the social act of forbidding generates relative obligations. This seems *ad hoc*: if forbidding generates relative obligations, then allowing should generate relative liberties. Indeed, forbidding and allowing belong to a common kind (together with obliging/commanding): both are other-directed, both bring about deontic status in their addressees (respectively, interdiction and permission); both require that the persons performing them have some legal power over their addressees. Finally, the logical relations between allowing and forbidding closely map the logical relations between permission and obligation. In the same way as *not being permitted to F* is equivalent to *being obligated to not-F*; *not allowing S to F* seems to have the same correctness conditions as *forbidding S to F*. Also, in the same way that *being permitted and forbidden to F* is contradictory, *allowing and forbidding S to F* is contradictory. One way to bring out that worry is to compare the deontic status of Ann in the present example with her deontic status had her father instead commanded her to go to the party. In such a case, Reinach would say (correctly) that Ann is under two incompatible relative obligations: the obligation, relative to her father, to go to the party; and the obligation, relative to her mother, not to go to the party. Why, when her father simply allows her to go to the party, should we treat the deontic conflict she finds herself in differently? Why shouldn't we see it as a conflict between two relative deontic states?

8.8 A RECONCILED ONTOLOGY OF RIGHTS

Let us take stock. Hohfeld maintains that all liberties are relative and have no-rights as correlatives. He faces objection stemming from cases such as property rights, in which liberties appear to be absolute. Reinach, for his part, maintains that all liberties are absolute and therefore lack correlatives. He faces objection from cases in which liberties appear to be relative, such as the liberties that arise from allowing. At this juncture, the way out seems obvious: a complete ontology of liberties should include both absolute and relative liberties.

However, this proposal raises an immediate worry: how should we distinguish liberties from claims? Hohfeld holds that they are distinct in virtue of having distinct correlatives (respectively, no-rights and relative obligations); Reinach holds that they are distinct in virtue of being respectively relative and absolute. If we welcome both absolute and relative liberties, we cannot distinguish them from claims based on either of these two criteria. Reinach, fortunately, provides us with another criterion: the key difference between claims and liberties is not to be found in their correlatives, but in their content. Liberties bear on the action of their holder, claims bear on the action of their addressees. We can thus retain most of Reinach's detailed account of the contrast between claims and liberties:

	Claims	**Liberties**
Content	Bear on the action of another	Bear on one's action
Parties	Have opposing parties	~~Lack opposing parties~~
Correlatives	Have relative obligations as correlatives	~~Lack correlatives~~
Satisfaction	Are fulfilled	Are exercised
Dynamics	Tend towards their fulfillment	Rest until they are exercised
Duration	Cease to exist when fulfilled	Continue to exist while being exercised
Waiving (1)	Essentially can be waived	Sometimes cannot be waived
Waiving (2)	Cease to exist when waived	Do not cease to exist when waived
Transferring	Can only be transferred with consent of the counterparty	~~Can be transferred without any consent of the counterparty~~

On top of avoiding all the worries raised above, this proposal reveals why absolute claims are impossible: since claims bear not on one's own action, but on the action of another, they necessarily must have a counterparty. The following figures contrast the proposed ontology of rights with that of Hohfeld and Reinach:

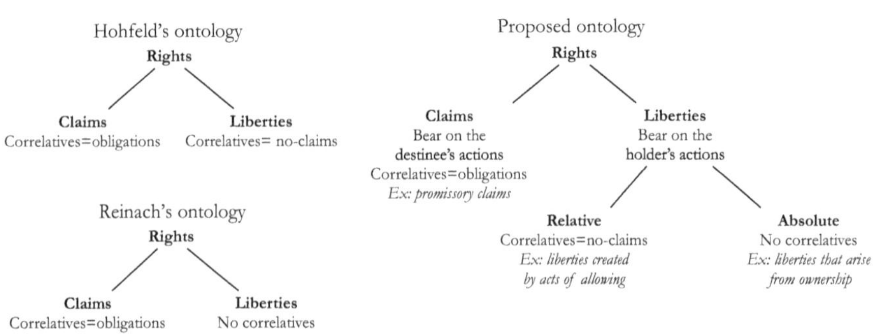

Based on this ontology, two Reinachian 'essential laws' can be formulated. To introduce the first, recall the distinction made by Reinach between social acts that are other-directed, and those that are not.[65] All speech acts need to be heard, and hence have an addressee, yet not all of them are other-directed. The acts of promising, commanding, or granting a right are other-directed, by contrast to the acts of enacting or waiving.[66] Based on this distinction, the first essential law states:

(1) Other-directed social acts cannot generate absolute rights and obligations.

Promising, commanding, and granting only generate relative rights and obligations. (Likewise, submitting, another other-directed act, generates in its addressee the *relative* legal power to bring about legal effect in the person who submitted.[67]) Absolute rights and obligations, on the other hand, arise from the nature of ownership, of persons, or from social acts like that of enacting, which is not other-directed. It is indeed possible to transfer an absolute right, and transferring a right is other-directed, according to Reinach, but this is no exception to the present law since transferring does not generate any right.

The second essential law concerns the condition of transfer. The owner of a thing, we saw, can transfer his liberty to use that thing without any further ado, while the person that has been granted the right to use a thing cannot transfer that liberty without the consent of the owner. This suggests the following essential law:

(2) All relative rights (be they relative claims or relative liberties) require the consent of their counterparty in order to be transferred by their holder, in contrast to absolute rights.

In the absence of countervailing factors, absolute liberties can be transferred without the consent of anybody. The transfer of relative liberties, by contrast, always requires the consent of the counterparty.

8.9 CONCLUSION

I have compared Reinach's and Hohfeld's contemporaneous ontologies of rights and argued that their main disagreement lies in their understanding of liberties. While Hohfeld sees liberties as relative, correlated with no-rights, Reinach claims that liberties are absolute, lacking any counterparties. I then argued that both start from a correct insight, but that they each then overgeneralize this insight to all liberties. This led me to propose an ontology of rights that makes room for both relative and absolute liberties.

Among the other points of disagreement between Hohfeld and Reinach that deserve further investigation, the nature of legal power is perhaps the most

[65] Reinach (n 2) 32.
[66] ibid 32, 105.
[67] ibid at 111.

interesting. While Hohfeld argues that legal powers constitute a *sui generis* kind of legal relation, on top of duties, claims, and liberties, Reinach sees legal powers as a subspecies of liberties, namely liberties to perform actions that modify rights. A strong reason to follow Reinach here is that powers bear on their holder's action, which is the mark of liberties. A strong reason to follow Hohfeld, though, is that the view that powers and liabilities are correlatives is highly plausible (and must be rejected by Reinach since powers, qua liberties, must lack correlatives). Here again, I surmise, the Reinachian framework could accommodate Hohfeldian liabilities, disabilities, and immunities, provided that it abandons the problematic assumption that liberties are always absolute. More precisely, the hypothesis would be that legal powers come in two kinds, absolute and relative, that relative powers have liabilities as correlatives, and, that liabilities are a kind of no-claims.[68]

BIBLIOGRAPHY

Feinberg J, 'Duties, Rights, and Claims' (1966) 3 American Philosophical Quarterly 137
Gilbert M, Rights and Demands: A Foundational Inquiry (Oxford University Press 2018)
Halpin A, 'No-Right and Its Correlative' (2020) 65 The American Journal of Jurisprudence 147
Hohfeld WN, 'Some Fundamental Legal Conceptions as Applied in Judicial Reasoning' (1913) 23 Yale Law Journal 16
'Fundamental Legal Conceptions as Applied in Judicial Reasoning' (1917) 26 Yale Law Journal 710
Hurd HM and Moore, MS, 'The Hohfeldian Analysis of Rights' (2018) 63 American Journal of Jurisprudence 295
Kanger S and Kanger H, 'Rights and parliamentarism' (1966) 32 Theoria 85
Kocourek, A, 'The Hohfeld System of Fundamental Legal Concepts' (1920) 15 Illinois Law Review 24
Koslicki K and Massin O, 'A Plea for Descriptive Social Ontology' (2023) 202 Synthese 59
Kramer M, 'On No-Rights and No Rights' (2019) 64 The American Journal of Jurisprudence 213
Lyons D, 'Rights, Claimants, and Beneficiaries' (1969) 6 American Philosophical Quarterly 173
'The Correlativity of Rights and Duties' (1970) 4 Noûs 45
Massin O, 'The Metaphysics of Ownership: A Reinachian Account' (2017) 27 Axiomathes 577
McNamara P and Van De Putte F, 'Deontic Logic' The Stanford Encyclopedia of Philosophy, EN Zalta and U Nodelman (eds), https://plato.stanford.edu/archives/fall2022/entries/logic-deontic/
Merrill, TW and Smith, HE, 'The Property/Contract Interface' (2001) 101 Columbia Law Review 773
'What Happened to Property in Law and Economics?' (2001) 111 Yale Law Journal 357

[68] I am very grateful to Marietta Auer, Robin Bianchi, Simon-Pierre Chevarie-Cossette, Malte Hendrickx, Jonathan Simon, Kathrin Koslicki, Jed Lewinsohn, Marco Marabello, Anne Meylan, Paul Miller, James Toomey, Alessandro Salice, and Henry Smith, for their precious comments and criticisms.

Mullock, P, 'The Hohfeldian No-Right: A Logical Analysis' (1970) 56 Archives for Philosophy of Law and Social Philosophy 265

Penner, JE, The Idea of Property in Law (1997) Oxford University Press

Reinach, A, 'On the Theory of the Negative Judgment' in B Smith (ed and tr) Parts and Moments. Studies in Logic and Formal Ontology (Philosophia Verlag 1982), originally published as A Reinach, Zur Theorie des negativen Urteils, *Munchener Philosophische Abhandlungen*, Festschrift for T Lipps, A Pfander (eds) (Barth, 1911) 196–254

'The Apriori Foundations of the Civil Law' (John F Crosby tr., 1983) 3 Aletheia 1–142, reprinted in Adolf Reinach, *The Apriori Foundations of the Civil Law Along with the Lecture 'Concerning Phenomenology'* (John F. Crosby ed., Ontos Verlag 2012), originally published as Adolf Reinach, Die apriorischen Grundlagen des bürgerlichen Rechtes, 1 (2) *Jahrbuch für Philosophie und phänomenologische Forschung* (Max Niemeyer 1913), 685–847

Sreenivasan G 'Duties and Their Direction' (2010) 120 Ethics 465

Thomson JJ, *The Realm of Rights* (Harvard University Press 1990)

Van Duffel S, 'The Nature of Rights Debate Rests on a Mistake' (2012) 93 Pacific Philosophical Quarterly 104

Williamson T, 'Converse Relations' (1985) 94 The Philosophical Review 249

PART III

Reinach and Legal Concepts

9

Adolf Reinach and Gerhart Husserl on the Foundations of Legal Phenomenology and the Temporality of Law

Stephan Kirste

9.1 INTRODUCTION

Edmund Husserl's work has been studied with regard to his phenomenology of the state, less so his phenomenology of law – probably because the scattered reflections on it did not seem to yield rich results.[1] However, A. Reinach, G. Husserl as well as A. Troller and others adopted phenomenological methods in their works on the philosophy of law[2] which were particularly fruitful concerning the concept of time and law.

For legal phenomenologists, time is not a structure external to law, as it belongs to the social world and thus also to the realm of law.[3] Drawing on Edmund Husserl's phenomenology, Adolf Reinach and Husserl's son Gerhart emphasized the importance of time for the understanding of the nature of law. To reveal the temporality of law, both begin with a qualitative time based on the temporal dimensions of present, future and past. They then distinguished this time from an objective and external

[1] Sophie Loidolt, *Einführung in die Rechtsphänomenologie: Eine historisch-systematische Darstellung* (Mohr Siebeck 2010); Karl Schumann, *Husserls Staatsphilosophie*, vol 29 (Praktische Philosophie 1988); Nils Brandenburg, 'Phenomenology of Law' in Stephan Kirste and Mortimer Sellers (eds), *Encyclopedia for the Philosophy of Law and Social Philosophy*, vol 4 (Springer International 2024). However, Husserl did exert an influence on Felix Kaufmann and other legal philosophers, cf. Genki Uemara, 'Husserl, Edmund' in Stephan Kirste and Mortimer Sellers (eds), *Encyclopedia for the Philosophy of Law and Social Philosophy*, vol 2 (Springer International 2024) 1383, 1385: In fact, Husserl later received and expanded Reinach's concept of the social act and also gave the concept of the norm a stronger meaning.

[2] Alois Troller, 'Das Bewußtseinsbild im Rechtsdenken' (1980) 13 ARSP Supplement 243; Alois Troller, 'Erkenntnistheoretische Parallele von Widerspiegelungstheorie und Phänomenologie im praktischen Rechtsdenken' (1983) I/3 *ARSP Supplement* 51.

[3] Schütz: 'The question of social meaning is a problem of time', 'das Sinnproblem [ist] ein Zeitproblem', Alfred Schütz, *Der sinnhafte Aufbau der sozialen Welt* (Springer 1932) 9, 10, 55 ff. repeatedly referring to Husserl and emphasizing the concept of duration as important for social meaning.

time series of 'earlier-than/later-than'.[4] Duration or extended present thus becomes the central temporal event for this qualitative time. In this way, both legal phenomenologists opened up conceptual possibilities for the understanding of the temporality of law that is distinct from natural and other social times. However, while Gerhart Husserl was able to work with his father's lectures on the 'Phenomenology of Internal Time Consciousness' published in 1928,[5] Reinach's approaches were devised independently and, in many ways, represent pioneering work for the exploration of the temporality of law based on the earlier Realistic Phenomenology. Reinach's early death, at the age of thirty-three, meant he only managed to deal with the temporality of law in a fragmentary way in his 'Die apriorischen Grundlagen des bürgerlichen Rechtes' ('The Apriori Foundations of Civil Law'), determining it as an essential structural element of the special existence of law. Gerhart Husserl, on several occasions, analyzed questions of law and time from the perspective of transcendental phenomenology and even Heidegger's 'Fundamental Ontology'.[6] Even if the presented elements of a theory of time and law remain very abstract, both succeed in determining time – far more than space – as a basic dimension of law. Considering the procedural character of modern law as well as the necessary temporality and historicity of legal discourses, both Reinach and Husserl thus throw a new light on an essential aspect of the structure of law. This alone is reason enough to take a closer look at some of the key points in the writing of both.

9.2 ADOLF REINACH'S APPROACHES TO A THEORY OF LAW AND TIME

Reinach accomplished for the structure of law what Rudolf Stammler worked on for its ethical content: the determination of an essential a priori.[7] Reinach focused on an 'ontology of law' or an 'apriorische Gegenstandslehre' ('a priori theory of objects'). What, for Stammler, was the 'correct law' ('Richtiges Recht') in the sense

[4] John M. Ellis McTaggart, 'The Unreality of Time' (1908) 17 Mind 457ff; John M. Ellis McTaggart, *The Nature of Existence*, vol 2 (Cambridge University Press 1927) 9 – 10; Neither Brentano, Reinach nor Husserl refer to him. However, Brentano deals with the same distinction between time series A consisting of present, future and past and series B comprised of 'earlier-than'/'later-than', insisting that series B holds primacy over series A because in 'earlier-than'/'later-than' would entail the determination of future and past would be present. Franz Brentano, *Philosophische Untersuchungen zu Raum, Zeit und Kontinuum* (Meiner 1976) 154.

[5] Edmund Husserl, *The Phenomenology of Internal Time-Consciousness* (Indiana University Press 1964).

[6] Although he did not refer to him much.

[7] However, Stammler criticizes Reinach for his theory, stating that 'legal will is not a phenomenon which could be recognized in its essence by direct observation'. Rudolf Stammler, *Lehrbuch der Rechtsphilosophie* (2nd edn, De Gruyter 1923) 48 and n 2.

of a 'natural law with changing content'[8] or an unconditional ideal for all changing content of natural law.[9] was for Reinach the 'social act' of law.[10] Reinach took into account the changeability of the living conditions of law but maintained that the content of positive law has its origin in a priori structures of legal social acts.[11] While Stammler's ideal form allows for changing natural law content as a measure of positive law, Reinach viewed every social act that produces positive law as having an a priori nature.[12] This essence is not normative for positive law but contains its substantial characteristics. At the same time, this essence gives the ontological foundation of contingent positive law. Reinach's approach distinguishes him from both legal positivists and natural law theorists: He is not looking for essential *normative* foundations of positive law or of right principles in a *moral* sense of natural law theory but for the essence of concrete legal rules. Reinach saw the temporality between the timelessness of logical and mathematical objects on the one hand and the simple being in time of physical and psychological objects on the other as belonging to the a priori structures of law.

For Reinach, the neglected study of the specific temporal structure of legal objects by his contemporaries was a major reason for his phenomenological analysis of the a priori foundations of law.[13] Legal ontology is supposed to lead us to new kinds of objects, which differ in structure from nature, namely the objects of psychology and ideal things. While temporality is an important element of their structure,[14] Reinach did not elaborate on his phenomenology of the temporality of law systematically. It is almost like Augustine, whom Reinach quoted with a statement from the 'Confessiones': 'If you do not ask me what it is, I believe that

[8] Rudolf Stammler, *Wirtschaft und Recht nach der materialistischen Geschichtsauffassung: Eine sozialphilosophische Untersuchung* (Veit 1896) 184–188; although he rejects the idea of an a priori law, this notion of natural law comes close to it.

[9] Rudolf Stammler, *Die Lehre von dem richtigen Rechte* (Wissenschaftliche Buchgesellschaft 1964) 81–90.

[10] Carl A Emge, 'Über den Charakter der Geltungsprobleme in der Rechtswissenschaft' (1920/21) 14 ARWP 146, 148: 'Reinachs Verdienste geben ihm seinen Platz bald nach Stammler. Was dieser für die Rechtsphilosophie bedeutet, bedeutet Reinach für die positive Rechtswissenschaft', cf. also 161 ff.

[11] It is interesting to note that Reinach misinterprets Stammler here by insinuating that the latter was concerned with an 'ideal law with immutable content', Adolf Reinach, 'The Apriori Foundations of the Civil Law' (John F Crosby tr, 1983) 3 Aletheia 1, reprinted in Adolf Reinach, *The Apriori Foundations of the Civil Law Along with the Lecture 'Concerning Phenomenology'* (John F Crosby ed, Ontos Verlag 2012), originally published as Adolf Reinach, Die apriorischen Grundlagen des bürgerlichen Rechtes, 1(2) *Jahrbuch für Philosophie und phänomenologische Forschung* (Max Niemeyer 1913) 685–847. Cf. also Neil Duxbury, 'The Apriori and the Legal' (1990) 21 Rechtstheorie 297, 309.

[12] Reinach (n 11) 133; Duxbury (n 11) 308 f.; Neil Duxbury, 'The Legal Philosophy of Adolf Reinach' (1991) 77 ARSP 314–347, 466–492, at 316 and 491.

[13] Reinach (n 11) 9: 'Claims and obligations, by contrast, arise, last a definite length of time, and then disappear again. Thus, they seem to be temporal objects of a special kind of which one has not yet taken notice'.

[14] ibid 6.

I know. But if you ask me, then I no longer know it'.[15] Augustine then developed his theory of time from this question. Reinach leaves us with many ideas regarding a phenomenology of time in his works,[16] although in them he criticizes sciences that are only concerned with proving the existence of certain phenomena 'at some point of objective time'.[17] He deemed that just as it would be wrong to describe the essence of red in physical terms of wavelength oscillations, it is also wrong to base the temporality resulting from the essence of law on an objective time.[18] The mistake here lies in trying to explain a color by using something else, in this case, a limited metric like the wavelength of light. As such, Reinach's phenomenology sought to avoid this problem by leading to the essence of the experienced phenomenon itself. To do this, he claimed that we have to 'put ourselves in the place' ('hineinversetzen') of law and its temporality and not try to explain it through something else.[19] Therefore, both the timelessness of the a priori foundations of law and the temporality of positive law tell us something important about Reinach's view of the nature of law. Both aspects are grounded in the structures of this essence ('Sein'/'Being') of law, which constitutes the legal a priori.

9.2.1 *The Timelessness of the Legal A Priori*

If one were to analyze law exclusively in terms of positivist legal theories, then, according to Reinach, one could only observe the constant changes in its enactment and expiration over time – where time means natural (astronomical or atomic) time.[20] One could neither demonstrate the generalizable structures of law nor do justice to legal temporality.[21] However, law does not neatly fall into a seemingly given and objective time and history but has its specific temporality which only becomes clear once its a priori structures are revealed.

15 In Reinach's words, Adolf Reinach 'Concerning Phenomenology', in John F Crosby (ed), *The Apriori Foundations of the Civil Law Along With the Lecture, 'Concerning Phenomenology'* (Ontos Verlag 2012) 143–167; Augustine Confessions, XI, XIV, 17, 162, 'What, then, is time? If no one asks me, I know what it is. If I wish to explain it to him who asks me, I do not know. Yet I say with confidence that I know that if nothing passed away, there would be no past time; and if nothing were still coming, there would be no future time; and if there were nothing at all, there would be no present time'.

16 Reinach (n 15) 145.

17 ibid 145.

18 ibid 147.

19 Adolf Reinach, 'Die Überlegung; ihre ethische und rechtliche Bedeutung (1912/13)' in Karl Schuhmann and Barry Smith (eds), *Adolf Reinach: Sämtliche Werke. Textkritische Ausgabe in 2 Bänden* (Philosophia Verlag 1989) 279–312, 282.

20 Positivists assume this, as did Reinach (n 11) 2, 'that there is simply no such thing as legal principles which stand in themselves and are timelessly valid, such as we find for instance in mathematics'.

21 Criticizing the legal positivisms of his time that ignored the timeless structures of a priori law, Reinach (n 11) 1.

Like the classical theories of law and time, Reinach also began with the timeless structures of law. However, unlike ancient and medieval metaphysics and their natural law theories,[22] he did not presuppose the existence of eternal laws. Nevertheless, Reinach shared their goal: the search for eternal truths that underlie the law:[23] 'We are concerned with descending down to the ultimate elements of right, which that authority cannot "create", and to the essential laws, to which it is indeed not bound but which have an eternal being which it cannot touch'.[24] Neither induction and abstraction from positive law nor new legal principles are sufficient to demonstrate the existence of prepositive legal principles as the latter exist independently and have timeless validity. Here, Reinach follows Edmund Husserl's concept of the 'material apriori'[25] in the early phase of his eidetic-realistic approach.[26] Any new period of history will likely negate these abstractions, and new legal principles will have to change with new moral convictions and economic developments. Law and jurisprudence gain their principles from the 'constantly changing content from the content of the times'.[27] However, this does not mean that the a priori legal structures change with positive law. Rather, every sentence of positive law is necessarily preceded by an a priori structure: '[T]hese structures and relations subsist antecedent to law; they are not defined by reference to it', as Duxbury puts it.[28]

Like other German legal theorists at the end of the nineteenth century, Reinach wanted to base jurisprudence as a scientific discipline on principles that were timeless as in other sciences.[29] What stood in the way, in his view, was the positivist assumption that all law – in form and substance – was produced by social action and that no legal foundations can be found prior to this production: 'We really do find what one has so emphatically denied: the positive law *finds* the legal concepts which enter into it; *in absolutely no way does it produce them*'.[30] Reinach argued that the foundations of law are not exhausted in their positive form and only positivism

[22] Stephan Kirste, *Die Zeitlichkeit des positiven Rechts und die Geschichtlichkeit des Rechtsbewußtseins* (Duncker & Humblot 1998) 26 ff. and 116 ff.

[23] Reinach (n 11) 137. However, as much as the search for natural law was justified and even 'finds its fulfillment in the apriori doctrine of law', the a priori foundations of every law are not law itself, but its essence.

[24] ibid 66.

[25] Edmund Husserl, *Erfahrung und Urteil. Untersuchungen zur Genealogie der Logik* (7th edn, Meiner 1999) 409 ff.; Brandenburg (n 1). Husserl considered this path from phenomenology to material a priori truths to be open to all sciences, including legal theory, ibid 428).

[26] Loidolt (n 1) 76.

[27] Reinach (n 11) 2.

[28] Duxbury (n 11) 305.

[29] For this endeavor see Stephan Kirste, 'The German Tradition of Legal Positivism' in P Mindus and T Spaak (eds), *The Cambridge Companion to Legal Positivism* (Cambridge University Press 2021).

[30] Reinach (n 11) 4. This is not to say that positive law raises a claim to correctness, ibid 51.

dwells on the laws of ought created by the legislator himself, while legal ontology goes back to the laws of being.[31] Furthermore, he noted that the search for non-positive foundations of law does not have to resort to purely formal, logical or methodological principles nor does law find its independent foundation merely in eternal material principles alone, as the doctrine of natural law asserts. Rather, for him all law is based on structures which it does not create, but which it must presuppose. Reinach laid great stress on the assumption that there are principles of all positive law that 'are independent of our grasp of them, just as are the laws of mathematics'.[32] These constitute the being or essence of law.[33] Thereby Reinach wanted to establish law as an independent sphere between physics or psychology and logic.[34] Ontology is supposed to give us insights into the essential structures of independent objects. It is to teach us about the essential foundations of law 'which stand in themselves and are timelessly valid'.[35] Thus, unlike Immanuel Kant's approach, Reinach held that the a priori foundations are not transcendental conditions of the possibility of knowledge, but of being itself.

The whole purpose of his 'Apriori Foundations of Civil Law' is to analyze these 'essential laws' with an 'eternal being'.[36] Positive law can depart from them and even ignore them but is still based on them. They subsist in positive law and are already there when it formulates its propositions.[37] For Reinach, positive law is therefore neither cognitively nor normatively conditioned by the a priori structures but rather by social fact. Positive law can indeed deviate from such structures, although it can never change them. If the connection is true, then positive law is the embodiment of these a priori structures. The temporal legal acts then temporalize the timeless a priori structures: Whenever an event occurs at moment M, a certain consequence F (e.g., a claim) must occur. This 'clear determination of temporal existence' by the

[31] ibid 124.

[32] ibid 5 f.

[33] ibid 161, 'In truth, the realm of the apriori is incalculably large. Whatever objects we know, they all have their "what," their "essence"; and of all essences there hold essence-laws. There is no reason at all for restricting the apriori to that which is in some sense "formal". Apriori laws also hold true of the material—in fact, of the sensible, of tones and colors'.

[34] Adolf Reinach 'Einleitung in die Philosophie' (1913) in Karl Schuhmann and Barry Smith (eds), *Adolf Reinach: Sämtliche Werke. Textkritische Ausgabe in 2 Bänden* (Philosophia Verlag 1989) 369–514, 424.

[35] Reinach (n 11) 2.

[36] These a priori principles, however, are 'eternal truths'. Even if it is not the main task of the a priori doctrine of law to prove them, it nevertheless finds them and, in this respect, shares a concern with the doctrine of natural law, ibid 137. The difference with the doctrine of natural law, however, is that the a priori doctrine of law only proves that these principles are not bound to historical circumstances, concrete human actions and positive law. Strictly speaking, it proves only their timelessness, but not their eternity. Also, ibid 66: 'We are concerned with descending down to the ultimate elements of right, which that authority cannot "create", and to the essential laws, to which it is indeed not bound but which have an eternal being which it cannot touch'.

[37] Duxbury (n 12) 327, 334, 336.

a priori legal structures creates a certainty of orientation.[38] The pure concepts of law are embedded in these structures[39] and the search for them is also a legitimate concern of natural law doctrines.[40] These doctrines were wrong not to take into account the changeable conditions of life on which the validity of such permanent principles is based. Despite this critique of natural law, however, Reinach tried to avoid falling into the trap of positivist theories. While some natural law theories assume timeless or even variable but not arbitrarily changeable principles of good, correct positive law, the a priori structures necessarily underlie all law – morally good as well as bad. The a priori foundations of law do not denote a higher or better law but simply the essence of law as it is.[41]

9.2.2 *The Temporality of Law*

As with his consideration of many other aspects of law, Reinach did not develop a full theory of its temporality. However, he emphasized the temporality of law as an important structure and gave many examples of it. The following traces these examples and brings them together within the framework of some common principles.

According to Reinach, when one looks at legal entities and structures from a phenomenological perspective, one can recognize a separate group of objects with their own mode of existence. These objects 'do not belong to nature in the proper sense, which are neither physical nor psychical and which are at the same time different from all ideal objects in virtue of their temporality'.[42] Their temporality is a crucial factor in understanding the nature of legal objects. As such, the following begins by looking at Reinach's notions of temporality and then presents his theoretical approaches to social and legal time.

9.2.2.1 Time and Space

Reinach developed a conception of the temporality of legal objects between the timelessness of the essential foundations of law and the temporality of natural objects. The a priori foundations of law have an atemporal nature: They exist without relation to a specific time. While we have seen that Reinach calls them 'eternal', this timelessness of the a priori foundations of law tells us little about the temporality of law itself. Reinach wanted to show that in addition to natural things which are, of course, 'in' time, there are also objects of knowledge in the form of

[38] Reinach (n 11) 14: 'principle of the definite determination of temporal existents'.
[39] ibid 98: His analysis was focused on 'the eternal laws of being which are grounded in the most basic pure categories of right'.
[40] ibid 137.
[41] ibid 135.
[42] ibid 6.

social acts which exist in their own temporal world.[43] In addition to their characteristic need to be consciously perceived ('Vernehmungsbedürftigkeit') and the presence of other characteristics common to social acts, namely intentionality, spontaneity and other-directedness, their temporality is an essential feature.[44] Social acts exist in their 'own world of temporal ... objects' (in German: 'eigene Welt zeitlicher ... Gegenständlichkeiten').[45] However, we already know that Reinach assumed that all law is based on a timeless foundation of the being or essence of its principles. This must also include the ontological foundations of the temporal structures of law itself. Just as law has an independent being that distinguishes it from all other objects, it also has a time structure that is not simply absorbed into the time structure of logical, natural things or the psyche. As little can be determined of the necessary properties of law from an examination of positive law alone, similarly, little can be determined about law's temporal structure by examining only its historical emergence and passing away or from dates, periods, deadlines and so forth. As such, Reinach sought the foundations of the temporality of law in its a priori foundation.

For Reinach, the concept of temporality ('Zeitlichkeit') is logically ambiguous. The diagnosed ambivalence lies in the fact that processes 'constitute themselves in time ... but a thing *is* in time'.[46] Here, the preposition 'in' is used for both processes and things. For clarity's sake, instead of 'constitute' and 'are', one could probably be allowed to say that processes bring themselves forth in time and things fall into time.

[43] For his theory of social acts and its influence on Speech Act Theory, cf. Armin Burkhardt, *Soziale Akte, Sprechakte und Texillokutionen. A. Reinachs Rechtsphilosophie und die moderne Linguistik* (De Gruyter 1986) 46 ff.

[44] Reinach (n 11) 18–20; Loidolt (n 1) 85.

[45] Reinach (n 11) 109. The English translation is inaccurate in this important point: 'We have in this work shown that in addition to the well-known sphere of natural objects, that is, of the physical and the mental, there is a world of its own consisting of entities and structures which are in time, though they do not belong to nature in the usual sense, and which derive from the social acts.' The full German text is, 'Wir haben neben der allbekannten Sphäre der Naturgegenstände, d. h. des Physischen und Psychischen, eine eigene Welt zeitlicher, aber nicht zur Natur im üblichen Sinne gehöriger, aus sozialen Akten erwachsender Gegenständlichkeiten herausgehoben', Adolf Reinach, 'Die apriorischen Grundlagen des bürgerlichen Rechts (1913)' in Karl Schuhmann and Barry Smith (eds), *Adolf Reinach: Sämtliche Werke. Textkritische Ausgabe in 2 Bänden* (Philosophia Verlag 1989) 141–279, 246.

[46] Adolf Reinach, 'Notwendigkeit und Allgemeinheit im Sachverhalt' in Karl Schuhmann and Barry Smith (eds), *Adolf Reinach: Sämtliche Werke. Textkritische Ausgabe in 2 Bänden* (Philosophia Verlag 1989) 352. My translation, 'The concept of temporality is ambiguous. Processes, e.g. thunder, constitute themselves in time, things not, but a thing *is* in time. In the same way, facts are not constituted in time, but they are in time because they are provided with temporal predications. It is a different matter when temporal elements are incorporated into the facts themselves'. In German, 'Der Begriff Zeitlichkeit ist zweideutig. Vorgänge, z. B. Donner, konstituieren sich in der Zeit, Dinge tun es nicht, aber ein Ding i s t in der Zeit. So konstituieren sich auch Sachverhalte nicht in der Zeit, aber sie sind in der Zeit, so weil mit zeitlichen Prädikationen versehen. Etwas anderes ist es, wenn zeitliche Elemente in den Sachverhalt selbst aufgenommen werden'.

Thus, by virtue of 'constituting', processes have a more active relation to time than things. It will soon become apparent that this difference between an active 'bringing forth' and a passive 'falling into time' is important for the temporality of social acts and law. Furthermore, Reinach held that processes are built up over time: they come into being, last for a while and then come to an end.[47] In contrast, states ('Zustände') lack this dynamic: they are in a certain sense complete and exist for a while, so they last. Whether one agrees with this or not, it is clear how Reinach tried to identify essential temporal differences between the phenomena of 'process' and 'state'.[48] From an ontological perspective, this is precisely where ideal, natural and social or legal objects differ: Ideal objects are timeless – like the a priori foundations of law; natural objects fall into a time that is external to them while social and especially legal objects bring forth a particular characteristic of time. This is true even if they, in a certain respect, also fall into a natural time and may refer to natural time. Nevertheless, this relation to natural time remains external to them. With the foregoing in mind, it seems appropriate to provide a closer analysis of Reinach's approach.

Reinach distinguished space, time and duration as different forms of continuity.[49] One finds continuity in both a line that is spatially continuous and a duration that is temporally continuous. What such a line and duration have in common is that their continuity is not composed of their parts. That is to say that many points do not result in a continuous line, nor do many moments result in a continuous time. They can only limit the continuum, not create it: Just as the beginning and end points limit a straight line, moments can limit time. However, this does not change the fact

[47] Reinach (n 34) 406, in German, 'beginnt, dauert, endet'.

[48] ibid 396: 'Every process has a temporal expansion (analogous to the spatial expansion), arises in it and is completed in it ... [In contrast, a] state enters the world complete [and] can last. States do not have temporal expansion in the sense that they build up in time in the sense of constitution and completion in time'. In German, 'Jeder Vorgang hat zeitliche Ausbreitung (analog der räumlichen), entsteht darin und vollendet sich darin ... [Dagegen ein] Zustand tritt fertig in die Welt [und] kann dauern. Zustände haben keine zeitliche Ausbreitung in dem Sinne, daß sie sich in der Zeit aufbauen im Sinne von Konstitution und Vollenden in der Zeit'.

[49] It would be very interesting to compare Reinach's 1914 theory of continuity with Franz Brentano's work 'Philosophische Untersuchungen zu Raum, Zeit und Kontinuum' from the same year. This is because Reinach's empirical approach to continuity and time is much closer to Brentano's than to Husserl's concept of the inner time consciousness, which departs from the empirical approach in phenomenology, Husserl (n 5) 29–40 (mostly referring to Brentano's early concept of time). Brentano also bases his theory of time on a discussion of continuity where the temporal is a relative quality in Brentano's concept of time: It is only in continuity with past and future. Brentano (n 4) 210. Edmund Husserl again criticizes Brentano's concept of time and continuity by assuming that the 'point of now' in continuity of past and future would merely be fictitious, Edmund Husserl, *Zur Phänomenologie des inneren Zeitbewußtseins*. Mit den Texten aus der Erstausgabe und dem Nachlaß. 1. Auflage. Hg. v. Rudolf Bernet. (Felix Meiner Verlag, Philosophische Bibliothek, 649, 2013) 328. For Brentano's concept of a plurality of times, cf. Brentano (n 4) 193 ff.: 'es gibt kein Individuum "der Raum" und kein Individuum "die Zeit" weder an sich noch als Phänomen'.

that time remains a continuum and even its smallest part does not become a moment. The parts of time always remain time and do not become something else, namely noncontinuous moments. Duration is a temporal continuum, however, according to Reinach, it can be interrupted. Thus, he argued that when it is divided, there is no duration between the two 'pieces' of duration, only time. This is because duration refers to a process that starts, goes on for a while and then stops. It is, therefore, characterized by the process and the process takes time. Duration is that which has a beginning and an end in time.[50] Because the process consumes something of time, it presupposes time. Although the process produces its duration, it leaves the primary time unchanged and can therefore be measured by it. This is why Reinach also speaks of time as the 'primary' and duration as the 'secondary' continuum. Duration, however, is peculiar to the process, 'Every process has its duration, which belongs to it alone, while several processes can take place in the same time'.[51] One could say, then, that duration is time that is determined by a process, in that this process begins, has a certain course and ends. The consideration provided here will, therefore, call the temporality of duration based on the nature of social acts as processes 'qualitative time'. In contrast, following Reinach's terminology, time as a 'primary continuum' is not characterized by processes and, it is therefore referred to here as 'objective time'.[52]

Not all temporal phenomena are continua, for example, moments.[53] The beginning and end of the durations are moments that are not continuous, although they

[50] Adolf Reinach, 'Die obersten Regeln der Vernunftschlüsse bei Kant' (1911), in Karl Schuhmann and Barry Smith (eds), *Adolf Reinach: Sämtliche Werke. Textkritische Ausgabe in 2 Bänden* (Philosophia Verlag 1989) 57.

[51] Adolf Reinach, 'Über das Wesen der Bewegung' in Karl Schuhmann and Barry Smith (eds), *Adolf Reinach: Sämtliche Werke. Textkritische Ausgabe in 2 Bänden* (Philosophia Verlag 1989) 577: My translation, 'Duration is – or rises and grows – only if something happens. There is no analogy for this in the line. The line is more independent than duration. Accordingly, one cannot distinguish moments of duration from moments of time like points of the line from the places of the space they fill'. In German, 'Die Dauer ist—bzw. hebt an und wächst—nur, sofern etwas geschieht. Dafür gibt es bei der Linie kein Analogon. Sie hat eine größere Selbständigkeit als die Dauer. Entsprechend kann man auch nicht Momente der Dauer von den Momenten der Zeit unterscheiden wie Punkte der Linie von den Orten des Raumes, den sie einnehmen.'

[52] Above note 17.

[53] Reinach was also interested in the temporal structure of his research subjects in other studies and gave examples of continuous and punctual temporal phenomena. In his short treatise on the 'Theory of Negative Judgment', for example, he writes 'Überzeugung sowohl als Behauptung, realisieren sich in der Zeit; es läßt sich der Zeitpunkt angeben, in welchem sie ins Dasein treten. Aber während wir von einer beliebigen Dauer der Überzeugung reden können, läßt die Behauptung ihrem Wesen nach eine zeitliche Ausbreitung nicht zu; sie verläuft nicht in der Zeit, sondern hat ein gleichsam p u n k t u e l l e s Sein'. (Adolf Reinach, 'Zur Theorie des negativen Urteils' (1911) in Karl Schuhmann and Barry Smith (eds), *Adolf Reinach: Sämtliche Werke. Textkritische Ausgabe in 2 Bänden* (Philosophia Verlag 1989) 99 f.; Author's translation, 'Both belief and assertion realize themselves in time; the point in time at which they come into existence can be specified. However, while we can speak of a shorter or

are still temporal. They have a different temporal structure than the duration that they limit and the time to which they refer. They depend on the process whose beginning and end they mark. Moments do not become, they simply are. Similarly, a state ('Zustand') does not become, it just is. Processes, however, become. Additionally, if this becoming has the temporality of duration, then Reinach can say that moments and states are nontemporal,[54] however, they still refer to objective time.

The difference between the line as a space continuum and the duration as a time continuum lies in their genesis. Reinach did not seem to accept Kant's view that the unity of such a line can be explained by the temporal activity of drawing it.[55] It is not subjective consciousness or activity that creates the distance or the duration, it is the particular quality of the process. What is important for an understanding of the temporality of law, however, is the duration. Social acts are the processes that create duration and, correspondingly, legal acts such as a promise or a determination produce legal duration. This duration of legal processes as a temporal phenomenon can then also be related to the time they take. Thus, social time is not constituted by a line of independently fixed points in time that are earlier or later in the sense of an

longer duration of belief, assertion, by its very nature, does not allow for temporal expansion; it does not pass in time but has, as it were, a punctual existence'. Conceptions have a duration, whereas the verbal expression of opinions would have a similar 'punctual temporal natural' ibid 102. Finally, a conviction detaches itself from the perceived objects and also outlasts their perception. Its longer duration is therefore part of the nature of conviction ibid 107, 125; Adolf Reinach 'Zur Phänomenolgie der Ahnungen' (1916/17) in Karl Schuhmann and Barry Smith (eds), *Adolf Reinach: Sämtliche Werke. Textkritische Ausgabe in 2 Bänden* (Philosophia Verlag 1989) 589–591, 591. Furthermore, in his manuscripts from 1916/17, Reinach dealt with 'Ahnungen' (perhaps: presentiments or anticipations). He notes that the presentiment of a future event would not be a simple emotion. Rather, 'the presentiment adds something new to the overall store of knowledge – in the broadest sense of knowledge; the subject seems here, rightly or wrongly it remains to be seen, to grasp something from the flow of future occurrences by means of the presentiment that was not accessible to him before'. In German: 'Vielmehr fügt die Ahnung dem Gesamtwissensschatze – im weitesten Sinne des Wissens gesprochen – etwas Neues hinzu'. It is neither certain knowledge about the future nor a vague feeling about it but a sense of something new approaching, ibid 590–591. Reinach even considered how a praying person, in his concentration, can get out of temporality and into contact with the absolute presence or eternity of God also: Monica Adamczyk, 'Zwischen Endlichkeit und Ewigkeit. Adolf Reinachs Konzept des religiösen Erlebnisses' (2014) 28 *Poznanskie Studia Teologiczne* 115–130, 123. Furthermore, another aspect of time interested Reinach in 'Reflection: Its Ethical and Legal Significance Introduction'. On p. 81 he summarized his analysis of reflexions, 'reflectively we present to ourselves the reflective behavior itself. Here it becomes clear how differently the presentification can manifest itself in individual instances … We posit as the first type of reflection the inner behavior of the subject who is in the questioning stance, which leads from sheer understanding or the sudden appearing ['Aufblitzen'] of a thought, through presentification of the content, to insight and conviction'.

[54] Reinach (n 51) 580.

[55] Immanuel Kant, *Critique of Pure Reason* (Paul Guyer and Allen W Wood eds, Cambridge University Press 1998) 258.

arrow of time but by the relative social acts that shape the present and, in relation to it, the future and the past. Social time – and with it legal time – is relative to the associated acts. The fact that social acts and law have their own temporality does not mean that they cannot be related to natural time, which can be measured by clocks. However, for Reinach, it was something else to examine the particular kind of present – instantaneous or extended in time – and to answer this question in the essence of the act or to relate it to measurable time.[56]

If one accepts the validity of Reinach's approach, he can help to understand that, firstly, the qualitative time of duration becomes an expression of the essence of processes, secondly, that these processes are social acts, and, therefore, thirdly, that unlike a spatialized time of 'earlier than' or 'later than', this concept of time is relative and not absolute.

9.2.2.2 Legal Temporality Based on Social Acts

For Reinach, the general ability to endure is a prerequisite for becoming a subject of law.[57] Mathematical objects do not have this ability. They do not participate in the coming into being and passing away of judged and measured natural things as, among other things, they are extratemporal.[58] Feelings and other mental events arise and pass away with a corresponding mental agitation. Legal entities such as a right or obligation are neither extratemporal nor do they arise or pass away with a psychical impulse or as a result of simple natural events. They continue even after the psychic impulse has ceased and independently of natural events unless the law explicitly refers to them.[59] This duration is necessarily part of the essence of the claim, as Reinach pointed out: Legal objects 'seem to be temporal objects of a special kind of which one has not yet taken notice'.[60] This temporal structure – that they are neither merely natural-temporal nor extratemporal – is essential to legal objects.[61]

56 Cf. again, the quote in n 14 above.

57 However, Reinach also acknowledges other entities, 'which are in time without having a duration. Such an event also exists, for example, when something lights up for me: it happens at a certain moment'. In German, 'die in der Zeit sind, ohne Dauer zu haben. Ein solches Geschehen liegt z.B. auch vor, wenn mir etwas aufleuchtet: das geschieht in einem bestimmten Moment', Reinach (n 51) 578. Reinach (n 11) 109.

58 Reinach (n 11) 108.

59 ibid 9, 11: 'claim and obligation can last for years without change, but there are no experiences which last like this'. J Dubois and B Smith, 'Adolf Reinach', in *Stanford Encyclopedia of Philosophy*, https://plato.stanford.edu/entries/reinach/, at 3.4.

60 Reinach (n 11) 9.

61 Adolf Reinach, 'Nichtsoziale und soziale Akte' in Karl Schuhmann and Barry Smith (eds), *Adolf Reinach: Sämtliche Werke. Textkritische Ausgabe in 2 Bänden* (Philosophia Verlag 1989) 358: 'Anspruch und Verbindlichkeiten [sind] nichts Physisches, auch nichts Psychisches, keine Erlebnisse … Vielleicht [sind sie dann] ideelle Gegenstände [im Sinne Husserls]? Aber [sie sind] keineswegs außerzeitlich wie Zahlen u. dgl. Anspruch und Verbindlichkeit haben Dauer, fangen an [usw.]. [Sie sind also ein] eigenartige Art, [eine] neue Klasse von Gegenständen' ('Claims and liabilities [are] nothing physical, also nothing psychological, no experiences …

First of all, it is noticeable that Reinach did not base his analysis of the a priori foundations of law on the concept of norms as, for example, Hans Kelsen does, but on social acts that can bring about 'determinations' ('Bestimmungen') as 'normations' ('Normierungen').[62] Not only does he criticize the polysemy of the term 'norm'[63] but his starting point is different. Following Reinach, in contrast to natural law theories, not even the a priori foundations of law produce normative permissions or prohibitions.[64] They are 'eternal laws of being', not normative propositions.[65] If one adds the a priori structures, one can say that eternal a priori laws of being lay the foundation for the temporal social acts that produce 'being-ought' ('Sein-Sollen') through 'determinations'. This is an essential preliminary decision for the temporality of law: whereas norms, as propositions, ought to aim at binding the future, the primary time dimension of acts is the present. Reinach even admitted that the ought-to-be[66] set by a legislator cannot be realized immediately. He distinguishes this from a provision in private law, which – like the waiver of a right – has immediate effect.[67] However, he avoids the consequence that in a legal system these legislative provisions – and thus norms – are the normal case that only provide the framework for the directly effective 'determinations'. In other words, the legislator's binding of the future only creates the legal precondition for the immediate effectiveness of civil law provisions.

Reinach, in contrast, started from the social act that is effective now and looks from there to the future binding of the ought-to-be. Social acts are intentional and spontaneous actions that are directed at another person and must be consciously perceived by that person.[68] The norm is, therefore, simply something that social acts

Perhaps [they are then] ideal objects [in Husserl's sense]? But [they are] by no means non-temporal like numbers and the like. Claim and connection have duration, begin [etc.]. [They are therefore a] particular kind, [a] new class of objects').

[62] Reinach (n 11) 4, 105, 133. He apparently understands norm strongly in the context of positive legal standardization: 'Normierung' – 'norming'. Here he speaks of Enactment of norms, not merely of the result of that act, the norm itself. He contrasts this with the ontological being of the social acts that establish law. His criticism of the concept of the norm does not mean that Reinach does not know the 'ought to be' ('Seinsollen'); he only wants to trace it back to its moral (Reinach (n 11) 105) and social (Reinach (n 11) 137) essence. And distinguishes three forms of it (Reinach (n 11) 109). On the linguistic aspects of his concept of norm as normal cf. Maria Gołębiewska, 'Normativity of Prescriptions in Adolf Reinach's Aprioristic Theory of Right' (2020) 90 *Acta Universitas Lodziensis* 41. Also, Stanley Paulson, 'Demystifying Reinach's Legal Theory' in Kevin Mulligan (ed), *Speech Act and Sachverhalt. Reinach and the Foundations of Realist Phenomenology* (Martinus Nijhoff Publishers 1987) 133–154, 145 f.

[63] Reinach (n 11) 104 f. Gołębiewska (n 62) 54 f.

[64] Rather, it they produce an impossibility, let's say, to transfer something which does not belong to a person (Reinach (n 11) 111). The essential being is at the same time, what ought to be (Reinach (n 11) 124).

[65] Reinach (n 11) 98.

[66] About the 'ought-to-be' in Reinach, cf. Duxbury (n 12) 480 f.

[67] Reinach (n 11) 115 f.

[68] Reinach gives several examples of social acts, cf. also Marta María Albert Márquez, 'Reinach, Adolf' in Mortimer Sellers and Stephan Kirste (eds), *Encyclopedia for the Philosophy of Law and Social Philosophy* (Springer Nature 2023) 3040, 3042. Dubois and Smith (n 59) 4.

can produce. In any case, in this way, he fails to conceptualize the structural principle of the hierarchical construction of norms as future obligations, which is characteristic of differentiated modern legal systems. Therefore, he misses a characteristic element of differentiated modern legal systems, according to which the determination of norms takes place in a tiered system of competences and procedures ('Stufenbau der Rechtsordnung'). What is crucial to understand here is that by focusing on the social act as the foundation of law rather than the norm, the present becomes the defining dimension of the law rather than the future obligation.

The temporality of social acts is thus the basis for the temporality of law. In this sense, for example, conviction and assertion differ essentially in their temporality: While a conviction lasts, an assertion has no temporal extension.[69] As was the case for Franz Brentano, the present is also the central temporal dimension for Reinach. When a social act is performed, 'something new enters the world'[70] and 'something is thereby changed in the world'.[71] The social world of 'other-directedness' is not as it was before. Therefore, the social act is historical. In contrast, the past only generates 'cold knowledge'.[72] Moreover, social acts have a teleological structure, namely they are aimed at a future event.[73] The minimal future event is that social acts become effective only when they are consciously perceived ('vernommen') or the addressee becomes aware of them ('innewerden').[74] Such a social act can be aimed at or produce a certain future, just as a question may be phrased in a manner that elicits a particular response. In the case of the social act of questioning, an extended present is simultaneously created in which the questioner waits for the answer.[75] Much natural time may pass during the waiting period, which can be measured with a watch, however, the question lasts until it is answered or until an answer can no

69 Again, see the quote in n 53.

70 Reinach (n 11) 9.

71 ibid 22.

72 ibid 38.

73 'An obligatory relationship strives towards its end, towards fulfillment', in German, 'Ein obligatorisches Verhältnis strebt seinem Ende zu, der Erfüllung' (Reinach (n 61) 360).

74 Reinach (n 11) 37, 91, 102, 19: 'We designate the spontaneous acts which are in need of being consciously perceived, social acts'. As far as I can see, Reinach uses the terms 'vernehmen' and 'innewerden' interchangeably, although 'innewerden' refers more to the internal aspect of perceiving, which can mean a certain awareness. 'The effect of social acts always comes about only when they are perceived', in German 'die Wirkung sozialer Akte stets erst dann eintritt, wenn ich ihrer innewerde', and for this, simply 'hearing' – as a minimal form of perception – is not enough (Reinach (n 11) 28). Hearing – as Crosby translates it – captures only one aspect of 'vernehmen' and in doing so omits the aspect of consciousness (Duxbury (n 12) 321, n. 27). Crosby's translation that 'if the promise is simply heard (vernommen) there arises a claim in the one who hears and an obligation in the promisor' contradicts Reinach's explicit observation – and his own translation – 'It is also not enough that the promisee perceive the external signs, for instance hear the words, without understanding them'. 'Vernehmen' and 'Innewerden' mean 'a certain conscious perception', for which hearing is necessary, but not in itself sufficient.

75 The act of questioning is itself a temporally punctual act that emerges from the questioning attitude as the basic phenomenon and itself a permanent attitude, Reinach, 'Reflection: Its Ethical and Legal Significance – Introduction', 69.

longer be expected. The expression of the answer is a responding act that closes the future opened up by the question.[76] Successful communication requires the simultaneity of speaking and listening.[77] The fact that this time is also measurable in a natural time is not essential to communication, but only an external circumstance. If one follows Reinach to this point, one must distinguish duration, which is an expression of the subject, from this external relation to a time.

However, for Reinach not all social actions have the present as their characteristic temporal dimension as many may have a nature that is related to the past. When one apologizes, congratulates, thanks, praises and so forth, such acts necessarily refer to the past.[78] Other social actions cannot refer to the past, such as obligation and demand, which refer to the future.[79]

9.2.2.3 The Temporality of Legal Acts

As noted above, for Reinach many social acts refer specifically to the temporal dimensions of the future, present and past. However, within these categories, acts can be distinguished between, such as with a command from a request: A command opens a social present that can only be closed by a future act – the fulfillment of the command. In this scenario, as with a question and answer, the first social act requires a future responding act.[80] Commands and questions are social acts that open a future that remains until the intended act – fulfillment, response – occurs.[81] Here, an intended future opens an extended present.[82]

Reinach shows that an offer and acceptance also have a specific temporal structure, resulting from their nature. One cannot accept an offer through information or a communication, but only through a specific utterance of a presentistic nature. One should, therefore, temporally distinguish the 'rigid' legal act of acceptance of 'I hereby accept' from the narrative 'I have already inwardly agreed' and a declaration of intent, namely 'I will agree'.[83] Like the 'I do' of the bridal couple in a church or before the registrar, acceptance is a performative act that can only take place and fulfill its meaning in the present. The groom, who holds out the prospect of saying 'I do' to his bride and does not actually say 'I do' is signaling to her that he is

[76] Baeyer (n 82) 60.
[77] Reinach (n 11) 21.
[78] Burkhardt (n 43) 328 f. calls these acts 'expressive'.
[79] Reinach (n 61) 358.
[80] In the sense of Speech Act Theories, one could mention other 'directives' with a similar temporal nature like requests, permissions, prohibitions, warnings, Burkhardt (n 43) 327 f.
[81] Reinach (n 11) 21.
[82] For this explanation of social temporality constituted by social acts cf. Alexander von Baeyer, 'Adolf Reinachs Phänomenologie' (doctoral thesis, University of Heidelberg 1969) 86.
[83] Burkhardt (n 43) 46 and 329: Other examples for such 'declarative' acts that have a present nature would be declaring war, sentencing somebody to prison, a coach removing a player from the sports field or appointing somebody to a position.

not serious about his intention and wants to think it over. The same is true for any potential contracting partner who only indicates acceptance. If the potential partner does not give any reasons for this, the delay in making his or her intention known is a reason to doubt if an intention to enter into the contract exists.[84]

As is well known, for Reinach, the basic legal act is the promise. Promises have a particular temporal structure because, as social acts, promises are processes with a specific temporal duration.[85] While a message can refer to the present, the future and/or past, a promise, like a command or request, 'always refers to a future time'.[86] However, while the behavior of others is central to commands and requests, a promise is centered on the person making the promise.[87] For Reinach, the promisor irrevocably binds his or her future in the presence of the promisee, even without the other's acceptance, when the promise is consciously perceived ('vernommen'). In this way, the promisor initiates 'a train of events'.[88] The claim and obligating nature of a promise arises immediately when it is made.[89] Unlike experiences, a claim or an obligation arising from a promise 'can last for years'.[90] Reinach can show that a promise has a teleological structure, 'an inherent tendency to an end and to dissolve'.[91] Unlike the transfer of property, for example, which exhausts itself in its efficacy,[92] a promise refers to future action.[93] With Franz Brentano one could say that the still unreal future only becomes reality through the binding nature of the promise because it is made present.[94] The temporal structure of promises, claims and obligations is thus an important distinguishing feature from other phenomena such as experiences. From this structure, Reinach concluded that claim and obligation 'seem to be temporal objects of a special kind'.[95]

In his discussion with Wilhelm Schuppe, Reinach returned to this temporal structure. Whereas Schuppe believed that the immutability of the obligation results from the trust of the recipient rather than from the promise, Reinach countered that the obligation follows from the nature of the promise itself. Irrespective of whether the promisor has granted the promisee a right of revocation or has made a

84 Reinach (n 11) 22 f.

85 'It can, according to its essence, last ever so long, but on the other hand it seems to have an inherent tendency towards meeting an end and a dissolution' (Reinach (n 11) 8).

86 ibid 35.

87 ibid 27.

88 ibid 25.

89 ibid 27, even if the promisor ties the content of the obligation already entered into to certain conditions, namely a 'promise with conditional content'.

90 ibid 9, 11: 'claim and obligation can last for years without change'.

91 ibid 8.

92 ibid 67.

93 ibid 11.

94 Brentano (n 4) 107, summarizing 'I believe I recognize that the real as real must be extended in time' and at 210, 'Thus it is certain that nothing exists except what is temporal or present' and at 214, 'that real that is that is present'.

95 Reinach (n 11) 9.

conditional promise, the promise is irrevocable 'from the outset'. This means that a promise creates its future obligation and the extended present the moment it is made and consciously received.[96]

The declaration of a promise establishes the present of the future obligation of that promise even without the acceptance of the addressee of the promisee. The promisor may, of course, make his promise conditional on the acceptance of the addressee.[97] In this case, if the addressee does not accept the promise or rejects it, no claim or obligation arises. This acceptance of the promise has a different time structure than the promise itself and, as has already been explained, it can only take place in the present.[98] Neither the person who indicates acceptance nor the person who promises to accept has actually accepted. An acceptor must accept by stating, for example, 'I hereby accept'. This 'I hereby accept' establishes the present necessary for acceptance. Acceptance can only take place as a performative, present declaration[99] – or as Reinach would later say, 'determination'. With Reinach we can conclude that, while a promise necessarily has a temporal structure of the future, an acceptance necessarily has a temporal structure of the present.

It seems appropriate at this point to follow an interesting modification that Reinach made when he introduced 'conditional promises' and 'promises with conditional content'.[100] In both cases, a promisor modifies the extended present, albeit in different ways. With both modifications, one may ask: How are we to understand the time between the act of promising and the occurrence of the condition? In a 'conditional promise', the promisor makes the efficacy of the resultant obligation dependent on a possible future event.[101] For example, at time t, a promisor says: 'I will only commit myself to action X when (time t') I know that you will commit yourself to action Y'. Only when the condition is fulfilled is the promisor obliged to do X, without any further acts being required from either the promisor or the promisee.[102] For the act at time t, it is essential that the occurrence of the future event of the condition is open. In other words: by its very nature ('essentially required', according to Reinach), the condition has the character of an open future. If the future event were already certain when the promise is made, the effectiveness of the obligation could, at best, be limited in time.[103] In contrast, in a case involving a 'promise with conditional content', the promisor enters into an obligation immediately but ties its content to certain conditions that must be

96 As a duration, the extended present only exists if something happens that can produce it (Reinach (n 51) 577).
97 Reinach (n 11) 28 f.
98 ibid 44.
99 ibid 29 f.
100 ibid 22 ff.
101 It is necessary that the occurrence of this event is possible and not necessary, 'their efficacy is tied to something which may occur later' (Reinach (n 11) 23).
102 ibid 27.
103 ibid 23.

fulfilled: 'I promise now (time t) to start doing X until Y happens (time t')'. This obligation arises immediately when the promise is made, and thus represents the normal case of a promise.

What is interesting about both modifications of a promise is how to understand the time between the making of the promise and the fulfillment of the condition (t – t'). In the case of a 'conditional promise', this extended present has an 'at first' or provisional character, that is, it is oriented toward the occurrence of the condition and ends with the corresponding event. If the promisor makes a conditional promise, then the claim and obligation arise with the occurrence of the event specified in the condition ('conditional promise') and expire as if the promise had never been made the moment it becomes clear that the specified event will not occur.[104] In the meantime, the obligation does not exist and, therefore, it is not yet possible to waive the performance of the promise. Here, 'initially' means that the promisee's waiver only becomes effective when the condition occurs, namely, in the period of time limited by the occurrence of the condition set by the promisor when the promisee can waive the claim just as conditionally. The same moment t' becomes the condition for the emergence of the claim and the condition for the waiver: 'The coming into existence of the claim is here the immediate cause of its death'.[105] The period of time t – t' has the character of the provisional. In the case of conditional renunciation, the period lasts until the moment t', which acquires the character of a common present through the condition of its obligation set by the promisor and the condition of its renunciation set by the promisee. Conversely, in the case of a 'promise with conditional content', the obligation is created immediately. Following Reinach, therefore a promisee may waive the relevant obligation during the entire period. This possibility to waive does not arise with the occurrence of the substantive condition but ends then. It is only in this respect that it is provisional: It is not a promisor's obligation that is provisional, but rather only the performance of that obligation. In the time span t – t' everything is related: the promise and the possibility of renunciation. Thus, by modifying the promise, a promisor has the power to make the extended present t – t' temporally as provisional toward a future event ('conditional promise') or already as fully realized ('promise with conditional content').[106] At any moment of the extended present t – t', the promisee can react with a renunciation. In both cases, the character of this time span t – t' does not result from natural time sequences, rather, it is characterized by the promise and the possibilities of the promisee to react to it; whether it has the character of the provisional or is the present depends on them. According to Reinach, this entire structure of a promise is based on the timeless a priori of law

[104] ibid 23.
[105] ibid 27.
[106] Reinach further distinguishes the promises with a conditional content – but only these – into acts with 'future conditions which put an end to an obligation and those which let the obligation come into being' (Reinach (n 11) 23).

('wesensgesetzlich gefordert', 'essentially required'). No matter how manifold the acts of a promise and its acceptance are, no matter how inadequate the legal regulations of this, 'their pure ideas are based on secure and immutable laws'.[107]

Therefore, one can agree with Reinach stating that promises and acceptances are 'temporal objects that have a character of their own and are neither physical nor psychological',[108] as long as one adheres to their ontological properties and distinguishes them from the experiences in which they appear to us. However, they are neither timeless nor out of time like the a priori structures. Rather, the declaration of a promise and its perception simultaneously generate a duration that is essential for social acts, and both acts only relate to each other because they constitute an extended present.[109] This duration is opened by the declaration of a promise and closed by its fulfillment. Acceptance – if necessary – falls into this present as a point in time constituted by the acceptor.

Taken together we can see with Reinach that a promise is a social act and as a social act, it is a process with a beginning of a certain permanence and an end, that is, it has a duration. However, a particular character of this duration follows from the nature of promises: The duration is directed toward a future realization of the promise in question. The beginning, continuation and end of this duration can be modified as continuous or provisional by conditions. The temporally structured present in this way is not an arbitrary construction of a promisor but follows from the nature of the promise given and the conditions or time limit set. This duration takes place based on objective time, which makes it possible to measure the moments of the social act of the promise in question, of the entry into the condition and of the time limit. However, what is measured – the social act of the promise – does not derive its duration from this time but from the essential process. As with a movement, the measurable moments do not define the duration of the process but are its expression, namely, its beginning and its end.

Reinach did not examine other legal acts with the same level of detail as he did the promise as a basic legal act. However, the examples below show how he anchored temporality in the nature of the respective social legal: Although Reinach did not explicitly speak of future commitment, he did say that the obligatory relationship tends toward its realization and it has a purpose. An obligation is related to 'the time at which it should be fulfilled'.[110] Correspondingly, a claim is directed toward its fulfillment. Such terms signal the teleological and thus future-oriented character of the relationship between the promisor and the promisee. At the moment when a claim is either fulfilled or a waiver becomes effective, that claim expires. Reinach also made a temporal distinction between relative rights,

[107] ibid 33.
[108] ibid 10.
[109] Baeyer (n 82) 90 f.
[110] Reinach (n 11) 32.

such as claims, and absolute rights that, for example, relate to property. While claims have a provisional temporal structure because they are ordered toward an end, absolute rights have something finite about them.[111] If a claim is fulfilled by the conduct of another party, it ends. However, rights arising from property can be exercised at any time. As such, both claims and absolute rights can have time-bound content.[112]

In addition, for Reinach a contract also has a specific, a priori existing temporality which results from the connection of the temporality of the mutual declarations: In the extended present, the contracting parties instantiate a future structure. This binds the future of the obligor and opens the future of the obligee.[113] In the case of reciprocal obligations, therefore, there are mutual future commitments, and the resultant extended present is not closed until all the contractual obligations have been fulfilled. For Reinach, this necessary temporal structure of contracts results from the necessary temporality of the social acts underlying contracts.[114]

Finally, there are social acts, such as judgments, that directly change something in the world. Reinach called them 'determinations' ('Bestimmungen') and these are relatively commonplace as they arise with an acceptance of an offer and the enactment of laws and statutes. 'Determinations' are not rooted in previous structures – although they may be shaped by them – but bring something new.[115] 'Determinations' are not future-oriented but have an immediate effect – which is the existence of a claim or property.[116] In contrast to a command, which is realized only if it is obeyed in the future, a 'determination' is realized immediately. Take § 1 of the German Civil Code (BGB): 'The legal capacity of a human being begins with the completion of birth'.[117] The indicative of the formulation shows that this effect occurs when its precondition is fulfilled. The legislator 'enacts that claim and property ought to be, and presently something is changed in the world. What is posited by the enactment is not merely something which ought to be and is waiting to be realized, rather it becomes real at the moment of the positing and through the positing: property and claim exist in virtue of the enactment'.[118] Transfer would be another example.[119] The present here has a very different character from the

[111] ibid 58.
[112] ibid 61.
[113] Baeyer (n 82) 94.
[114] ibid 89.
[115] Reinach (n 11) 108.
[116] ibid 52, 'There are rights to actions with an immediate efficacy in the world of right – we already encountered some of them: the right to waive, to revoke, and the like. These are social acts the exercise of which produces an immediate effect in relations of right, such as ending them or modifying them'.
[117] Paulson (n 62) 149.
[118] Reinach (n 11) 110.
[119] ibid 66 f., 'Both promising and transferring are social acts with immediate legal efficacy. But only transferring reaches its final goal with this efficacy'.

teleological present of a promise:[120] The act of transfer exhausts itself in the present. However, in the case of enacting laws, this does not mean that a legislator establishes a norm that contains an obligation. In its application, the law then becomes a command from the user to the person subject to the norm to do this or that. 'Determinations' and commands remain distinct social acts. This command then – like other commands – has a reference to the future and is not exhausted in the present of its utterance.[121] While a promise creates a claim and an obligation with its conscious perception, it only becomes effective with the fulfillment of its resultant obligation where the transfer of rights is a social act that is realized in the presence of the transfer. It closes the future that was opened, for example, by the establishment of the obligation. Furthermore, these direct social acts can do this because their meaning does not refer to a future and there is, therefore, a certain freedom in the 'determinations'.[122] As Reinach states, 'Only that which can be and can also not be, which can have a beginning, duration, and an end in time, is the possible content of "determinations"'.[123] That, which is in itself timeless and necessary – like the a priori structures – cannot be included in the content of 'determinations'.[124]

Just as social acts are not phenomena of consciousness, such as emotions or cognitions, this temporality does not arise from consciousness, as in Husserl's transcendental second phase, but for Reinach is objectively grounded in the nature of the corresponding acts.[125] Admittedly, the past plays a subordinate role in legal relations and, perhaps as a consequence, Reinach hardly mentioned it. Nevertheless, it is clear that the past becomes important around the time of the acceptance of a promise: A promise made in the past must still exist at the time of the conscious perception or, if necessary, its acceptance. Reinach shows that the

[120] ibid 111, 'The promise is by its very nature incapable of generating an immediate efficacy for the enactment'.

[121] Paulson (n 62) 150.

[122] Duxbury (n 12) 475 ff. translates 'Bestimmungen' as 'Enactments', whereas Paulson translates them as 'legally issued norms' or 'issuances' (Paulson (n 62) 148). 'Bestimmungen' seems broader to me and also encompasses concretizations: it is an act which precedes the enactment and its possible result, the norm (Reinach (n 11) 111).

[123] Reinach (n 11) 108 f.

[124] How about the morally right then? Is it also not a possible content of a 'determination'? It is the present author's view that what Reinach tries to avoid here is to make the morally right a matter of a 'determination'. As such, the morally right is not a matter for a 'determination'; however, 'determinations' can reflect the morally right (Duxbury (n 12) 482).

[125] As far as the present author can see, there is only one example of the significance of the inner consciousness of time in Reinach's 1916/17 notes: 'There is no measure of duration in itself, any more than there is a measure of extension in itself. Cf. Malebranche I, p.71: God can cause – by allowing us to experience a great deal in a very short time – that a single hour appears to us like several centuries. (Of course, even these experiences, however rapid, would pass one after the other)', Adolf Reinach, 'Notizen auf losen Zetteln' (1916/17) in Karl Schuhmann and Barry Smith (eds), *Adolf Reinach: Sämtliche Werke. Textkritische Ausgabe in 2 Bänden* (Philosophia Verlag 1989) 592–604, 595, my translation. However, this had no significant influence on his philosophy.

interaction of the a priori temporally structured social acts then results in a specific present: A question opens up a present that is closed by its answer. A promise opens up a present that extends as far as its hearing and can be closed by the fulfillment of that promise or its renunciation and can be structured in time by the promisor through conditions. Absolute rights grant their holders an unchangeable, permanent present in which they are authorized to make use of these rights. By their very nature, provisions are temporally punctual social acts, however, they open up an extended present in which new rights or obligations exist for the person concerned: The transfer of a right now allows the recipient to make use of it. An enacted law is valid for a certain or indefinite period. When an acceptance of an offer is required, an extended present of contractual obligations is also required. Through these social acts, an extended present or duration is brought forth which can have a future-oriented, teleological character toward their fulfillment or take on a more static, unchanging character.

This duration – or extended present in the Bergsonian sense – is an essential characteristic of legal time.[126] It is precisely demonstrated by the fact that essentially founded legal institutions can exist independently of fluctuating sentiments and interests. For Reinach, it is an essential characteristic that claims, obligations and other legal forms 'arise, last a definite length of time, and then disappear again'.[127] They 'can last for years without change', because they are independent of emotions or other experiences. Rights over things ('Sachenrechte') 'survive a change in the owner of the thing … without any respect of the person of the owner at a given time'.[128] These rights can 'survive the change in the owner'.[129] It is in the nature of these rights to endure and not to be limited by temporal events that the law does not consider relevant, as in the case of deeply personal rights ('höchstpersönliche Rechte').[130] These enduring phenomena are the basic social phenomena, from which temporally punctual acts, such as the attitude of questioning and the explicit question, can be explained.[131] Again, this extended present of duration can be measured and quantified in natural time even though it arises from the nature of rights, claims and obligations.

Reinach thus showed that acts, especially social acts, have their own temporality which distinguishes them from natural time on the one hand and from the extra-temporality of a priori structures on the other. While intentionally future-oriented, presently effective or permanent acts and legal structures can certainly be measured

[126] Reinach (n 51) 557 ff.; on Bergson see also Stephan Kirste, 'Longue Durée de la Loi' in George Kadige (ed), *De La Pérennité et de la Temporalité du Droit* (Publications de l'USJ 2015) 67.
[127] Reinach (n 11) 9.
[128] ibid 71; Reinach (n 34) 424.
[129] Reinach (n 11) 123.
[130] ibid 82.
[131] ibid 282.

in natural time, their temporality is not determined by it.[132] Reinach's phenomenology of legal time is realistic, not because it adheres to the superficial temporality of natural events, but because it takes social legal acts as its starting point and examines their nature in terms of their own temporal structures. For this reason, he also distinguished between natural objects, which simply fall into time, ideal objects, which are extratemporal or even eternal, and social acts, which must be temporal but whose temporality is to be substantiated concretely from their essence and not from their natural appearance. However, precisely because this time is essential time, it is not a subjective time of a time consciousness or even a social construction.[133] In these social, and especially legal, acts one finds those events that produce duration and thus time in the sense shown above. Social and legal times for Reinach thus arose from social acts, although not from their arbitrariness but from their essential structure. Accordingly, it is not surprising that this structure of time does not consist of an external quantitative 'earlier-than'–'later than' or 'before-after'. Rather, this legal time is a qualitative time that emerges from the specific temporality of social acts. It exists as a shared social present where the future emerges from the meaning of a promise and its declaration. Intentionality is the structural aspect of the social act that characterizes the future. It is opened as another possibility for a promisee and closed as an obligation for the promisor. In this way, the future is also a social future that emerges from the actions of those involved.

9.2.3 *To Sum Up*

All in all, Reinach took the first steps toward the recognition of a legal time as a distinct form of time, which one can distinguish from other times, but which can also serve as the basis for the synchronization of the other social times.[134] However, one can also find problematic aspects both in his theory of time and his theory of law.

Although Reinach said that the temporality of legal acts is one of their essential characteristics, distinguishing them from both ideal and purely empirical objects of knowledge, his theory of time is nevertheless fragmentary. It had to be reconstructed

[132] This is not to say that Reinach does not recognize natural time. He deals with it in his discussion of the Zenonian paradox of movement (Reinach (n 51) 574), although even here he is always concerned with qualitative differences: For example, he distinguishes a pause within a piece of music from an interval between two pieces of music. If both are measured in terms of natural time, they may be the same length and, in this respect, there is no difference. However, in terms of their quality, a pause and an interval are two completely different presences.

[133] This becomes clear if one looks at Reinach's critique of Kant's theory of space and time as mere forms of perception (Reinach (n 34) 444 f.).

[134] Stephan Kirste, 'The Temporality of Law and the Plurality of Social Times: The Problem of Synchronizing Different Time Concepts through Law' in M Troper and A Verza (eds), *Legal Philosophy: General Aspects. Concepts, Rights and Doctrines* (ARSP-Beiheft 2002) 23–44.

here from very different passages of his works. Many aspects of the temporality of law have already been decided by essential a priori structures. This may be one reason why for Reinach, as it does for Brentano, the present plays a prominent role. In contrast, both the openness of the future, which makes free action possible, and questions concerning the past, play only a subordinate role. Throughout his writing, it becomes clear how Reinach's pioneering work on a theory of the temporality of law did not draw on the groundbreaking insights of Edmund Husserl's investigations into the phenomenology of inner time consciousness and Heidegger's fundamental ontological foundation of 'Being and Time'. However, while for both Husserl and Heidegger the social dimension is not very important, from the outset, Reinach constructed his theory of the temporality of law from the a priori foundations of social acts, thus revealing a worthwhile path for later attempts.

By their social acts and especially by determining the law through its positivization, people can deviate from the a priori structures.[135] In this respect, they have a negative freedom but lack the positive freedom to create new essential structures. The inherent justification of discourses that produce something genuinely new from the convictions of the participants thus is outside Reinach's understanding of the temporality of law. Whenever a legal discourse produces new values, principles or rules, the a priori doctrine of law will claim that their essence already exists. However, since values differ, discourse and normative guidance are needed to agree on what is produced. For this reason, the concept of the norm would also have to be placed at the center of the analysis of the temporal structure of law, which Reinach does not do.

Process and norm come together when one considers the importance of the futurity of social action, something also emphasized by Reinach. Law, by virtue of its norms, implies a commitment to the future because human action is shaped by the awareness of an open future of options. Norms should guide human actions and correct them where necessary. Since this freedom also refers to the process of norm-setting in, for example, contracts, laws and criminal norm assertions, there is a need for a reflexive structure of law. Law subjects the open future horizon of norm-setting, norm interpretation and norm enforcement to norms in turn. These are norms that relate, for example, to the conclusion of contracts, the legislative process, and enforcement. A working theory of the temporality of law would have to take into account both a qualitative understanding of the dimensions of time and the normativity of law, something Reinach failed to do but that he did, arguably, open the door toward.

9.3 GERHART HUSSERL

To better appreciate Adolf Reinach's pioneering work on a theory of law and time and, at the same time, to gain some perspective on the direction in which a

[135] Reinach (n 11) 5 f.

phenomenological theory of legal time may develop, it is helpful to take a look at Gerhart Husserl's work. This is because the latter's theory has an advantage over Reinach's work by having a more detailed legal basis and by assuming a greater plurality of temporal experiences.

In the context of his phenomenological investigations of the relationship between law and time, Gerhart Husserl[136] did not explicitly refer to his father's 'Lectures on the Phenomenology of the Internal Consciousness of Time'.[137] However, it is likely that when he published an article entitled 'Recht und Welt' ('Law and World') in the Festschrift for his father in 1929, Gerhart was aware of the lectures held in 1905 and that were edited in 1928 by Martin Heidegger and published in volume XI of the 'Jahrbuch für Philosophie und phänomenologische Forschung'. Husserl had already committed himself to a phenomenological approach in his graduation thesis of 1925, which he dedicated to his father.[138] He did not thematize it but applied the method of phenomenological reduction. In the years that followed he returned to phenomenological considerations and, in 'Time and Law', he went into explicit detail and, among other things, provided a vivid example using the 'shoe' to explain the nature of functional objects and then also of the law.[139] Besides applying his approach, the completely different 'Eigenart' (specific character) of Martin Heidegger left some traces in Husserl's work.[140] Heidegger's first main work on

[136] On him cf. Britta Böhler, 'Gerhart Husserl: Leben und Werk' (doctoral thesis, University of Freiburg 1992).

[137] Husserl thanks his father in the preface to his essay on 'Rechtskraft und Rechtsgeltung' and admits that 'the example of the phenomenological method of research had a lasting influence' on his own work. However, it is not a work 'of the phenomenological school' because it is a legal-dogmatic and not a philosophical work; Gerhart Husserl, *Rechtskraft und Rechtsgeltung: Eine rechtsdogmatische Untersuchung*, vol 1 (Springer 1925) VII. However, he agrees with Reinach that the search for the 'essential prerequisites of law' is one of the tasks of jurisprudence. He sees himself connected to Reinach in the application of an intuitive method that has enabled a fruitful problem orientation.

[138] He has stronger transcendental phenomenological roots that he himself reveals, Loidolt (n 1) 187.

[139] Gerhart Husserl, *'Recht und Zeit': Fünf rechtsphilosophische Essays* (Klostermann 1955) 14–17, 17, 'We wanted to use the example of a shoe to make it clear that general statements can be made about things in our practical environment. Our explanations moved in the region of the a priori of physical things. Neither did we speak of the thing (which has the purpose of a shoe) as we encounter it in a certain historical reality, nor of a fictitious thing of this kind imagined in the imagination, but rather of the thing "shoe", reduced to its idea: the purpose of the thing that wants to be a shoe' (as with all quotes from Husserl: my translation). In German, 'Es kam uns darauf an, an dem Beispiel eines Schuhes andeutungsweise klar zu machen, daß über Dinge unserer praktischen Umwelt allgemeingültige Aussagen gemacht werden können. Unsere Darlegungen bewegten sich in der Region des Apriori physischer Dinge. Wir sprachen nicht von dem Ding (das den Zwecksinn eines Schuhes hat), wie es uns in einer bestimmten geschichtlichen Wirklichkeit begegnet, aber auch nicht von irgendeinem, in der Phantasie vorgestellten Ding dieser Art, vielmehr von dem Ding "Schuh" reduzieren auf seine Idee: den Zwecksinn des Dinges, das ein Schuh sein will'.

[140] Manfred Sommer, *Lebenswelt und Zeitbewußtsein* (Suhrkamp 1990) 200.

fundamental ontology 'Being and Time' was published in 1927 in Volume VIII of the aforementioned yearbook.

9.3.1 *Abstract and Concrete Time of Law*

9.3.1.1 The Abstract Time of the Works of Art and Law

Husserl's analysis of the relationship between law and the world is based on the principle of experience. A priori propositions have a legal meaning but are not valid law; they must first be transformed into social reality to attain legal validity.[141] Here, Husserl is thus distancing himself from Reinach.[142] He starts by viewing a human being as 'being in the world'. This being in the world can be naive, immediate or ecstatic.[143] In the experience of nature there is doubt, everything is uncertain, and everything is as transitory or temporary as man himself. Indeed, in natural attitudes, Gerhart Husserl emphasized the omnipresence of a death consciousness even more strongly than Edmund Husserl. This did not yet lead the former to the preeminent position of the future for Dasein ('existence'), as Heidegger did in 'Being and Time'.[144] Thus, one finds only echoes of fundamental ontology in Husserl's works.

By turning to transcendental ideas, people overcome these doubts and uncertainties in, what Husserl calls, 'an ecstatic attitude'. This attitude does not mean escaping from the world, even if it entails alienation from the world, but taking the situation of doubt seriously and fully investing one's own person in this world. The ecstatic attitude then becomes the conscious assumption of the world in which a naive person simply finds themself and it seeks to provide an affirmative attitude toward this world. In this transgression of the consciousness, a transcendent time

[141] Husserl (n 137) 9: 'Law, however it is developed in detail, derives its legal content to an essential (and determinable) part from such conceptual material of an a priori social and legal doctrine. But it is only possible to speak of "law" in our sense when the facts have been given the value of legal validity. What is not cast in the form of legal validity is a pre-legal fact'. 'Das Recht, wie immer es im einzelnen ausgestaltet wird, gewinnt seinen Rechtsinhalt zu einem wesentlichen (und bestimmbaren) Teile aus solchem Begriffsmateriale einer apriorischen Sozial und Rechtslehre. Aber von "Recht" in unserem Sinne kann erst dann gesprochen werden, wenn dem Sachverhalte der Seinswert der Rechtsgeltung zuteil geworden ist. Was nicht in die Form der Rechtsgeltung gegossen ist, ist vorrechtlicher Sachverhalt.'

[142] ibid 46, emphasizing the autonomy of the legislator with respect to a priori structures. He emphasizes the contingency of the law with respect to these structures (Husserl (n 139) 22). They are truths about law but not themselves normative legal provisions (Husserl (n 139) 14).

[143] Gerhart Husserl, 'Recht und Welt' in Gerhart Husserl (ed), *Recht und Welt: Rechtsphilosophische Abhandlungen* (Klostermann 1964) 67.

[144] Husserl (n 143) 69: 'The world made comprehensible to the naturally behaving human being is rooted in his historical existence, in which the experienced past lives on in a decisive way' ('Die dem natürlich sich verhaltenden Menschen erschlossene Welt wurzelt in seinem geschichtlichen Dasein, in dem erlebte Vergangenheit bestimmend fortlebt').

structure is also experienced: in religion, eternity, and also in pictorial works of art, we hold to our present against the current of experience.[145]

The time of a work of art is essentially negatively determined – a nonnatural, 'illusory time'. First of all, a musical composition has an 'abstract time', which only enters into concrete time-being through its 'temporalization' in the performance. The composition is only a 'norm' for its repeated reproduction, which can and must then be concretely experienced and kept in consciousness ('retendiert')[146] if it is to be perceived as an experience in the natural world. The determination of the composition as a norm and its being in time as 'abstract time' is also to be kept in mind for an analysis of law. Husserl does not understand the 'ecstatic transcendence' of naturally naive world behavior as a transition into a fully valid temporality of one's own; rather, he sees it only as an abstraction into an illusory time. The composition receives its concrete reality only through its reentry into the natural-bodily world. Only in this way does the norm become the object of time consciousness.[147]

In a subsequent step, Husserl compared the creation of art to the realization of law.[148] In doing so, law is also put into a state of 'abstract time' and must then be 'temporalized'. While Reinach distinguishes between the timeless form of the a priori foundations of law and legal temporality, Husserl moves from the 'abstract time' of norms in books to the more concrete temporality of the realization of legal norms. This approach will be examined in more detail below.

9.3.1.2 Detemporalization of Law

For Gerhart Husserl, law was a 'work of will' of the legal community ('Rechtsgemeinschaft').[149] He believed that like a work of art, law has its own being in time, although not in natural time. Law is not eternal nor is it designed for a temporal end and, while it is valid, it is not regarded as coming from the past and being carried out to a future end.[150] It is not an object of memory or expectation and it exists beyond our experienced present.[151] Just as law is valid in an abstract way, it also has an 'abstract time'. Law has this abstract temporality because it does not refer

[145] Husserl (n 143) 71 f.

[146] Edmund Husserl distinguishes 'Retention' and 'Protention'. By 'retention' the consciousness keeps an impression alive, like a sound that has faded but is still in our ears. So, we have not forgotten it and remember it, we hold it in our consciousness, so to speak. Husserl (n 49) S. 26/ English 44. However, while I hear the first note within a melody that I know, I can complete the rest of the melody in my consciousness. Husserl calls this 'protention'. It is not an expectation of something to come, but the start of something beginning, Husserl (n 49) 39/ English 58.

[147] Husserl (n 143) 77.

[148] Husserl (n 137) 21.

[149] Husserl (n 143) 77 and 89. This brings him close to the concept of law espoused by his father, Loidolt (n 1) 186.

[150] Husserl (n 143) 79.

[151] ibid 78.

to a singular social fact or 'spatio-temporal reality'.[152] In this 'abstract validity', it has not yet reached either legal reality or legal temporality. The abstract time of a legal norm is produced by an abstract formulation of the facts. Here, possible courses of action are recorded against a developing future and, once created, a law becomes a product of will ('Willenswerk') that exists as a norm detached from legal consciousness, 'even if all subjects of law under its spell sleep dreamlessly'.[153] Like Reinach, Husserl viewed legal validity as abstract in terms of the psychological attitudes that may or may not realize it, but while Reinach ties this abstraction to the a priori structures of law, Husserl referred to the abstract legal norms in books.

Essentially, this abstract time means 'timelessness' because no temporal element can be named for law in this form. Thus, law has lost its temporal reality and has been transformed into a potentiality. From there it must be transformed into legal reality by the deliberate acts of 'legal comrades'. Here, in Husserl's theory, legal comrades are persons and legal orders that mutually support each other; however, man would lose his legal personhood and a legal order its validity if the attitudes of the community toward the law were to change. They would thus leave the world of law and fall back into a natural world. This inaccessible 'will'-attitude guarantees permanence in that the individual cannot dispose of it and therefore cannot 'reject' it.[154] At the same time, however, law depends on every human being for its validity.[155]

Husserl's desire to hold on to consciousness as the basis for the temporality of law seems to require an objective consciousness of the legal community in the case of laws. The duration of law as the basis of its abstract time is dependent on the duration of a permanent collective will of the people. For this, he relied on the constant expression of this will. However, there are some doubts about this aspect of his concept: On the one hand, this attitude is supposed to lift the individual out of the naively experienced world into a legal world to justify and support him; on the other hand, however, this will is not supposed to be available to him. This raises the question: Why should our (collective) will and the law not be changed for good

[152] Husserl (n 137) 17.

[153] ibid 7. It is remarkable that Husserl refers here to the remarks by Reinach.

[154] Husserl (n 143) 80: It is the attitude of will 'which awakens and maintains the community of law to its selfhood; it consequently carries the legal order ... A collapse of this sense of will in the members of the legal community suspends the law (in a revolutionary way). At the same time, however, this would entail a collapse of the person himself, who gave away his sense of right. Because in legal connectedness the - right-want is not a today-and-tomorrow-want but a permanent attitude of will, which constitutes an essential element of existence'. It is this 'Willensgesinnung', 'welche die Rechtsgemeinschaft zu ihrem Selbstsein erweckt und aufrechterhält; sie trägt folgeweise die Rechtsordnung ... Ein Zusammenbruch dieser Willensgesinnung bei den Gliedern der Rechtsgemeinschaft setzt das Recht (auf revolutionäre Weise) außer Kraft. Es würde das aber zugleich einen Zusammenbruch der Person selbst, die ihre Rechtsgesinnung preisgab, nach sich ziehen'.

[155] Husserl (n 143) 100.

reasons? Another concern here is that this 'attitude of will' seems to be a mere fiction. However, if law is to be moved from existing in abstract time into concrete and perceptible time, the permanent attitude of will also needs to be empirically proven. It remains unclear in Husserl's work what this will is. In a defense of a psychological justification of law, Husserl objects to calling it somehow emotional, just as Reinach did not want to rely on psychological facts for the construction of law. The reason for both men having this somewhat common perspective is that the 'abstract' being of law should not be the object of a feeling, which, if it were, would lose its objectivity.[156]

9.3.1.3 Putting Law into Time

Husserl's second step in the constitution of experiential law further concretized law by placing it in time ('Verzeitung' ~ temporalization). In this regard, he noted: 'In fact, it is a matter of crossing over from the other side of the timeless world of law to this side of the reality of the will, which lies in the natural flow of time, to which the legal proposition, as one affected by norms, is concretely related'.[157] This is the task of the judge in particular as in the legal force of his judgment, the law acquires concrete validity and 'world-shaping power'.[158] This fixes law in time and, as long as it is determined in this way, it can be the object of personal feelings and the like and has become evident.

Therefore, Husserl makes an important exception to the necessity of 'temporalization', namely, constitutions. For him, constitutions represent 'the legal being of the legal community' with a particular temporality. They do not require an explicit application to be concrete because they are – again – 'supported and held by the permanent will of the legal community, which is beyond the experience of today, but at the same time has its roots in the living personhood of the respective existing human beings'.[159] In fact, a constitution represents the will of the relevant legal community.[160] It is not clear here whether Husserl now introduces another tempor-

[156] Husserl (n 143) 104.
[157] ibid 82.
[158] ibid 88.
[159] ibid 93.
[160] ibid 93: 'The constitution, which represents the legal being of the legal community (not necessarily verbally formulated), applies itself, so to speak: it is sustained and held by the permanent will of the members of the legal community, which stands beyond the experiential present, but at the same time has its essential roots in the living personhood of the people who exist in each case. The Constitution is the beginning and the end of the law'. 'Die Verfassung, die ja das rechtliche Sein der Rechtsgemeinschaft (nicht notwendig verbal formuliert) darstellt, wendet sich sozusagen selbst an: Sie wird von der permanenten Willensgesinnung der Rechtsgenossen, die jenseits des erlebnishaften Heute steht, zugleich aber im lebeniligen Personsein der jeweils daseienden Menschen ihre Wesenswurzeln hat, getragen und gehalten. Die Verfassung ist des Rechtes Anfang und Ende'.

ality besides the natural and the abstract one; however, doing so seems to be necessary: Constitutions certainly cannot have natural temporality because they are based on a certain will-intent with its own temporal structure that is different from the natural temporality of emotional acts. What was needed here was not an 'ideation' involving the natural time-transcending commitment of the 'legal comrades' but only an 'awakening of the constitutional will-intent'.[161] However, this entails constitutions being either transferred into a world of psychic experience, resulting in their temporalization ('Verzeitung'), or them remaining as they are, awakened in the mind itself. This means they cannot be natural-temporal because a will attitude that brings a constitution into being, according to Husserl, only brings about abstract temporality. A constitution should not be, however, in abstract time because it already has reality in the common will of the people. Here, too, Husserl's theory of the attitude of will ('Willensgesinnung') does not lead to a clarification of the question of temporality.

At the next level of concretization, Husserl argued that administrative action should not seek temporization or the creation of new law but the abstract normative facts should be given a concrete and adequate form. An official simply makes use of his or her authority and performs an act of will which is then legally evaluated. He 'moves in the sphere of action of natural experience. He places his work in the flowing time in which social things come into being and pass away. His effort is to create the permanent, not the once and for all'.[162] The contact with the interests of the natural social world makes the other decisions uncertain. Their actions are all still legally open and thus in the natural realm of doubt. Judges are tasked with freeing the law and its concretization from this doubt and determining the law. Only the judge's decision represents a real, certain, 'Verzeitung' of the abstract law. More specifically than Reinach, Husserl shows here that the extended present with an open future of a legal process of concretization can only be closed by certain legal acts, namely judgments.

With this subjective approach, Husserl certainly contributes to a foundation of the temporality of law on the consciousness of law and time. However, it does not do justice to the manifold possibilities of acts applying the law. One need only think of the force of validity ('Bestandskraft') of administrative acts and with the rules of limitation or *res judicata*. How can the acts of judges do so if they do not put law into time? The failure of natural acts to obey temporal constraints clearly has legal consequences. Yet, this did not have a place in Husserl's theory of the temporality of law. This already shows that the limitation of the temporalization to the courts is too narrow and does not sufficiently take into account other forms of transforming temporally abstract laws into concrete legal time.

161 ibid 95.

162 ibid 106 f.

9.3.2 *Doubts and Revisions of the Temporality of Law Based on Legal Consciousness*

From the above brief reconstruction of Husserl's theory,[163] one can conclude that two aspects are decisive for the temporality of law: on the one hand, the 'de-temporalization' of the content of law to a legal order that is in a form supported by an individually unavailable will and where law is in abstract, nonexperiential time. On the other hand, law must be 'temporalized' to be able to have a world-shaping effect. This happens in court decisions which definitively establish the law and make it capable of experience in space-time as only in this form is the law accessible to the consciousness of time. As plausible as these two steps are, problematic aspects remain: first, the foundation of the permanence of 'abstract law' on the attitude of will and, in general, its closer determination and, second, the limitation of the temporalization to the activity of the judge. Despite all the differences that have become apparent with regard to the conception of the 'phenomenology of inner time consciousness', the insufficiency of a foundation of time on this subjective time remains with respect to objective structures such as law.

Husserl himself may have had doubts about his conception, a notion borne out by his later considerations where he shifted the focus and wrote more intently about the temporalizing moments in the action of the legislator.[164] In 1955, in 'Law and Time', he emphasized more strongly the relationship of the legal order to the concrete historical situation and linked the fate of the norm to the legal community. This was a notable shift from both the first part of his work on the validity of law in 1925 and in 'Law and the World' from 1929.[165] In 'Law and Time', he argued that the application of norms now affects their temporal structure and they reach back into the past, whereas in his earlier works, legal norms seemed to have no past. The legislative act becomes the keystone of this past. In the act of reception of this prehistory of laws, Husserl presents this keystone initially as an act of 'de-timing' ('Entzeitlichung'), which here means a reduction of the legal propositions to their 'core of meaning'. As long as they are 'untimed' ('entzeitet'), they have no normative force and must first be incorporated into a legal order. In this respect the act of the legislator is the keystone of prehistory. However, the arm with which he reaches into the future is of finite length and the ongoing actualization of the law is a matter of its application, with the latter remaining the focus of his concept. Thus, while in his earlier works Husserl emphasized the abstract temporality of norms that are lifted out of the flow of temporal events, he eventually took into account the fact they change and that they are dependent on historical time as a time filled with historical content. Indeed, he noted that abstract time in this

[163] For a more thorough analysis cf. Kirste (n 22) 254–256.

[164] Husserl (n 139) 10 f.

[165] ibid 23; he also gives up his comparison with works of art (Husserl (n 139) 26).

context means objective, measurable time.[166] In his later works, historicity began to play a more important role in Husserl's work and fundamental ontological thinking gained greater traction. One can almost perceive Heidegger's influence when Husserl speaks of the temporal structure of the legal claim, which has the nature of a tool and is directed toward an end.[167] This is then distinguished from the temporal structure of continuing obligations, which are not directed toward their end but are carried by the ongoing fulfillment of meaning.[168]

Husserl's clarifications lead to a more differentiated view of the temporality of legal objects. The abstract comparison of subjective and objective time has receded somewhat, giving way to a broader view of the multiple temporalities of legal content.

9.4 CONCLUSION

In conclusion, the foregoing has briefly contrasted Reinach's approaches to a theory of the temporality of law with Gerhart Husserl's theory of the temporality of legal consciousness. This was done to show the different conceptions of the temporal structure of law arrived at by the various approaches of phenomenology. While Reinach made his observations based on realist phenomenology, Gerhart Husserl worked with the transcendental and, to some extent, the fundamental ontological method. This led Reinach to anchor the temporality of law in the timeless a priori structures of fundamental legal acts and an objective temporality of law. Husserl, in contrast, excludes this sphere and understands timelessness itself as a social structure, namely the abstract time of the laws, borne by a permanent attitude of will. He is interested in the temporality of positive law as it results from the temporalization by the users of law. Both philosophers arrived at a point where they saw a specific temporality of law; for Reinach, this resulted from essentially structured legal acts while for Husserl it was born from legal consciousness.

Ultimately, for Reinach, the temporality of law rested in the unchangeable a priori temporal structures of legal acts in which everything seems to have already been decided. For him, everything rests on their realization, even though a legislator can deviate from this in its 'determinations'. However, the fact that concrete law is also an expression of deliberations, evaluations, optimizations and considerations, while not excluded by Reinach, was not sufficiently included in his theory of the temporality of law. After World War I, the emergence of democratic, administrative and judicial procedures with their different temporal structures and novel ideas about a newly anticipated future, presenting the past and a will to maintain the legal state, played a greater role than at the end of Germany's constitutional monarchy

[166] Husserl (n 139) 31 f.
[167] ibid 32 f.
[168] ibid 37.

when Reinach developed his theory. In his writings during the Weimar Republic and later on, Gerhart Husserl was able to incorporate these historical legal developments into his theory of the realization of law as temporalizing. In contrast to Reinach, he does not distinguish between a timeless a priori sphere and a temporal one but between an abstract time of the enacted law and its realization in concrete legal acts.

Both Reinach and Husserl broke new ground, each in his own way, laying the foundations for a theory of the temporality of law. However, the positive law of the present is more than determining timeless a priori structures or expressing a temporal consciousness of law. This is because it produces its own temporality, one grounded in the extended present of the law's validity, which opens up a future horizon in which legal persons can rely on predictable meanings of their legal acts. Law regulates its own present, future and past and herein lies its temporality. Adolf Reinach and Gerhart Husserl, as legal phenomenologists, opened the door to approaches to a theory of law's temporality that can be further developed. Finally, and despite the incompleteness of their respective works, they have shown that contrary to the ancient idea of a possible approximation of positive law to an immutable natural law, law has its own temporality.[169]

BIBLIOGRAPHY

Adamczyk M, 'Zwischen Endlichkeit und Ewigkeit. Adolf Reinachs Konzept des religiösen Erlebnisses' (2014) 28 Poznanskie Studia Teologiczne 115–130

Augustine A, *Confessions* (AC Outler tr and ed, Hendrickson Publishers 2004)

Baeyer A v, 'Adolf Reinachs Phänomenologie' (doctoral thesis, University of Heidelberg 1969)

Böhler B, 'Gerhart Husserl: Leben und Werk' (doctoral thesis, University of Freiburg 1992)

Brandenburg N, 'Phenomenology of Law' in Stephan Kirste and Mortimer Sellers (eds), *Encyclopedia for the Philosophy of Law and Social Philosophy*, vol 4 (Springer International 2024) 2659

Brentano F, *Philosophische Untersuchungen zu Raum, Zeit und Kontinuum*' (Meiner Philosophische Bibliothek, Bd. 293, 1976)

Burkhardt A, *Soziale Akte, Sprechakte und Texillokutionen. A. Reinachs Rechtsphilosophie und die moderne Linguistik* (DeGruyter 1986)

Dubois J and Smith B, 'Adolf Reinach', in *Stanford Encyclopedia of Philosophy*, https://plato.stanford.edu/entries/reinach/

Duxbury N, 'The Apriori and the Legal' (1990) 21 Rechtstheorie 297

'The Legal Philosophy of Adolf Reinach' (1991) 77 ARSP 314–347, 466–492

Emge C, 'Über den Charakter der Geltungsprobleme in der Rechtswissenschaft' (1920/21) 14 ARWP 146

Gołębiewska M, 'Normativity of Prescriptions in Adolf Reinach's Aprioristic Theory of Right' (2020) 90 *Acta Universitas Lodziensis* 41

Husserl E, *The Phenomenology of Internal Time-Consciousness* (Indiana University Press 1964)

[169] Some aspects can be found here: Kirste (n 134) 23–44.

Zur Phänomenologie des inneren Zeitbewußtseins. Mit den Texten aus der Erstausgabe und dem Nachlaß. 1. Auflage. Hg. v. Rudolf Bernet. (Felix Meiner Verlag, Philosophische Bibliothek 2013) 649

Husserl G, *Rechtskraft und Rechtsgeltung: Eine rechtsdogmatische Untersuchung*, vol 1 (Springer 1925)

Recht und Zeit: Fünf rechtsphilosophische Essays (Klostermann 1955)

'Recht und Welt' in Gerhart Husserl (ed), *Recht und Welt: Rechtsphilosophische Abhandlungen* (Klostermann 1964) 67

Kant I, *Critique of Pure Reason* (Paul Guyer and Allen W. Wood (eds), Cambridge University Press 1998)

Kirste S, *Die Zeitlichkeit des positiven Rechts und die Geschichtlichkeit des Rechtsbewußtseins* (Duncker & Humblot 1998)

'The Temporality of Law and the Plurality of Social Times – The Problem of Synchronizing different Time Concepts through Law' in M. Troper and A. Verza (eds), *Legal Philosophy: General Aspects. Concepts, Rights and Doctrines. Proceedings of the 19th World Congress of the IVR, New York* (ARSP-Beiheft Nr. 82 2002) 23–44

'Longue Durée de la Loi' in George Kadige (ed), *De La Pérennité et de la Temporalité du Droit* (Publications de l'USJ 2015) 67

'The German Tradition of Legal Positivism' in P Mindus and T Spaak (eds), *The Cambridge Companion to Legal Positivism* (Cambridge University Press 2021)

Loidolt S, *Einführung in die Rechtsphänomenologie: Eine historisch-systematische Darstellung* (Mohr Siebeck 2010)

Márquez MMA, 'Reinach, Adolf' in Mortimer Sellers and Stephan Kirste (ed), *Encyclopedia for the Philosophy of Law and Social Philosophy* (Springer Nature 2023) 3040

McTaggart JME, *'The Unreality of Time'* (1908) 17 Mind 457

The Nature of Existence, vol 2 (Cambridge University Press 1927)

Paulson S, 'Demystifying Reinach's Legal Theory' in Kevin Mulligan (ed), *Speech Act and Sachverhalt. Reinach and the Foundations of Realist Phenomenology* (Martinus Nijhoff Publishers 1987) 133–154

Reinach A, 'The Apriori Foundations of the Civil Law' (John F Crosby tr, 1983) 3 Aletheia 1–142, reprinted in Adolf Reinach, *The Apriori Foundations of the Civil Law Along with the Lecture 'Concerning Phenomenology'* (John F Crosby ed, Ontos Verlag 2012), originally published as Adolf Reinach, Die apriorischen Grundlagen des bürgerlichen Rechtes, 1(2) *Jahrbuch für Philosophie und phänomenologische Forschung* (Max Niemeyer 1913), 685–847.

'Notwendigkeit und Allgemeinheit im Sachverhalt' (1910) in Karl Schuhmann and Barry Smith (eds), *Adolf Reinach: Sämtliche Werke. Textkritische Ausgabe in 2 Bänden* (Philosophia Verlag 1989) 351–354

'Die obersten Regeln der Vernunftschlüsse bei Kant' (1911), in Karl Schuhmann and Barry Smith (eds), *Adolf Reinach: Sämtliche Werke. Textkritische Ausgabe in 2 Bänden* (Philosophia Verlag 1989) 51–66

'Nichtsoziale und soziale Akte' (1911) in Karl Schuhmann and Barry Smith (eds), *Adolf Reinach: Sämtliche Werke. Textkritische Ausgabe in 2 Bänden* (Philosophia Verlag 1989) 355–360

'Zur Theorie des negativen Urteils' (1911) in Karl Schuhmann and Barry Smith (eds), *Adolf Reinach: Sämtliche Werke. Textkritische Ausgabe in 2 Bänden* (Philosophia Verlag 1989) 95–140

'Die Überlegung; ihre ethische und rechtliche Bedeutung' (1912/13) in Karl Schuhmann and Barry Smith (eds), *Adolf Reinach: Sämtliche Werke. Textkritische Ausgabe in 2 Bänden* (Philosophia Verlag 1989) 279–312

'Die apriorischen Grundlagen des bürgerlichen Rechtes' (1913) in Karl Schuhmann and Barry Smith (eds), *Adolf Reinach: Sämtliche Werke. Textkritische Ausgabe in 2 Bänden* (Philosophia Verlag 1989) 141–279

'Einleitung in die Philosophie' (1913) in Karl Schuhmann and Barry Smith (eds), *Adolf Reinach: Sämtliche Werke. Textkritische Ausgabe in 2 Bänden* (Philosophia Verlag 1989) 369–514

'Über das Wesen der Bewegung' (1914) in Karl Schuhmann and Barry Smith (eds), *Adolf Reinach: Sämtliche Werke. Textkritische Ausgabe in 2 Bänden* (Philosophia Verlag 1989) 551–588

'Notizen auf losen Zetteln' (1916/17) in Karl Schuhmann and Barry Smith (eds), *Adolf Reinach: Sämtliche Werke. Textkritische Ausgabe in 2 Bänden* (Philosophia Verlag 1989) 592–604

'Zur Phänomenolgie der Ahnungen' (1916/17) in Karl Schuhmann and Barry Smith (eds), *Adolf Reinach: Sämtliche Werke. Textkritische Ausgabe in 2 Bänden* (München Philosophia Verlag 1989) 589–591

'Concerning Phenomenology' in Adolf Reinach and John F Crosby (eds), *The Apriori Foundations of the Civil Law*, vol 8 (Ontos Verlag 2012) 143

Schütz A, *Der sinnhafte Aufbau der sozialen Welt* (Verlag von Julius Springer 1932)

Sommer M, *Lebenswelt und Zeitbewußtsein* (Suhrkamp 1990)

Stammler R, *Wirtschaft und Recht nach der materialistischen Geschichtsauffassung: Eine sozialphilosophische Untersuchung* (Veit 1896)

Lehrbuch der Rechtsphilosophie (2nd edn, De Gruyter 1923)

Die Lehre von dem richtigen Rechte (Wissenschaftliche Buchgesellschaft 1964)

Schumann K, *Husserls Staatsphilosophie*, vol 29 (Praktische Philosophie 1988)

Troller A, 'Das Bewußtseinsbild im Rechtsdenken' (1980) 13 ARSP Supplement 243

'Erkenntnistheoretische Parallele von Widerspiegelungstheorie und Phänomenologie im praktischen Rechtsdenken' (1983) I/3 ARSP Supplement 51

Uemara G, 'Husserl, Edmund' in Stephan Kirste and Mortimer Sellers (eds), *Encyclopedia for the Philosophy of Law and Social Philosophy*, vol 2 (Springer International 2024) 1383

10

How to Make Gifts with Words

Emma Tieffenbach

10.1 INTRODUCTION

Speech act theorists, such as John Austin, Peter Strawson, Zeno Vendler, John Searle, Michael Hancher or Mitchell Green,[1] take a gift to be among the range of things we can do with words. From their perspective, a gift is an illocutionary act, an act performed in uttering a meaningful sentence. In the right circumstances, saying, for example, "This bike is yours" is what it takes to gift it to you.[2] The consensus is that the utterance, whether implied or expressed, is a necessary component of the act.

Speech act theorists give their insights about gifts *in passing*. Once compiled, their scattered remarks reveal some remarkable disagreements and aspects left in the dark. One disagreement regards to what extent the giftee participates in the act. Most speech act theorists require gifts to be taken in by their recipients. As for any other illocutionary acts, the need to be heard and understood is taken to be among its felicity conditions. However, Peter Strawson contemplates the possibility of a gift unknown to its recipients in the form of a "will that is never read".[3] Speech act theorists who insist on the need of an uptake diverge about whether the giftee is

[1] John L Austin, *How to Do Things with Words* (JO Urmson and Marina Sbisà, eds, 2d edn Harvard University Press 1975); Peter Strawson, 'Intention and Convention in Speech Acts' (1964) 73 The Philosophical Review 89; Zeno Vendler, *Res Cogitans: An Essay in Rational Psychology* (Cornell University Press 1972); John R Searle, *Speech Acts: An Essay in the Philosophy of Language* (Cambridge University Press 1969); Michael Hancher, 'The Classification of Cooperative Illocutionary Acts' (1979) *Language in Society*, 1; Mitchell Green, 'Speech Acts', in Edward N. Zalta (ed), *The Stanford Encyclopedia of Philosophy* (Fall 2021 Edition) URL: https://plato.stanford.edu/archives/fall2017/entries/speech-acts/.

[2] Following Austin (n 1) 90, the illocutionary act of making a gift can be further distinguished from the "locutionary act" of saying "This is yours", on the one hand, and from the contingent effects (the joy, the gratitude, or the felt burden to express the latter) brought about in the person to whom the uttering is addressed (the "perlocutionary act"). Only the illocutionary act of making a gift is under focus here.

[3] Strawson (n 1) 448–449.

further required to *accept* the gift for the act to be completed. Besides these points of division, speech act theorists have neglected the deontic dimensions of gifts. If I give you my bike, what I seem to be giving you is the *right* to use it forever while *ipso facto* losing mine. John Austin hints at the related deontic changes when he classifies gifts (together with ordering, prohibiting, enacting law) among "exercitives" by which "powers, rights and influence" are conferred.[4] Likewise, Zeno Vendler includes gifts among "operatives" (along with "arrest, sentence, condemn, fine, offer, surrender") issued when "I say something and the social, ritual, or legal effect *ipso dicto* takes place".[5] Austin and Vendler do allude to the deontic effects of gifts but leave it at one's guess what they precisely are. These are quandaries about gifts, at best quickly addressed in the past, providing the occasion, seized in the present chapter, to expound on the topic. To further reflect on how gifts are made with words, I mobilize Adolf Reinach's *The Apriori Foundations of the Civil Law*, first published in 1913.[6] Reinach has written very few and sparse remarks on gifts.[7] However, his theory of "social acts", developed almost fifty years before *How to Do Things with Words* (1962), provides the notions and distinctions that are useful to elucidate the aspects of gifts which Austin and his followers have parenthetically addressed or neglected. As many commentators have stressed, what Reinach calls "social acts" are very much like Austin's "illocutionary acts".[8] Following the crowd,

4 Austin, (n 1) 151.

5 Vendler (n 1) 22.

6 Adolf Reinach, 'The Apriori Foundations of the Civil Law' (John F Crosby tr, 1983) 3 Aletheia 1, reprinted in Adolf Reinach, *The Apriori Foundations of the Civil Law Along with the Lecture 'Concerning Phenomenology'* (John F Crosby ed, Ontos Verlag 2012), originally published as Adolf Reinach, Die apriorischen Grundlagen des bürgerlichen Rechtes, 1(2) *Jahrbuch für Philosophie und phänomenologische Forschung* (Max Niemeyer 1913) 685–847.

7 Reinach briefly alludes to gifts twice (n 6), and each time in order to illustrate how the positive law departs from the *a priori* laws. In certain legislations, Reinach notes, "[. . .] the oral promise to give someone a house [does] not establish any claim even if [it is] accepted" (ibid 102) in implicit contrast with *a priori* law being such that "a claim is always and without exception generated by a promise" (ibid 116). Reinach points to a similar deviation when he notes how, in certain legislations, "a promise to give something as a gift needs to be notarized in order to be valid" (ibid 103) in implicit contrast to *a priori* law about promises, whether uttered or written, giving rise to obligations (ibid 8–9).

8 The similarity is stressed by Armin Burkhardt ("Zunächst soll jedoch die in ihren Umrissen skizzierte Geschichte der Sprechakttheorie um eine Position ergänzt werden, die wesentliche Aspekte der sprechakttheoretischen Betrachtung bereits vorwegnimmt und bisher fast völlig unbeachtet geblieben ist. Es handelt sich um die Theorie der sozialen Akte' des Rechtsphilosophen und Husserl-Schülers Adolf Reinach, die – neben ihrer philologischen Bedeutung – geeignet ist, einige Probleme der Sprechakttheorie in neuem Lichte anzugehen"), in Armin Burkhard, *Soziale Akte, Sprechakte und Textillokutionen. A. Reinachs Rechtsphilosophie und die moderne Linguistik* (Max Niemeyer 1986); by Kevin Mulligan ("The topics on which Reinach wrote most illuminatingly, speech acts (which he called 'social acts')", in his *Speech Act and Sachverhalt: Reinach and the Foundations of Realist Phenomenology* (Dordrecht 1987); by Arkadiusz Chrudzimsk ("Many people still believe that the idea of speech acts, and particularly of their performative function, was invented by Austin. In fact it was Adolf Reinach who introduced it some forty years before under the label 'social

I will also assume that "they are the same acts"[9] and, to avoid confusion, I use the slashed terms "social/illocutionary" to refer to both at once.

The discussion is structured around the previously outlined issues. Section 10.2 addresses Strawson's example of the will that is never read. This example does not refute the giftee's need to grasp the utterance in which gifts are made, I argue, because the act of writing a will is not yet the social/illocutionary act of making a gift to one's heir. The question whether gifts need to be accepted is discussed in Section 10.3. In light of Reinach's discussion of acceptance of promises, I argue that, although a gift need not be accepted, to refuse it blocks its completion. Section 10.4 critically examines Austin's intuitive view of a gift as always involving a "gesture", in the usual form of a handing over of something. This view, I argue, misguidedly focuses on the *things* that are gifted, whereas it is in fact the *ownership* over these things that is in all cases *transferred* to the giftee. Relying on Reinach's insights on transfers and ownership, I put forth the "Ownership View of Gifts", as I call it. I then consider the alternative view of charity-gift proposed by Waldron in Section 10.5. According to Waldron, a gift can be made by *waiving* property rights.[10]

acts'"), in 'Reinach's Theory of Social Acts' (2015) *Studia Phaenomenologica* 281; by James Dubois and Barry Smith ("Reinach developed his theory of *social acts* [...] a theory which bears striking similarities to the theory of speech acts later developed by Austin and Searle", in their 'Adolf Reinach', in Edward N. Zalta (ed), *The Stanford Encyclopedia of Philosophy* (Fall 2018 Edition), URL: https://plato.stanford.edu/archives/fall2018/entries/reinach; by Barry Smith ("Adolf Reinach [...] is of principal note as the inventor, in 1913, of a theory of speech acts (or 'social acts' to use Reinach's own terminology) which in some respects surpasses the later work of thinkers such as J.L. Austin and Searle") in his 'Reinach, Adolf (1883–1917)', *The Routledge Encyclopedia of Philosophy* (Taylor and Francis 1988); by Karl Schuhmann and Barry Smith ("Historical research has recently made it clear that, prior to Austin and Searle, the phenomenologist Adolf Reinach (1884–1917) developed a full-fledged theory of speech acts under the heading of what he called 'social acts'") in their 'Elements of Speech Act Theory in the Work of Thomas Reid' (1990) 7 History of Phenomenology Quarterly 47; by John F. Crosby ("I tried to show that Reinach's 'social acts' correspond to the 'illocutionary acts' of speech act theory") in his 'Introduction to the Reprint of Two Works of Adolf Reinach' in Adolf Reinach and John Crosby (eds), *The Apriori Foundations of the Civil Law: Along with the Lecture 'Concerning Phenomenology* (De Gruyter 2012) VII–VIII; and by Emmanuel Picavet ("L'une des raisons de relire attentivement Reinach aujourd'hui est la préfiguration, chez cet auteur, d'une théorie des actes de langage apparentée à celle qui devait renouveler profondément, au cours des dernières décennies, la compréhension philosophique des rapports entre validité, signification et interprétation") in his 'Formes sociales et actes sociaux. L'originalité du point de vue de Reinach'in J Benoist and J Kervégan (eds), *Adolf Reinach : Entre droit et phénoménologie* (CNRS Éditions 2008); by Marietta Auer ("The parallels between the speech act theory developed by mid-twentieth century philosophers of language, on the one hand, and Reinach's theory of linguistic social acts as the legal a priori, on the other, are striking") in her 'Promising, Owning, Enacting, Adolf Reinach's Phenomenology of Legal Speech Acts', Chapter 1, this volume.

9 John F Crosby, 'Speech Act Theory and Phenomenology' in JF Crosby and A Reinach (eds), *The Apriori Foundations of the Civil Law. Along with the Lecture, 'Concerning Phenomenology'* (JF Crosby ed, Ontos Verlag 2012) 167–191.

10 Jeremy Waldron, 'Welfare and the Images of Charity' (1986) 36 The Philosophical Quarterly 463.

While I show that Waldron's view does not withstand scrutiny, I also show how a gift can be made by an act of waiving one's claim over someone else's property rights. It is the main result of the present Reinachian inquiry that most of the puzzles raised by gifts dissolve once attention is redirected from its physical aspects – from the gestures, the thing that is gifted, its change of location – to the metaphysical underpinning of the speech act that is performed.

10.2 DOES THE GIFTER NEED TO SECURE UPTAKE?

The present inquiry focuses on those gifts that are made in the performance of a locutionary act.[11] Relevant examples of the latter are "I hereby give you my bike", "Here is a gift for you", "Look what I got for you!", "Have some wine", or simply "My gift!" while pointing at the thing thus being gifted. The act done in each of these utterances is a gift.[12] Giving birthday presents, giving cash gifts, writing a will, making a bequest, distributing grants, bestowing prizes, donating money, almsgiving, etc. are commonly taken to be instances of gifts. Are they all genuine instances of the kind? The nature of gifts – what a gift fundamentally is – is a question that has been largely neglected.[13] It is also one that need not be resolved for the purpose of the present inquiry. Nothing should be presumed about the *genus* of gift, not even that the alleged instances of gifts listed above have any common properties in virtue of which they are gifts. It suffices that certain utterances have the social/illocutionary force of a bequest, of a birthday gift, of almsgiving, etc., and that the latter are commonly described as "gifts" in ordinary language.

As a social/illocutionary act, a gift depends on the linguistic competencies of its two parties. I focus on the illocutionary acts of *making* a gift, in contrast to *requesting* one ("Will you give me your bike?"), to *promising* to make one ("I pledge to give 10 percent of my income to the poor"), to *discouraging* ("No tipping") or to *encouraging* one ("Give What You Can"). Verb-terms and expressions commonly spoken to express the making of a gift are "to give",[14] "to bring something as a gift" or

[11] It is an interesting question to ask, although not addressed in the present chapter, whether the linguistic expression (the uttering) is essential to *all* cases of gifts. It suffices for the present inquiry that it is essential to *some* of them.

[12] Since the noun-term "a gift" designates an act, it would be less confusing to refer to it as "an act of gifting".

[13] One recent exception is D Elder-Vass, 'Defining the Gift' (2020) 16 Journal of Institutional Economics 675.

[14] Many things which in ordinary talk are given require no utterance at all and, for this reason, fall outside of the present inquiry. If I say: "Will you give me more time to do it?", I am not asking for a gift, however grateful I will be if you grant me the requested delay. Likewise, another meaning of "to give" is "to produce something", as in "cows give milk" – utterances not being required to that effect. Also, not relevant for the present inquiry are some instances of a so-called "gift for music" which someone owes to nature, as it were, and surely not to someone else who has given it to that person.

simply "to gift".[15] Some clarifications are in order. First, the utterance through which a gift is made need not contain the term "gift" nor any similar expressions. "Take it!", "Have it!", "I bought it for you!" are efficient alternatives.[16] Moreover, the same utterance can serve different illocutionary acts. In some context, someone may say "The pen is yours!" to *give* it to you, to *order* you to grab it, to *warn* you against the risk of losing it, etc. Reinach admits that a social/illocutionary act can be performed silently as long as it is "expressed in mien, *gestures*".[17] In some circumstances, nodding, raising one's eyebrows, smiling while pointing at the bike are the outward signs of the illocutionary act. Finally, let us note that the verb *give* can serve other illocutionary acts than a gift. If I say: "I am giving a party next Saturday", "giving" means "organizing", so it is correct to understand what I say as me *announcing* the event.

Both for Reinach and Austin, a social/illocutionary act must be heard and understood. Austin speaks of the "need to secure correct understanding"[18] of the audience. According to Reinach, an uptake is a necessary condition of a social/illocutionary act. "The turning to *another subject*", he claims, "and the need of being heard [by that subject] is absolutely essential for every social act".[19] Social acts need "to be announced or communicated" in contrast to "internal acts" (such as forgiving, deciding) which "can lack any announcement to others".[20] However, Strawson wonders if securing uptake applies to the case of a bequest that remains undisclosed to its recipient:

> [...] a man may, for example, actually have made such and such a bequest, or gift, even if no one ever reads his will or instrument of gift... Might not a man really have made a gift, in due form, and take some satisfaction in the thought, even if he had no expectation of the fact ever being known.[21]

The case of a will that is never read is not meant to refute, but merely to downplay, the need to secure uptake. The latter, as Strawson grants,

[15] While the term "gift" is more frequently used as a noun, "gift" as a verb does exist, according to *Merriam-Webster Dictionary* (11th edn 2023). The term means "to give something in an official or formal way", hence excludes the informal phenomena to which the present Reinachian investigation also focuses.

[16] Austin's distinction between "explicit" and "primitive" performatives is relevant here. In an *explicit* performative, the verb-term refers to the act performed through the utterance. For example, "I give you my bike" or "Let me make it a gift to you!". In a primitive performative, by contrast, the utterance refers to no act, although it does serve the goal of carrying one out. For example, if I say: "This is yours" or if I just sing "Happy Birthday to you" while handing you the flowers.

[17] Reinach (n 6) 20 (my emphasis).

[18] Austin (n 1) 36.

[19] Reinach (n 6) 160–161.

[20] Reinach (n 6) 18.

[21] Strawson (n 1) 448.

remains "essentially *a standard, if not an invariable*"[22] element of all social/illocutionary acts.

Against Strawson, one may insist that making sure the utterance is understood is not a mere desideratum, but an essential aspect of illocutionary acts. As Reinach argues, the utterance "is not something that is added thereto as an incidental extra; rather, it stands in the service of the social act and is necessary in order that this should fulfill its announcing function".[23] That announcing function is precisely not satisfied in Strawson's case of the will that will never be read. However, merely restating the necessity of being read (heard, understood, having an uptake, etc.) of all social/illocutionary acts does not suffice to rule out Strawson's case. Indeed, isn't the point of that example to cast doubt on the necessity of uptakes that both Austin and Reinach take to be necessary to social/illocutionary acts: to suggest that unbeknownst gifts really are gifts?

There is an ambiguity in the act of making a will which may have mislead Strawson into thinking that it qualifies as an illocutionary/social act. The ambiguity is between the act of *writing* a will and the *outcome of that act* in the form of a legal document named "a will". The suggestion here is that the need to secure uptake is true about that document, but not about the act of writing that document. Reinach's subtle distinction between acts that are "other-directed" and acts that are "addressed" is relevant to capture Strawson's confusion. Reinach defines "other-directed acts" as acts that are "essential[ly] directed to a subject other than the originator".[24] For instance, to forgive or to envy are always to forgive and to envy *someone*. By contrast, acts that are addressed to someone require the participation of another person who "consciously takes in" the act: who hears and understands the utterance through which the act is made. While all social/illocutionary acts are thus "addressed" according to Reinach, they are not all other-directed. Indeed, "other-directedness" characterizes certain "internal acts" such as forgiving *you* and being afraid of *you*. The addressed/non-addressed distinction and the directed/non-directed distinctions are hence orthogonal. Promises are both other-directed and addressed. Declarations and enactments are addressed (therefore social/illocutionary acts) but are not other-directed.

These distinctions may have eluded Strawson and led him to mistakenly assume the other-directedness of the act of writing a will makes it a social/illocutionary act. However, once one rather focuses, as Reinach invites us to, on the need to be addressed, it becomes clear why the act of writing a will is not an instance of the social/illocutionary kind. The writing of a will, like any other act of writing, is fully completed before it is read by anyone. "A good thing done", the testator may think once she is (indeed) done with the task. However, the mere writing of the will, while a crucial step in the making of a gift, is not (yet) a gift. It is only when the outcome of

22 ibid 448.
23 Reinach (n 6) 20.
24 ibid 20.

the writing – the written document – is read and understood by the court and the heirs at the testator's death that the latter really are gifted what is left to them in the will. Until then, the document has not fulfilled its purpose: no gift has been effectively made. In short, the will *qua* a document must be addressed to the heirs and taken in by them. The sheer act of writing is not addressed in the related Reinachian sense of the term but also does not count as a gift, either legally or from *an a priori* point of view.[25]

The necessity of hearing and understanding the utterance by which gifts are made (discussed and defended in this section) is different from the necessity or the mere conceptual possibility of accepting them, which is discussed in the next section.

10.3 DO GIFTS REQUIRE ACCEPTANCE?

In *How to Do Things with Words*, John Austin asks: "Are you required to accept the gift if I am to give you something?", then notes that "in formal business, acceptance is required",[26] but then wonders if it also features in casual gifts. If so, what appears to be the act of one person – a "unilateral act" as Austin names it – turns out to be the act of two, namely, a "bilateral act". In the latter case, the giftee participates in the act in a more demanding form than by simply hearing and understanding the utterance in which it is made. He would have to accept the act.[27] The question is not whether gifts can be refused (of course, they can). The question is whether a gift has been made in the circumstance where it is refused. If a gift is a bilateral act, refusing it prevents it from being brought into completion. Austin then ponders if the seeming bilaterality of gifts is a defining feature of all social/illocutionary acts: "The question here is how far can [illocutionary] acts be unilateral. Similarly the question arises as to when the act is at an end, what counts as its completion?"[28]

Is acceptance of a gift essential to its making? If the gift causes trouble to its recipient (think of a dog), it seems that the giftee must have the option to do something to prevent the act. The other intuition relates to the contrary case where the giftee, being wholly pleased with what she is gifted, would rightly consider accepting it as unneeded. The asymmetry between the cases of the unwanted gift

[25] Legal documents are *tangible objects* and thus differ from speech acts which are performed through *utterances*. However, as shown by Barry Smith, documents are sufficiently analogous to speech acts for approaching them as "documents acts", that is, as "acts in which people use documents, not only to record information, but also to bring about a variety of further ends, thereby extending the scope of what human beings can achieve through the mere performance of speech acts" (Barry Smith, 'Documents Acts' in A Konzelmann Ziv and HB Schmid (eds), *Institutions, Emotions, and Group Agents. Studies in the Philosophy of Sociality* (Springer 2014) 19).

[26] Austin (n 1) 37–38.

[27] The content of acceptance is the act, while the content of the grasping is the propositional content of the act.

[28] Austin (n 1) 37.

and that of the welcome gift is not well accounted for if gifts are (merely) thought of as either unilateral or bilateral acts.

Reinach's insights on acceptance, I submit, provide a way to reconcile the two intuitions. Reinach clarifies the term by distinguishing between five different meanings of acceptance, among which is the "purely inner experience, an inner 'saying yes' an inner assent"[29] to some social/illocutionary act. Accepting a gift is just the experience of the internal act of *approving of* it, of finding it to one's taste. Alternatively, accepting can itself be "a social act in its own right".[30] To accept is, in this other sense, always to accept or express a response to another social/illocutionary act (an invitation, to take a bet, an offer, etc.). Three possibilities can be distinguished in this regard. Accepting a social/illocutionary act can either be:

(i) a *possible* response to that act
(ii) an *impossible* response to that act
(iii) *necessary* to the completion of that act.[31]

Let us look at the related three cases more closely with the view to figuring out which one, if any, is relevant to the cases of accepting the gift. First, acceptance is a *possible* response vis-à-vis those social/illocutionary acts which do not depend on it for being done. Nominations and invitations are cases in point. While you do have the option to either decline or accept my invitation to dinner, I have invited you regardless. Not so, it seems, as far as gifts are concerned, if it is true that a gift has not been made in the case its recipient refuses it. Unlike refusing an invitation, refusing a gift does stop its completion.

Secondly, acceptance is *impossible* vis-à-vis certain social/illocutionary acts which are such that to either accept or decline does not make sense. Reinach holds commands and requests to be examples of acts that are not meant to be accepted nor declined. Reinach writes that "with [commands and requests] it is a question of imposing an obligation on the addressee of the social act, and this of course really does not need some acceptance".[32] For example, a teacher who commands a late student to arrive on time next time imposes an obligation on that student. The teacher should not worry about securing the student's acceptance although she might not be indifferent as to whether the student takes her command seriously or whether she internally assents to it. Obligations created by commands and requests are such that the option to accept, or, for that matter, to decline them, is just not there. To be sure, commands can be obeyed or disobeyed, and requests can be answered or left unanswered. However, to disobey is to not act as one is commanded to act, but the important point is that the command has been fully made

[29] Reinach (n 6) 29.
[30] ibid 29.
[31] I thank Kevin Mulligan for drawing my attention to these three options.
[32] Reinach (n 6) 31.

independently of whether it is obeyed or not. Unlike a command, however, a gift is such that the option to refuse it is there.

A third way acceptances relate to illocutionary/social acts is by being a *necessary* component of such acts. Acceptance is here required for the completion of the illocutionary/social act of which it is the necessary response. According to Austin, a bet is a relevant instance of the latter. "For a bet to have been made", Austin notes, "it is generally necessary for the offer of the bet to have been accepted by a taker (who must have done something, such as to say 'Done')".[33] A bet is an instance of a "bilateral act", and the question is whether a gift is, as Austin also suggests, another *bona fide* instance of the kind. The idea is that it takes two for one to make a gift, the giftee playing his part of the act by accepting the gift, either explicitly or implicitly.

Michael Hancher concurs with this hypothesis.[34] The bilaterality of certain social/illocutionary acts, Hancher argues, is brought to light by the redundancy of adding "and he accepted the act" to any description of the related act. In particular, the bilaterality of appointment is underlined by noting that, in the following two sentences, "the extra clause [in (b)] goes without saying":[35]

[a] Smith appointed Jones to the committee.
[b] Smith appointed Jones to the committee and John accepted it.

Applying Hancher's argument to gift, one may note the same stylistic awkwardness in:

[c] Julie gave her bike to Paul, and Paul accepted it.

Acceptance is already featured in (what is misguidedly described as) Julie's act. Julie's act is a bilateral act, one may further argue, because, unlike declining an invitation, declining a gift prevents it from being made. And this is in accordance with the intuition, previously described, about how the refusal of gifts which carry obligation results in their cancellation.

However, construing gifts as bilateral acts fails to account for the asymmetry underlined previously between the cancelling effect of refusing unwelcome gifts and the superfluity of accepting wanted gifts. The related asymmetry may be explained, I shall argue, in light of Reinach's view about how the acts of accepting and declining *respectively* relate to promises. Reinach holds acceptance to be an unnecessary component of promises. Acceptance is not required "for the efficacy of the promise" according to Reinach and "can at most serve to confirm" it.[36] It is "not necessary to a promise that it be accepted." The addressee of the promise, Reinach claims, only needs to "take cognizance of the act of promising".[37] Acceptance is

33 Austin (n 1) 9.
34 Hancher (n 1) 11.
35 ibid 11.
36 Reinach (n 6) 28–29.
37 ibid 28–29.

therefore a *possible* response to a promise (akin to acceptance being a possible response to an invitation). However, Reinach also holds conversely that "an act of declining [a promise] prevents both claim and obligation from coming into being".[38] For example, if you decline my promise to invite you to play tennis with me once a month, you prevent me from incurring the obligation to invite you to play. The option of blocking a promise toward oneself seems important to secure when the promise gives rise to an obligation to act in some unwanted way. In the contrary case, accepting a promise appears as a superfluous addendum. Reinach's view about the distinct jural effects of accepting and of declining promises points toward the following fourth hybrid case in which:

(iv) on the one hand, accepting a social/illocutionary act is an impossible response to that act and, on the other hand, declining the same social/ illocutionary act brings its performance to a close.

The asymmetry previously outlined regarding accepting and refusing gifts, I submit, is another instance of these fourth hybrid cases. While it is not necessary for a gift to be accepted, declining a gift prevents its completion. The underlying explanation for the related asymmetry could be analogously related to the importance of not imposing on the recipient of a gift any potentially unwanted obligations. In particular, when a gift entails the transfer of certain obligation(s),[39] the option to prevent the gift from being made by refusing it should be at the giftee's disposal.

The important point to retain is that whereas a gift does not require acceptance for being done, refusing a gift does block its completion. The distinct roles of accepting and refusing gifts, to which Reinach draws our attention through his analysis of acceptance of promises, seem to have been overlooked by Austin and Hancher. Having resolved the questions of the essential role of uptake (Section 10.2), and of the unessential role of acceptance (Section 10.3), I shall now emphasize the deontic dimensions of gifts.

10.4 GIFTING BY TRANSFERRING OWNERSHIP

A gift is intuitively visualized as someone handing something over to someone else. Austin has done a lot to show what is wrong with that view, redirecting our attention from the physical actions – here the handing – to the utterance. The latter, as Austin claims, is "a, or even, *the* leading incident in the performance of the act".[40] However, Austin also remains faithful to the intuitive view by granting a key role

38 ibid 29.

39 Think of the obligation to feed the dog received as a present or of the duty to repair the roof of the inherited house.

40 Austin (n 1) 9.

to the gesture. "It is hardly a gift if I say 'I give it you' but never hand it over".[41] The gesture associated with a gift need not be a handing. It can be a passing, a pointing, etc. In all cases, the intuitive idea seems to be that whatever is gifted to someone must be put at her disposal. To be sure, as it has certainly not escaped Austin, certain giftables (cars, houses, lands, etc.) are not liable to be handed over.[42] Implicit in the received view are therefore metaphysical limits as to what can be gifted. Only entities that are liable to be held and relocated are "giftables".[43] These properties appropriately disqualify concepts, feelings, numbers, weddings as possible objects of gifts. However, the view also restricts "giftables" to "movables", unduly ruling out gifts of things that are too heavy for being handed to anyone (cars) or gifts of things that by their nature (lands) remain where they are.[44] Be that as it may, it is tempting, following Austin, to assume that the handing, or some cognate gesture, is necessary to most other central cases of gifts[45].

In this section, I show why that intuitive view is not correct, and not even an accurate account of the restricted range of cases of movable gifts (flowers, rings, etc.) it is supposed to be. The main problem of the intuitive view is that it targets the *things* (the bike, the flowers, the glass of wine) involved in gifts as *what* is given to the giftee, whereas it is in fact their *ownership* that is fundamentally targeted by the act. When I give you my bike, what I fundamentally do is to convey to you the ownership I have over it. The revision suggested here is meant to be commonplace. Still, the change of focus from the object of gift to its ownership also has important implications, as I intend to show, which speech act theorists have disregarded as the result of their focus on the things that are gifted instead of the change of ownership that these things undergo when they are brought to someone as gifts.

Let us remark, first, that the distinction between the *thing* that is owned and the *ownership* that someone has over that thing is sometimes hidden in ordinary talk. French people refer to what they own as "ma propriété" ("my ownership") as if ownership was a generic category that comprises all the things that someone owns. Likewise, one commonly hears of "someone *having* ownership over something". This misleadingly suggests that ownership can be *had* by someone, therefore being

[41] ibid 9. The related intuitive view is also one Hancher adopts when he stresses the "commissive aspect" of a gift which someone fails to honor when, uttering "Have some wine!", fails to put forth any. Hancher (n 1) fn 4, 6.

[42] As Henry Smith told me (private communication), in many of these cases, the gift is made by the delivery of a stand in or part (a key, a deed, etc.) of the whole unmovable thing.

[43] In the metaphysical jargon, giftables fit in the category of "endurants" defined as entities that endure over time, yet lack temporal parts, and float free from their creators, producers or makers (cf. Barry Smith 'Basic Concepts of Formal Ontology' in Nicolas Garino (ed), *Formal Ontology in Information System Guarino* (IOS Press 1988).

[44] The constraint imposed by the intuitive view also rules out services (hair-cutting, medical advising, lecturing) from the category of giftables. Because services are acts (i.e., metaphysical "occurents"), they cannot be *handed* to anyone.

[45] Austin (n 1) fn I, 37. As Austin also admits, it is not clear whether the handing is essential to the completion of the act or among its felicity conditions.

itself liable to enter into another ownership relation, in a *regressus ad infinitum* inasmuch as this new ownership relation would also be liable to be owned, etc.

Reinach's theory of ownership, to which I now turn, scrupulously prevents the confusion.[46] This is because Reinach conceives ownership[47] as a dyadic *relation* between someone (the owner) and a thing.[48] To have the ownership of a bike is to relate to that bike in a particular way. Reinach further qualifies the ownership relation as a "thoroughly 'natural' relation which is no more artificially produced than is the relation of similarity or of spatial proximity".[49] Reinach also holds ownership to be a *prelegal* relation, one that "comes into being even where there is no positive law".[50] The island on which Crusoe is shipwrecked provides the fictitious law-free environment in support of that view. "When Robinson Crusoe produces for himself all kinds of things on his island, these things belong to him".[51] The ownership relation is further qualified as *a primitive* relation, that is, as one that "cannot be further resolved into elements".[52] Moreover, but no less crucially, it is, Reinach claims, ownership over a thing which confers to the owner "the right to deal in any and every way with the thing".[53] Against the proponents of the bundle of rights theory of ownership, Reinach urges us not to conflate the ownership relation with "the absolute right [of the owner] to deal in any way he likes with the thing which belongs to him".[54] These absolute property rights, while distinct from the ownership relation, are also "grounded" in the latter. Reinach subscribes to the view that ownership "is itself not a right over a thing, but rather a relation (*Verhältnis*) to the thing, a relation in which all rights over it are grounded".[55] As Olivier Massin suggests, the grounding relation between the absolute property rights and ownership is an essential relation.[56] It is in virtue of the essence of ownership that whoever owns a thing also has the absolute right to use that thing in whichever way she desires.

The ownership relation between an owner and what she owns stands in contrast to other kinds of relations between persons and things. In particular, the ownership relation differs from the relation of *possession* that someone has over the thing he has

46 The present discussion only focuses on the aspects of Reinach's theory of ownership that cast doubt on the intuitive view of gift.

47 My presentation draws on Olivier Massin's reconstruction of Reinach's theory of ownership in Olivier Massin, 'The Metaphysics of Ownership: A Reinachian Account' (2017) 27 Axiomathes 577.

48 Reinach (n 6) 54.

49 ibid 54.

50 ibid 46.

51 ibid 56.

52 ibid 56.

53 ibid 70.

54 ibid 55.

55 ibid 56.

56 Massin (n 47) 582–583.

at his disposal. If the ownership/possession distinction sounds otiose, it is because *often* the owner of a thing also possesses it. However, it is among the sophistications of Reinach's theory of ownership to accommodate the cases where possession is dissociated from ownership. The dissociation occurs when someone steals something. While the thief now has possession of the bike, he has not acquired its ownership.

Once ownership, so defined, is recognized as the target[57] of gifts, it becomes clear why the gestures (the handing over, passing, putting forth, etc.) included in the intuitive view are not relevant to the act. Ownership occupies no space, has no weight, nor has the three-dimensions of its two *relata*. If so, while the thing that is gifted may be liable to be grasped, handed over to the giftee and be thus relocated, its ownership moves nowhere, and, in fact, is nowhere. And yet, it is really the ownership over the thing – being conveyed, as it were, from the gifter to the giftee – that undergoes the crucial ontological change *in all cases*. The complexity of gift as a "four-legged act" (involving a *gifter*, a *thing* that is gifted, the *ownership* of that thing, and the *giftee*) is revealed. We may accordingly redescribe a gift as an act by means of which someone (namely, the gifter) makes someone else (namely, the giftee) the new owner of a thing.

The alternative and presumably refined view of gift here outlined – the Ownership View of Gift (hereafter "OVG"), as I name it – differs from the intuitive view in several respects. First, the intuitive view, because it focuses on the *thing* that is gifted, is attentive to what now appear to be contingent features (the change of location, the episodic nature of the act). The OVG focuses on the *ownership* over that thing as the necessary target of gifts. From this perspective, a gift is an instantaneous act (while it takes time for a thing to be handed over to someone, the change of ownership undergone by that thing takes no time).

Secondly, whereas the intuitive view ascribes a central role to the *physical* gestures by which the gift is carried to the giftee, the OVG urges the neglect of these gestures and puts forth the (implied or explicit) utterances through which gifts are made as essential to their performance.

Thirdly, whereas, on the intuitive view, a gift is one by which the gifter gives a good to someone, the OVG offers a different view of the nature of the illocutionary of the act – one that makes someone the new owner of something[58] – that is performed when a gift is made.

57 What is here described as the target of gift seems the same thing as what Searle and Vanderveken would term its "illocutionary point", i.e., the characteristic aim that individuates one illocutionary act from another (John R Searle and Daniel Vanderveken, *Foundations of Illocutionary Logic* (Cambridge University Press 1985).

58 While a "deed" (or a "title deed") is the legal term for such an act, there is no casual term for designating the prelegal form of the act that is under scrutiny here. In English as in other languages, the term "appropriation" designates the act of making oneself the new owner of a thing. Interestingly, there is no term, as far as I know, for the other-directed equivalent act.

Fourthly, whereas the intuitive view of gift, focusing as it does on the thing that is being gifted, is prone to identify the "commissive" aspect of gift (i.e., the fact that the speaker is committed to bring that thing to the giftee), the OVG, emphasizing the underlying ontological change of ownership, redirects attention to the power of gifts to change reality. As Reinach insists, the ontological change taking place when "a thing is conveyed 'into the [ownership][59] of another' [...] is more than a linguistic turn of phrase. It is really the case that the supporting member of the relation of owning (i.e. the owner) modifies the relation by his own act in such a way that he drops out of the relation and someone else takes his place, though for the rest the thing and the relation remain identically the same".[60] To understand the nature of the power of the transfer of ownership, Searle's distinction between speech acts with a "word-to-world" and those with a "world-to-word direction of fit"[61] is helpful. The typical utterances ("this is yours") through which gifts are made have both directions of fit. Their propositional content not only "represents the reality as being so changed",[62] it also modifies the reality to make it match the content. The distinctive power of gifts to change reality is one the intuitive view, fixed as it is on the contingent changes of location sometimes undergone by the thing that is gifted, cannot properly register. Uttering "I hereby transfer to you the ownership of the bike"[63] is more truthful, even if admittedly clumsy, to the ontological changes involved in gifts than "I hereby give you my bike".

Fifthly, the two views differ in their conception of the illocutionary force of the utterances (how that utterance should be interpreted[64]) through which gifts are made. Whereas the intuitive view refers to the illocutionary force of the utterance as *to give*, the OVG takes it to be *to make someone the new owner of something*. To my knowledge, there is no single English term for that illocutionary force – a noteworthy *lacuna* given the use of "appropriation" for the act of making *oneself* the new owner of a thing.

While all these differences vindicate the OVG, indeed revealing its greater accuracy, a proponent of the OVG also faces additional challenges from which advocates of the intuitive view are spared. In particular, if the illocutionary force of a gift is, as the OVG has it, the making of someone else the owner of a thing, it is

59 Reinach uses two terms, namely "Eigentum" and "Gehören", uniformly translated by John Crosby as "property". I use the term "ownership" over a thing to enhance the contrast, stressed by Reinach, with the "property rights" over that same thing.

60 Reinach (n 6) 70.

61 John Searle Jr, *The Making of Social Reality* (Cambridge University Press 2010) 27–28.

62 ibid 12.

63 The stylistic short-cut is not entirely benign as it misleadingly assumes that properties are not metaphysically different from any other entities (named "continuants" in metaphysics) that can be *owned* which is nonsense. The ownership of x cannot itself be something that the owner of x owns in addition to his ownership of x.

64 Austin (n 1) 70.

presumably an act that has the effect of altering the deontic status of both the gifter (who loses the ownership of the thing and property rights over that thing) and the giftee (who correlatively acquires both). Following Reinach, we may refer to "the jural power to produce, modify, etc. rights and obligations through his own social acts" and the "natural ability" to, say, hand over something to someone.[65] The proponent of the OVG is expected to specify *who* has the related jural power to make someone the owner of a thing, and also *which social/illocutionary act* that person has to perform to that jural effect. The OVG will readily provide the requested clarifications as follows. For X (the gifter) to have the jural power to make Y (the giftee) the new owner of *a*, it needs to be the case that:

[1] X is the *owner* of *a*.
[2] X *transfers* ownership of *a* to Y.

Both requirements are commonsensical. In his entry "Speech Act" of the *Stanford Encyclopedia of Philosophy*,[66] Mitchell Green gives voice to [1] when he points to the "preparatory conditions" that must be met for the speech to not misfire, illustrated by the case of a person who "cannot bequeath an object unless she already owns it".[67] As far as the role of transfer in gift, it is widely recognized among legal theorists.[68] However, although scholars correctly point to the role of transfer in gifts, they fail to notice, let alone think through, as Reinach does, the ontological change and deontic aspects that transfers of ownership have the power to bring about.

First, the ontological change realized by a transfer of ownership is "to change the relation of belonging by changing its bearer".[69] The content of the transfer – *what* is transferred – need not be an ownership relation. A transfer can, alternatively or additionally, bear on property rights, on a relative obligation, on a claim or on a jural power. In each case, however, the act of transfer is such that, as Edmund Husserl puts it, "through it" an entity "passes from one person to another".[70] In other words, a transfer unfolds in such a way that at the beginning the transferor has the entity and the transferee does not have it, whereas at the end, the transferee has the entity and the transferor does not.[71]

65 Reinach (n 6) 86; on the distinction between natural powers and jural powers cf. Reinach (n 6) 174.
66 Green (n 1).
67 ibid.
68 I shall content to refer to Richard Hyland, *Gifts: A Study in Comparative Law* (Oxford University Press 2009) as evidence of the commonality of the assumption.
69 Reinach (n 6) 63.
70 Edmund Husserl 'Obituary Notice' in John Crosby (ed), *The A Priori Foundations of the Civil Law: Along with the Lecture Concerning Phenomenology* (Ontos Verlag 2012) xiii, originally published in (1919) 13 Kant-Studien 147.
71 Olivier Massin and Emma Tieffenbach 'The Metaphysics of Economic Exchanges' (2017) 3 *Journal of Social Ontology* 182.

Secondly, both legal scholars and speech act theorists who reflect on gifts fail to register that "[t]he transferring of [ownership] also presupposes a power to transfer insofar as owning essentially implies the right to deal in *any and every* way with the thing, the power to transfer the thing into the ownership of others is contained in this right".[72] The power (or right) to transfer ownership is just one of the "absolute rights" that the ownership relation, in virtue of its nature, confers to owners. "It is grounded in the essence of owning", Reinach claims, "that the owner has the absolute right to deal in any way he likes with the thing which belongs to him".[73] The jural powers grounded in ownership stand in contrast to the jural powers that have their source "in the person as such".[74] Following Kevin Mulligan, the distinction between those jural powers that are grounded in ownership and those that have their source in personhood may be further explicated as follows. While being a person is all that is needed for having the jural power to "apologize, promise, accept promises, order, ask questions, answer questions, inform, grant, request, submit himself, thank",[75] merely being a person does not suffice for being endowed with the jural powers to condemn, to declare (war), to baptize, to dissolve the government or to petition for bankruptcy. Likewise, I submit, being a (thin) person does not suffice for having the jural power to transfer to someone the ownership of a thing. Only those (thick) persons who have the ownership of that thing in the first place have the jural power to transfer its ownership to someone else. By extension, one may say that gifters do not have the power to make a gift of a thing they do not own. Speech act theorists, such as Hancher, point to the "commissive" dimension of gifts,[76] suggesting that utterances such as "Have some wine" commit the gifter to making what is gifted readily available. However, it may now appear that the March Hare's misfired gift to Alice could instead be a matter of the March Hare not having the jural power of gifting the wine to Alice.

Because the OVG confines the category of gift to the transfer of *ownership*, it conceptually rules out the gifts of stolen things. Approached in consideration of Reinach's distinction between ownership and possession, the gifts of stolen things would correspond to the case where what is transferred is the possession of a thing. Someone who has stolen a bike possesses the bike without owning it. She can transfer the possession of the bike to someone else without thus transferring the ownership of the bike. If Julie steals John's bike, Julie possesses it while John still owns it although he has lost the power to use it. Julie can then transfer her possession of John's bike. Paul is now the new possessor of the motorcycle, while

[72] Reinach (n 6) 51.

[73] ibid 55.

[74] ibid 86.

[75] Kevin Mulligan, 'Persons and Acts: Collective and Social. From Ontology to Politics' in Alessandro Salice and Hans Bernhard Schmid (eds), *The Phenomenological Approach to Social Reality* (Springer Verlag 2016).

[76] Hancher (n 1) 6.

John remains its owner. Now the pressing question is: Has Julie gifted John's bike? The answer to that question is not entirely clear and depends on whether a transfer of possession that is dissociated from a transfer of ownership can have the illocutionary force of a gift. I shall point to two implausible implications as decisive considerations in support of ruling out the related case. First, it would entail that the recipient of the gift possesses that which she is gifted without being further endowed with its ownership or with the property rights to use the thing. While the recipient would be able to make use of the thing, she would not have the property rights to act accordingly.

It is time to recap the sequences that, on the OVG, unfold in many central cases. For X (a gifter) to gift her *a* to Y (the giftee), it needs to be the case that:

(i) X initially owns *a*.
(ii) X utters, either implicitly or explicitly: "I hereby transfer the ownership of *a* to Y".
(iii) Y hears and understands X's utterance.
(iv) Y does not decline the transfer of ownership.
(v) As the result of (i)–(iv), Y becomes the new owner of *a*.

The OVG, as it is outlined here, may appear to achieve generality at the cost of being at odds with the intuitive understanding of the act. One may object that it is at odds with the ordinary use of the term "gift" which does bear on things, not on their ownership, let alone a relation between someone and a thing. However, the OVG does not conflict with the widespread view that the objects of gifts are things. It really is the bike (not its ownership) that I bring to you as a gift. The rectification that the OVG urges to make regards technical aspects of gifts. In particular, the OVG presses for reconsidering the illocutionary act by which a gift is done in terms of a transfer of ownership from oneself to the recipient of that gift. The OVG also presses for reconsidering the illocutionary force of a gift as making someone the new owner of a thing.

10.5 JEREMY WALDRON'S ENCOUNTER: HOW TO MAKE GIFTS BY WAIVING OWNERSHIP

Jeremy Waldron also purports to define "what charity[77] is and what it involves".[78] Waldron intends to refute both the view "that charity involves a positive act of assistance"[79] and the correlated claim that "withholding charity can be seen as an

[77] The notions of charity and gifts are not strictly identical. Only those gifts which are driven by benevolent concern are instances of charity acts. And there are other ways of performing the latter than by gifting one's resources. Still, the two categories do overlap in the case, discussed by Waldron (n110), of the food that is given to the weary travelers.

[78] ibid 469.

[79] ibid.

omission – a mere failure to act".[80] As he notes, "[t]his image of charity derives from the old biblical story of the Good Samaritan", the latter being usually seen as actively doing what is needed to rescue the man. In the biblical story, "charity means putting oneself out, actively intervening for someone else's benefits".[81] As a plausible alternative, Waldron proposes "a different image of charity" as being achieved "by doing nothing"[82] (or almost nothing, as I will shortly explain).

Waldron tells two variants of the biblical story. In the first, two bad Samaritans actively prevent some weary travelers from helping themselves to the foods displayed on a table in their house. In the second version, one good Samaritan inactively lets weary travelers help themselves to the food. What the latter version reveals, Waldron argues, is that charity can consist in "passively allowing another to help himself to the resources":[83]

> As we noted earlier, charity involves giving but giving – the exercise of the power of alienation of one's property – need not involve any active or onerous expenditure of effort. If you have physical possession of my typewriter already (you were carrying it home for me, say, as a favor), and I say, "Keep it – it's yours", the only action I have to perform is the purely symbolic or gestural one of saying that a gift has been made. To give you something, I do not have to put myself out for your sake or come actively to your assistance. The airiest waiver of my property rights is reasonably sufficient.[84]

The central claim here is that waiving property rights over something (in the present case, a typewriter) suffices for giving it to someone just in case the latter is able to help himself to, or is already in possession of, the thing. The conception of gift defended here advances two requirements. One is the "waiving of property rights", which Waldron correctly conceives as being performed in the mere uttering "Keep it – it's yours". The other requirement is on the recipient of the gift, who is expected all by herself to enter into possession of that which is gifted.

According to Waldron, the originality of this conception is that it dispenses with the physical acts (such as "putting myself out for your sake") which, on a more conventional conception, are necessary for making a gift. From this perspective, Waldron seems to endorse a version of the OVG presented in Section 10.4. However, Waldron's view does depart from the OVG when, instead of a transfer of property rights,[85] it puts forth a waiving of these property rights as the act by which the change of ownership is brought about.

80 ibid.
81 ibid.
82 ibid.
83 ibid 471.
84 ibid 470.
85 Waldron does not dissociate, as Reinach does, ownership and property rights, assuming that owning something is just to have the property rights over it. While one may object to the related conflation, the latter does not affect Waldron's view of gift.

Waldron is right to note that the mere waiving of property rights does not suffice for making anyone the bearer of these property rights. Waiving property rights over *a* leaves *a* un-owned. Waldron is also right to claim that entering into a relation of possession with something can in itself create an ownership relation with that thing. However, Waldron is wrong to infer that the performance of these two amalgamated acts – a waiving on one side matched by an act of appropriation on the other – amounts to the making of a gift. Reinach's insights about the social/illocutionary act of waiving can be mobilized to explain why it is so. Waiving, as Reinach notes, is "a social act which lacks the moment of other-directedness. Waiving refers merely to that which is waived, in this case to the claim; it is not directed to a person".[86] Waiving, like declaring, revoking and enacting, belongs to the sub-category of social acts which are not other-directed. In support of that observation, one may note that the following sentence:

[d] "I hereby waive my property right over that thing to you."

does not sound correct. The important point is that if a waiving is *not* other-directed, the act fails to display the other-directedness that is essential to gifts: the fact that the propositional content of the sentence through which a gift is made always refers to the recipients of that gift.

Although a gift cannot be done by merely waiving a property right over a thing, the social/illocutionary act of waiving can be involved in genuine cases of gift. Consider the case of Julie who promises to give Paul her bike *if* he gives her CHF100. Julie's conditional promise is a defining feature of economic exchanges.[87] Suppose that Paul gives to Julie the requested amount and then changes his mind: he no longer wants to buy Julie's bike and is also willing to not ask Julie to give him back the CHF100 that he transferred to her. Maybe Paul has been told that Julie put her bike on sale because she urgently needs the money. Because Paul wants to be kind to Julie, he is now disposed to gift her the CHF100 which he initially transferred in exchange for the bike. What Paul can do (and this is, in fact, the only thing he can do) so that Julie has the right to keep both his money and her bike is to waive his claim over Julie's bike.

The fictitious example described here illustrates a way of making a gift other than by transferring the ownership of the thing that is gifted. Paul has already transferred the CHF100 to Julie, but the transfer was done in the context of an economic exchange between the two. The ownership of the CHF100 was shifted to Julie when she and Paul were still engaged in buying and selling each other's goods. What makes the case tricky is that Paul makes Julie the new owner of his CHF100 not by transferring to her his ownership over the money, but by waiving his claim over

86 Reinach (n 6) 32.

87 Massin and Tieffenbach (n 71).

Julie's bike. The money is *what* Paul gifts to Julie. But the social/illocutionary *act* that Paul performs in order to gift the money to Julie is to waive his claim over Julie's bike. It is a case of an economic exchange that evolves into a case of gifts as the effect of a social/illocutionary act, namely a waiving of a claim, that modifies the nature of the interaction. It is a case in which a buyer (Paul) takes the role of a gifter while the seller (Julie) becomes *ipso facto* the beneficiary of a gift.

10.6 CONCLUSION

This chapter is a follow-up to dispersed and occasional remarks on gifts that speech act theorists have made. Far from having the ambition to be a speech act theory of gifts, the upshots of the present inquiry can nonetheless be assembled in the form of a (non-exhaustive and provisional) list of conditions for the (illocutionary-)making of gifts. It is time to recap the main findings and also to gesture at some of the issues that a full-blown speech act theory of gifts would have to tackle.

I have first shown that a gift has not been made if the giftee has not grasped the utterance through which it is made. Strawson may have been misled by the other-directedness of the writing of a will that is never read into supposing that it is a *bona fide* instance of a speech act. While the orthodox view about the utterance being essential to the illocutionary act remains unchallenged, it is not entirely clear, as Maryam Ebrahimi Dinani rightly points out, what from Reinach's perspective "the general requirement of grasp" precisely means.[88] In the case of gifts, it is an interesting question to ask the extent of the understanding that is implied in the grasping. While it seems reasonable to require that the addressee understands the nature of the act (as an instance of a gift) as well as the role (that of its recipient) she is ascribed in the act, it is less clear whether the addressee is also further expected to grasp the nature of the social/illocutionary act (an act of transfer) performed and also the illocutionary force of the utterance (making her a new owner) through which the act is made. What knowledge of these various hidden aspects of the gift should be expected on the part of the addressee? The level of understanding that the general requirement of grasp presupposes needs to be specified to avoid a theory of gift that is too cognitively demanding, because it is at odds with the intuitive, pre-theoretical understanding of the act that manifestly suffices for its successful performance.

A second result of the inquiry is that a gift may not be the "bilateral act" that Austin has in mind if its acceptance, in the form of a social/illocutionary act, is superfluous, as I have argued. Granted: the intended recipient of a gift has the option to prevent the act from being completed. However, if this is what is at stake, the option can be chosen simply by declining the gift in the relevant circumstance.

[88] Maryam Ebrahimi Dinani, unpublished Doctoral Dissertation (2023 Paris) 226.

It seems unnecessary, I have argued, that the recipient also does her part of the act, as it were, by accepting the gift in the alternative circumstance where she wants it.

There is another reason for rejecting the requirement of acceptance. It tends to confound what is fundamentally a single act with a collective one. The way the giftee is essential to the act of gifting is not by *co*-performing the act, but simply by uptaking it. The utterance through which the gifter makes a gift has to be heard and understood by the giftee, but the gifter is the only agent making that gift.[89] Thus, although a gift involves two persons, it remains the act of one person only. There is no we-gift, only an I-gift matched by a You-uptake.

Finally, it is a third result of the inquiry to press for a shift of focus from the thing that is the object of the gift to the ownership over that thing that is transferred to the giftee. The merits of the shift of attention are threefold: to lay bare the metaphysical underpinning of the act, to confront us with its conceptual boundaries, and to accommodate a greater range of cases. The unexpected variety of gifts is maybe the most striking result of the present inquiry. To gift my bike to you, I can either *transfer* its ownership to you, *grant* you the right to revoke your promise to pay for it or *waive* the right I have over the amount of money you owe me. One can also suppose that the actual diversity of the act is not fully laid bare by these three sub-cases, and therefore the subject matter warrants further exploration.[90]

BIBLIOGRAPHY

Auer M, 'Promising, Owning, Enacting: Adolf Reinach's Phenomenology of Legal Speech Acts' (this volume)

Austin JL, *How to Do Things with Words* (JO Urmson and Marina Sbisà, eds, 2d edn Harvard University Press 1975)

Burkhardt A, *Soziale Akte, Sprechakte und Textillokutionen. A. Reinachs Rechtsphilosophie und die moderne Linguistik* (Max Niemeyer 1986)

Chrudzimsk A, 'Reinach's Theory of Social Acts' (2015) 15 *Studia Phaenomenologica* 281

Crosby JF, 'Speech Act Theory and Phenomenology', in Crosby JF and eds, *The Apriori Foundations of the Civil Law. Along with the Lecture, 'Concerning Phenomenology'* (Ontos Verlag 2012)

'Introduction to the Reprint of Two Works of Adolf Reinach', in JF Crosby eds, *The Apriori Foundations of the Civil Law. Along with the Lecture, 'Concerning Phenomenology'* (Ontos Verlag 2012)

89 Alessandro Salice and Olivier Massin make a similar observation about promises being the single act of the promisor, even if a promise requires being taken in by the promisee (Alessandro Salice and Olivier Massin, 'So Close and Yet So Far, Reinach and Gilbert on Promises', Chapter 11, this volume.

90 I thank Marietta Auer, James Toomey, Henry Smith, Sara Amighetti, Francis Cheneval, Julien Deonna, Felix Koch, Jed Lewinsohn, Kevin Mulligan, Alessandro Salice, Peter Schaber, Regina Sibylle Surber for their precious comments. The research done for the present article was funded by the Swiss National Science Foundation as part of the Research Project # 212804 "Essentialism and Mentalism in Austrian Economics".

DuBois J and Smith B, 'Adolf Reinach', in Zalta EN ed, *The Stanford Encyclopedia of Philosophy* (Fall 2018 Edition), URL: https://plato.stanford.edu/archives/fall2018/entries/reinach/

Ebrahimi Dinani M, Unpublished Doctoral Dissertation, prepared at Ecole Normale Supérieure, Paris

Elder-Vass D, 'Defining the Gift' (2020) 16 Journal of Institutional Economics 675

Green M, 'Speech Acts', in Zalta N ed, *The Stanford Encyclopedia of Philosophy* (Fall 2021 Edition). URL: https://plato.stanford.edu/archives/fall2017/entries/speech-acts/

Hancher M, 'The Classification of Cooperative Illocutionary Acts' (1979) Language in Society 1

Edmund Husserl, 'Obituary Notice', in John Crosby (ed), *The A Priori Foundations of the Civil Law: Along with the Lecture 'Concerning Phenomenology'* (Ontos Verlag 2012), originally published in (1919) 13 *Kant-Studien* 147

Hyland R, *Gifts: A Study in Comparative Law* (2009 Oxford University Press) (Oxford University Press 2009)

Massin O, 'The Metaphysics of Ownership: A Reinachian Account' (2017) 27 *Axiomathes* 577

Massin O and Tieffenbach E, 'The Metaphysics of Economic Exchanges' (2017) 3 *Journal of Social Ontology* 167

Mulligan K, *Speech Act and Sachverhalt: Reinach and the Foundations of Realist Phenomenology* (D. Reidel 1987)

'Persons and Acts: Collective and Social. From Ontology to Politics', in Salice A and Schmid HB eds, *The Phenomenological Approach to Social Reality* (Springer Verlag 2016)

Picavet E, 'Formes sociales et actes sociaux. L'originalité du point de vue de Reinach', in Benoist J and Kervégan J eds, *Adolf Reinach : Entre droit et phénoménologie* (2008 Paris CNRS Éditions)

Reinach A, 'The Apriori Foundations of the Civil Law' (John F Crosby tr, 1983) 3 *Aletheia* 1–142, reprinted in Adolf Reinach, *The Apriori Foundations of the Civil Law Along with the Lecture 'Concerning Phenomenology'* (John F Crosby ed, Ontos Verlag 2012), originally published as Adolf Reinach, Die apriorischen Grundlagen des bürgerlichen Rechtes, 1(2) *Jahrbuch für Philosophie und phänomenologische Forschung* (Max Niemeyer 1913), 685–847

Salice A and Massin O, 'So Close and Yet So Far; Reinach and Gilbert on Promises', (this volume)

Schuhmann K and Smith B, 'Adolf Reinach: An Intellectual Biography', in K Mulligan ed, *Speech Act and Sachverhalt. Reinach and the Foundations of Realist Phenomenology* (Kluwer 1987)

'Elements of Speech Act Theory in the Work of Thomas Reid' (1990) 7 History of Philosophy Quaterly 47

Searle JR, 'A Classification of Illocutionary Acts' (1976) 5 Language and Society 1

Speech Acts. An Essay in the Philosophy of Language (Cambridge University Press 1969)

The Making of Social Reality (Cambridge University Press 2010)

Searle JR and D Vanderveken *Foundations of Illocutionary Logic* (Cambridge University Press 1985)

Smith B, 'Basic Concepts of Formal Ontology' in Garino N ed, *Formal Ontology in Information System Guarino* (IOS Press 1988)

'Reinach, Adolf (1883–1917)', in *The Routledge Encyclopedia of Philosophy* (Taylor and Francis 1998)

'Towards a History of Speech Act Theory' in A Burkhardt ed, *Speech Acts, Meanings and Intentions. Critical Approaches to the Philosophy of John R. Searle* (de Gruyter 1990)

'Documents Acts', in AK Ziv and HB Schmid eds, *Institutions, Emotions, and Group Agents. Studies in the Philosophy of Sociality* (Springer 2014)

Strawson P, 'Intention and Convention in Speech Acts' (1964) 73 The Philosophical Review 89

Vendler Z, *Res Cogitans: An Essay in Rational Psychology* (Cornell UniversityPress 1972)

Waldron J, 'Welfare and the Images of Charity' (1986) 36 The Philosophical Quarterly 463

11

So Close and Yet So Far

Reinach and Gilbert on Promises

Alessandro Salice & Olivier Massin

11.1 INTRODUCTION

Promises are ubiquitous in our social life: we plan our conduct based on the promises that we make and those addressed to us. We build our reputation on the promises we honor. We blame those who do not fulfil their promises, and we apologize if we are not able to deliver what we promised. The concept of a promise is also of crucial importance to disciplines such as law and economics, as promises arguably lie at the heart of contracts and economic exchanges.[1]

Given the pervasiveness of promises in our social world, it should not be surprising if they come in many shapes and forms. In line with considerations about promises developed by Adolf Reinach[2] and Margaret Gilbert,[3] this paper focuses on the "informal" or "everyday" sense of promise according to which, if something qualifies as a promise, it imposes an obligation on the promisor and an equivalent claim (or: demand-right) on the promisee, regardless of whether or not the speaker uses the term "promise."[4] One key question for any theory of promises, so

[1] Kent Bach, 'Terms of Agreement' (1995) 105 Ethics 604, responding to Margaret Gilbert, 'Is an Agreement an Exchange of Promises?' (1993) 90 Journal of Philosophy 627. See also Olivier Massin and Emma Tieffenbach, 'The Metaphysics of Economic Exchanges' (2017) Journal of Social Ontology 167 and Alessandro Salice, 'Wilhelm Schapp and the Standard Theory of Exchanges' (2023) 19 New Yearbook for Phenomenology and Phenomenological Research 132.

[2] Adolf Reinach, 'The Apriori Foundations of the Civil Law' (John F Crosby tr, 1983) 3 Aletheia 1, reprinted in Adolf Reinach, The Apriori Foundations of the Civil Law Along with the Lecture 'Concerning Phenomenology' (John F Crosby ed, Ontos Verlag 2012), originally published as Adolf Reinach, Die apriorischen Grundlagen des bürgerlichen Rechtes, 1(2) Jahrbuch für Philosophie und phänomenologische Forschung (Max Niemeyer 1913), 685.

[3] Margaret Gilbert, *Rights and Demands: A Foundational Inquiry* (Oxford University Press 2018).

[4] Gilbert (n 3) and Margaret Gilbert, 'Three Dogmas about Promising' in H Sheinman (ed) *Understanding Promises and Agreements* (Oxford University Press 2011), 80 reprinted in Margaret Gilbert, *Joint Commitment: How We Make the Social World* Oxford University Press 2014) 296. We will be quoting from the 2014 reprint.

understood, is: how do promises generate obligations and claims? This chapter addresses this question by comparing Gilbert's theory of promise with the remarkably similar, and yet importantly different account developed by Reinach at the start of the twentieth century. This is the plan ahead.

In Section 11.2, we present Gilbert's background motivations for her account of promises. The account aims at vindicating two intuitions about promises and at rejecting three "dogmas," which she identifies as core to contemporary debates about promises. In this section we also show that Reinach warmheartedly shares Gilbert's intuitions and that therefore he, too, rebuts the three dogmas.

In Section 11.3, we introduce Gilbert's account of promises. According to her view, promissory obligations and claims are brought about by certain commitments that promisor and promisee jointly enter. Hence, the reason why promises generate claims and obligations is that promises are to be explained in terms of joint commitments, and joint commitments generate claims and obligations.

Sections 11.4 to 11.6 marshal ideas borrowed from Reinach's theory of promise to reject the account: while endorsing Gilbert's background motivations, Reinach's theory rejects the possibility for promises to have a (or any) substantive explanation and, thus, provides reasons for dismissing Gilbert's positive account of promise in terms of joint commitments. In particular, Section 11.4 argues, *contra* Gilbert, that promises do not necessarily require acceptance. Section 11.5 claims that Gilbert's account misidentifies the authors of promises and Section 11.6 that it misconstrues the content of promises.

While the result of our discussion is mainly negative, Section 11.7 maintains that Gilbert's research program of understanding the capacity of promises to generate claims and obligations without falling prey to the three dogmas remains wide open. We suggest that progress in this research program can be achieved by taking seriously Reinach's idea that the search for a substantive explanation of the fact that promises generate claims and obligations is pointless and that promises generate those normative entities in virtue of their nature or essence.[5]

11.2 THREE DOGMAS VS. TWO INTUITIONS

Three dogmas, according to Gilbert, steer contemporary debate about promising: the Moral Requirement dogma, the No Willing dogma, and the Immoral Promises dogma.[6]

[5] Karl Mertens develops an insightful comparison between Gilbert's and Reinach's theories of promises, which is equally critical of both and, in particular, of Reinach's metaphysical presuppositions. See Karl Mertens, 'On the Essence and Sources of Obligation: A Critique of Reinach's and Gilbert's Accounts of Promises', (2023) 19 New Yearbook for Phenomenology and Phenomenological Research 90. If our attempt to establish the point that promises cannot be subject to substantial explanation is successful, then Reinach's idea of promises carrying a nature (or an essence) becomes a viable way of understanding promises and Mertens' criticism of Reinach could be put to rest.

[6] Gilbert is wary that these assumptions are not universally shared and that they are not blindly followed by all participants in the debate about promises. However, she adds that "they tend not to be examined with a critical eye," although they should be (Gilbert (n 3) 214; see also Gilbert

The Moral Requirement dogma goes back at least to Thomas Scanlon's understanding of promissory obligations: "When promises give rise to [...] obligation, these can be accounted for on the basis of general moral principles."[7] Scanlon's idea is that honoring a promise is dictated by a moral requirement, which derives from moral principle(s) and that these moral principles do not depend on contingent agreements or other conventional arrangements among people.

Moral Requirement dogma: When promises give rise to obligations, they do so in virtue of some moral principles.

The Moral Requirement dogma, Gilbert argues, is the most important among the three assumptions because it directly sustains the other two, as we will soon see.

The second dogma, called "No Willing" dogma, is expressed in Hume's notorious passage "'Tis impossible that we could ever will a new obligation,"[8] which can be reformulated this way:

No Willing dogma: Mere willing cannot bring about obligations.

In a nutshell, this dogma captures the idea that a personal (private or inner) act of the will does not have the normative power to generate an obligation. The Moral Requirement dogma and the No Willing dogma are related: given that the obligation to honor a promise is a moral requirement and given that moral requirements are not grounded in voluntary agreements or arrangements among people, mere acts of the will cannot bring about promissory obligations. Finally, we have the

Immoral Promises dogma: Immoral promises do not put their subject under an obligation to act as promised.

Gilbert argues that this third dogma, too, gains persuasive force from the Moral Requirement dogma. For, if promissory obligations are moral requirements, then promises with an immoral content do not generate obligations. The moral requirement the promisor is actually subject to is *not* to keep immoral promises.

Gilbert contrasts these dogmas with two intuitions. The first intuition is what she calls "Inevitability Point."[9] This point relates to Prichard's view that "[o]nce call

(n 4) 299). Interestingly, those assumptions were already circulating at Reinach's time. As Gilbert, so does Reinach discuss Hume's theory as representative of the No Willing Dogma; the Immoral Promises and the Moral Requirement dogmas are exemplified in the theory of contract developed by German philosopher Wilhelm Schuppe. Reinach also tackles Theodor Lipps' psychologistic theory of promises, but that discussion is of no concern to this paper.

7 Thomas Scanlon, *What We Owe to Each Other* (Harvard University Press 1998) 315.

8 David Hume, *A Treatise on Human Nature* (Oxford University Press 2000) 332.

9 Gilbert (n 3) 113; also called "Prichard's point" in (n 4) 303.

some act a promise [*sic*], and all question of whether there is an obligation to do it seems to have vanished."[10] She formulates the intuition as follows:

Inevitability Point: "[I]f someone has made a promise to do something, then he is obligated to it, by virtue of his promise."[11]

Reinach concurs: "The promising produces a unique bond between two persons in virtue of which the one person [. . .] can claim something and the other is obliged to perform it or to grant it."[12] So, Reinach agrees with Gilbert that promises inevitably generate obligations. However, it is worth noting that Reinach here goes beyond Gilbert's "inevitability point" as stated above, for her "point" does not state that the noted obligation correlates with a claim. However, we will soon see that, for Gilbert too, promissory obligations correlate with claims (or demand-rights).

The Inevitability Point, Gilbert adds, is something that is known a priori.[13] Reinach, again, agrees: "[. . .] claim and obligation are grounded with essential necessity in the act of promising as such."[14] It is noteworthy that this last point can have two different readings: a strong and a weak one. The weak reading is this:

Inevitability Point (weak reading): If someone has made a promise to do something, then, *in the absence of sufficiently powerful countervailing considerations*, he is obligated to do it by virtue of his promise.

Yet, Gilbert and Reinach both insist that only the strong reading properly captures our intuitions on this matter:

Inevitability Point (strong reading): If someone has made a promise to do something, then he is obligated to do it by virtue of his promise.

They are not claiming that one is obliged to keep one's promises, no matter what. Their position tacitly builds on the distinction between *pro tanto* and *pro toto* obligations.[15] *Pro toto* obligations are *resultant* or *all things considered* obligations: these are obligations which result from weighing all – possibly conflicting – *pro tanto* obligations that are attached to one and the same action.[16] Promissory

[10] Harold Arthur Prichard, *Moral Obligation and Duty and Interest* (Oxford University Press 1968) 198.

[11] Gilbert (n 4) 303.

[12] Reinach (n 2) 8.

[13] Similar ideas can be found in Austin ("'I promise but I ought not' is parallel to 'it is and it is not'," John Austin, *How to Do Things with Words* (JO Urmson and Marina Sbisà, eds, 2d edn Harvard University Press 1975) 51; and in Searle ("I say if a person promises he is committed to doing the thing promised, and this is purely in virtue of the meaning of 'promise'," John Searle, *Speech Acts* (Cambridge University Press 1969) 190f).

[14] Reinach (n 2) 46.

[15] Gilbert (n 3) 135–143; Reinach (n 2) 45.

[16] On that notion of resultant/overall/pro toto obligation, see David Ross, *The Right and the Good* (Oxford University Press 2002), 28–29; Charlie Dunbar Broad, 'Some of the Main Problems of Ethics' in H Feigl and W Sellars (eds) *Readings in Philosophical Analysis* (Appleton-Century-Crofts

obligations may conflict with and be overrun by other obligations, and then be contrary to resultant or *pro toto* obligations.[17] Against this backdrop, Gilbert and Reinach's strong reading of the Inevitability Point is that an obligation is necessarily brought to existence by the promise, but this obligation is only *pro tanto*, so that it may conflict with and be overrun by other obligations.

On this strong reading, the Inevitability Point is incompatible with the Immoral Promises dogma. For, if promises always generate obligations, then so do immoral promises, *contra* the Immoral Promises dogma. Furthermore, this suggests, *contra* the Moral Requirement dogma, that promissory obligations are not moral obligations because moral principles cannot generate obligations with morally heinous content.

The second intuition Gilbert endorses is that promissory obligations are relational, that is, they are directed at somebody else: the promisee. Gilbert captures this idea by talking of "directed" obligations and "directed" claims (or "demand-rights"[18]): it is because the promisor's obligation is directed to the promisee that the promisee (and only them) have the "standing to demand" the promised action of the promisor. If Laura has an obligation to Sam to call him, then Sam can authoritatively demand of Laura that she call him. In a certain sense, Laura owes it to Sam to call him, and Sam therefore has the standing to demand that of her: if Laura does not do that, Sam is in a position to rebuke her. This suggests that any promissory obligation of the promisor, in virtue of its directedness, is equivalent to a promisee's claim against the promisor:

Directed Obligations (and Claims): Promissory obligations (and claims) are relational.

The relationality of obligations and claims also is at the core of Reinach's theory: "There [...] exists a correlativity between [promissory] claim and obligation: each has identically the same content, and the relations of bearer and partner are mutually interwoven according to strict apriori law."[19]

1949) 552; John Searle, 'Prima Facie Obligations' in J Raz (ed) *Practical Reasoning* (Oxford University Press 1978) 81–90.

17 "Its existence [i.e., the existence of the promissory obligation] is not affected, however, even by the existence of factors such that all things considered one ought not to fulfill it" (Gilbert (n 4) 319). "We can know whether a [promissory] obligation should be fulfilled only by going beyond it to the moral duty grounded in it. For only in this sphere is a comparison with other duties possible. *The extra-moral obligation remains untouched by all this*" (Reinach (n 2) 45, our emphasis).

18 In what follows, we will use the term "claim" to design the right of the promisee that is equivalent to the promisor's obligation (as we have seen, Gilbert's own term for "promissory claim" is "demand-right"). We use "claim" because of the ambiguity between liberty-rights and claim-rights (see Wesley Newcomb Hohfeld, 'Fundamental Legal Conceptions as Applied in Judicial Reasoning' (1917) 26 Yale LJ 710). Clearly, the right acquired by the promisee is not of the same kind as the right to free speech or the right to do what we want with what is ours.

19 Reinach (n 2) 12.

This second intuition is in tension with the Moral Requirement dogma because it assigns a particular standing to the promisee, which the Moral Requirement dogma is not able to accommodate. Why? Recall that, according to the Moral Requirement dogma, promissory obligations are moral requirements.[20] When a moral requirement is violated, everybody has the same "standing to demand compliance, if anyone does." If so, the Moral Requirement dogma leaves unexplained Laura's *special* standing towards Sam, which is captured by the idea that Sam has an obligation directed towards Laura (and, conversely, Laura has a claim that is directed towards Sam).

The interim conclusion of this discussion is that the two intuitions put unsurmountable pressure on the Moral Requirement dogma. In addition, given that the No Willing dogma and the Immoral Promises dogma are directly supported by the Moral Requirement dogma, if this goes, they too stand on shaky ground. Gilbert and Reinach agree on all this: a good account of promises should preserve the two intuitions and reject the three dogmas. Put differently: promises are intentional acts,[21] which necessarily give rise to nonmoral, relational claims and obligations. They part ways, however, when it comes to the positive account of promises.

11.3 THE JOINT COMMITMENT ACCOUNT OF PROMISING

Endorsing the two intuitions and, thus, rejecting the three dogmas leaves one with the proverbial elephant in the room: if promissory obligations necessarily arise from promises, though not in virtue of some moral principles, how do promises bring them about? To provide an answer to the question, Gilbert introduces her joint commitment account of promises:[22]

[20] It is worthwhile emphasizing that, according to the Moral Requirement dogma, the moral principles generating promissory obligations are general. A moral principle qualifies as general if it is valid unconditionally insofar as it applies to every moral agent (e.g., "one ought not to lie"). As such, they are different from non-general moral principles, i.e., from moral principles that are valid conditionally because they do not apply to every moral agent (as an example, consider the special moral obligations that only parents have towards their children). While the obligations generated by the latter principles, insofar as they are directed obligations, are similar to promissory obligations in some respect, they differ from them. We have already seen that it is possible to carry a promissory obligation, which has an immoral action as its content (whereas moral principles cannot generate obligations with immoral content). In addition, promissory obligations are created by free acts and can be modified by free acts (e.g., transferred to other persons under specific conditions or assumed by other persons), but this is impossible in the case of directed (and undirected) moral obligations. Reinach devotes important considerations to this matter, see Reinach (n 2) 13ff.

[21] Gilbert and Reinach concur that an act of a mere inner will is not capable of generating relational obligations and claims. However, they do insist upon the idea that the promise, which has that power, is intentional in the sense that it stands under the promisor's (and, according to Gilbert, the promisee's) voluntary control. Accordingly, while the will alone is inefficacious in creating promissory obligations and claims, this is not to say that it plays no role at all in the explanation of how those obligations and claims are brought about.

[22] It merits attention that Gilbert's account is based upon her influential and sophisticated theory of plural subjects. Despite the importance of her positions to many areas of philosophical

Joint commitment account: X has made a promise to Y if and only if (1) X and Y are jointly committed to endorse as a body a particular plan of action P, and (2) X and Y created this joint commitment by virtue of appropriate, explicit expressions on the part of each, in conditions of common knowledge and (3) P specifies an action for X.[23]

Promises are accounted for in terms of (joint) commitments. What are commitments? Although "committing oneself" has a psychological connotation, on Gilbert's understanding, *commitments – personal or joint –* are *normative*, nonpsychological phenomena.[24] The psychological process of committing oneself should not be conflated with its normative product: "to commit" and "committing" are psychological; "to be committed" and "commitment" are normative.[25]

Against this background, *personal* commitments are normative phenomena created by acts of the individual will, namely intentions or decisions.[26] In this sense, commitments are "creatures of the will."[27] Although normative, no moral valence is attached to commitments: "[t]o commit oneself [in this sense] is to make it the case that one has sufficient reason to do a certain thing."[28] If Laura decides to kill Sam, Laura now has a sufficient reason to do so because her decision has brought about a personal commitment, independently of its immoral content. (One could add that the commitment at stake is *pro tanto*, given that other reasons, and especially moral reasons, which may speak against the action, accrue to her.) Importantly, a personal commitment can be reneged on by its very bearer *solo*, as it were. Changing one's mind is a personal affair, which may be difficult and may come with psychological costs, but which is possible without the subject consulting with anybody else. Yet, this very possibility is precluded when it comes to *joint* commitments. Why is that and, more generally, what are joint commitments?

A joint commitment is one commitment (not a combination of commitments) of two or more persons by these two or more persons. Roughly put, the form of joint commitments is this: "A and B are jointly committed to φ as a body" (where φ is an agential or psychological predicate). A joint commitment is brought about when individuals express their readiness for a particular joint commitment with one

research, the scope of this paper forces us to address only those parts of her general theory that are immediately relevant to the discussion of promises. Also, note that this paper only objects to the relationship between promises and joint commitments, but it targets neither Gilbert's notion of joint commitments as such nor its heuristic value in accounting for other social phenomena.

23 Gilbert (n 3) 204.

24 ibid 161, 181.

25 Margaret Gilbert, 'Introduction' in *How We Make the Social World* (Oxford University Press 2014) 6.

26 Gilbert (n 3) 162.

27 Margaret Gilbert, 'Rationality in Collective Action' (2006) 36 Philosophy of the Social Sciences 1, 6.

28 Gilbert (n 4) 310.

another, under conditions of common knowledge.[29] Importantly, "expressing readiness" should be understood as "expressing that state of [the] will that is readiness [...]."[30] Imagine Laura telling Sam "should we go for a walk?" and Sam "sure, lets!"[31] In this case, Laura and Sam have expressed, under conditions of common knowledge, their relevant states of the will that is each one's readiness jointly to commit to taking up as a body the goal of going for a walk. They are, therefore, jointly committed to doing so. Thus, in the same way in which personal decisions create personal commitments, so expressions of states of the will that are readiness to jointly commit (under conditions of common knowledge) create joint commitments. A joint commitment (just as with a personal commitment) provides each of the parties sufficient reason to conform to it: "If [...] one is jointly committed [...], [o]ne therefore has sufficient reason for performing actions that conform to the commitment, sufficient reason that is independent of one's inclinations and self-interest." Interestingly, Gilbert continues by stating that: "in the case of a personal decision, intention, and so on, the normative force of this commitment can be eradicated by one's own fiat. Failing special background understandings, that is not so in [the] case [of joint commitment]."[32]

So, joint commitments, in contrast to personal commitments, cannot be rescinded by a single party unilaterally (barring special background understandings). Why? Because a joint commitment, Gilbert claims, creates a set of directed obligations and correlative rights. These obligations and rights block the possibility for a single individual to renege on a joint commitment unilaterally. Put another way, each party of a joint commitment not only is obligated to the others to conform to the commitment, they can also authoritatively demand conforming actions of the others. Note that these obligations and rights are content-independent, meaning that they are not moral and do not derive from moral principles. As long as a joint commitment is in place, corresponding obligations and rights arise, regardless of the moral content of that commitment.

Before assessing the joint commitment of promises, three clarifications are in order.

First, Gilbert's position on what X and Y are committed to, when X makes a promise to Y, has evolved through time. In a former version of her theory,[33] X are Y are held to be jointly committed to the *decision* that X performs a certain action. In the last version presented here,[34] X are Y are jointly committed to an *action plan*

[29] On common knowledge, see Margaret Gilbert, *A Theory of Political Obligation* (Oxford University Press 2008), 138ff.

[30] Gilbert (n 3) 216.

[31] Margaret Gilbert, 'Walking Together: A Paradigmatic Social Phenomenon' (1990) 15 Midwest Studies in Philosophy 1, 1–14.

[32] Gilbert (n 29) 156.

[33] Gilbert (n 4).

[34] Gilbert (n 3).

that specifies an action of X. While the distinction between commitment to decisions to act and commitment to plans to act matters in various respects, we shall consider the two versions of theory to be equivalent for the purposes of our paper given that our objections do not hang on that point.

Second, it should be stressed that, despite its name, *the joint commitment account does not equate promises with joint commitments*. As we have seen, commitments are normative phenomena that ensue from the persons' acts of *committing*. The distinction between the joint commitment and the actions of X and Y that give rise to it is reflected in the use of the present and past tense in Gilbert's definition. This is perhaps more easily seen in Gilbert's earlier formulation of her view:

> for one person to make a promise to another is *for them jointly to commit themselves*, by an appropriate, explicit process, to the decision that one of them ("the promisor") is to perform one or more specified actions.[35]

We infer from this that, on the joint commitment account, making a promise consists in the acts of jointly committing, not in the (normative) state of being jointly committed.

Thirdly, a clarification about the notion of "jointly committing" is in order. The acts of jointly committing mentioned in Gilbert's account of promises must not, on pain of circularity, be understood as joint actions in a collective sense, according to which an action is joint if it is performed upon a shared intention.[36] For her notion of shared intention is explained by that of joint commitment: in brief, the intention to φ is shared by X and Y iff X and Y are jointly committed to intend as a body to φ.[37] So, if joint commitment were created by joint acts of committing (in the collective understanding of "joint acts," which presupposes shared intentions), then her theory would become vulnerable to a charge of circularity. Therefore, the appeal to the notion of "jointly committing" in her account should be read in the noncollective (or "distributive") sense, according to which X's act of expressing personal readiness for the joint commitment in question and Y's act of expressing personal readiness for the same joint commitment do *not* presuppose X and Y's shared intention to perform the relevant acts. Once the necessary expressions have been made under condition of common knowledge, then the joint commitment will be in place, as is understood by the parties.

We now have all the elements required to appreciate Gilbert's account of promises. Laura's promise to Sam to call him later is Laura and Sam's joint commitment to decide or endorse as a body the plan that Laura calls Sam later (a

35 Gilbert (n 4) 317, our italics.

36 David P Schweikard and Hans Bernhard Schmid, 'Collective Intentionality' in *The Stanford Encyclopedia of Philosophy* (Edward N. Zalta, ed., https://plato.stanford.edu/archives/win2020/entries/collective-intentionality/ 2020).

37 Margaret Gilbert, 'What Is It for Us to Intend?' in G Holmström-Hintikka and R Tuomela (eds), *Contemporary Action Theory*, Vol. II (Dordrecht: Kluwer 1997) 65–85.

joint plan arrived at by a particular process e.g., Laura's saying "I promise..." and Sam offering an accepting response; on such a "response" more later).

Why should one favor the joint commitment account of promises? Gilbert gives four arguments in its support.

1. The first argument is that the joint commitment account vindicates the two intuitions. Thus, the account explains why a promise necessarily generates an obligation and why that obligation is relational.
2. Second, the joint commitment account jettisons the three dogmas. It rejects the Moral Requirement dogma because no moral principle is appealed to in order to explain the *pro tanto* obligation of a promisor to perform the promise. The No Willing dogma is also dismissed: while the obligation, as a matter of fact, *is* willed into existence, but its creation does not happen merely in virtue of the *individual* will of the promisor, but in virtue of *two* individual wills.[38] Finally, the Immoral Promises dogma, too, is subject to rejection: promissory obligations are content-independent, which means that, regardless of their content, they are brought into being by the joint commitment.

Gilbert adds what in her eyes constitutes two further advantages of her view:

3. If promises are joint commitments to the decision that the promisor φs, then the jointness of that commitment requires that not only the promisor, but also the promisee, is active in a certain sense. This conforms to our intuitions, according to Gilbert, so that: "one point in favor of the joint commitment account of promises is that [...] the promisee must do something of an accepting rather than a rejecting nature"[39] (note that acceptance does not have to be verbal, but it is not mere uptake or acknowledgment[40]).
4. Finally, Gilbert claims that her view entails that, when a promise is made, not only the promisor but also the promisee takes on some obligation (whose content is not specified in the content of the promise). She takes this to be a welcome consequence of her account, which again is supposed to conform to our intuition: imagine Laura promises to call Sam on the phone, Sam accepts that, but then he takes his phone off the hook. On Gilbert's account, Laura can rebuke Sam authoritatively because Sam has the obligation to Laura not to make her calling him impossible.[41] Since joint commitments generate both obligations and rights, on each of its parties, this intuition is also explained by the account.

38 See Gilbert (n 4) 321, and (n 3) 214f.
39 Gilbert (n 4) 318.
40 Gilbert (n 3) 108ff.
41 See Gilbert (n 4) 318.

In the next three sections, we mount several objections against Gilbert's theory of promises. These objections are grounded in elements of Reinach's theory of promises. While we flag these elements by referring to Reinach's text, our objections are substantive, rather than historical or exegetical.

11.4 FIRST OBJECTION: ACCEPTANCE

One important element in Gilbert's theory of promises, which has been mentioned only briefly in the previous sections is this: "[p]romising," she writes, "is understood to include whatever is necessary to supplement the actions of the promisor in order to complete the promise; *this* [...] *includes the promisee's acceptance*."[42] Gilbert specifies that acceptance is a kind of concurrence as opposed to mere acknowledgment: "if Jeremy were to make a prediction, such as 'I think I'll be calling you tonight, it's going to be hard being home alone,' Julia might respond with 'I hear you.' This would be a case of acknowledgment without acceptance in the sense at issue."[43] However, Gilbert otherwise does not elaborate extensively on the credentials of this act. In this section, we follow Reinach in canvassing various senses of "acceptance" and show that none of them are necessary for the promise.[44]

First, "acceptance" could point to (1) an act of inner assent, which can be described as the experience of saying "yes" to a certain content that *p* as contrasted with the experience of merely entertaining the content that *p* or refusing it. The specific credentials of this act (e.g., whether it is a dispositional belief or an episodic action) are not of interest for our present purposes. What is important, though, is that this act (just as beliefs and other mental actions) is internal in the sense that it does not stand under the requirement of being expressed to others.

The second sense of acceptance (2) discussed by Reinach is the – nonintentional and noncommunicative – expression of (1), for example, nodding while reading a contract we are asked to sign. This sense of acceptance bears little or no relevance to our discussion, which is why we won't dwell on it, but it allows us to distinguish a third sense of acceptance, which is (3) the intentional act of informing somebody about one's acceptance of *p* in the sense of (1). In contrast to (2), (3) demands an addressee: informing your colleague that you have accepted the contract is an intentional act, which has to be distinguished from your (nonintentional) nodding in the presence of the colleague.

The fourth act is a *sui generis* intentional social or speech act of acceptance (4), which is performed, for example, when one accepts the contract by saying "I hereby accept the terms of the contract." One might wonder whether (3) genuinely differs from (4). The following consideration shows that it does: while (3), in principle, can

[42] See Gilbert (n 3) 113 n 25, our emphasis.
[43] Gilbert (n 4) 318.
[44] Reinach (n 2) 28–31.

be addressed to anybody, (4) can be addressed sensibly only to the relevant person in the relevant given communicative situation: while one can inform their colleague about their inner assent to the contract, one cannot accept the contract in front of their colleague (in the fourth sense), unless they are or represent the other party of the contract. Furthermore, (3) can be repeated *ad libitum*, but (4) can meaningfully and efficaciously be performed only once. Finally, (3) can be made in the present, past or future tense ("[I inform you that] I have accepted" or "I accept" or "I will accept the contract"), but (4) admits only of the present tense.

Is acceptance in at least one of these four senses necessary for promises? Start with the first sense of acceptance. Inner assent, it can be contended, is irrelevant to promises: We have seen that the No Willing dogma declares mere internal willing unable to alter the space of interpersonal normative reasons, that is, to bring about normative entities like directed obligations or claims. But if mere internal willing does not have that power, neither does inner assent insofar as it is a personal (private and internal) act. Interpersonal reasons are just not the kind of entities that are created by individual and internal acts, be they acts of the will or of inner assent.

Since acceptance in the second sense merely is the nonintentional expression of (1), the inner assent's irrelevance to promises extends to (2) as well. Hence, promises' capacity to generate relational obligations and rights does not hinge on nonintentional expressions of inner acts. More importantly, it does not hinge on the *intentional* expression of internal assent either (in the sense of (3)). To see why, consider these two ideas. First, one can inform anybody about their assenting to a promise, but that does not amount to accepting the promise in the sense at stake here. Suppose Laura promises to Sam: "I will call you this afternoon!" and Sam, unbeknownst to Laura, informs Pam that he has assented to Laura's promise. While one can grant a sense in which Sam, towards Pam, has "accepted" Laura's promise and while this might have repercussions in the normative relations between Sam and Pam, no normative relation between Laura and Sam has been established by Sam's act of informing Pam about his assent. Because of that, this act is not relevant to promises. Second, the promisee can inform the promisor of their assent. Admittedly, this act can be confused with the proper act of acceptance. However, its linguistic expression will help disambiguate the communicative situation. If the subject's utterance is in the past or in the future tense ("I have assented to your promise" or "I will assent to your promise"), chances are that they are merely informing the promisor about their inner act. The same consideration holds if they repeat their utterance several times. In these cases, the promisor is likely to request clarification on what the promisee is doing. But no such request will be raised if the promisee's utterance is in the present tense and/or if they complement it with relevant adverbs like "hereby."[45] For these are linguistic signals that the promisee is performing a genuine act of acceptance.

[45] On the relevance of this adverb see Reinach (n 2) 30 and Austin (n 13) 57.

Is acceptance *qua* specific intentional speech or social act different from (1)–(3) necessary for promises? Sometimes, this act is indeed required. Imagine Laura telling Sam: "I will call you, only in case you agree," and Sam replying: "I hereby agree." Laura is here issuing a *conditional promise*: its efficaciousness is contingent on an event, which is Sam's act of acceptance – in the fourth sense illustrated above. For the promissory obligation to get off the ground, Sam has to accept Laura's promise by performing an intentional act of a specific kind. (In this particular case, the promise is contingent on an act of acceptance, but promises could be made contingent on all sort of events: for example, "if it rains, I promise I'll bring the dog for a walk.")

However, not all promises are conditional. Imagine Laura who struggles to keep up with her jogging schedule. To motivate herself, she tells Sam, her flatmate, while he is doing the dishes: "I promise to go for a run at 5 pm." In uttering those words, Laura creates a promissory obligation that motivates her to go for a run at 5 pm. Now, it is true that Laura's motivation to make the promise is entirely private (she wants to keep her jogging schedule). However, this doesn't mean that she has not entered a promissory obligation. In fact, the motivational power Laura intends to elicit precisely derives from its relationality: since Laura cannot renege on the obligation unilaterally, she is bound to honor it. The promissory nature of Laura's obligation can also be inferred by the fact that Sam acquires a content-identical claim. This claim may well have practical insignificance to Sam, but this is not to say that it does not exist. Under specific circumstances, Sam may decide to enforce it. For instance, imagine that Sam schedules an online meeting for 5 pm, which requires the use of Laura's room. Around that time, he notices that she hasn't yet prepared for jogging and demands that she honors her commitment to go for a jog. Sam's demand carries normative force, meaning that if Laura fails to meet it, Sam is entitled to rebuke her. This normative force wouldn't exist if Laura had merely informed Sam of her intention to go for a jog at 5 pm. Having established all this, let's go back to Laura's promise; while Sam is doing the dishes, she tells him: "I promise to go for a run at 5 pm." Does Sam need to accept the promise in a case like this? No, he can continue doing the dishes without saying a word.[46]

For at least some promises, acceptance is therefore not necessary: call these promises "unconditional." It is true that many promises that are explicitly unconditional appear to be tacitly conditional. So, for example, promises like "I will sell you the house at the best price" or "I will take care of your children for the next three days" are not explicitly formulated in conditional terms, but do require acceptance

[46] Interestingly, Gilbert makes a similar example, but draws a different conclusion (see Gilbert (n 3) 111). Another example: "I may promise someone in person, face to face, to come and visit him in hospital tomorrow. He receives the promise stone-faced, saying nothing and moving not a muscle. My promise is binding, and it requires some imagination to claim that it has been accepted." Joseph Raz, *The Roots of Normativity* (U Heuer ed., Oxford University Press 2002) 205.

on the promisee's end to generate obligations and rights. These observations suggest that conditional promises may be more ubiquitous than usually thought. But this does not imply that all promises are conditional. We surmise that the view that all promises require acceptance stems from a natural, but ultimately overbroad generalization from conditional to unconditional promises.[47]

Perhaps acceptance-based accounts of promises[48] are motivated by a concern to include a mechanism that safeguards the interest of the promisee, for example, in a case where they perceive the promise to endanger them (e.g., the promise of transferring shares in a company that involve liability). Charles Fried writes in this vein: "I admit unease [...] about insisting on acceptance in the case where the promise is clearly communicated and where it would be captious to doubt that the promisee is delighted the promise." But he then continues: "Since [...] any putative benefit may in fact be unwanted by a particular (putative) promisee, there must at least be the option to refuse or reject not just the benefit but the promise of the benefit."[49] We think that the concern is legitimate, but misplaced. For the promisee can avail themself of a mechanism to protect their interest unrelated to acceptance. In fact, the promisee has the power to release: in waiving their claims, they, by the same token, release the promisor of their obligation and make the promise null and void. (As we will see, one of the criticisms we raise in the next section against Gilbert's theory is that it disavows this power.)

Our interim conclusion is that promising as such does not require acceptance. To dismiss this conclusion, defenders of an acceptance-based account of promises should dismiss the notion of unconditional promise as inconsistent and empty. However, this notion does not involve any internal contradiction and, hence, is not inconsistent. Also, many of our promises do appear to be unconditional.

[47] Reinach is not alone in endorsing the existence of unconditional promises: Raz, as we saw above, concurs. But this idea has a long history: Thomas Aquinas (and other medieval philosophers) do as well, see James Gordley, *The Philosophical Origins of Modern Contract Doctrine* (Clarendon Press 1991) 45. John Searle only mentions the promisee having "knowledge" (not "acceptance") of the promise as condition for successfully promising (Searle (n 13) 60). For what it's worth, promises not conditional on acceptance are recognized to give rise to "unilateral obligations" (in contrast to "mutual contracts") in Scottish law, see Gloag and Henderson: *The Law of Scotland* (H MacQueen and The Right Hon Lord Eassie, eds W. Green/Smith and Maxwell) 5.1.

[48] In addition to Gilbert, a number of other philosophers impose an acceptance-condition on promises. Some recent contributions that emphasize the role of acceptance include: Stephen Darwall, 'Demystifying Promises' in H Sheinman (ed) *Promises and Agreements: Philosophical Essays* (Oxford University Press 2011) 256; Abraham Sesshu Roth, 'Intention, Expectation, and Promissory Obligation' (2016) 127 Ethics 88); Brendan de Kenessey, 'Promises as Proposals in Joint Practical Deliberation' (2020) 54 Noûs 204.

[49] Charles Fried, *Contract as Promise. A Theory of Contractual Obligation* (Oxford University Press 2015) 43.

11.5 SECOND OBJECTION: THE AUTHORS OF PROMISES

We ordinarily think of promises as actions of the promisor. However, the joint commitment account misidentifies the authors of the promises by equating the promisor's singular act of promising with actions performed by promisor and promisee: "for *one* person to make a promise to another is for *them* jointly to commit..."[50] It is true that, on Gilbert's theory, there is more to promises than that (e.g., appropriate and explicit expressions on the part of promisor and promisee must have occurred). While these details are important to Gilbert's general account,[51] our focus in this section will be restricted to the idea that what appears to be an act of an individual (the promisor's *promising*) directed at another (the promisee) turns out to be a plurality of acts of those individuals (the promisor's and promisee's *committing*). This amounts to a strongly revisionary account of the authors of promises.

Note, first, that our point is not that the promisor/promisee asymmetry gets lost on the joint commitment account. It does not: the promisor – not the promisee – figures *as the author of the decided action* in the content of the decision to which the promisor and the promisee commit. Our point rather is that what distinguishes the promisor from the promisee is not *just* that the promise bears on the promisor's action. The distinction between the promisor and the promisee is first and foremost content-independent: the promisor is not only the author of the promised action, he also is the author of the promise (or, as Reinach calls him, the "originator"[52] of the promise). Gilbert's account fails to capture that aspect of promises.

In answer, Gilbert might simply challenge the notion that promises, as we submitted, are, in fact, ordinarily conceived of as acts of the promisor and not as acts of the promisor and the promisee.[53] However, the following considerations suggest that that is very much the case indeed:

1. We tend to ascribe the authorship of promises to the promisor alone:
   a. Suppose that, after Laura promised Sam to call him, Jim asks Sam: "Did *you* commit together with Laura to the decision that she will call you?" Sam is likely to answer in the negative: "No – this is Laura's commitment!" If Laura were asked the same question, a similar answer may be expected – perhaps accompanied by an element of remonstration: "No, what I promise is entirely up to me, why should have I consulted with Sam in advance on what to promise to him?".

[50] ibid 317, our italics.

[51] They, for instance, help Gilbert distinguish between promises and agreements, see Gilbert (n 3) 204f.

[52] Reinach (n 2) 18.

[53] Note that, as we make explicit below, we do not deny that there can be promises made by two or more individuals *together*. Here, we are only putting pressure on the claim that *all* promises are joint actions.

b. Imagine an evil demon announcing that he will kill the first person who makes a promise after *t*. In a heroic sacrificial act, Sam shouts "I promise never to forget you Laura!". Should the demon kill them both?

c. A promisor can plan to make a promise, without any uncertainty being caused by the possible lack of cooperation of the promisee. One's promises are easy to plan, in contrast to agreements and joints actions.

2. The contrast between individual and collective promises ("I promise" vs. "we promise") is, on the face of it, content-independent:[54] it is simply the contrast between the promise made by a single subject and the promise made by a plurality of subjects. The joint commitment account has to reject this. On the joint commitment account, the difference cannot depend on the number of subjects performing the act (one *versus* many). Rather, what distinguishes individual from collective promises pertains to their content: individual promises are joint commitments bearing on individual actions, while collective promises are joint commitments bearing on collective actions (more on the content of promises in the next section).

So, the ways in which we conceive of, plan, and evaluate promises converge in showing that promises are acts *of the promisor*. The joint commitment account is, as mentioned above, robustly revisionary in that respect. Couldn't Gilbert bite that bullet? We doubt it. First, this revision concerns such a core feature of promises that one may wonder whether an account denying that promises are acts of the promisor can still legitimately claim to be *about promises*. Second, the revision entails four further problematic consequences to which we now turn.

(i) *Too many obligations for the promisee.* Let us start by formulating a worry concerning the standard obligation of the promisor, that is, the "performance obligation" to act as promised, which is at stake in the Inevitability Point. The worry is this: if X and Y jointly commit to endorse the decision that X will φ, then both X and Y should have an obligation to that effect. However, this is not so in the case of promises.

Gilbert denies that X and Y's joint commitment entails that performance obligations accrue to both, X and Y: "[...] the only performance obligations associated with a promise X makes to Y are those of X [...]."[55] But if the promisee incurs no performance obligation, then we confess to lose grip on the very idea that, when X promises Y to φ, X *and* Y *are jointly committed to endorse the decision that* X will φ.

[54] See Reinach (n 2) 24.

[55] Gilbert (n 3) 204.

That is, we doubt that there is any ordinary notion of joint commitment such that X and Y are jointly committed to an action of X, without Y incurring any (performance) obligation as a result.[56] It just doesn't seem that Y has committed to anything in such a case.

However, it is important to note that, in denying that X and Y's joint commitment entails that performance obligations accrue to both X and Y, Gilbert is not denying that other, "ancillary" obligations accrue to the promisee. She writes: "the promisor's performance obligation is not the only obligation arising, inevitably, in the context of a promise." What are these obligations? "A promisee's ancillary obligation," she continues, "is at a minimum an obligation to his promisor not to act in ways that prevent his promisor from fulfilling the promise."[57]

Does the existence of ancillary obligations deflate our criticism? Let us reply by highlighting that we do not dispute the existence of such ancillary obligations. However, we resist the idea that they are generated by the promise. Instead, we suggest that these obligations are generated by a general moral principle. While the exact formulation of this principle is the topic for another paper, we can state it in a loose manner as follows: one ought not to thwart the realization of somebody else's intention (barring special circumstances: e.g., if the intention carries a morally heinous content). Since honest promises presuppose the promisor's intention to perform the promised action, the promisee (and, actually, given the moral nature of the principle at stake: anybody else) ought not thwart the realization of the promisor's intention (barring special circumstances). So, if Laura promises Sam, in the presence of Robert, that she will meet Sam at the pub at 5 pm, then not only Sam but also Robert should refrain from actions that would hinder Laura from fulfilling her promise.

(ii) *Loss of power of release for the promisee.* A second problematic consequence of the joint commitment account pertains to the rescission of a promise. Gilbert claims that, since not only the promisor, but also the promisee, places himself under an obligation when a promise is performed, then the promisee cannot, on the face of it, unilaterally rescind the promise. This is in contrast with the widely accepted idea that the promisee has a "power of release."[58] Gilbert offers two replies to alleviate the tension with this widely endorsed idea.

Her first reply is to question the systematic existence of such a power of release. Gilbert suggests that we are under the impression that such a power exists because, in our analyses of promises, we selectively focus on promises that the promisor has

56 In her works, Gilbert repeatedly contends that her notion of joint commitment is "a fundamental everyday concept," ibid 164.

57 ibid 114.

58 Reinach (n 2) 75.

no personal desire to perform. These are cases in which the promise has been solicited by the promisee. While looking at this specific class of promises, it may sound plausible that the promisee has a power to release, given that the promisor has no interest in the promise. However, Gilbert claims that if the promisor *does* have the desire to promise, then the promisor will be justified in resisting the promisee's attempt to waive their right unilaterally (thereby making the promise null and void). This is the example Gilbert makes to illustrate the point:

> [. . .] suppose Joe promises to return Jane's book on Tuesday. Jane calls him to say that it is not that important for her to have the book, so he may keep it. He might then say 'No, I promised to return the book on Tuesday and that's what I'll do.' It is at best not clear that Jane is [in] a position to say 'But the promise is over, I just said so'.[59]

We disagree: it seems to us that Jane is very much in a position to do so. We suspect that confusion is at play here between Jane's rescinding the promise and Jane's forbidding Joe from returning the book. Of course, Jane is in no position to issue such an interdiction. While Jane's rescinding of the promise destroys Joe's obligation to return the book, his permission to do so remains intact.

If you are nonetheless under the impression that Jane is in a position to forbid Joe to return the book, then perhaps, Reinach argues,[60] you conceived of Joe's "promise" as a promise *together with some nonpromissory act*. For instance, it might be that by uttering the word "I promise to return your book on Tuesday," Joe performed not one, but two acts: a promise to return the book *and* a request to Jane that she accept that he will return the book on Tuesday. Of course, if Jane accedes to the *request*, she takes on an obligation. This is the obligation to accept that Joe returns the book, and it is one that she cannot revoke unilaterally. While Jane retains the power to waive the claim deriving from Joe's promise, she cannot exercise that power, given the obligation she entered by accepting Joe's request. In this scenario, Jane therefore is under an obligation that she cannot rescind, but this is not, as the joint commitment account would have it, because the promisee is tied by the promise that was made to her, but because she is tied by her having accepted the concomitant request of the promisor.

Gilbert's second reply is to point out that should one insist on the promisee's power of release, one could modify the joint account so as to accommodate it in the following way: "a promise is a joint decision that one party, 'the promisor,' is to do something – a joint decision entered into by an appropriate explicit process – *with which is associated the understanding that it stands at the pleasure of the other party – 'the promisee'*."[61] Our reply is that while promisor and promisee may have

[59] Gilbert (n 4) 318f, and (n 3) 210f. Note that the example is slightly confusing, given that we have a duty to give back what we lent independently of any promise.

[60] Reinach (n 2) 32f.

[61] Gilbert (n 4) 319, our italics.

that understanding and may even render it explicit in the process of making the promise, a great many promises are *not* associated with that understanding simply because the parties do not possess it. And yet, even in those promises, we would maintain that the power of release accrues to the promisee. So, for example, Laura promises Sam that she will call him at 5 pm. Sam (and, for what it's worth, Laura too) might not be aware that Sam can release Laura (perhaps they have never reflected on these matters). Yet Sam does possess that power (even though, due to his ignorance on the matter, he will not exercise it). If that is correct, it goes to show that the power of release does not depend on such an understanding.

(iii) *Too much responsibility for the promisee.* Intuitively, the responsibility for a promise accrues to the promisor in a way that does not accrue to the promisee. Thus, in the case of immoral and, especially, unconditional promises, the promisor is blameworthy in a way the promisee is not. Likewise, the promisee does not get any credit for the courageous or generous promises made by the promisor. Since on the joint commitment account both the promisor and the promisee perform the promise together, such asymmetries in responsibility ascription run the risk of getting lost.

Gilbert may reply by relying on the fact that her account does not erase the difference between the promisor and the promisee but traces it back to the content of the joint commitment: the promisor, to recall, is the one whose action figures in the joint commitment. Thus, on the joint commitment account, it may be argued that the promisor incurs the responsibility of the promised action because that action is hers. By extension, if the promised action is immoral, then the promisor – not the promisee – is blameworthy.

However, there are two reasons why such a view fails to capture the relevant asymmetry in responsibility. First, given that both the promisor and the promisee are jointly committed to the decision that the promisor will perform the immoral action, the promisee, on the joint commitment account, should still incur some responsibility for that blameworthy action, should it be performed. But if Sam makes the unconditional promise to Laura to kill a cat for fun, how is Laura even partly responsible if Sam delivers on his promise?[62]

[62] One might object that whether Laura incurs responsibility depends on how she reacts to this unconditional promise, which is left unspecified in the example. Laura might (i) ignore Sam's promise; (ii) insist on Sam's delivering the promise; (iii) exercise her power to release Sam. Admittedly some form of responsibility accrues to Laura in scenario (i) and surely in (ii) – but not in the third scenario (iii). However, that responsibility, we submit, is not for Sam's action (she is not the one who, after all, has killed the cat), but rather the responsibility for not deterring Sam to act, as in (i), or for encouraging him to act, as in (ii). At this juncture, it is interesting to recall that Gilbert's theory deprives Laura of the power to release. Because of that, the joint commitment account precludes Laura to evade whatever form of responsibility Laura might incur in (i) by activating that power. Finally, it should be mentioned that moral

Second, one might be blameworthy (or praiseworthy) for a promise without this deriving from the blameworthiness (or praiseworthiness) of the promised action. Suppose it is forbidden to make promises on Mondays. If Sam nevertheless unconditionally promised to Laura on Monday, Laura does not incur any responsibility for violating the interdiction. However, in such a case the asymmetry in blameworthiness cannot be traced back to the blameworthiness of the promised action. Indeed, the promised action may well not be blameworthy. In such a case, if Sam is blameworthy and Laura is not, this cannot be because they jointly commit a blameworthy action of Sam. In short, differences in blameworthiness of promises cannot always be derived from differences in blameworthiness of promissory contents.

(iv) *Second-order promises and Euthyphro.* Consider this second order promise: Sam promises Laura that he will promise to call her. On the joint commitment account, such a second-order promise amounts to Sam and Laura jointly committing to the decision that Sam will promise to call Laura, which in turn amounts to Sam and Laura jointly committing to the decision that Sam and Laura will jointly commit to the decision that Sam calls Laura. Let us focus on the wide scope, second-order promise. That promise is, *ex hypothesis*, a promise made by Sam. On the joint commitment account, this should mean that the promise bears on an action by Sam. However, the joint commitment account entails that this is not the case: the content of that second-order joint commitment is an action of Sam and Laura – namely a first-order joint commitment. This highlights that the joint commitment account is in no position to maintain that, with respect to the second-order promise, Sam is the promisor.

The natural reply on behalf of the joint commitment account is that the first-order joint commitment (of Sam and Laura to the decision that Sam will call Laura) is a promise by Sam, because it bears on an action by Sam (calling Laura). If so, the second-order joint commitment bears on an action by Sam – a first-order promise – so that it is itself, in turn, a second-order promise by Sam.

This reply, we submit, brings to the fore how wrong-side-up it is to identify the promisor via the content of the promise.[63] To determine whether a second-order joint commitment of Sam and Laura corresponds to a promise by Sam, by Laura, or is not a promise, we must look into the content of that second-order order

consequences bearing on Laura would have reverberated if Sam's promise was conditional on Laura's acceptance and Laura accepted it.

[63] To be sure, this is not the only way in which the role of the promisor is identified by Gilbert's theory. For instance, the promisor is also identified by the ritual in which the relevant joint commitment is entered: the promisor, though not always, is the one who utters "I promise" and the promisee is the one who accepts the promise.

commitment. Since that is another joint commitment, we have to look further and check the content of that first-order commitment. This puts the cart before the horse. We need not know what is promised to determine *who* has promised. Gilbert is certainly right that our promises necessarily bear on actions of ours. But they are not our promises because they bear on actions of ours. They bear on actions of ours because they are our promises.

For all these reasons we conclude that authorship of promises should not be attributed to both the promisor and the promisee, as entailed by the joint commitment account. We now turn to our third objection to the joint commitment account of promises.

11.6 THIRD OBJECTION: THE CONTENTS OF PROMISES

In this section we argue that the joint commitment account of promises mischaracterizes the *contents of promises* by equating them with decisions to act (or endorsement of action plans) and not with actions *tout court*. Remember Gilbert's account:

> **Joint commitment account:** X has made a promise to Y if and only if (1) X and Y are jointly committed *to endorse as a body a particular plan of action P*, and (2) X and Y created this joint commitment by virtue of appropriate, explicit expressions on the part of each, in conditions of common knowledge, and (3) P specifies an action for X.[64]

On this view, "Laura promised to Sam that she will call him" ought to be paraphrased into "Laura and Sam jointly committed to endorse the plan [or 'decide'] that Laura calls Sam."[65] However, what we typically promise is neither to *decide* to act nor to *endorse* an action, but *to act* (sometimes, Reinach argues, the promisor promises *results* rather than actions – but these results still are results of the promisor's actions[66]). All in all, Gilbert's *analysans* is more complicated than the *analysandum* in two respects. First, promises – which *prima facie* are individual acts – are analyzed in terms of a plurality of acts. Second, promises – which *prima facie* have a first-order content directed at the action of the promisor – are analyzed in terms of committal acts of the will directed at a *joint decision to act* (or at the *joint endorsement of some action plan*). A first order individual act is analyzed in terms of a plurality of second order acts.

64 Gilbert (n 3) 204, our italics.

65 Couldn't one read the account in such a way that the content of the joint commitment simply is the action of one of the two committers (rather than their joint endorsement of a plan of action)? We come back to this alternative interpretation in the final part of this section where we show that, in addition to going against the letter of Gilbert's account, it also is uncharitable to it as it generates a number of problematic consequences.

66 Reinach (n 2) 11f.

In principle, one could maintain that promises are in fact more complex than they seem to be by arguing that this complexity is a cost worth paying – for instance, because joint commitments allow analysis of a wide variety of other phenomena, such as agreements. However, we submit that such gains are overridden by substantial costs which, all things considered, should advise us against endorsing the joint commitment account of promises.

To begin with, there is a cost in intuitive simplicity: promises are something else than what they appear to be. Preferring an elaborate account of promises to our intuitive grasp of them stands in tension with Gilbert's laudable attempt to stick to appearances in other places. For instance, elsewhere she argues against the view that agreements are exchanges of promises by raising the worry that an "agreement, for one, does not look like a pair of promises, mutual, exchanged or whatever."[67] We agree, but by parity of reasoning, one should also note that promising does not look like jointly committing to a decision to act.

Furthermore, although one chief aim of the joint commitment account is to explain the Inevitability Point (according to which if X promises to φ, then X is, without exception, under the *pro tanto* obligation to φ), equating promises to joint commitments to a *decision* to act might be incompatible with that point. To see that, suppose that Laura promises to call Sam. If Laura and Sam are jointly committed as a body to the decision that Sam calls Laura, then it seems that Laura now has an obligation *to espouse as a body the decision* that Laura calls Sam. If that is the case, Laura will have promised to call Sam without ever having been under the obligation to call Sam (*contra* the Inevitability Point).

One could object to our reconstruction and note that, in this scenario, Sam and Laura are not committed to decide or endorse as a body the plan that Laura will call Sam, rather they have jointly decided that.[68] Accordingly, neither of them has an obligation to decide anything (unless it is a decision to accord with the joint decision). And since the joint decision has been made, it is incumbent upon Laura to make the call, if she is to accord with the decision they have made. Hence, the theory preserves the Inevitability Point. We welcome the objection because it enables us to specify that our criticism rests on two general assumptions about commitments as such. Below we provide reasons for endorsing these assumptions. Our criticism, therefore, is conditional: if those assumptions are misplaced, it fails.

Our first assumption concerns a general point about commitments, already highlighted in Section 11.4: a commitment (personal or joint) to φ is a sufficient reason for φ-ing (e.g., acting or forming a certain attitude). This goes to show that, at the moment in which the joint commitment has been formed, φ *has not yet happened*, rather the agents are motivated to make it happen. Note that the creation

[67] Gilbert (n 4) 315.

[68] This is, as a matter of fact, the objection Margaret Gilbert has raised to us in private correspondence.

of the joint commitment might well lead to the immediate realization of its content. Perhaps, this is how joint commitments lead to the formation of, especially, psychological attitudes (in contrast to actions). But our assumption concerns the motivational or normative nature of the relation between the joint commitment and its content, not its temporal determination. It is at least in principle possible for the (personal or joint) committer to disregard the commitment: in this case, the commitment does not necessitate the committer to φ (regardless of the temporal relation that binds the commitment and φ in the case where the committer conducts themselves according to their commitment).

The second assumption relates to the idea, again discussed in Section 11.4, that a joint commitment cannot be unilaterally rescinded because it generates directed obligations and claims on X and Y. As Gilbert writes: “If Anne and Ben are jointly committed to doing something as a body, each owes the other appropriate actions by virtue of their joint commitment.”[69] It stands to reason that these appropriate actions must be in accordance with the joint commitment. Hence, our second assumption here is that the obligations inherit, as it were, the content of the joint commitment. So, e.g., if Anne and Ben have jointly committed to φ, where φ is to climb a mountain together, then each of them has the obligation against the other to climb the mountain (the same, of course, applies to cases where φ is a psychological and not an agentive predicate).

Now, according to Gilbert's account, Laura has made a promise to Sam to call him if, among other conditions, Laura and Sam are jointly committed to endorse as a body a particular plan of action φ. Based on the first assumption, it seems to follow that the content of the joint commitment is to endorse as a body the particular plan of Laura's calling Sam. Hence, Laura and Sam have a sufficient reason to endorse as a body that particular plan of action. But this means that the agents are motivated to endorse that plan, which *has not yet happened* at the moment when they have formed the commitment

Further, the joint commitment cannot be unilaterally rescinded because Laura and Sam have acquired directed obligations. What is the content of the obligation accrued to the promisor, and in our example, to Laura? Based on our second assumption, this is the same content of the joint commitment. In other words, this is an obligation Laura has against Sam to endorse as a body the particular plan of calling Sam.

If our assumptions are on the right track, then Laura, in promising Sam to call him, acquires the obligation to jointly endorse the plan to call him – she does not acquire the obligation to call him. But then, as we highlight above, this infringes upon the Inevitability Point. Our two assumptions seem to consistently square with the two ideas about commitments and directed obligations presented in Section 11.4.

69 Margaret Gilbert, *Sociality and Responsibility. New Essays in Plural Subject Theory* (Rowman & Littlefeld 2000) 56.

Yet nothing in what we have argued excludes the possibility that that the Joint Commitment Account of Promises can do without the two assumptions. Though doing so, we presume, will come at the cost of revising other principles of the general theory of joint commitments. We won't explore this possibility, but ask further whether Gilbert's theory of joint commitments couldn't be amended (or interpreted) in another way so as to obviate the mischaracterization of the promises' contents and to salvage the general idea that promises are joint commitments?

Consider the scenario in which a child and their parents, after a disastrous parents–teacher meeting, enter the joint commitment that the child will spend more time doing his homework. This seems to be a case of joint commitment the content of which is the action of *only one* of the commitment's parties. Based on this idea, Gilbert's theory of promises could be revised by now claiming that promises are joint commitments whose content is the promisor's decision only (and not a joint decision of promisor and promisee): for example, if Laura promises to call Sam, then Laura and Sam jointly commit to Laura's decision that she calls Sam. The revised version of the account secures the Inevitability Point (Laura's promise obligates Laura to the decision of calling Sam) and correctly attributes a first-order content to promises, while maintaining that promises are joint commitments.

Unfortunately, this amendment appears to have all the advantages of theft over honest toil (which is why, we presume, Gilbert nowhere hints at this possibility). For one can only commit to what is up to oneself or to what is (on some salient interpretation) under one's control: actions or attitudes of another are not something one can commit to.[70] Accordingly, the subject of the psychological predicate in the commitment's content can only be the subject of that very commitment and this holds for both singular and joint commitments. Our joint commitment is a commitment of ours that has an action or an attitude of ours as its content – something that is up to us or stands under our joint control.

[70] See Annette Baier, 'Doing Things with Others: The Mental Commons' in L Alanen, S Heinämaa, and T Wallgren (eds) *Commonality and Particularity in Ethics* (St. Martin's Press 1997) 15; Frederick Stoutland, 'Why Are Philosophers of Action So Anti-social?' in L Alanen, S Heinämaa, and T Wallgren (eds) *Commonality and Particularity in Ethics* (St. Martin's Press 1997), 45; J. David Velleman, 'How to Share an Intention' (1997) Philosophy and Phenomenological Research 29. Suppose one successfully rebuts this general point about commitments, as it is sometimes held in theories of joint actions (see Abraham Sesshu Roth, 'Shared Agency and Contralateral Commitments' (2004) 113 Philosophical Review 359 as one example among others). What would follow for our critique against Gilbert? Not much, we contend. Let us assume for the sake of the argument that the commitment of Laura and Sam to the action that Laura calls Sam is a genuine case of joint commitment. It would follow from this that all parties – Laura *and* Sam – incur performance obligations. And yet, when Laura promises Sam to call her, it is only upon Laura, not Sam, that a performance obligation accrues. To come back to the relevant point raised in Section 11.5: using "joint commitment" to describe cases like promises in which (performance) obligations accrue only to one committer, strikes us as a misnomer.

If that is correct, then alleged cases of joint commitments which have the action of a committer as their content are not genuinely joint. Going back to the previous example, the putative case of joint commitment that the parents and the child have turns out to be a combination of two different commitments: the child's commitment to spend more time doing homework and the parents' commitment that they will do their best to facilitate the child doing their homework. These two commitments have different contents and therefore do not qualify as one joint commitment.

Because it imposes an acceptance-condition on all promises and because it mischaracterizes the author and content of promises, we conclude that the joint commitment account of promises must be rejected. Of course, this result is doomed to reignite the original question: How should one then explain the Inevitability Point? If promissory obligations and claims are not grounded in joint commitments, then what grounds them? While we won't be able to fully answer these questions in this paper, the next section advances a suggestion on how progress could be made in these matters.

11.7 GILBERT, REINACH, AND A FOURTH DOGMA ABOUT PROMISES

A general consideration shall conclude our assessment of the joint commitment account of promises: in addition to the three dogmas about promises discussed in Section 11.3, we suggest the existence of a fourth dogma. In a nutshell, this dogma assumes that the fact that promises generate claims and obligations calls for a substantive explanation. In order to better clarify what we mean by this "fourth dogma," it might be helpful to come back to Reinach's account of promises.

As we have seen, Reinach insists that all promises, including immoral ones, generate *pro tanto* obligations – this is in accordance with Gilbert's Inevitability Point (strong reading) as well as with Gilbert's rejection of the Immoral Promises Dogma. Furthermore, Reinach maintains that promissory claims and obligations are not moral, which is in accordance with Gilbert's rejection of the Moral Requirement Dogma. Also, Reinach argues that promises are speech acts that bring about obligations – and this, again, is in accordance with Gilbert's rejection of the No Willing dogma. Finally, Reinach holds that promissory claims and obligations are relational or directed – in accordance with Gilbert's Directed Obligation. Thus, Reinach and Gilbert independently arrive at the same five key desiderata for an account of promises.[71]

While one can only be struck by these many affinities, there is one fundamental divergence between the two accounts. Gilbert rejects – correctly, we believe, with Reinach – substantive explanations of the binding character of promises that equate promises to expectation triggers, solicitations of trust, useful social practices, etc., or

[71] Their respective analyses actually converge on even more issues. To mention but one, both pinpoint an easily overlooked distinction between unconditional promises with conditional content (I promise that if p, I φ), and conditional promises (If p, I promise that I φ) – see Gilbert (n 1) and Reinach (n 2) 22–23.

that appeal to moral constraints. However, she concurs with these accounts of promises in that she accepts that some substantive explanation has to be given as to why promises generate obligations and claims. In fact, her main contribution to the debate is to propose a new explanation that, by accounting for promises in terms of joint commitments, is alternative to those previously theorized.

Reinach, on his part, rejects all substantive explanations of the binding character of promises: promises – so his claim goes – generate obligations and claims in virtue of their very nature. On his view, this is a truth that does not need to be grounded in any other: promises are what they are and not anything else. More precisely, promises are generators of obligations and claims. Obviously, this does not mean that nothing else informative can be said about promises: Reinach agrees that we still need to clarify what kind of event a promise is, what kinds of obligations and claims promises generate, whether promises need to be heard and/or accepted in order to have force, and more. But looking for some explanation of why promises generate obligations and claims is, in his view, a pointless endeavor. It is pointless because promising is a primitive kind of action and cannot be reduced to other, more primitive kinds of action.

Does Reinach's position matter in this context? We submit that it does – for two main reasons. First, it matters because, if Reinach is right, then the view that the Inevitability Point demands a substantive explanation may be a fourth dogma about promises (a dogma to which even Gilbert has fallen prey). Second, it also matters because, if it can be shown that abiding by the fourth dogma generally dooms an account to failure, then the question of whether Reinach is right is an urgent one. However, tackling the question of whether – and/or to what extent – Reinach is right can only be a topic for future research.

11.8 ACKNOWLEDGMENTS

This chapter underwent a lengthy development process and benefited from feedback and discussions with numerous colleagues. We are grateful to John Michael and Donnchadh O'Conaill for their comments on previous drafts and to Jed Lewinsohn for discussing the acceptance of promises with us. We presented the chapter detail at events in Cork, Frankfurt, Lugano, Oxford, and Warwick, where we received very valuable feedback from the audience. Finally, we would like to express our deepest gratitude to Margaret Gilbert for her generous feedback on our chapter, which has greatly contributed to refining our arguments, although we suspect she remains unpersuaded.

BIBLIOGRAPHY

Austin J, How to Do Things with Words (JO Urmson and Marina Sbisà, eds, 2d edn Harvard University Press 1975)

Bach K, 'Terms of Agreement' (1995) 105 Ethics 604

Baier A, 'Doing Things with Others: The Mental Commons' in L Alanen, S Heinämaa, and T Wallgren (eds) *Commonality and Particularity in Ethics* (St. Martin's Press 1997) 15

Broad CD, 'Some of the Main Problems of Ethics' in H Feigl and W Sellars (eds) *Readings in Philosophical Analysis* (Appleton-Century-Crofts 1949)
Darwall S, 'Demystifying Promises' in H Sheinman (ed) *Promises and Agreements: Philosophical Essays* (Oxford University Press 2011), 256
de Kenessey B, 'Promises as Proposals in Joint Practical Deliberation' (2020) 54 Noûs 204
Fried C, *Contract as Promise. A Theory of Contractual Obligation* (Oxford University Press 2015)
Gilbert M, 'Walking Together: A Paradigmatic Social Phenomenon' (1990) Midwest Studies in Philosophy 1
'Is an Agreement an Exchange of Promises?' (1993) 90 Journal of Philosophy 627
'What Is It for *Us* to Intend?' in G Holmström-Hintikka, R Tuomela (eds) *Contemporary Action Theory*, Vol. II (Kluwer 1997)
Sociality and Responsibility. New Essays in Plural Subject Theory (Rowman & Littlefeld 2000)
'Rationality in Collective Action' (2006) 36 Philosophy of the Social Sciences 6
A Theory of Political Obligation (Oxford University Press 2008)
"Three Dogmas about Promising', in H Sheinman (ed) *Understanding Promises and Agreements* (Oxford University Press 2011), 80, reprinted in M Gilbert *Joint Commitment. How We Make the Social World* (Oxford University Press 2014) 296
'Introduction' in *How We Make the Social World* (Oxford University Press 2014)
Joint Commitment: How We Make the Social World (Oxford University Press 2014) 296
Rights and Demands: A Foundational Inquiry (Oxford University Press 2018)
Gordley J, *The Philosophical Origins of Modern Contract Doctrine* (Clarendon Press 1991)
Hohfeld WN, 'Fundamental Legal Conceptions as Applied in Judicial Reasoning' (1917) 26 Yale Law Journal 710
Hume D, *A Treatise on Human Nature* (Oxford University Press 2000)
MacQueen H and The Right Hon Lord Eassie (eds) *Gloag and Henderson: The Law of Scotland* (W. Green/Smith and Maxwell)
Massin O and E Tieffenbach, 'The Metaphysics of Economic Exchanges' (2017) 3 Journal of Social Ontology 167
Mertens K, 'On the Essence and Sources of Obligation: A Critique of Reinach's and Gilbert's Accounts of Promises' (2023) 19 New Yearbook for Phenomenology and Phenomenological Research 90
Prichard HA, *Moral Obligation and Duty and Interest* (Oxford University Press 1968)
Raz J, *The Roots of Normativity* (U Heuer ed Oxford University Press 2002)
Reinach A, 'The Apriori Foundations of the Civil Law' (John F Crosby tr, 1983) 3 Aletheia 1–142, reprinted in Adolf Reinach, The Apriori Foundations of the Civil Law Along with the Lecture 'Concerning Phenomenology' (John F Crosby ed, Ontos Verlag 2012), originally published as Adolf Reinach, Die apriorischen Grundlagen des bürgerlichen Rechtes, 1(2) Jahrbuch für Philosophie und phänomenologische Forschung (Max Niemeyer 1913), 685–847
Ross D, *The Right and the Good* (Oxford University Press 2002)
Roth AS, 'Shared Agency and Contralateral Commitments' (2004) Philosophical Review 359
'Intention, Expectation, and Promissory Obligation' (2016) 127 Ethics 88
Salice A, 'Wilhelm Schapp and the Standard Theory of Exchanges' (2023) New Yearbook for Phenomenology and Phenomenological Research 132
Scanlon T, *What We Owe to Each Other* (Harvard University Press 1998)

Schweikard DP and HB Schmid, 'Collective Intentionality' in *The Stanford Encyclopedia of Philosophy* (Edward N. Zalta, ed., https://plato.stanford.edu/archives/win2020/entries/collective-intentionality/ 2020)

Searle J, *Speech Acts* (Cambridge University Press 1969)

'Prima Facie Obligations' in J Raz (ed) *Practical Reasoning* (Oxford: Oxford University Press 1978)

Stoutland F, 'Why Are Philosophers of Action so Anti-social?' in L Alanen, S Heinämaa, and T Wallgren (eds) *Commonality and Particularity in Ethics* (St. Martin's Press 1997) 45

Velleman JD, 'How to Share an Intention' (1997) 57 Philosophy and Phenomenological Research 29

12

The Conceptual Foundations of Contract Formation

*Crescente Molina**

The aim of this essay is to analyze the basic concepts that underlie contract formation. I start from one axiom about the nature of contracts. Contracts, that is, the set of deontic relations (i.e., rights, obligations, etc.) that constitute a contract, are necessarily a product of both parties' assents. Thus, contracts presuppose some kind of *agreement*: We simply cannot acquire a contractual right or obligation against or towards another person unless we and that person in some form agree to us having such a right or obligation. Accordingly, this axiom (the 'Necessity of Agreement Axiom' or simply 'NOA') entails that one cannot *unilaterally* create or assume a contractual right or obligation, namely create or assume a contractual right or obligation against or towards another person without the assent of one's obligor or obligee. Contractual rights are, necessarily, those that are formed, created or brought about by agreement.

I will explore NOA's implications for our understanding of contract formation. I maintain that if we adopt NOA, there are at least two different ways through which two persons can enter into a contract, that is, two mechanisms by which one may form contractual agreements. One is well known to anyone familiar with any modern system of positive contract law: 'offer and acceptance'. The other, interestingly neglected by most contract lawyers and theorists, is what I call 'contractual subscription'. I develop the concept of contractual subscription, and then proceed to discuss the notions of offer and acceptance. Drawing on Reinach's idea of a 'social act', I provide an account of 'juridical acts'.[1] Juridical acts, I argue, are a type of

* Assistant Professor of Law; Rutgers Law School; crescente.molina@rutgers.edu. Many thanks to Felipe Jimenez, Manuel González and the participants of the 'Reinach and The Foundations of Private Law' conference in Frankfurt for their helpful comments. I'm especially grateful to the editors of this volume, Marietta Auer, Paul Miller, Henry Smith and James Toomey.

1 Adolf Reinach, 'The Apriori Foundations of the Civil Law' (John F Crosby tr, 1983) 3 Aletheia 1, reprinted in Adolf Reinach, *The Apriori Foundations of the Civil Law along with the Lecture 'Concerning Phenomenology'* (John F Crosby ed, Ontos Verlag 2012), originally published as Adolf Reinach, Die apriorischen Grundlagen des bürgerlichen Rechtes, 1(2) *Jahrbuch für Philosophie und phänomenologische Forschung* (Max Niemeyer 1913), 685–847. Unlike other

social act, and contractual offers are a kind of juridical act. Finally, I analyze the role of another important notion in contract formation, that of a 'promise'.

Many writers have argued that contractual relations are necessarily constituted by promises. Here I contend that promises are not only not necessary to enter into a contract but that, in their elementary form at least, promises are never sufficient to form a contract. I distinguish between what I call a 'basic promise' and a 'promissory offer'. Developing a Reinachian insight, and against other philosophers and jurists, I argue that promises in their basic form produce their deontic effects immediately once they're apprehended or known by the promisee. They thus bind without the promisee's assent mediating. Therefore, if we remain committed to NOA and basic promises can create rights without the promisee's agreement intervening, these rights cannot be contractual rights. We shall see that promissory offers (and offers more generally) are not essential to the process of contract formation. But only promises that are promissory offers and not basic promises can begin the process of contract formation.

This chapter is about the basic theoretical architecture of contract formation, and thus proceeds at a relatively high level of abstraction. It should, however, shed light on some traditional topics in contract law doctrine, such as the discussion about the structure of so-called 'unilateral' contracts, the problem of the moment of contract formation, and the status of the power to revoke an offer. Furthermore, I do not explore the related yet largely independent issue of the morality of contract formation, namely the moral principles that should (and typically do) inform our views about contract formation. I hope, however, that the views I defend about the conceptual structure of contract formation will clear up the territory for new forms of moral or normative inquiry in the domain of contract law. Our examination of the conceptual bases of contract formation will motivate normative questions such as: is there any value that requires contracts to be formed only by offer and acceptance and not by what I refer to as contractual subscription? Are we morally better off endorsing or rejecting NOA? What is the moral significance of the distinction between basic promises and promissory offers? I briefly elaborate on only one of these questions (Section 12.4), but I do hope that the account I offer of the rich landscape of concepts that govern contract formation will set up a framework for the careful study of these and other questions in the morality of contract. Let's begin by exploring NOA.

essays in this volume, my main focus here is not on Reinach's work. Yet the present essay is Reinachian in spirit in three central ways. First, it assumes that a fundamental form of legal theory consists in exploring the basic conceptual structure of legal notions such as right, obligation, promise, contract, property, etc. Second, it assumes that the basic structure of such notions is, to a significant extent at least, determined by facts different from the mere dictates of the positive law. Third, it draws on important insights, concepts and distinctions developed by Reinach to elaborate an account of contract formation. Reinach himself left out of the *Foundations* the '[...] interesting and difficult phenomenology of contract'. Reinach, 'Foundations' (n 1) 50 (n 26). Here I undertake part of the task.

12.1 THE NECESSITY OF AGREEMENT AXIOM

The NOA axiom holds that a contract binds only if all the contracting parties agree or give their mutual assent.[2] One may identify at least two versions of NOA by distinguishing different forms of ontological dependence of contractual rights upon the parties' assents.

One of them, which we may call 'modal-dependence', holds that contractual rights' existence or bindingness is simply conditional upon the parties' mutual assent, that is, that their mutual assent is *necessary* for the existence or bindingness of their contractual rights. This view, however, leaves open the question of whether the parties' mutual assent is what ultimately *grounds* their contractual rights, that is, whether such rights ultimately obtain *because of* or *in virtue of* the parties' mutual assent. For instance, according to the modal-dependence version of NOA, contractual rights' ground may be a legislative act which in turn makes the parties' mutual assent an enabling necessary condition for the bindingness of such rights. If this is the case, contractual rights' bindingness is conditional upon the parties' assents, yet they are grounded in an act of legislation (i.e., in a law that makes the parties' mutual assent necessary for contract formation). By contrast, according to a version which we may call 'ground-dependence', all contractual rights necessarily obtain because of or in virtue of the parties' mutual assent: a right is contractual in kind only if it is grounded in, and not merely modally dependent upon, the parties' mutual assent. Later I further elaborate on this distinction and contend that these two different ways of understanding NOA have important implications for our views about the structure of contract formation. For the moment, however, we should stress that according to both the ground-dependence and modal-dependence versions of NOA, a person cannot hold a contractual right against another unless both parties have given their assent to the creation or bindingness of such right.[3] Therefore, under either of these versions, NOA entails that persons simply cannot bring about a binding contractual right *unilaterally*, that is, without their contracting party's assent mediating.[4]

[2] Throughout the chapter, I refer to the parties' 'agreement', their 'mutual assent' or their 'assents' as synonyms.

[3] There is an even more inclusive understanding of NOA, which holds that it is sufficient for a right of content A to be contractual in nature that such right's existence or bindingness depends upon the parties' assents to a contractual right of content A, *or* B, C, D, etc. For instance, according to this version of the NOA, a statute may impose a right of content A to parties who agree to the creation of a contractual right of content B, and the right of content A may still be contractual in nature even if the parties never agreed to it. In this case, right A's existence is still conditional upon the existence of a right-modifying agreement between both parties, even if of a different content. I argue for this way of understanding the relationship between contractual agreements and some kinds of contractual obligations and rights in 'Contracting Without Promising' (University of Toronto Law Journal, forthcoming).

[4] The reader must distinguish this sense of unilaterality (i.e., the idea that one person can form a binding contract without their contracting party's assent mediating) from the notion of a *unilateral contract*, which standardly refers not to a contract created by just one of the parties'

Though widely accepted, I do not think NOA is what we may call a 'commonsense truth' about the nature of contracts, that is, an undeniable fact about their nature that we can know by simple observation of the pre-theoretical phenomenology of contracting. Indeed, we will see that some legal systems appear to consider what below I call basic promises (which are unilaterally binding) as sufficient grounds for legal liability, and contract theorists have offered serious arguments in favor of their contractual character. Thus, if NOA is not a commonsense truth about contracts, it requires justification: a theory of contract must make the case for (or against) the agreement-dependency of contractual rights. In this essay, I will assume the soundness of NOA and focus primarily on analyzing some of its implications for our understanding of the structure of contract formation. However, at the end of Section 12.4 I sketch the beginnings of a thesis regarding NOA's justification.

Once we endorse NOA, we can think of different possible mechanisms of contract formation, that is, different ways through which persons can reach a contractual agreement. Let's explore two of these contract formation mechanisms.

12.2 CONTRACT FORMATION AND CONTRACT-ENABLING NORMS

We can think of at least two ways in which persons can give their mutual assent to a contractual relation. First, they can form a contractual agreement through the process standardly known as 'offer and acceptance'. Second, they can reach a contractual agreement by assenting to a set of contractual terms (i.e., rights, obligations, etc.) that are not fixed by a contractual offer in the first place. In this case, they form their contract through what I call 'contractual subscription'.[5] Though some recognize the limits of the offer and acceptance model of contract formation,[6] contract law scholars have neglected the task of providing a theoretical analysis of other possible ways of reaching contractual agreements.[7] Consider the case of contractual subscription.

assents but to the fact that only one of the involved parties assumes an obligation towards the other. *See e.g.*, the French *Code Civile*, art. 1106; and the canonical case *Carlill v. Carbolic Smoke Ball Co.* [1893] 1 Q.B. 256. Yet some contract theorists argue that unilateral contracts must be understood precisely as contracts formed unilaterally by one of the involved parties. Thus understood, unilateral contracts would constitute an exception to NOA. See below at note 49.

[5] I am grateful to Paul Miller for suggesting the term.

[6] *See e.g.*, Allan Farnsworth, 'Precontractual Liability and Preliminary Agreements: Fair Dealing and Failed Negotiations' (1987) 87 Columbia Law Review 217, 219; Andrew Burrows, *A Restatement of the English Law of Contracts* (Oxford University Press 2016) 52–53. Yet contrast, *e.g.*, Marvin Chirelstein, *Concepts and Case Analysis in the Law of Contracts* (7th edn, Foundation Press 2013) 36.

[7] It is likely that the dominance of offer and acceptance as a model for understanding the structure of contract formation is a product of the shift from thinking of contracts as constituted by the broader idea of *consensus* (i.e., agreement) to the idea, started in the late scholastic period but consolidated in the work of early modern thinkers like Grotius and Pufendorf, that

If A and B are contracting parties to a contract C, they formed such contract through contractual subscription and not offer and acceptance if: 1) they both agreed to being subject to the terms of C (i.e., to the rights and obligations C constitutes) *and* 2) the terms of C were not fixed, in the way I specify below, by an offer from A or B. Though below I will offer another example, we may first use the case of entering into a marriage contract as a way of illustrating contractual subscription.

Marital relations entail a cluster of legal obligations and rights that spouses owe towards, and have against, each other. Spouses have no or little power to determine the content of many of these obligations and rights. Yet in modern societies at least, legal marital rights and obligations are contractual in the sense we identified above: their bindingness is conditional upon the involved parties' assents. However, even if marital rights and obligations are in this sense contractual, it would be mistaken to hold that spousal assent must be preceded by a process of offer and acceptance. It is not that it is merely odd or counterintuitive to portray spouses as making reciprocal offers and acceptances when manifesting their spousal assent, the point is that we need not think of their assent to form a marriage contract as mediated or constituted by the process of offer and acceptance. To see why, we must abstract out of the example of marriage for a moment.

Consider the following thesis: The formation of a contractual agreement necessarily presupposes an antecedent 'legal norm'[8] which fixes the content of certain rights and obligations and makes their bindingness conditional upon the parties' mutual assent. We may call this type of norm a '*contract-enabling norm*'. Contract-enabling norms have roughly the following structure: they make it the case that if A and B assent to being subject to terms C (i.e., rights and obligations of content C), then they are thereby bound by C. In themselves, contract-enabling norms do not constitute contractual relations (i.e., contractual obligations or rights), yet they are, according to this thesis, necessary to enable the creation of contractual relations by way of establishing conditional rights and obligations whose bindingness holds upon two persons' assents. Thus, there must be *conditional* rights or obligations in the first place for even the possibility of contractual assent. This is because, according to this view, assenting or agreeing *to a contract* is precisely fulfilling the condition stated by a norm which fixes a right or obligation which *would bind* the parties if they give their assent.

I think a thesis along these lines informs the widespread view that contracts must be formed by the two-step process of offer followed by acceptance. Offers, according

contracts are made of *accepted promises*, which are constituted by two acts: a promise (offer), and the acceptance of the promise by the promisee (the offeree). *See* Reinhard Zimmermann, *The Law of Obligations: Roman Foundations of the Civilian Tradition* (Oxford University Press 1996) 567–69. I discuss the role of promising in contract formation below (Section 12.4.1).

8 A legal norm is broadly any fact (e.g., the issuing of a statute, the existence of a custom, etc.) which the officials of a given legal system take to make it the case that someone is under a certain legal obligation or acquires certain legal right (power, etc.) in such legal system.

to this view, are precisely contract-enabling norms, which acceptances turn into fully fledged, binding contractual relations. Therefore, the view goes, since contract-enabling norms are necessary for contract formation, offers are of the essence of contract formation too. One may of course dispute this way of understanding the nature of contractual agreements and hold that persons can reach contractual agreements, that would bring about contractual rights, without anything like a contract-enabling norm mediating. But let's assume, *arguendo*, that the thesis is sound, and thus that contractual agreements, which constitute contractual relations, necessarily presuppose the existence of contract-enabling norms in the first place. The point I wish to stress here is that there are different legal facts that may create or constitute contract-enabling norms. Offers, as I argue below, are *just one of them*. Offers are thus not necessary for contract formation even if contract-enabling norms are. To flesh out this idea, let's go back to the case of marriage.

For the case of the modern contract of marriage, we can think of a marriage contract-enabling norm as established by civil *legislation*. For instance, Section 1312 of the *BGB* (German Civil Code) states that: '[o]n the occasion of the marriage, the registrar as a rule is to ask the parties contracting the marriage separately whether they intend to enter into marriage with each other and, after the parties contracting the marriage have answered this question in the affirmative, state that they are now, by operation of law, lawfully joined spouses [. . .]'.[9] Thus according to this provision, if the spouses declare to the relevant legal official their assent to getting married, they become lawful spouses and thus acquire a series of reciprocal legal obligations and rights. Among them, for example, they acquire the obligations and rights established by Sections 1353, 1356–59, or 1360 which holds that: '[t]he spouses are reciprocally obliged to appropriately maintain the family through their work and with their assets. If the household management is left to one spouse, that spouse as a rule performs their duty of contributing to family maintenance through work by managing the household.'[10] Section 1312, in conjunction with the other cited and other provisions, constitute a contract-enabling norm: they fix a set of conditional legal obligations and rights that two persons render reciprocally binding by providing their assent in the legally required form. Since in this case legislation already establishes a contract-enabling norm for the contract of marriage, such contract may be formed by the parties by subscription, namely by manifesting their mutual assent in the form required by the legislated contract-enabling norm established in the *BGB*. No offer is needed in this case.

Marital rights and obligations are not the only type of legal right and obligation that persons may incur by contractual subscription. Another prominent example is the case of some forms of fiduciary duty. For instance, in many legal systems, corporate directors acquire a set of legal obligations, notably duties of loyalty and

[9] §1312 *BGB*.
[10] ibid §1360.

care towards the shareholders of the corporation which appointed them. These duties and their correlative rights are conditional upon both the appointed directors and shareholders' assent: a director A is only under a fiduciary duty towards the shareholders of corporation B if both A and the shareholders of B assented, in the legally specified way, to A becoming a director of B.[11] Thus, if this is the case, directors' fiduciary duties are contractual in kind: their binding force is conditional upon both parties' assents. However, as in the case of marriage, to a large extent the content of such duties is fixed by contract-enabling norms created by judicial precedents (typically in common law jurisdictions) and legislation (in civilian jurisdictions). These legislative or judge-made contract-enabling norms establish such fiduciary duties while rendering their binding force conditional upon the reciprocally bound parties' assents. In this case the parties, corporate shareholders and directors, bind themselves through the mechanism of contractual subscription and not offer and acceptance.[12]

Contractual offers constitute *one* distinct class of contract-enabling norms. As I contend later in more detail, a contractual offer is a contract-enabling norm created by a contracting party, that is, by one of the at least two persons whose rights will be modified by entering into the contract. In preliminary terms, we may hold that a person A makes a contractual offer to person B if she creates an obligation or right of content C, whose bindingness is conditional upon B giving her assent to C (i.e., to the bindingness of C). Thus, revisiting the definition provided above, we can maintain that a contractual agreement is formed by contractual subscription if both parties have assented to being subject to the terms fixed in conditional form by a contract-enabling norm *different from an offer* (i.e., a contract-enabling norm not

[11] On the mutual assent dependency of some fiduciary duties see Paul Miller, 'The Fiduciary Relationship' in Andrew Gold and Paul Miller (eds) *Philosophical Foundations of Fiduciary Law* (Oxford University Press 2014) 74. For the case of corporate directors see ibid 81–82.

[12] It is worth thinking about the connection between the idea of contractual subscription and the operation of some legal *statuses*. In most modern legal cultures, the obtaining of some legal statuses (e.g., being a 'spouse') is conditional upon the status holder's assent. It is the law (e.g., legislation, precedents) that shapes the obligations and rights attached to these statuses, yet their binding force is conditional upon the status holder's assent. However, we must be careful in noting that not all cases of contractual subscription are ones in which persons assent to a change in their legal status. Think, for instance, of all the detailed default and mandatory terms (i.e., rights, obligations, etc.,) that modern sale of goods legislation imposes on those who enter sales agreements. These terms are not the product of an offer by the buyer or seller, but of a set of legislated provisions. *See e.g.*, arts. 30, 35, 53 of the widely adopted United Nations Convention on Contracts for the International Sale of Goods. Plausibly, those who enter sales agreements incur these obligations and rights through contractual subscription, and not offer and acceptance. Yet when doing so, they have not changed their legal statuses. On the notion of legal status, *see* Paul Miller, 'The Concept of Personality in Private Law' in Samuel L. Bray et al (eds) *Interstitial Private Law* (Oxford University Press 2024). Particularly relevant is the connection between Miller's notion of 'nominate' statuses, and the idea of contractual subscription.

created by any of the involved contracting parties). Conversely, as we will see later in more detail, if the agreement is ultimately formed by the assent of one of the parties to the conditional obligations and rights fixed by a contract-enabling norm created by the other contracting party, the contractual agreement is formed by the process of offer and acceptance. Thus, contractual agreements need not be preceded by an offer, which is just one type of contract-enabling norm. As we saw in the case of marriage and corporate directors' fiduciary duties, legislative enactments and judicial precedents can also constitute contract-enabling norms. Furthermore, not only legislation, judicial precedents and offers are capable of constituting contract-enabling norms. We should remain open to the idea that other legal norm-creating facts such as, in certain circumstances, customs or social practices may also constitute contract-enabling norms.

I have mentioned different possible sources of contract-enabling norms (i.e., legislation, judicial precedents, offers and, arguably, customs), which in turn lead to at least two different possible mechanisms of contractual agreement formation, namely offer and acceptance, and contractual subscription. Some may dispute this claim by arguing that in certain jurisdictions the law recognizes only offers and not legislation, judicial precedents or customs as facts that may create contract-enabling norms, and thus that in such legal systems contractual agreements can only be formed through offers followed by acceptances and not by contractual subscription. Others, perhaps invoking the value of contractual freedom, may contend that the moral value of contract law requires that only offers, which are contract-enabling norms created by the parties, and not those created by legislation, judicial precedents or custom should be capable of producing genuine contractual agreements. I think both views are mistaken. The first one is descriptively flawed, for all the jurisdictions at least I am familiar with comprise legislated, judge-made and, or customary contract-enabling norms. The second one ignores the plurality of values that may justify different aspects of our contractual practice.[13] Yet in any case, these queries are not our concern here. My aim is to lay out the basic *theoretical possibilities* of contract formation and not the ways in which such possibilities are instantiated in particular legal systems, or the limits on such possibilities imposed by our preferred theories about the morality of contract.[14] The key points we should take away for our subsequent discussion are the following: 1) contract-enabling norms, I have assumed, are necessary for persons to reach contractual agreements; 2) offers are just one way of establishing contract-enabling norms; and 3) if a contract-enabling

[13] I discuss in detail the sense in which legislation and customs can constitute sources of contractual obligations and rights, and argue against 'monistic' approaches to morality of contract law in 'Contracting Without Promising' (n 3).

[14] Yet, as I said at the outset, later (Section 12.4) I will venture a thesis about the connection between NOA and the morality of contract.

norm is constituted by a legal source (e.g., legislation, judicial precedents or custom) different from an offer, the parties subject to that norm reach their contractual agreement, and thus form a contract, by contractual subscription and not by offer and acceptance.[15]

Let's now explore in more detail offer and acceptance as a mechanism of contractual agreement formation. Later on, I will move on to analyzing offers' relationship with another notion that has been central to the development of the law of contracts: promise.

12.3 OFFERS AND ACCEPTANCES

We are not concerned here with all kinds of offers. The offers that are relevant in the domain of contract formation are what we may call 'juridical' offers. People *offer* to others their condolences, their advice, etc. Yet these offers, or at least some of them, need not have juridical effects: they need not bring about any modification in the offeror's or offeree's *rights*.[16] Offers, in our sense, are a type of *juridical act*, that is, belong to the class of acts that necessarily have an *immediate effect in the world of right*. Thus, before exploring offers, we must take a slight detour and look at the notion of a juridical act.[17]

[15] What if our power to make contractual offers is ultimately conferred on us by the positive law, and thus that, at a certain level at least, *all* contract enabling norms emanate from law (e.g., from legislation or judicial precedents)? Here I cannot discuss the interesting and difficult question of what makes a power (or an obligation or right) legally created or conferred in kind by contrast to nonlegally created or 'prelegal'. For our purposes, it suffices to make clear that even if ultimately our power to make contractual offers derives from the positive law, we must still draw the distinction between: 1) forming a contract by the process of offer and acceptance, in which one of the contracting parties, by exercising her (arguably) legally conferred power to offer, is the one who fixes the content of the parties' contractual rights and obligations; and 2) the process of contractual subscription, in which both parties assent to certain reciprocally owed rights and obligations whose content was fixed not by them but by legislation, judicial precedents or custom. The importance of distinguishing these two mechanisms of contract formation holds regardless of the answer we give to the question of whether the power to offer is an artifact of the positive law or a prelegal power. I thank Marietta Auer for pressing me to clarify this point.

[16] Indeed, many offers have 'moral' effects (e.g., they change the aptness of some morally significant emotions and dispositions) yet do not impact our rights. Other offers have no juridical *or* moral effects. Here I am interested only in offers that have an effect on our rights, that is, juridical offers.

[17] The notion of juridical act I propose here is meant to be an elaboration of the one (*actus iuridicus* or *negotium iuridicum*) that has for a long time been present in European legal thought. For a helpful historical account of this notion *see* Alejandro Guzmán Brito, 'Para la historia de la formación de la Teoría General del Acto o Negocio Jurídico y del Contrato, IV: Los orígenes históricos de la noción general de Acto o Negocio Jurídico' (2004) 26 *Estudios Histórico-Jurídicos* 187. Although, to my knowledge, no express references are made in the *Foundations*, it would be surprising if Reinach's account of 'legal power' was not influenced by this idea. *See* below at n 23.

12.3.1 *Juridical Acts*

As I will understand it here, a juridical act is *any (intentional) public act which, at least under one true description, produces an immediate effect on our rights*. The concept of a juridical act has three important components.[18]

First, juridical acts are 'intentional' acts. Unlike what we may call mere juridical *facts*, juridical acts are constituted by intentional acts, that is, by what persons *intentionally do* rather than by what simply happens to them or by what they inadvertently do. An example of a juridical fact is, for instance, the fact of being born. The fact of a person being born has some immediate effects in the domain of right, that is, it makes it the case that such person acquires various rights. Yet such rights (i.e., the ones that hold in virtue of being born) are obviously not grounded in any intentional act by such person, for, we may assume, being born is not an intentional act. Juridical *acts*, by contrast, are made of intentional acts and this, among other things, means that one cannot (genuinely) perform a juridical act (e.g., make a contractual offer) inadvertently, that is, without one knowing that one is doing so.[19]

Second, juridical acts are constituted by (intentional) *public* acts, that is, they are at least in part made of acts that are not purely mental in kind. I thus cannot perform a juridical act (e.g., make a contractual offer) *merely* by thinking. In order to perform a juridical act, a person must (intentionally) perform an act which is external in kind (e.g., pronounce some words, sign a document, etc.). The public character of juridical acts derives from a more basic aspect of their nature: they are *social* in kind. As Reinach puts it, social acts are necessarily *other-directed*. They are necessarily *addressed to others*, and, accordingly, they are completed as acts insofar as they can imprint themselves in their addressees' experience.[20] Since these acts can only imprint themselves in their addressees' experience if the addressees are capable of *knowing* or *apprehending* these acts in the first place – and, we may assume, we cannot know each other's thoughts but through external facts – juridical acts, like all social acts, must be at least in part constituted by public facts.[21]

Although all juridical acts are, in Reinach's sense, social acts, not all social acts are juridical acts in our sense. Acts such as to threaten, warn, insult, congratulate, etc.,

[18] I elaborate in detail on the claims presented in this subsection in 'The Power in the Law' (unpublished MS, available upon request).

[19] Of course, the positive law deals with cases in which juridical acts (e.g., offers) appear to have been intentionally made but the (putative) juridical agent declares to have not made them intentionally but by mistake. The answer to the question regarding how the law should decide on this and other related issues (e.g., coercively extracted juridical acts, etc.) will depend on multiple factors besides our views about the nature of juridical acts.

[20] '[T]he one who performs them and *in the performance itself*, are as it were cast towards another person in order to fasten themselves in his soul'. Reinach, 'Foundations' (n 1) 20.

[21] Reinach seems to grant that if this limitation would not exist (e.g., if we could read each other's minds) purely *in foro interno* social acts would be possible. See ibid 20.

are also social in kind: they are necessarily addressed to others and are thus completed as acts once they can be apprehended by their addressees.[22] Yet unlike these social acts, social acts that are juridical acts have *immediate effects in the domain of right.*[23] This leads us to the third element of our definition.

The fact that juridical acts have what I call immediate deontic effects means, first of all, that juridical acts (if validly made) *necessarily* produce certain deontic effects (i.e., a right, obligation, etc.). This is what distinguishes them from other social acts, like congratulating or threatening someone, which can but do not necessarily produce any deontic effect. Furthermore, this feature of juridical acts entails that there is a special kind of *constitutive explanatory relationship* between a juridical act and its immediate deontic effects: the obtaining of juridical acts' immediate deontic effects is, in a distinctive way, explained by such juridical acts. Elsewhere I argue that this kind of special explanatory relationship, which I call an *essential explanatory dependency*, holds because juridical acts metaphysically *ground* their immediate deontic effects.[24] For instance, (validly made) promises – which we will see below are a kind of juridical act – essentially explain the obtaining of promissory rights and obligations, and they do so because (validly made) promises ground promissory rights and obligations. This way of understanding the relationship between juridical acts and their immediate deontic effects allows one to draw an important distinction between the immediate deontic effects of a juridical act and those deontic effects whose obtaining is merely conditional upon, yet not grounded in, such acts. For instance, in many legal systems, those who enter sales contracts (which are often made of juridical acts) incur an obligation towards the government to pay sales taxes. However, though its bindingness is conditional upon the making of a sales contract, such an obligation is not grounded in the contract as, we may assume, the seller's obligation to deliver the goods or the buyer's obligation to pay the price are. The tax obligation, we may say, *modally depends* on the existence of the parties' sale agreement (i.e., the agreement is necessary for the tax obligation to become binding on the buyer and seller), yet it is not grounded in it, namely it is not an immediate deontic effect of the juridical acts that constitute the parties' contract.[25]

22 Some juridical acts are not completed once they *can* be apprehended by their addressee, but once they are *indeed apprehended* by their addressee. One may hold that offers belong to the latter class of acts.

23 *See* Reinach, 'Foundations' (n 1) 66, using this formulation to characterize the notion of legal power. He holds that a legal power '[...] reveals itself in the fact that the action to which it refers, produces an immediate effect in the world of right [...]'. Perhaps we could say that legal powers in Reinach's sense are abilities to perform a subclass of social acts, namely juridical acts.

24 'The Power in the Law' (n 18). For a helpful recent survey on the relationship between grounding and explanation, see Alexander Skiles and Kelly Trogdon, 'Should Explanation Be a Guide to Ground?' (2021) 178 Philosophical Studies 4083.

25 To be sure, the point is that the parties' tax obligation is not grounded in *the parties'* juridical acts even if its bindingness is conditional upon their contractual agreement. Yet of course, the parties' tax obligation is an immediate deontic effect of a juridical act of the legislature, that is, of the juridical act of *legislating*.

After these remarks on the nature of juridical acts in general, we are ready to turn to offers.

12.3.2 *What Is an 'Offer'?*

In broad, preliminary terms, we may characterize an offer as a juridical act in virtue of which a person (i.e., the offeror) creates or modifies a right, or assumes an obligation towards, another person whose assent is a condition for the bindingness of such right or obligation. The 'offeree' is the person to whom the offer is addressed and whose rights (in addition to the offeror's) will be bindingly changed if she gives her assent. The assent given by the offeree to an offer is her 'acceptance'.

As juridical acts, offers have all the basic properties of such acts: they are intentional public acts which have certain immediate deontic effects. What distinguishes offers from other juridical acts is the peculiar structure of the deontic effects they generate, namely the fact that they create rights whose bindingness is conditional upon the offeree's assent. Yet before focusing on offers' distinctive deontic effects, a remark on the (intentional and public) *acts* that may constitute the juridical act of an offer is needed.

It is, to an important extent, a task for social conventions and the positive law to specify the intentional public acts that may count as capable of producing certain immediate deontic effects, that is, the public acts whose intentional performance by a person constitutes a juridical act. And, of course, such conventional or legal act-specification admits a large range of possible acts counting, by virtue of law or convention, as constituents of juridical acts. Some may be tempted to maintain that contractual offers (and arguably other juridical acts too) are necessarily constituted by a special kind of public act: *speech acts*.[26] Yet this view should be rejected. It is certainly possible to make an offer by the offeror saying, using verbal or written words, to the offeree that she thereby grants the offeree a certain right under the condition that she assents. But even if we hold that we always have the power to make offers by using words, it is mistaken to hold that we can only make offers in this way. For instance, in many legal systems (silently) taking a good from a shop's shelf to the counter counts as an offer, that is, as an intentional public act whereby a person assumes an obligation to pay for the good under the condition that the seller accepts the deal and transfers possession over the good to the purchaser. It would be implausible to hold either that such acts cannot constitute offers, or to understand them as necessarily involving some kind of hidden speech act. Though there is certainly more to be said about the relationship between offers made through speech

[26] For an analysis of offer and acceptance along these lines see e.g., Peter Meijes Tiersma, 'The Language of Offer and Acceptance: Speech Acts and the Question of Intent' (1968) 74 California Law Review 189. *See* also Robert A Samek, 'Performative Utterances and the Concept of a Contract' (1965) 43 Australasian Journal of Philosophy 196.

acts and through other acts,[27] what distinguishes offers from other juridical acts is primarily the structure of the deontic effects that offers generate. It is this aspect of offers that will occupy us in what follows.

As mentioned before, an offer produces a right (or obligation, etc.) whose binding force is conditional upon its addressee's (the offeree's) assent. This broad formulation of the concept of an offer, however, comprises different possible kinds of offer. We may at least distinguish offers by the specific *type of deontic entity they generate* and by the *mode of acceptance* they require. Let's consider the first distinction.

By making an offer, a person may be aiming at (and succeed in) creating different types of conditional rights. For instance, A may offer to B a property right over an object that he owns, O. In this case, we may understand A as creating in B an *in rem* entitlement or right over O, only in case B assents to the acquisition of such right.[28] Other offers do not purport to modify our property or *in rem* relations but only our *in personam* or *obligational* relations. For instance, A may assume an obligation to perform an act under the condition that B assents. In this case, A creates a claim-right or *in personam right* in B that A performs said act, whose bindingness is conditional upon B's assent. Furthermore, offers can create other types of deontic entities. For instance, A may create in B a *power* (e.g., a power to act on A's behalf or 'power of attorney'), whose bindingness is conditional upon B assenting to the acquisition of such power. Many contemporary legal cultures operate under the idea that contracts only involve a modification in the parties' obligations or *in personam* rights, and thus assume that only obligational or *in personam* offers are distinctively contractual in kind.[29] I think this view is mistaken. Contracts often modify *in rem* rights, powers, and other deontic incidents that cannot be reduced to obligations or *in personam* rights. A conceptual framework for analyzing contracts that confines contracts to the purely obligational domain overlooks the richness of the landscape of possible contractual agreements.

There is, however, a narrower conception of contractual offers that deserves careful scrutiny. According to this view, contractual offers necessarily create one distinctive type of deontic entity in the offeree, namely the *legal power of acceptance*. The identification of this view of what it is to make an offer leads us to a second form of classifying offers and, as we will see, to two possible ways of understanding the role of acceptance in contract formation.

[27] For instance, we should remain open to the idea that some juridical acts are less sensitive to conventional or legal act-specification mechanisms, and perhaps there is a more fundamental connection between these juridical acts and speech acts.

[28] *In rem* rights are, using Reinach's terminology, a type of 'absolute right'. They are rights of persons over things. See Reinach, 'Foundations' (n 1) 12–14, 52–53. For a persuasive defense of the notion of absolute rights *see* Olivier Massin's contribution, Chapter 8 in this volume, 'The Ontology of Liberties: Reconciling Reinach and Hohfeld'.

[29] Though just in passing, a broader sense of offer (i.e., one that it is not exclusively obligational in kind) is acknowledged by Arthur L Corbin, 'Offer and Acceptance, and Some of the Resulting Legal Relations' (1917) 26 The Yale Law Journal 169, 171.

12.3.3 *What Is an 'Acceptance'?*

I have so far characterized offers as juridical acts whereby persons create rights whose bindingness is conditional upon the offeree's assent. I will call this way of understanding offers the 'mutual assent' conception of an offer. Contrast now this conception of an offer with what we may call a 'power-conferring' conception of offers. According to the power-conferring conception, for A to make a contractual offer to B it is not sufficient that she merely creates a right or obligation in or towards B whose bindingness is conditional upon B's assent. This view holds that offers must grant the offeree a *legal power to accept* A's offer, that is, the ability to bind the offeror to the terms of her offer by the offeree performing a special kind of *juridical act*.[30] The performance of such juridical act is what constitutes the offeree's acceptance. There are several important differences between these two conceptions of contractual offers.

According to the power-conferring conception, an offer must create in the offeree a legal power to bind the parties to the terms of the offer. A legal power, as I shall understand it here, is the ability to perform a juridical act, namely, as we saw, a public (intentional) act which has certain immediate deontic effects.[31] An offer is thus a juridical act that confers on its addressee, the offeree, the power to perform another juridical act, namely the act of accepting an offer. By contrast, it is not necessarily a juridical act, but an act of what we may call 'mere assent', that is sufficient to constitute an acceptance for the mutual assent conception of an offer.[32] Again, according to this conception, to make an offer is simply to create a right in the offeree whose bindingness is conditional upon the offeree's mere assent, assent which may well be a purely mental act. Of course, this view, which entails that one may in principle accept an offer *in foro interno*, is compatible with the fact that offerors may qualify their offer and make part of the offer's terms that the offeree's assent must be, even if not constituted by public acts, *manifested* or *expressed through* specifically defined public means (e.g., by sending a letter to the offeror, by signing a document, etc.). Furthermore, the mutual assent conception of offers is compatible with the view that holds that the positive law should use objective standards to *ascertain* or *discover* the parties' assents, and thus that, from the point of view of the positive law, the offeree accepts an offer when it is reasonable for an external observer to believe that she has done so. Yet as a conceptual matter, the mutual assent conception states that, whilst offers in themselves are juridical acts,

[30] Seemingly adopting this conception see Wesley N Hohfeld, *Fundamental Legal Conceptions as Applied in Judicial Reasoning* (Yale University Press 1964) 56 and Corbin, 'Offer and Acceptance, and Some of the Resulting Legal Relations' (n 29) 171.

[31] Reinach, 'Foundations' (n 1) 66. See also n 23.

[32] Making a similar distinction regarding the notion of acceptance, see ibid 28–33. See also n 42.

acceptances need not be so and thus they may well be made of the offeree's purely internal or private assent.

Different sorts of considerations may militate in favor of the positive law adopting a set of rules about offer and acceptance that come closer to a mutual assent instead of a power-conferring conception, or vice versa, and it's not my aim to explore these considerations here. We must note, however, that the soundness of one of these conceptions or the other is intimately connected to our understanding of the nature of the Necessity of Agreement axiom, that is, to our views about the type of ontological dependence that holds between contractual rights and the parties' agreement. Let's see.

If we adopt what I called the modal-dependence version of NOA, rights and obligations are contractual in kind insofar as their binding force is conditional upon the parties' assent. Assuming this way of understanding NOA, I have proposed that it is sufficient to form a contractual agreement that there is what I called a contract-enabling norm, that is, a norm which creates a certain deontic effect whose bindingness is conditional upon the parties' (mere) mutual assents. We saw that offers, if we adopt the mutual assent conception, are a way of creating contract-enabling norms. By contrast, if we adopt what I called the ground-dependence view of NOA, contractual rights and obligations are those that necessarily obtain in virtue of the parties' agreement. Therefore, if we follow this version of NOA, contractual rights and obligations must be necessarily *grounded in*, and not merely conditional upon, *both* parties' assents. Hence such 'assents' must be constituted by *juridical acts* and not by what I referred to as mere assents; and, accordingly, the only type of legal norm that can make possible the creation of contractual agreements are precisely norms that confer or regulate legal powers; legal powers to contract either created by offers, or created or recognized by other kinds of legal source (e.g., legislation). By contrast, if we adopt the modal-dependence view of NOA, *both* offers that constitute mere contract-enabling norms and those that confer the legal power of acceptance are capable of creating a contract if acceptance follows.

I believe the modal-dependence view of NOA provides a better theoretical model for analyzing contract formation than the ground-dependence view. Whilst committed to the necessity of mutual assent for contract formation, it gives us a more malleable way of conceiving the relationship between contractual rights and obligations and different sources of law, and between different types of juridical acts (offers qua power-conferring or qua contract-enabling) and the formation of contractual agreements. This more nuanced and flexible understanding of the relationship between contractual agreements and different legal sources and juridical acts may be needed to make sense of the complexities of the modern social practice of contract. My aim here, however, is not to offer a defense of this claim (for this obviously requires separate, careful treatment), but to reveal different possible ways of thinking about the connection between the nature of contractual agreements and the rich array of notions that comprise the structure of contract formation. Let's now finalize by discussing another important notion in contract formation.

12.4 PROMISES AND CONTRACT FORMATION

There are of course many ways of modelling the act of making a promise. Yet maintaining the theoretical framework used so far, we may define promising as a juridical act whereby a person (the promisor) assumes an obligation to act or refrain from acting in a given way towards another person (the promisee), who in turn acquires a claim-right to performance, namely an *in personam* right to performance directed towards the promisor. A great deal of contemporary contract theory, mostly in the Anglo-American context, is devoted to the examination of promising, assuming perhaps that the notion of a promise constitutes the most basic element contracts are made of.[33] Under this view, promising is necessary for contracting; one simply cannot enter into a contract without making or accepting a promise. There are, however, good reasons for rejecting this view.

From our previous discussion, we may quickly infer that there are at least two ways in which, under the proposed framework, we may form a contractual agreement without making a promise. First, promises' immediate deontic effects are exclusively *obligations* and their correlative *in personam* rights. Yet as we saw, and as I argue elsewhere in detail, some contracts only modify the parties' *in rem* or property rights: their immediate deontic effects are only *in rem* and not *in personam* in kind.[34] Thus, if there are contracts of this kind, they cannot be made of promises, for again all promises, even when they constitute contractual offers (as I discuss below), have only *in personam* effects as their immediate deontic effects. Thus, when made of the parties' juridical acts, *in rem* contracts must be made of juridical acts which have *in rem* effects, and again, promises cannot be such acts.[35] Second, we saw that if we adopt the modal-dependence version of NOA, the parties may enter into a contractual agreement without any of them performing any juridical act: they may enter into a contractual agreement by what I called contractual

[33] *See, e.g.*, Charles Fried, *Contract as Promise: A Theory of Contractual Obligation* (Harvard University Press 1981); Stephen A Smith, 'Performance, Punishment and the Nature of Contractual Obligation' (1997) 60 Modern Law Review 360; Seana V Shiffrin, 'The Divergence of Contract and Promise' (2007) 120 Harvard Law Review 708; Daniel Markovits and Alan Schwartz, 'The Myth of Efficient Breach: New Defenses of the Expectation Interest' (2011) 97 Virginia Law Review 1939.

[34] 'Contracting Without Promising' (n 3).

[35] Of course, other juridical acts (e.g., legislation) or other sources of norms such as customs may attach different deontic effects to our promises (e.g., in rem effects). The point is that deontic effects different from obligations and claim-rights cannot be *immediate* deontic effects of promises. I can promise to give you a property right over O, and thus assume an obligation and grant you a claim-right that I do so. But I cannot *give you property* over O (i.e., an *in rem* right over O) by *simply promising* to give you property over O. Again, such a property transfer must be grounded in another juridical act or norm.

subscription. If there is a contract-enabling norm created by legislation, judicial precedent, custom or by any other legal sources different from an offer (like we saw for the case of marriage and corporate directors' fiduciary duties), the assenting persons enter into a contractual agreement by giving what I called their *mere assents* (and, if applicable, by complying with the formalities established by the contract-enabling norm). If this is correct, contracting parties may enter into contractual agreements and assume contractual obligations and rights without any of them performing any juridical act, either a promise or of another kind. Yet even if not necessary for contracting, is the making of a promise ever *sufficient* for contracting?

When formulating this question, we are of course not concerned with whether according to the positive law a promise is sufficient for contracting, because it is well known that in many legal systems the law adds other conditions than promising for contract formation (e.g., consideration, certain formalities, etc.); and furthermore in other legal systems, mostly in the civilian tradition, the notion of a promise is largely absent in the law of contract formation. Our question is theoretical in kind. We are asking whether the juridical act of a promise creates obligations and rights in the form required by NOA, namely whether promissory obligations and rights' bindingness depends upon the promisor *and* promisee' assents. The answer to this question, however, depends on our views about the nature of promising. Since at least the seventeenth century, the question of whether a promise requires acceptance or uptake by the promisee in order to bind has received significant attention. Some theorists have argued that promises are binding only insofar as the promisee assents to the bindingness of the obligation and right proposed by the promisor's promise. According to this view, promises are essentially a kind of offer, a juridical act whereby the promisor (the offeror) creates in the promisee (the offeree) an obligation and correlative claim-right only if the promisee assents to the bindingness of such obligation and right. By contrast, others hold that promises are not offers, their bindingness is not conditional upon the promisee's assent. According to this view, promises bind *unilaterally*, that is, without the promisee's assent mediating, even if the promisee may, once the promise is formed, waive his right to performance thereby terminating the promisor's obligation.[36]

These opposing views are still well represented in contemporary work on the philosophy of promising. Joseph Raz, for instance, argues that it is a mistake to claim that someone has accepted a promise if, upon receiving it, she simply remains 'stone-faced, saying nothing and not moving a muscle'. It is clear to Raz that there is no acceptance in this case and yet the promise binds the promisor once made, even if the promisee may immediately waive her claim-right to performance.

[36] On the history of the problem of the necessity of the promisee's acceptance see Wim Decock, *Theologians and Contract Law: The Moral Transformation of the Ius Commune (ca.1500–1650)* (Martinus Nijhoff 2013) 187–92; and TB Smith, 'Pollicitatio – Promise and Offer' (1958) *Acta Juridica* 141.

He concludes then that there is no reason to hold that promises need to be accepted in order to bind.[37] The opposite conclusion is reached by Charles Fried, who invokes the example of a group of people who, without any request by Fried mediating, send him a letter promising they won't have more than two children. This promise, according to Fried, is not binding, and the reason is that promisees must have the capacity to decide whether to acquire a right to performance against promisors. Therefore, according to Fried, promisees must always accept the promises made to them for such promises to create any binding obligations or rights.[38] I believe both Raz and Fried's views capture important elements of the phenomenology of promise-making. We need a theory of the nature of promising that can make sense of cases in which promises appear to bind even if there is no acceptance by the promisee mediating *and* cases in which promises appear to bind only if the promisee gives her acceptance. In this respect, Reinach's account of promising proves helpful.

According to Reinach, a promise is a kind of social act. Therefore, as we saw, as a social act the act of promising must necessarily have an addressee (the promisee); and such act is completed once the promisee can apprehend the promise in her experience. As he puts it, the promisee '[...] *must take cognizance of the act of promising itself*, he must, as we would put it somewhat more exactly, *consciously take in the promising*'.[39] Moreover, as we saw, promises have certain immediate deontic effects. According to Reinach, such effects are an obligation to act as promised, and a correlative claim-right to performance (a claim-right which, once created by the promise, can of course be waived by the promisee).[40] Yet Reinach's account of the nature of promising suggests that the promisee's acceptance is not required for promises to produce their immediate deontic effects. A promise creates an obligation and claim-right once the promisee apprehends it in her experience, that is, once she knows of the promise and its central elements (i.e., the identity of the promisor, and the content of the obligation and claim-right created by it). Thus, if the promisee cannot apprehend these elements about a promise made to her, she

[37] Joseph Raz, 'Is There a Reason to Keep a Promise?' in Gregory Klass et al (eds) *Philosophical Foundations of Contract Law* (Oxford University Press 2014) 72. Holding a similar position *see* James Penner, 'Voluntary Obligations and the Scope of the Law of Contracts' (1996) 2 Legal Theory 325, 328–29; and Seana V Shiffrin, 'Promising, Intimate Relationships, and Conventionalism' (2008) 117 Philosophical Review 481, 491.

[38] Fried, *Contract as Promise* (n 33) 43 ff.; also maintaining this view *see* David Owens, *Shaping the Normative Landscape* (Oxford University Press 2012) 223–26.

[39] Reinach, 'Foundations' (n 1) 28 (emphasis added). See also ibid, Reinach's technical sense of 'hearing' a promise: '[i]f the promise is simply heard *(vernomen)* there arises a claim in the one who hears and an obligation in the promisor'. I believe Reinach's sense of 'hearing' means simply to *(consciously) apprehend by perception*. And of course, in this broader sense the promisee may 'hear' the promisor's promise without hearing the sounds of the words 'I promise' or indeed any other sound if, for instance, the promise is made silently, e.g., exclusively in writing.

[40] ibid 31–32.

cannot acquire any promissory right against the promisor. Therefore, according to Reinach's account, if the promise in Raz's example was appropriately apprehended by the promisee, the promisor is obliged. The same applies to Fried's example. The promise will indeed be binding if the promisors (i.e., the group of people who sent him the letter) know the identity of the promisee (i.e., Fried) and the promisee knows the identity of the promisors, and the content of the obligation and claim-right created by the promise. Reinach's theory, however, can accommodate cases in which promises bind only insofar as accepted by the promisee.

Reinach acknowledges that some promises are made under the condition that the promisee accepts the promise.[41] Promisors have the power to render their promise into what we may call a 'promissory offer'. Here again one may identify a power-conferring conception of promissory offers, that is, one which holds that promissory offers are juridical acts that besides creating a conditional obligation and claim-right to performance, confer a legal power to accept on the promisee, and thus that become unconditionally binding only if the promisee performs the juridical act of acceptance. Yet, as we did before, one may instead adopt a mutual assent conception of a promissory offer, according to which a promissory offer is a juridical act whereby a person (the promisor/offeror) only creates an obligation to perform and a correlative claim-right in another person (the promisee/offeree) whose bindingness is conditional upon the promisee giving her (mere) assent.[42] Promissory offers have in common with what I will call 'basic promises' the type of deontic effect they purport to ultimately generate, namely a fully fledged obligation in the promisor and correlative claim-right to performance in the promisee. Yet they are still offers, for the obligations and claim-rights they create bind only if their addressees assent to their bindingness. Thus, according to Reinach, among the different juridical acts that persons may choose to perform, they can make basic promises, which as we saw bind once apprehended by the promisee, and promissory offers, which bind once apprehended *and* accepted by the promisee. Furthermore, there is another important difference between basic promises and promissory offers.

As we saw, it is in the nature of promises to create a claim-right to performance in the promisee. The fact that promises create claim-rights to performance means that the promisee acquires a form of *personal authority* or *exclusive deontic control* over the promisor in the matter of the promise: it is exclusively up to the promisee to demand performance or to release the promisor from his obligation by waiving her promissory right. Among other things, the relationship of exclusive deontic control that promises generate entails that promisors do not have the unilateral power *to revoke their promise*, for again, if promises grant the promisee entitlements to

[41] ibid 29.

[42] Reinach makes an equivalent move by distinguishing acceptance as a social act and acceptance as an act of 'inner assent' by the promisee, inner assent which may well be expressed or communicated by the promisee to the promisor, but that, even when expressed, it does not amount to the social act of acceptance. See ibid 29–30.

exclusive deontic control over the promisor in the matter of the promise (i.e., a claim-right to performance), only the promisee and not the promisor can have the power to release the promisor.[43] To be sure, by mutual agreement, the parties to a relationship of obligation can entitle *both* the obligee and the obligor with the power to revoke such relationship.[44] Yet this type of deontic relationship differs from that created by promises which, as I have characterized them here at least, necessarily amount to relationships of right or exclusive deontic control by the promisee over the promisor in the matter of the promise.[45] The essential irrevocability (by the promisor) of promissory relationships helps us to further distinguish basic promises from promissory offers. Unlike a basic promise, there is nothing in the concept of a validly made promissory offer that prevents it from being revoked by the promisor before accepted by the promisee. This is because offers, once apprehended by the offeree, do not constitute binding relationships of right (i.e., of exclusive deontic control) until accepted. Yet once accepted, a promissory offer produces a relationship of exclusive deontic control and therefore the promisor lacks the ability to revoke the promise (unless, as we said, the promisee has agreed to the promisor having such capacity and in such case their relationship is not a promissory deontic relationship any longer but one of a different kind).[46]

Let's now conclude by analyzing the consequences of this way of understanding the nature of promises for the problem of contract formation.

12.4.1 *Promises and the Necessity of Agreement*

If we remain committed to NOA, promises in their basic form are not in themselves sufficient to initiate the process of contract formation, since basic promises produce obligations which are not conditional upon both involved parties' assents. Thus only promises that constitute promissory offers can count among the facts that can get contract formation started.[47] A theory of contract that purports to give promises an essential role in the process of contract formation must thus either propose an

[43] Of course, other cancelling factors besides the promisee's release (e.g., the promisee's death) may liberate the promisor of her promissory obligation, but she cannot have a power to liberate herself by sheer fiat or choice.

[44] *See* Reinach, 'Foundations' (n 1) 33–34.

[45] I explore our power of self-release and its bearing on the idea of obligation in 'Promises, Commitments, and the Nature of Obligation' (2023) 25 Journal of Ethics and Social Philosophy 59.

[46] To be sure, this claim about the inherently revocable nature of promissory offers is compatible with the fact that the offeror may indeed render his promissory offer 'irrevocable' by making a (basic) promise not to revoke his promissory offer. Here, the offer *becomes* irrevocable, but only because the offeror has performed an *additional* (irrevocable) juridical act (i.e., a basic promise not to revoke his offer) which purports to alter the revocable nature of his offer.

[47] Basic promises, like many other facts, can *causally* contribute to the formation of a contract (e.g., your basic promise to marry someone, may motivationally contribute to you and that person afterwards entering into a marriage contract). Yet this kind of contribution is not

alternative conception of promising whereby promises bind only insofar as the promisee gives her assent,[48] or simply abandon NOA and endorse the view that at least some contracts may bind unilaterally.[49] To be sure, the idea that basic, unilaterally binding promises do not constitute the foundations of contractual liability is of course compatible with holding that the positive law may consider them as capable of generating a *sui generis* or a merely legal, noncontractual form of liability. Indeed, this seems to be the case in the legal systems in which unilateral promises' binding force is legally recognized.[50] At this stage, however, one may wonder why we should remain committed to NOA. Is there any reason we should maintain that only those rights whose bindingness depends on both parties' assents should be deemed contractual in nature? In this chapter, my aim has been to map out some of the relevant notions that make up the conceptual landscape of contract formation if we assume NOA to be true. A defense of NOA, however, should amount to explaining the *normative* point, function or value of the fact that contractual rights and obligations can only be a product of both parties' assents. It therefore entails getting into the terrain of the moral or normative foundations of contract, and I, of course, cannot embark on such an enterprise here. Let me finish, however, by outlining a thesis regarding where the justification of NOA may lie.

One may defend the soundness of NOA by invoking a view regarding the justification of the *enforceability* of contracts. According to this view, both basic

juridical in kind, that is, it doesn't even partially constitute the grounds in virtue of which contractual rights may obtain. Basic promises, as such, are never contract-enabling norms.

48 See n 38.

49 Arguing for this alternative, *see* Peter M Tiersma, 'Reassessing Unilateral Contracts: The Role of Offer, Acceptance and Promise' (1992) 26 U.C. Davis Law Review 1, 24–41. Following Tiersma on this point see Stephen A Smith, *Contract Theory* (Oxford University Press 2004) 183–84.

50 For a helpful general overview see Martin Hogg, 'Promise: The Neglected Obligation in European Private Law' (2010) 59 International & Comparative Law Quarterly 461. A clear illustration of the role of unilateral promises as a source of legal and not contractual liability is provided by the Italian *Codice Civile*, which contains a title (IV) on unilateral promises, and states that 'a unilateral promise to a performance *only* produces obligatory effects in the cases *stated by the law*'. Art. 1987 (emphasis added). Articles 1988–89 enumerate these cases, which include a unilateral promise made in recognition of a previous debt and, in certain circumstances, a promise made to the public (e.g., a reward promise). Some cases of so-called promissory estoppel may fall into the category of noncontractual, legally imposed liability too. However, in the paradigmatic case of promissory estoppel, although there is no consideration, the promisee has accepted the promise, for it is plausible to hold that otherwise she wouldn't rely on it. Perhaps a more accurate example in American contract law is the case of irrevocable or firm offers. An irrevocable offer is one made together with the offeror's basic promise not to revoke the offer (*see* note 46). In this case, the law appears to dictate the legal enforceability of such promises (i.e., to legally bind the offeror to keep his offer open) under a special regime, for it enforces these promises only if they comply with certain legal formalities that are typically not required for contracts (e.g., being in writing). *See* Uniform Commercial Code, art. 2. § 205. In other words, in this case an offeror is *legally obliged* to maintain his offer open, yet the offer becomes *a binding contract*, and he incurs distinctively contractual obligations, only once the offeree accepts the offer.

promises and contractual agreements entail the parties immediately affecting (i.e., creating, modifying, terminating) their rights by choice or fiat. However, the view goes, there is a basic principle in the morality of rights which holds that one cannot, by sheer unilateral choice, change the basic principles that determine the *permissible use of force*, that is, produce a change in our *enforceable rights*. According to this principle, whilst I can unilaterally make it the case that I simply owe it to you, by making a basic promise, to give you $10, I cannot without your assent mediating grant you a claim *to enforce such right* against me – namely a claim that entitles you to exercise necessary and proportionate force (either directly or through institutional mechanisms) to extract performance or compensation upon my breach.[51] If this moral principle is sound, contractual agreements but not unilateral juridical acts can create enforceable rights. Of course, a just legislature can also create enforceable rights and thus *render* a unilateral promise, which is in principle unenforceable, legally enforceable.[52] Yet individuals, under this view, without the backing of such an additional collective juridical act (i.e., legislation) cannot create enforceable entitlements unless all the parties involved (i.e., obligors and right-holders) have assented to the creation of such entitlements. Thus, if it is in the nature of enforceable legal rights that they cannot be unilaterally created *and* validly made contracts create not merely binding but enforceable rights, then NOA must be sound.

BIBLIOGRAPHY

Bray et al (eds). *Interstitial Private Law* (Oxford University Press 2024)

Burrows A, *A Restatement of the English Law of Contracts* (Oxford University Press 2016)

Chirelstein M, *Concepts and Case Analysis in the Law of Contracts* (7th edn, Foundation Press 2013)

Corbin A, 'Offer and Acceptance, and Some of the Resulting Legal Relations' (1917) 26 The Yale Law Journal 169

Decock W, *Theologians and Contract Law: The Moral Transformation of the Ius Commune (ca.1500–1650)* (Martinus Nijhoff 2013)

Farnsworth A. 'Precontractual Liability and Preliminary Agreements: Fair Dealing and Failed Negotiations' (1987) 87 Columbia Law Review 217, 219

Fried C, *Contract as Promise: A Theory of Contractual Obligation* (Harvard University Press 1981)

Gold, A. and P Miller (eds). *Philosophical Foundations of Fiduciary Law* (Oxford University Press 2014)

Guzmán Brito A. 'Para la historia de la formación de la Teoría General del Acto o Negocio Jurídico y del Contrato, IV: Los orígenes históricos de la noción general de Acto o Negocio Jurídico' (2004) 26 *Estudios Histórico-Jurídicos* 187

[51] The reader will identify the Kantian ring of this idea, yet of course a defense of it need not be committed to the Kantian theoretical apparatus. See Immanuel Kant, *The Metaphysics of Morals* (Cambridge University Press 1996) 6: 231, 261, 263, 271, 274.

[52] See n 50.

Hogg M, 'Promise: The Neglected Obligation in European Private Law' (2010) 59 International & Comparative Law Quarterly 461
Hohfeld W, *Fundamental Legal Conceptions as Applied in Judicial Reasoning* (Yale University Press 1964)
Kant I, *The Metaphysics of Morals* (Cambridge University Press 1996)
Klass et al (eds). *Philosophical Foundations of Contract Law* (Oxford University Press 2014)
Markovits D and A Schwartz 'The Myth of Efficient Breach: New Defenses of the Expectation Interest' (2011) 97 Virginia Law Review 1939
Miller P, 'The Fiduciary Relationship' in A Gold and P Miller (eds) *Philosophical Foundations of Fiduciary Law* (Oxford University Press 2014) 74
'The Concept of Personality in Private Law' in SL Bray et al (eds) *Interstitial Private Law* (Oxford University Press 2024)
Molina C, 'Promises, Commitments, and the Nature of Obligation' (2023) 25 Journal of Ethics and Social Philosophy 59
'Contracting Without Promising' (2025) 75 *University of Toronto Law Journal* 203
'The Power in the Law' (MS)
Owens D, *Shaping the Normative Landscape* (Oxford University Press 2012)
Penner J, 'Voluntary Obligations and the Scope of the Law of Contracts' (1996) 2 Legal Theory 325
Reinach A, 'The Apriori Foundations of the Civil Law' (John F Crosby tr, 1983) 3 Aletheia 1–142, reprinted in Adolf Reinach, *The Apriori Foundations of the Civil Law Along with the Lecture 'Concerning Phenomenology'* (John F Crosby ed, Ontos Verlag 2012), originally published as Adolf Reinach, Die apriorischen Grundlagen des bürgerlichen Rechtes, 1(2) *Jahrbuch für Philosophie und phänomenologische Forschung* (Max Niemeyer 1913), 685–847
Samek R, 'Performative Utterances and the Concept of a Contract' (1965) 43 Australasian Journal of Philosophy 196
Shiffrin S, 'The Divergence of Contract and Promise' (2007) 120 Harvard Law Review 708
'Promising, Intimate Relationships, and Conventionalism' (2008) 117 *Philosophical Review* 481
Skiles and K, Trogdon 'Should Explanation Be a Guide to Ground?' (2021) 178 Philosophical Studies 4083
Smith S. 'Performance, Punishment and the Nature of Contractual Obligation' (1997) 60 Modern Law Review 360
Contract Theory (Oxford University Press 2004)
Smith TB 'Pollicitatio – Promise and Offer' (1958) Acta Juridica 141
Tiersma, PM 'The Language of Offer and Acceptance: Speech Acts and the Question of Intent' (1968) 74 California Law Review 189
'Reassessing Unilateral Contracts: The Role of Offer, Acceptance and Promise' (1992) 26 U.C. Davis Law Review 1
Zimmermann R, *The Law of Obligations: Roman Foundations of the Civilian Tradition* (Oxford University Press 1996)

Index

For EU product safety concerns, contact us at Calle de José Abascal, 56–1°,
28003 Madrid, Spain or eugpsr@cambridge.org.

www.ingramcontent.com/pod-product-compliance
Ingram Content Group UK Ltd.
Pitfield, Milton Keynes, MK11 3LW, UK
UKHW040056310825
462435UK00019B/412

* 9 7 8 1 0 0 9 4 4 5 9 9 3 *